Ancient Furies

Ancient Furies

A Young Girl's Struggles in
the Crossfire of World War II

ANASTASIA V. SAPORITO
WITH DONALD L. SAPORITO

Potomac Books
An imprint of the University of
Nebraska Press

Four lines from "The Fury of Aerial Bom-
bardment" From *Collected Poems 1930-1986*
by Richard Eberhart (New York: Oxford
University Press, 1986), 90. Reprinted by
permission of Oxford University Press, Inc.
Copyright 1960, 1976, 1987 Oxford Univ.
Press, and by the Richard Eberhart Estate.
All rights reserved
Manufactured in the United States of
America

Library of Congress
Cataloging-in-Publication Data

Saporito, Anastasia V., 1928-2007. Ancient
furies: a young girl's struggles in the crossfire of World War II / Anastasia V. Saporito
with Donald L. Saporito.
pages cm
ISBN 978-1-61234-633-5 (cloth: alkaline
paper)—ISBN 978-1-61234-634-2 (ebook) 1.
Saporito, Anastasia V., 1928-2007—Childhood and youth. 2. World War, 1939-1945—
Personal narratives, Yugoslav. 3. World War,
1939-1945—Personal narratives, Russian.
4. World War, 1939-1945—Serbia—Belgrade. 5. Russians—Serbia—Belgrade—
Biography. 6. Belgrade (Serbia)—Biography.
7. Blankenburg am Harz (Concentration
camp)—Biography. I. Saporito, Donald L.
II. Title.
D811.5.S259 2014
940.54'81497—dc23
2013031943

Set in Lyon Text by Laura Wellington.
Designed by J. Vadnais.

This book is dedicated to my children, who have a right to know more of their mother, her background, and therefore their heritage than time, or circumstance, or the pain of remembering ever permitted me to tell them; to my parents, who gave me both life and the "foundation" needed to prosper; to Kristina, who has lived always in my heart, and whose memory so often guides me in my own kitchen; to my husband, whose constant love, urging, and editing finally brought this memoir to completion; and finally to the millions who lie in unmarked and/or forgotten graves throughout the world, victims of armed conflicts they neither sought nor understood.

Anastasia Popova Saporito

You would feel that after so many centuries
God would give man to repent; yet he can kill
As Cain could, but with multitudinous will,
No farther advanced than in his ancient furies.

Richard Eberhart, "The Fury of Aerial Bombardment"

Contents

Foreword

This memoir had its beginning in 1967, when I was enrolled in graduate school at the University of Denver. Our children were enrolled in the first and second grades of grammar school, and Anastasia (Asya), without a teaching assignment at my new graduate school, found herself at home with time on her hands. The Vietnam War was raging, and several of our friends, drafted or enlisting, left for Vietnam, while others left for Canada to escape the draft.

Asya had spent most of her sixteenth year as a prisoner in a Nazi forced labor camp in Blankenburg am Harz, in eastern Germany. With antiwar sentiment enflaming most campuses, Asya, deeply antiwar because of her own experiences, thought, perhaps naively, that if others could understand the things which had overtaken her and her family during World War II, it might help to put a stop to what so many of us at the time found to be the insanity and senseless killing taking place in Southeast Asia.

Asya did not mention her efforts to me at the time, and it was only when we were packing to move to my first job after graduate school that I came across the manuscript. Astounded at the level of detail and honesty with which she had written, I told her that I would help her to edit it as soon as we were settled in the Chicago area. However, my new position at Argonne

National Laboratories was followed within eighteen months by our move to Dartmouth College, where a new teaching position for Asya, and raising our children, kept delaying the editing process.

Following Asya's graduation from Dartmouth College (a graduate degree in June 1978), we moved to Lafayette, Louisiana, where I held the position of director of university libraries at the University of Louisiana. Asya taught for only two semesters because it became clear that student interest in the Russian language was lacking. The university called on her, however, to ask if she would be willing to serve as interpreter for a trade delegation from Ukraine, a group of Soviet agricultural experts interested in agricultural developments in Louisiana.

For several days she accompanied the group throughout the area, and during one dinner conversation she mentioned her grandparents, Kuliabko-Koretskii, and the family estate, Kotchubeyevka. The family name didn't seem to ring any bells, but eyebrows went up at the mention of Kotchubeyevka. Kotchubeyevka, the Soviets told her, had become the largest collective farm in all of Ukraine. The group's recognition of the name of the family estate reignited her determination to complete her book.

In 1997 Asya and I visited Vienna and found the house on Mariahilferstrasse where Asya was reunited with her parents a few weeks before they were forced into the Klosterwerk forced labor camp in Blankenburg am Harz, Germany, in October 1944. Her mother, Maria Petrovna Popova, was killed by an American bomb April 20, 1945, during the liberation of the camps and is buried in the city cemetery in Blankenburg. Her father, Vasilii Mitrofanovitch Popov, died of a broken heart December 13, 1947, and is buried in Munich.

In 1999 we visited Blankenburg. The city archivist, Ingrid Glogowskii, gave most generously of her time and expertise, providing Asya with a copy of her mother's death certificate and leading us to her mother's grave, to the Klosterwerk tunnel, and to the site of the forced and slave labor camps. Asya learned from Ms. Glogowskii that Herr Mueller, who befriended Asya in the camp, had survived to become a well-known radio commentator in East Germany. Sadly, his wife had been sent to a Nazi death camp and did not survive. Asya also learned that a consignment of slave laborers from Belgium were held in the Klosterwerk, confirming her memory of the boy to whom she had given her scarf, who she thought was from Belgium.

Asya died December 6, 2007. At the time of her death, she left an original, double-spaced, typed manuscript of 321 pages which she had completed in 1968, plus six spiral-bound subject notebooks, several exam booklets, and a number of loose pages gathered together in groups, but unbound, all in longhand. Her original manuscript, written without chapter divisions, begins with the German invasion of Yugoslavia, just after the three-day bombing that terrorized Belgrade beginning on Palm Sunday, April 6, 1941, and ends when she is notified of the death of her father just two months after they were reunited in August 1947. That manuscript forms the last half of chapter 10 and continues through chapter 22.

The timeline in that original manuscript sometimes incorrectly juxtaposed wartime events with events from her adolescence. These have been rearranged, almost always with her knowledge and agreement, but there are some instances in which the changes were made after her death, based on our prior discussions. If there are errors in the timeline, they are mine. I insisted that she write about her parents and her early childhood experiences to provide background contrasting the trauma that had followed and because I felt it would be of special interest to our children and grandchildren. That material, also completed without chapter divisions, fills much of the spiral-bound notebooks and has been sharply reduced to form chapters 1 through 10 of this published memoir.

Asya had never written about the final arrangements and funeral of her father. Those two days of her life were still so emotionally heavy for her to bear. But she had told me about it in detail, and I felt it essential that she try to put it into writing with the same honesty I saw in everything she did. I reminded her several times over the years about that, and she always agreed—"but a little later." Obviously, the memory was still painful for her. After her death, while finally trying to edit all she had left into this final format, and faced with trying to write what she had told me of those two days surrounding her father's death and burial, I went again to the notebooks that she had completed, looking for any notes she might have made that would help.

Only then did I find her manuscript, folded and tucked into the back of an unused notebook—thirty handwritten pages covering the death and funeral of her father. The paper she used leads me to believe she wrote them in the early 1990s, perhaps following our return from Vienna when we found the place where she and her parents were reunited in 1944, just before they were taken to the forced labor camp. They were written without any significant corrections, probably done in a single afternoon, while I was working on a different part of her manuscript. She had not mentioned them to me. I believe they were too painful for her and that she had quietly put them aside intending to tell me about them when we reached that point in our editing. That material forms chapter 24.

The names Makharov, von Holzen, and von Stoiber are fictitious. The characters are real, but in spite of an extraordinary memory, Asya was unable to recall the correct names. Of course, they appeared in her life in minor roles at a most difficult emotional time. Although every effort has been made to ensure historical accuracy, the book is first and foremost a memoir.

For years Asya and I tried to identify the U.S. Army unit that had liberated the Klosterwerk camp where she and her parents were held in Blankenburg. We requested copies of military After Action Reports that seemed to be promising, always to be disappointed. Then when my final editing of this memoir was complete, I decided to try another internet search. I had no idea what, if anything, I did differently that time, but with my first press of the return key, there it was:

After Action Report, G2 Section, 8th Armored Division, 1–30 April 1945. Section 2: Enemy Operations during Period.

. . .

Subsection B. 12–30 April 1945: Between the 12th and 22nd of April 1945, the 11 Pz Army, defending the Harz Mountains, was completely smashed . . .

"On 20 April 1945, CCA and CCB attacked south. Due to the state of general confusion in the pocket, resistance was sporadic and unpredictable. Blankenberg [sic] fell to CCB by nightfall on 20 April. . . .

"PW's during the period: 10,295; PW's to date: 25881

Enemy tanks destroyed: 1

AT guns destroyed: 4

Motor Transport destroyed: 30.

It was the U.S. 8th Armored Division, the "Thundering Herd," that pushed into Blankenburg on April 20, 1945, smashing the German 11th Panzer Army by nightfall in the process, the battle which surrounded the terrified sixteen-year-old girl who would one day become my beloved wife. The name of the town had been misspelled Blankenberg in the After Action Report, and I must have inadvertently made the same mistake in typing my last search.

Asya and I met, quite by accident, one warm summer evening in 1958. We seemed to hit it off well, and when I took her home that evening, I asked for a date for the following week. The night we met happened to be my twenty-sixth birthday, which allowed me to forever claim her as the best birthday present anyone ever received. Throughout my early years, many people entered my life, most briefly, some lingering, all adding to my own life experience. I marvel at the wisdom I evidently had which allowed me to so quickly recognize the one among all who would always mean so much to me.

We were married about two weeks after that first following date. We would, in fact, be married three times: two weeks after our first date, when we sought a judge at the courthouse in Golden, Colorado, on August 22, 1958, to perform the ceremony; a second time, almost a year later, on July 4, 1959, when we were expecting a child and wanted a ceremony in a Catholic church; and a third time, just over forty-nine years later, when we began to fear that Asya might not make it to our fiftieth anniversary, and our parish priest visited our home to perform the ceremony August 30, 2007. We remained happily married for forty-nine years, three months, two weeks, and one day. Asya passed away in our bed, holding my hand, squeezing it very hard with her last breath, in a final farewell.

Asya was the most considerate, thoughtful, generous person I have ever met, always concerned with the feelings and well-being of others, always placing the welfare of others first. She had, of course, been tested in ways most of us cannot imagine and tempered by experiences none of us would ever seek. Those experiences had taught her, before her sixteenth birthday, those truths that most of us finally learn much later in life, sometimes too late, and that some of us never learn—that life itself is the most precious gift; that family background, advantages, wealth, and privilege count for very little in the end; that what is centrally important is our faith in God, what we do with the talents we have and the moral foundations we were provided, and the way we interact with and treat our fellows.

While editing Asya's work, Father Gregórii has intruded often in my thoughts. He withheld from Asya the touchstones of the cherished memories of her family and her childhood. Asya forgave him, of course, back in 1947. There was no room for rancor in her heart. His failure to understand also withheld from our children and grandchildren the touchstones of their heritage. I'm sure that I too will soon forgive him.

Asya taught me something every day of our life together, something about love and commitment, about honesty and values, about generosity and helping others, about respect for other people's views, about simple humility. I have not always been a good student, and one of her oft-repeated lessons—"If something needs to be done, do it, don't put it off"— was one of those lessons I seemed to have trouble with. As a result, this memoir languished for forty years, but I know she has forgiven me. There has not been one single moment since her death that I have not thought of her, have not consciously missed her, whether alone or with friends, whether reading or listening to music, whether watching television or, of course, editing this, her memoir. She is always in my thoughts . . . always gently on my mind.

On the night we were married in 1958, we sat together in front of a massive picture window in my small studio apartment in Golden, Colorado, the room flooded with light from a full moon. We were listening to records I had placed on the phonograph—the opera *La Boehme* and a collection of Italian folk songs, which included the beautiful Neapolitan song "Torna Piccina." I had no knowledge of her history then nor of the part that song had played in it. I left the room for just a moment as the song began and returned to find her crying softly. When I asked what was troubling her, she replied simply that she well knew how short life was, and that it saddened her that we had not met years before. Her father, she said, used to sing "Torna Piccina" to her when she was a little girl. I comforted her then, as we promised each other at least fifty years together.

I made two other promises to her that night. Although I then knew nothing of her wartime experiences, she had mentioned that she had always been afraid of dying alone—almost certainly the result of her mother's lonely death. I promised her first that I would be by her side to hold her hand as she drew her last breath on earth and second that I would follow her within fifteen minutes. God did not permit me to keep that second promise, but I am eternally grateful for having been able to keep the first.

One day in 1972, I returned from my office at the Dartmouth College Library and went to our bedroom, where I found a surprise gift on my pillow waiting for me—not an unusual event. The gift, however, was unusual. Asya had found a piece of bark that had fallen from a birch tree in our yard, the same tree so important throughout Russian literature, and had used it to write me a love note. Written in Russian, in the careful, clear Cyrillic script that she maintained all her life, the note, now framed, hangs in our bedroom. The translation that follows is mine. Although I would no longer claim extensive knowledge of Russian, I believe it is accurate:

8 December 1972

My Dearest Love,
I am so happy with you. I love you so, and am just so sorry that everything has a beginning and an end, and that life passes so quickly. But I am certain that love cannot simply end—and that somewhere, beyond this world, our love will be endless.

Asya

When our children were teenagers, we had adopted a phrase in our family, "Mom's always right," which reflected the fact that whenever she announced a decision, answered a question to settle a disagreement, or rendered an opinion, she was invariably proven correct. I look forward eagerly to being able to say, "Mom's always right" to her when we are reunited.

D. L. S.

Acknowledgments

This is the story, honestly told, of Asya's early years and the terrible trauma of World War II that ended her childhood and destroyed everything and everyone she held dear. My main work on the manuscript really began in the very trying months following Asya's death. Most of the friends who were so supportive remain unnamed, and I apologize to them. Organizing and editing the work, particularly shortening the initial manuscript for publication, proved far more difficult than I had anticipated, and there are several people who must be recognized for the great help they were to me.

Our daughter Tatiana and granddaughter Kristina patiently read the initial manuscript, searching out grammatical errors or possible historical errors, as I entered it into a computer.

Dr. Harold Bowman and his wife, Priscilla, read the first rough draft of a privately printed family edition and offered suggestions for refinement, but most importantly, at the time I most needed it, offered encouragement to pursue publication. Harold was a particularly dear friend and always supportive.

Günter and Barbara Dilssner, citizens of Blankenburg am Harz who became treasured friends, gave generously of their time and hospitality to Asya and me, strangers at the time, as we tried to locate the site of the former camps.

The mayor of Blankenburg am Harz, Heinz A. Behrens, graciously referred us to the city archivist, Ingrid Glogowskii, who gave most generously of both her time and her expertise. She provided Asya with the official death certificate for her mother and led us to the cemetery chapel, Asya's mother's grave, and the site of the former slave and forced labor camp where Asya spent most of her sixteenth year.

Finally, I owe a special debt of gratitude to three people: Don McKeon, editorial assistant at Potomac Books, for first recognizing the importance of the story and for recommending its publication, to Bridget Barry, acquisitions editor at the University of Nebraska Press, for her advice, guidance, and expert assistance in reducing the manuscript to meet publication requirements, and finally to Elaine Otto, copy editor, who provided invaluable guidance in the final preparation of the manuscript for typesetting.

D. L. S.

ONE

The Early Years

Winter can be both long and very cold in northern New England, yielding only reluctantly to something aptly called "Mud Season." By June, however, the Hanover Plain is bright with the color of early flowers and that special green of spring. I had been told that, by tradition, it did not rain on Commencement Day. So it was in 1978.

My teenage children watched proudly as I accepted a graduate degree, and my husband held my hand tightly, pride reflecting in his eyes, as a 1930s model car drove slowly by—the driver blowing the horn and happily waving his new degree. The sound of that old horn seemed to pierce my heart, when the memory of Mother returned and I wondered if she was watching, proud of this latest accomplishment. One of my earliest memories as a toddler was rushing to a large window to look for the car that would bring Mama back to pick me up—a memory, if truly a memory, which would prove both useful and confusing in the years ahead. The sound of an old horn always started a rush of so many memories. It seems only yesterday that I longed for the sound of that old horn with all my heart, but it was so very, very long ago . . .

We lived in Belgrade, Yugoslavia, in the heart of the capital's government and diplomatic sector. Our home was the large ground floor unit at No. 6

Dr. Kester Street, with four bedrooms, three baths, a large parlor, a dining room, a study that served as a music room and housed Mother's piano, and a small adjoining room that served as Father's office or den. A large kitchen and pantry and a maid's suite with private bath completed the unit. If I close my eyes in writing this, I can see all of the wonderful french doors, the beautifully polished parquet floors, and, best of all, the very large windows that lined the hallway leading to my bedroom, Aunt 'Lyena's bedroom, a shared bath, and a guest room. Those hallway windows overlooked one of two enclosed courtyards and would play a special part in my early childhood. I loved every inch of that home, but it was the people who filled my childhood who were important—my parents and the close family friends who had such an influence on me and my development. My story begins with them.

My father, Vasilii Mitrofanovitch Popov, was born in Penza, in the heart of Russia, in March 1895, one of seventeen children born to General Mitrofan Popov and his wife. Four of the seventeen died in infancy. All were born at the family estate near Penza, into a family of position and privilege, although not the great wealth once held by the family he would marry into.

Vasilii enrolled in the Imperial Military Academy and entered the Russian army as a commissioned officer upon graduation. He was always very proud of his service with the Drozdovsky Regiment and the raspberry colored uniform facings by which it was known.

When the revolution erupted, his unit was placed under the command of General Anton Denikin. Command soon changed to General Peter Wrangle, who renamed the White Army the Russian army, and Vasilii was promoted to the rank of captain. Wrangel led the army on a major offensive through Ukraine, entering Poltava victorious in the early autumn of 1920, and Captain Popov led a small detachment of soldiers into the central jail in Poltava to release any White prisoners confined by the Reds.

As he started unlocking cells, he found two young women—one an exceptionally beautiful girl of about nineteen, and her cellmate, close to the same age but handicapped. They were identified as Maria Petrovna and Elyena Petrovna Kuliabko-Koretskaya, daughters of the former governor general of Ukraine.

I have often tried to picture the scene that day in that Poltava jail cell—

the very dashing, handsome young captain who must have stood speech-less, at least for a moment, before the beautiful girl he found. I can almost see her drawn to her full height, demanding to know who this was that had entered the cell and stood now facing her and her sister.

Within weeks of the release of the two girls from jail, Wrangle's forces suffered crushing defeat at the hands of a newly reinforced Red Army, and Wrangel organized a mass evacuation on the Black Sea coast offering soldiers and civilian the free choice of evacuating with him, into the unknown, or remaining to face the Red Army.

Captain Popov, together with Maria and Elyena, elected to join the exodus with Wrangel to Constantinople. I know that the three then traveled on to stay at least briefly in Shanghai, where the girls had friends and at least one cousin, before returning to Constantinople. I like to think that he and Maria were already deeply in love, but they simply never talked about this time in their lives.

King Alexander of Yugoslavia soon issued an invitation to all tsarist forces, welcoming them to Yugoslavia, and General Wrangel quickly organized and led a mass immigration of his Russian followers to Belgrade. Captain Popov and his two charges decided to join them.

Once settled in Belgrade, a Russian émigré community was quickly organized, perhaps by General Wrangle, centered on activities of the Russkii Dom (Russian House), which quickly became a vibrant social center for the community, establishing a school for émigré children. Captain Popov and his two charges were founding members of this group.

I don't know where or even when my parents were married, but I was born in Belgrade, October 6, 1928, into a well-ordered household consisting of my parents, my aunt, and our housekeeper, Kristina. Russian children were always given the name of an Orthodox saint and a second name, a patronymic, which was the name of their father with an ending meaning "son of" or "daughter of" followed by the family name of the father. Accordingly, I was named and baptized Anastasia Vasilievna Popova—Anastasia (after the youngest daughter of the tsar), Vasilievna (after my father, Vasilii, with the *evna* feminine ending), Popova (with the feminine *a* ending). Russian is rich in the use of diminutives—pet names fondly used among family and close friends. I would be variously called Asinka, Anochka, or Asya, with Asinka used most frequently when I was a child and Asya commonly used as I became a young adult. Similarly, Father, Vasilii, was called Vasya, and Mother, Maria, was most often called Marusha by Father.

Father was the light of my life. Vasilii Mitrofanovitch Popov had dark brown hair and large blue eyes that exactly matched the color of the bachelor-button flower. The Russian word for this flower is Vasiliók, and I always imagined that the flower had been named after him because of his eyes. He was five years older than Mother, about six feet tall, broad-shouldered, slender, and athletically built. He was always very generous with his affections and took great pains to instill in me, from very early on, the importance of character. He often told me stories that he invented and that always held a moral—the importance of being truthful and earnest at all times, and *never* to forget that I was a Russian and his daughter.

"As you go through life," he said, "there will be times when you will be helpless. Disappointments will be found along the road of life, temptations and hurts that will weaken you, just as the walls of a house may be weakened by storms. But if the foundation is solid and strong, then one can reinforce the walls and the house will be made even stronger. So it may be in your life. But all the hurts and disappointments will only make you stronger. Never surrender your integrity! As long as your integrity, faith, and honesty are strong within you, then your foundation is solid and you will pass through all the ravages of life."

My mother, Maria Petrovna, was born on her family estate, Kotchubeyevka, near Poltava in Ukraine, November 4, 1900. She and her sister were born into a life of great wealth, position, and privilege. Only one or two years separated them. Elyena Petrovna, who I believe was the older and who I would come to know and love as Aunt 'Lyena, suffered a birth defect that left her slightly handicapped, with a palsy-like tremor and a speech impediment.

Both girls began their education at home, under the tutelage of nannies and private tutors. The girls excelled at all subjects, particularly languages, gaining fluency in several by the time they were six years old. When the time came for a more structured, formal education to begin, Maria was enrolled in a private boarding school in Lausanne, Switzerland. Elyena, because of her handicap, remained at Kotchubeyevka to continue with home tutoring.

Mother was exceptionally beautiful and accomplished. She had a fair complexion and never used makeup other than light lipstick. Her eyes were dark brown with almost black irises surrounded by lovely bluish whites and very slightly slanted, rather almond-shaped, and her jet-black hair just brushed her shoulders. With a tiny waist and long, slender legs, her figure was nearly perfect and always earned admiring glances from both men and women. She took great pride in her hands and insisted that a manicurist visit her at home twice each week to see to their care. Her voice was low and well modulated and commanded attention whenever she spoke. She never raised her voice, even when correcting me.

Mother had managed to keep a family album of photographs showing her family at Kotchubeyevka and of herself at boarding school in Lausanne. I always thought my own baby pictures looked out of place among the formal family portraits. I would often leaf through the album, examining the sepia-toned pictures. One was a portrait of Mother's father in riding clothes, with a pince-nez on the bridge of his nose. He was seated in a large chair, crossed legs highlighting his riding boots, arms resting comfortably on the chair arms, his right hand lightly holding a riding crop. He wore a leather device on his left hand—narrow leather straps extended between each of his fingers and were attached to a wide leather band that encircled his wrist. It looked terribly important to me, and I thought it must be something that only general governors wore.

I remember at about the age of six while looking at the album with Mother, I remarked once to her that I thought it must be wonderful to live in such a home, surrounded by so much art and beauty. Mother's look softened as she said, "Always remember, Asinka, they were very nice, but they were only 'things.' One's family and close friends are the treasures of life. They are the *real* treasures to be valued."

"Yes, Mama."

It would be many years before I began to appreciate Mother's wisdom, but without realizing it I quickly adopted her values.

Mother would always hug me warmly but never kiss me. I wanted so much to jump up, hug and kiss her, and bury my face in her neck. She always smelled so good. But she would always restrain me and limit my closeness. The seed of rejection can be planted early and grow rapidly. If a passing automobile sounded its horn at such times, I would recall a dim, dark "memory," perhaps a dream of being left someplace and being told by my mother to listen for the sound of the automobile horn. Told that the sound of the horn would mean that Mama was coming to get me, I would run to a large window and look out to the street for an automobile at the curb.

The "memory," or dream, never included the face of my mother, and I began to think that the wrong mother had picked me up—someone kind, but not as loving as a mother should be. I never related this "memory" to Mother. Perhaps my parents simply left me overnight with friends while they traveled someplace on business or a brief vacation, but the explanation, if any, is now gone forever. It would be many years before I began to guess at the reason for Mother's apparent distance.

Aunt 'Lyena was very frail with light brown hair streaked heavily with gray, softly falling to below her waist, but which she always twisted into a tight bun. She wore thick eyeglasses through which her very dark eyes appeared enormous to me. Her head twitched constantly and sharply to the right. Her hands trembled, and she held everything with both hands in order to avoid dropping it. She had a serious speech impediment, which caused her not to stutter but to draw out the length of many syllables so that good, for example, became goooood and bad became baaaaad. This often made it difficult to understand her and encouraged everyone to avoid any unnecessary conversation with her. I always understood her speech, and she remains sharply in my memory as the kindest, gentlest person I have ever known. It was Aunt 'Lyena who read me bedtime stories each evening, heard my evening prayers, and took me to church every Saturday evening and Sunday morning.

Church and religion were central to Aunt 'Lyena's life, and I always looked forward to our weekly attendance. Our Russian Orthodox church was, for me, a center of magic, mystery, and reverence. The interior of the church contained a gold adorned altar and a great many Byzantine icons and was dimly lit by large round candle stands filled with hundreds of burning candles. There were no pews. The congregation stood throughout the lengthy service, but the children were invited to sit on the steps of the altar. From my perch on the steps the candles cast a mysterious glow and flickering shadows on the faces of the saints in the icons, convincing me that I could see their eyes and lips moving in silent prayer and that they would keep us all safe. I could always see Aunt 'Lyena standing in front, deep in prayer. Aunt 'Lyena would remain a strong moral force and example to me throughout my life.

Kristina was our housekeeper, and I could always count on her for an extra measure of affection. Kristina was Slovenian—a kind-faced woman with blonde hair fixed in braids that she wore wound about her head. She lived with us, cooked our meals, and looked after me and my well-being. She had large blue eyes and a smile that would chase all the clouds away and bring a tingling happy sensation into my busy but dull and quiet routine. Kristina was to become my confidante—a substitute mother to whom I could run with childish secrets and the questions that would trouble my childhood. There was, however, one secret which I always kept from her.

As far back as I can remember, I had to take a daily dose of cod-liver oil. The bottle was placed on the sill of one of the enormous hallway windows, between the inner window and the storm window. It was my responsibility to get a spoon from Kristina, fill it with cod-liver oil, and drink the foul-tasting stuff. It took me only a few days, however, to discover that I could open the outer storm window. From then on I simply opened the inside window, filled the spoon with the terrible stuff, opened the storm window, and dumped the spoon outside. I would then close the windows and return the spoon to Kristina. She, of course, never failed to heap praise upon me, particularly when I returned an empty bottle every few weeks.

"Oh, Asinka," she would say, "what a good girl, and so grown-up."

The little twinges of guilt this always caused must have been a small price to pay for avoiding the terrible liquid. The routine continued for years until my parents felt that I no longer needed it. Once when Mother was not at home, I went to her bathroom, which looked out on the courtyard from the other end. I pulled back the curtain to look out and was horrified to discover a long, dark oily stain on the stones of the wall from a windowsill to the ground. I quickly closed the curtains and prayed that Mother would never look out through the curtains. It didn't alter my routine, however. I simply stretched my arm further out before dumping the spoon. My secret was never discovered.

The cod-liver oil must have been the result of some childhood anemia because it coincides in my memory with a special drink that Father always prepared just for me—eggnog that he prepared with fresh milk, an egg, and spices that I had to drink daily to "build me up." Father called it "Gogol-Mogul" and mixed it with great relish, handing it to me with a broad smile to encourage me. "Here you are, Asinka, Gogol-Mogul, delicious Gogol-Mogul." Whatever it was, I thought it delicious and never needed encouragement to drink it, unlike the cod-liver oil.

All the people who were important in my life had a definite role. Father was the developer of my character, Aunt 'Lyena looked after my religious and moral development, and Kristina was a source of endless love and affection. Mother saw to overall planning and constantly added "aesthetic" touches, and all of our friends added a touch here and there to improve demeanor and appearance. Mother hosted weekly, relatively "formal" dinners that almost always included the same close friends, each of whom always kept me under close, constructive scrutiny:

General Mikhail Fedorovich Skorodumov was a very impressive man—an impeccable dresser, tall, broad-shouldered with jet-black hair graying at the temples, piercing dark eyes, a Roman profile, and upward curling mustache. He wore a leather strap device on his left hand, which commanded my utmost respect. I had no idea of its purpose, but Grandfather wore the same device in his portrait in our family album, and I was convinced that it signified a person of great importance.

A few years older than Father, General Skorodumov had seen service and combat in WWI fighting against Germany. At some point after the start of the Revolution, he joined General Wrangle's White Army in the Crimea. Perhaps he joined the mass emigration of Wrangle's followers from Ukraine in 1920 and came to Yugoslavia just as my parents had. All of our close family friends were known and addressed by me as Uncle or Aunt So-and-so or by their name and patronymic, a proper Russian form of address, but General Skorodumov was *always* addressed as General! General Skorodumov's influence on me was particularly memorable on two occasions. When I was about five, he brought me a particularly thoughtful gift on Easter, and about two years later he taught me a lesson, rather traumatically, at a special dinner held to welcome Mother home from a trip to America.

The General's younger brother, Nikolai Fedorovich Skorodumov, was just the opposite in appearance and demeanor. He too was tall and quite handsome, but carelessly casual, almost sloppy in dress, and totally negligent in manners. I was permitted to address him, more familiarly, as Uncle Kolya. Nikolai Fedorovich was an accomplished actor in Russian theater abroad.

Boris Stepankovsky had served with Father in the White Army, but was the antithesis of a soldier. Dyadya (Uncle) Borya was a very quiet, gentle, almost meek person, very artistic, with a slender build and gliding, graceful gait. He was always in our home. He was simply always there whenever I returned from school or running errands with Kristina. He often sat quietly for hours, doing embroidery, a hobby I believe he had adopted to help heal the traumas of war. Our calico cat, Triska, was always in his lap to have her ears rubbed endlessly. When Uncle Borya wished to return to his embroidery, he would simply drape the cloth over the cat and Triska would purr contentedly for hours. He had apparently seen enough fighting and bloodshed. He held absolutely no interest in war, revolution, counterrevolution, or the endless dreams and plans that preoccupied the majority of our Russian émigré circle. He had only two interests, his embroidery and lovely women. He seemed always to have a pretty young woman fluttering about him.

Baroness Andersen was an eccentric lady in her late eighties or early nineties. She had snow-white hair, always with a diadem of precious stones and topped with a black lace mantilla. Her mantilla extended over a corseted, heavy brocade blouse with pearl embroidery, fitted at the waist to meet a wide black hoop skirt, which seemed to hover above black slippers also adorned with pearls and semiprecious stones. Her carefully manicured hands were seen through mesh gloves that extended almost to her elbows. When greeting someone, she would extend the tips of her fingers, aloofly keeping the person at arm's length.

One of the most colorful of the stories that emanated from and about the Baroness was her claim that she remembered so fondly the time she bathed in champagne with Napoleon. I must have been about eight years old when I first heard her relate this tale to someone. I was advanced in school enough to know that Napoleon Bonaparte had ruled France and was defeated in Russia in 1814, and I simply dismissed what I heard as the eccentric foolishness of a very old woman. The Baroness was old, I thought, but not over 120. However, Napoleon's son, Napoleon III, ruled France from 1852 to 1870, and his son, Napoleon Eugene, was proclaimed Napoleon IV following the death of his father. He was soon exiled to England and died in 1879. The Baroness, who had also spent time living in England, probably would have been about nineteen or twenty when Napoleon III died—old enough for a liaison with either father or son—and she never indicated otherwise. The truth is now gone forever, as perhaps it should be.

Aunt Lyalya, a close friend of Mother's, was considered by most to be flirtatious and frivolous. In truth, she was simply and completely uninhibited in social situations. At that time she had divorced husband number four and was seriously looking for number five, which may be the reason I seem never to have known her full name. I was always excited to see her because she dressed in the latest styles, with bright colors and knee-length skirts. I thought she was an extremely warm, affectionate person. I could speak to her without curtsying and could hug her at any time. She was so very different from the stiff, correct, and impeccable characters of most of our friends. If anybody criticized her, she would immediately collapse in a dead faint, and someone would rush for the smelling salts to revive her. Lyalya was also my mother's favorite among all our friends. I'm certain that she felt both affection and admiration for Lyalya. I believe she secretly envied her uninhibited good nature.

All of the people who attended Mother's formal weekly dinners were close family friends who monitored my development as much as my parents. General and Mrs. Nazimov (Aunt Nadia) were the only family friends who had children, which probably explains why they did not always attend Mother's dinners. They are the only friends whose home I remember visiting with my parents. The General was a serious, solemn person, but far more approachable than General Skorodumov.

General Nazimov and Aunt Nadia had two sons, Kolya and Yura. Kolya was about five years older than I, and Yura was perhaps three years older. Both boys attended military school, a sort of prep school outside of Belgrade. The boys were always home on school holidays and spent a lot of time in our home, where they tolerated my company and agreed to play quiet games with me—but always at a price. Father had given me a copper and steel bank, which was kept on a table in the living room. All our friends would smile at me as they entered our home and drop in a coin or two, jokingly saying that it was for my dowry. Father, too, frequently dropped in coins with a wink and a smile and the same comment. I liked to jiggle the bank to listen to the coins inside. Father kept the key somewhere in his desk. The two boys felt that it was a chore for them to play the "childish" games that I favored and decided that they were entitled to compensation for their efforts.

"Kolya," I would say, "let's play Parcheesi."

"Wel-l-l," he would always reply slowly. "All right, but it will cost you money."

While Kolya kept watch for any approaching adults, Yura would use his pocket knife to jiggle coins from the bank. I don't know if Father ever wondered why the bank didn't fill as fast as he expected, but I was delighted to have someone around who was at least a bit closer to my own age.

My day always began when Kristina awakened me at 7:00, bathed and dressed me, and prepared my breakfast, which *always* included hot cocoa—a treat which, over the years, I would learn to truly dislike and which would play an unfortunate part in a later episode of my life. Weather permitting, after breakfast I went outside to the courtyard to skip on the cobblestones, listen to the birds, and look at the flowers.

At 9:00 I was called back into the house, usually greeting my parents as they were finishing their breakfast, to begin my lessons in reading, writing, and basic arithmetic. Home tutoring was central to my life beginning at age three. Two tutors, Volodya and Zhora, both university graduate students, came to the house five days a week.

Volodya, who I remember as a very mild and pleasant young man who had enormous patience with my often stubborn and uncooperative nature, arrived to begin my lessons at 9:00, while Zhora began at 10:45 each morning.

Zhora tutored me in the same subjects but entirely in French. After lunch each day I was expected to read a children's book in Russian, Serbian, or French and to write a brief report in both Russian and Serbian for Volodya and in French for Zhora.

It seems so strange to remember this today. Surely the childish scrawl that first year was meaningless to both my parents and tutors, but my memory is clear concerning the pride I felt in surrendering my scrawls for review. The benefit, of course, is that the process quickly became routine. I simply have no memory of ever being able to speak only one language. My formal lessons ended at noon except for three afternoons each week when Zhora returned to give me piano lessons. Mother insisted on the piano lessons. She frequently filled the house with music.

Every two weeks Volodya and Zhora would arrive together and polish the parquet floors by removing their shoes, placing soft cloths under their feet, and skating throughout the entire house. These parquet days were my favorites because while studying my lessons for both, I could listen to Volodya as he skated through the rooms and sang Russian folksongs. He had such a beautiful tenor voice.

> January 30, 1933: Adolf Hitler of the Nazi Party was elected chancellor of Germany; accepting the chancellorship, he announced the Third Reich, which he predicted would last 1,000 years, and gave orders that the Nazi swastika flag would be flown beside the German flag.
> March 22, 1933: The Nazi Party opened a soon-to-be infamous detention camp in the lovely south Bavarian village of Dachau.
> March 23, 1933: The Reichstag passed the Enabling Act, effectively granting dictatorial powers to Adolf Hitler. By July 14, 1933, all German political parties except the Nazi Party had been outlawed.

In 1933 a very close friend or a relative passed away, and Mother, Father, Aunt 'Lyena, and I went to church for the funeral. As was the custom in the Russian Orthodox Church, my parents approached the casket together; first Mother and then Father stepped to the dais and slowly bent to bestow a final kiss on the face of the lady who lay in the casket. Aunt 'Lyena helped me up to be face-to-face with the body. I looked at the lady lying in the casket, eyes closed, hands folded across her chest, looking as if she were peacefully sleeping.

Aunt 'Lyena gently pushed my head toward the figure and told me to kiss her. I placed my lips on her cheek, and a shudder went through me. Her cheek felt icy cold, damp, and the candlelight playing on her face made me think she moved. My face and lips felt clammy, and my whole body felt slimy cold as I cried out loudly. Father lifted me quickly from the dais and held me tightly against his warm chest. It was a terrible, frightening experience that I would never forget.

> October 17, 1933: A young German physicist named Albert Einstein, fleeing Nazi persecution of the Jews, arrived in the United States.

August 19, 1934: Berlin: A Plebiscite approved the vesting of "sole executive power" in Adolf Hitler.

The summers in Belgrade were extremely hot, and Mother automatically disappeared during the worst of the heat, going off to the Swiss Alps to find some relief for a few days. I was allowed to go with Kolya and Yura and their parents on all-day excursions to Gypsy Island. To get there we had to take a trolley to the Danube and then take a small boat to the island. The island itself was isolated and very large, or so it seemed to me. It had a large, sandy beach and was half pine groves and half swampy areas with lots of water lilies, cattails, and interesting wild flowers that could not be found in Belgrade itself—wonderful for exploring. Gypsy Island became a very important part of my childhood and adolescence.

TWO

School Days

At the age of six, in September 1935, I was enrolled in the first grade of the Russian Girls School operated within the Russkii Dom. With the start of school, ballet lessons were added and German was introduced to my home language instructions. At the same time, Mother began a home "language calendar"—a large calendar on which she wrote a language for each day of the week and hung on the wall in my room. A different language, Russian, Serbian, German, or French, was written in for each day, Monday through Friday. She made a game of it, with each of us—Mother, Father, Aunt 'Lyena, and me—required to speak only in the language of the day, and with a small forfeit or penalty to be paid by any of us who made a mistake by speaking in a different language.

There were always many laughs when someone, usually Father, used a Russian word in the middle of a conversation in French. Weekends were a family favorite. Everyone was free to mix words from any of the languages listed on the calendar in any sentence or conversation. I thought it was great fun, and it kept me on my toes. Father, of course, enjoyed the weekends the most.

September 15, 1935: The Nuremberg Laws adopted by the German

Reichstag deprived German Jews of citizenship and made the swastika the official symbol of Nazi Germany.

One day in 1935 I suddenly developed a sharp pain in my side that grew more intense. Kristina, concerned, made me lie down, but nothing seemed to help. By the time Mother and Father returned home, the pain had grown severe, and I lay doubled over on the bed, now perspiring and complaining of nausea. Mother and Father, obviously concerned, called a taxi to take me to our regular family doctor. The doctor immediately diagnosed appendicitis and instructed my parents to take me directly to the hospital where he would meet us. At the hospital, we were met at the door by a nurse with a small wheelchair, which Father placed me in before following the nurse to a room. Father lifted me onto the bed, and he and the nurse undressed me carefully, replacing my clothes with a hospital gown, while Mother looked on with a worried expression. Then Father looked directly into my eyes.

"Now, Asinka, the doctor has decided that you need a small operation to take away that pain that is bothering you. I'm going to take you down to the operating room, but I'm not allowed to go in with you. When we get there, the nurse will take you into the room and the doctor will be there waiting. He will be wearing a small white mask, but that's just part of his uniform that must be worn in the operating room. You know the doctor, and you know what a nice man he is. Most important, you must remember that there is nothing to be frightened of. Now look at my eyes. Look closely. Do you see yourself there? Of course you do. That's because you are a part of me, and I am a part of you. You must remember that you are a *Russian* and that you are *my* daughter, and you know that we Russians are never frightened of anything."

I looked carefully, and there I was, magically reflected in his eyes.

"Yes, Papa," I replied solemnly, no longer afraid. "I remember."

Suddenly the pain seemed to go away as Father lifted me from the bed, placed me in the wheelchair, and began to push the chair out of the room with the nurse in attendance. Father kissed the top of my head as we reached the door of the operating room, and the nurse took over to push me through the doors. I saw the doctor waiting in the mask just as Father had told me. He stood next to the operating table and looked at me kindly.

He said, "Hello, Anastasia. We are going to put you up on top of this table now. Are you a little frightened?"

"No, sir," I replied, rising from the chair and starting to climb up on the table. "I'm a Russian, you see."

The doctor stopped me until the nurse provided a step stool, and then allowed me to continue my climb, although now with a little help. He then explained that I would be awake during the operation, but that he was going to make sure that it didn't hurt. The spinal tap, of course, ensured that there was no pain, and the doctor held up my ruptured appendix in a little bottle for me to see when he had removed it. I drifted off to sleep soon after that, and when I awoke, it was to see myself reflected in Father's eyes as he bent over my bed, anxiously looking at me. In a week or two I returned to school, armed with a greater sense of who I was.

At the end of that first school year, Mother announced that I was to spend part of summer vacation at a place called Hopova. My summer of 1936 would set the tone for several summer vacations and would prove to be a source of many cherished memories. Father and I boarded a train in Belgrade for the relatively short trip.

The Fruska Gora, a hilly, wooded region between the Sava and Danube Rivers, is home to many monasteries dating from the 1690s. One of these monasteries, Hopova, was founded during that period and had become a convent operated by an order of Russian nuns who offered a summer program for Russian children. The Mother Superior during my summers at Hopova was Matushka (Little Mother) Varvara, a Russian princess who had entered the convent after losing her husband during the 1914–18 fighting.

Hopova was a large stone three-story structure with two single-story wings enclosing a cloistered courtyard. The first floor had a huge kitchen, a large dining hall, and an ancient chapel adorned with icons and frescoes. A squeaky wooden door led from the kitchen into a large garden—rows of vegetables in the center, surrounded by brilliant flowerbeds. Beyond the gardens a formally landscaped area provided a place for the nuns to walk and to meditate, the silence broken only by the exotic calls of the many peacocks that strolled throughout the lawns.

A short walk through orchards and small flowerbeds beyond this area led to a grotto—a large rock outcropping within which a niche held a glass-encased icon. Water continuously poured from a spout protruding from the rock face below the icon into a large stone basin. We were given strict instructions that this was a sacred place that was to be revered. We could drink from the grotto when thirsty, but were never to play with it or near it.

The second floor of the main building held Matushka Varvara's office and sleeping quarters, the tiny cells that were occupied by the nuns, and several rooms that held religious artifacts. The third floor was a dormitory, a long room with a wide center aisle and beds on each side. Dormer windows, which had deep sills providing wonderful perches from which to view the courtyard and grounds below, separated the girls' beds. A narrow, winding staircase led to the monastery's bell tower.

Next to the main entry to the dormitory, a raised platform held a small cot and a tiny table and chair where a nun remained during the night to watch over her sleeping charges. Above the nun's cot an icon hung on the wall just above a small shelf which held a flickering oil lamp. A candle lit the tiny table in front of the nun on duty and cast mysterious shadows on the wall. The girls watched and waited patiently for the nun's head to nod, when they would begin to whisper and giggle over the events of the day until the nun stirred and all would grow silent again.

The days in Hopova were glorious and carefree. We rose very early and dressed in native costumes—an ankle-length skirt of green, red, and dark blue plaid, a white cotton blouse with puffy sleeves, a matching plaid vest, and a matching plaid babushka-style kerchief. We formed a single, orderly line, hands folded reverently, and followed a nun as she led us into the chapel for morning prayers and then to the dining hall.

After breakfast we followed the nun back to the dormitory, where we folded and put away our plaid outfits and changed into play clothes. There were no rules for play clothes, just whatever had been brought from home. Then we were let loose to run and play anywhere except the vegetable garden and the grotto.

While there were always two nuns to supervise us, we were free to climb the trees, sing, yell, and run barefoot through the orchards—so completely different from what I was accustomed to. While I was a bit inhibited at first, I soon joined in. In no time at all I learned to love climbing trees and wandering, alone or with another girl, the many winding paths that meandered throughout the orchards and the small meadows and wooded areas that bordered the orchards and gardens. Those winding paths of Hopova early formed a love of solitude and nature that would help me through the many difficult times that lay ahead. We ate lunch at picnic tables and lay quietly on the grass after lunch, but then it was glorious, free, do-as-you-please time again.

At 3:30 the nuns assembled us at the picnic tables to quietly read the books each girl had brought from home. My parents packed fairy tales and storybooks in French, German, and Russian for me. We read until 5:00, when we returned to the dormitory, washed, changed back into our plaid outfits, filed into the chapel for evening prayers, and then to the dining hall for dinner at 6:00. After dinner, we were asked to write a brief report describing what we had read earlier that day. The report was always written in Russian, regardless of the language of the book, and a nun checked the grammar. By 8:00 we were all in bed, watching the shadow on the wall and waiting for the nun on duty to begin to nod off.

Aunt 'Lyena came to stay for a few days that first summer, and although she spent most of her time in the chapel or at the grotto, we spent some time together. I remember walking with her to the grotto where we prayed silently.

"Aaalways reeemeemmmber, Anochka," she said softly, "the grrrootto is a veeery hooly plaaace."

She explained that several miracles had occurred when ill people washed at the grotto spring and prayed to the Virgin Mary. I remember watching Aunt 'Lyena deep in prayer and wondering if she ever prayed for some cure for her own ailments or whether, as I knew was her habit, she prayed only for the well-being of others.

Toward the end of that summer I fell out of a tree while climbing in the orchard. Bruised, scraped, and shaken, I cried as one of the nuns gently cleaned my scrapes.

"Don't you think, Sister," I asked through my tears "that we should wash them at the grotto so that they will get better?"

"Who has told you such a thing?" she asked, frowning.

"My Aunt 'Lyena visits the grotto often to pray," I replied solemnly. "She told me that the Virgin Mary answers prayers and that some people have been cured there."

The look on her beautiful face softened.

"Well, it is true that the grotto is a very holy place and that miracles have happened in the past when people have prayed earnestly and truly believed in God's goodness. But the grotto is not for healing scrapes and bruises. You should always keep the memory of the grotto in your heart, and in the years ahead if you find yourself in deep despair, think of the grotto and remember it."

She smiled, hugged me warmly, told me that my bruises were the prettiest she had ever seen, and sent me back to play. The memory of that little nun's lovely face and tender words would remain with me throughout my life. That night I lay awake thinking long and hard, trying to discover "despair" in my life without really understanding the meaning of the word. I finally decided that I was free of despair and fell asleep watching the flickering candle and the peacefully nodding shadow of the nun on the wall of the dormitory.

In the turbulent years that followed, I would recall the nun's words often and wish with all my heart to return to Hopova, to be able to seek solace in its serenity and its peaceful grotto, but that was never to be. I would spend at least a part of each of the following three summers at Hopova, and my summers there remain among the most treasured memories of my childhood. Meanwhile, although I was blissfully unaware of them, world events kept advancing rapidly.

> November 1, 1936: Benito Mussolini, speaking in Milan, described a recently formed alliance between Italy and Adolf Hitler's Germany to be an "axis" extending from Rome to Berlin. From then on his words were used to define the "Axis Powers" as Germany and her allies during World War II.

Mother added English to my home tutoring at the start of the 1937 school year, filling the language calendar from Monday through Friday with English, French, German, Russian, and Serbian. Mother spoke each of these languages, in addition to Polish, Ukrainian, Greek, Spanish, and Italian. Unlike Father, she spoke each language fluently and with no discernible accent, and she expected the same of me.

In midwinter 1937, an open sore formed on Father's chest, and he was hospitalized and isolated, seen only through a hallway window into his room. His doctors stated that this apparently unknown bacterial infection did not respond to treatment. As soon as they determined that there was no danger of contagion, he was released from the hospital, but at home he continued to feel ill and seemed to have lost all of his old energy. There was no change throughout that year. I remember Aunt 'Lyena gently chiding him: "Vaaashaa deear, Yooou shouuuld baaathe that woound with the waaater at Hoopova. I knoooow thaat the Bleeesssed Mooother wiill heeelp, aand that God willl aaaansweeer your prraaayers."

> March 12, 1938, Anschluss: Nazi Wehrmacht troops entered Austria to "symbolize" the unification of the German populations of Austria and Germany. This constituted the annexation of Austria into greater Germany. Austria would cease to exist as an independent nation until late 1945, not to regain full sovereignty until 1955.

In July 1938 Father borrowed an automobile from someone and drove me to Hopova for my summer vacation. He was still not feeling well and had to keep the sore in the middle of his chest bandaged.

"I'm going to stay at Hopova tonight," he told me as we drove out of Belgrade. "I want to say a few prayers and bathe the sore on my chest with the water at the grotto. Aunt 'Lyena is convinced that it will help."

We met after breakfast the following morning, and he asked me to show him the grotto. I took his hand and led him along one of the winding paths that led to the grotto, where we knelt together before the icon at the spring. Father prayed while he removed the bandages. Kneeling beside him, I could see the sore—now over two inches in diameter in the center of his chest. It looked like a very bad burn, moist and raw in the center and bright red and swollen around the edges. He prayed as he scooped water from the pool to wash the wound. He repeated this three times and then rebandaged his chest.

"Does it hurt badly, Papa?"

"No, Asinka, it doesn't hurt, but it just gets bigger. It won't close up and heal as it should, and it has been over six months since it appeared. I'm sure it's nothing to worry about," he said, adding, "Everything is in order," his usual reassurance. "You concentrate on having a good time with the nuns and the other girls and enjoying this beautiful place."

My third summer at Hopova proved even happier than the first two. There were new girls to become acquainted with, and since I was now an "experienced" summer boarder, I could show them all the neat places and walks that I had already discovered. I felt a little odd, though. Although many other girls were my age, the books they brought from home, I noticed, were childish compared to the books I brought, which then tended to be classic tales or novels in French or German. Mother had recently given me a copy of *The Adventures of Tom Sawyer* in English, but I had not yet attempted to read that. Aunt 'Lyena visited a week or two after Father had left, and I accompanied her again to the grotto where we both knelt in prayer. This time I heard her mention Father's name in her prayers, and as I was reminded of his chest, I too prayed for him.

The summer passed as quickly as the previous summers had, and when it was time to return to Belgrade, I remember feeling a bit sad at leaving. I think I was beginning to mature a bit and to recognize those things in my life which were to be treasured. And I think I understood that Hopova was one of those treasures and that it would soon belong to the past.

> September 30, 1938: British prime minister Neville Chamberlain and the leaders of France and Italy signed an agreement with Adolf Hitler in Munich to permit Germany to annex a large portion of Czechoslovakia in exchange for a promise of peace. Chamberlain hailed the accomplishment as "peace in our time." Hitler broke the agreement eleven months later.
>
> November 9, 1938: Nazi gangs smashed, looted, and burned synagogues and Jewish-owned businesses and homes in Germany and Austria. It came to be known as Krystallnacht, a "night of broken glass."

As 1939 began, there was every promise of it becoming a wonderful year. The soft sounds of Mother's piano filled the house, Father's health was steadily improving, my studies both at home and at school were interesting, and I was doing exceptionally well. The friends who joined us for dinner brought lively conversation and frequent laughter. I knew at a very early age that I was to attend the Sorbonne in Paris and that Kolya Nazimov and I were expected to marry after we had both finished our education. However, in 1939 my childhood would come to an end. My whole world would begin to change dramatically and rapidly.

Family dinner conversations gradually became more and more concerned with political events. I knew that Germany had absorbed Austria in a vote held in March of the previous year, but I still did not fully understand the long-range implications. I knew also that a territorial dispute existed between Germany and Czechoslovakia until, I thought, it had been settled by a treaty in the previous November. No one seemed alarmed, but during dinner conversations there was concern that Germany appeared to be strong and belligerent and that events could possibly result in hostilities.

> March 14, 1939: The Republic of Czechoslovakia was dissolved as Nazi Germany prepared to occupy the country.
> April 7, 1939: Italy invaded Albania. Less than a week later, Italy annexed Albania.

By late spring the sore on Father's chest had disappeared without leaving any visible scar. Aunt 'Lyena was overjoyed, since she had urged him to visit the grotto at Hopova.

> June 4, 1939: The liner ss *St. Louis* carrying over nine hundred Jewish refugees from Germany was denied permission to dock in the United States.

I left for Hopova in July 1939 for the last time. Perhaps I already anticipated my "new life" in Gymnasia, but I did not climb the trees in the orchards or run carefree and heedlessly through the lush green meadows. The summer was cut short, signaling that the pages of my life were beginning to turn more rapidly. Father appeared at the end of the second week to pick me up, explaining that there were a great many preparations for Gymnasia that must be attended to.

For many students, the completion of elementary school would mark the end of their education. Gymnasia offered a progressive program providing four years of intensive studies in preparation for university admission. It was roughly comparable to completion of high school plus the first two years of college in the United States, and it was normally entered at age fourteen or fifteen after eight years of elementary school. "Double promotions" in elementary school were not uncommon during the 1930s, but my progress was unusual. With the advantage of intensive home tutoring beginning at age three, I would enter Gymnasia just before my eleventh birthday. I remember several serious discussions that led to my parents deciding that all my home tutoring had prepared me well scholastically and that I was much more mature than the average eleven-year-old.

My parents had decided on the more progressive Trécha Zhénska Gymnasia Kralitse Maria (Third Women's Gymnasia of Queen Maria) instead of the Russian Gymnasia, and I was particularly excited because of the uniforms. The girls at the Russian Gymnasia wore very drab uniforms—a dark brown dress to mid-calf, a black, full apron, black socks, and high black shoes. Trécha Zhénska girls, however, wore short, navy blue pleated skirts, a white satin blouse with Peter Pan collar, white knee socks, black patent shoes, and a navy blue cashmere beret. The beret was worn at all times and displayed three gold chevrons indicating Third Women's Gymnasia, and gold roman numerals below the chevron indicating the grade. I could hardly wait to attend that school—really, to wear that uniform.

When we arrived home, Mother explained that there were many things to do in preparation for the start of school and that she had many things to tell me.

"Are you excited about entering Gymnasia, Asinka?" Mother asked in English. I had noticed that she spoke to me now more often in English when we were alone. It seemed a bit odd to me, but my thoughts were occupied with entering Gymnasia. "Sit here on the sofa, Anochka," she began. "This is to be a big year with many changes in all our routines. But first, tell me—did you enjoy Hopovo this year?"

"Yes, Mama, but it wasn't the same. I thought that the other girls were just children this year."

"Of course. That's because you are growing up. You're going to begin Gymnasia in just a few weeks and that will bring changes and new responsibilities. You'll soon become a young lady. The girls you meet in Gymnasia are older and already behaving like young ladies. You will have to behave accordingly and to study hard."

It seemed to me that between school and my tutors I studied constantly, and the words "study hard" made me wonder a bit, but I was excited about what was beginning.

"Now," Mother continued, "we are going to have a very important visitor in a few days. This is a gentleman I have known for many years. You are to be on your very best behavior, and you might practice your curtsy a bit. His name is Umberto, Prince Umberto. He is the son of King Emanuel of Italy and is now the Crown Prince of Italy. He will be in Belgrade on state business for just a few days. I expect you to be a perfect lady when he visits."

August 23, 1939: Nazi Germany and the Soviet Union signed a nonaggression treaty.

The house became a whirlwind of activity. Kristina polished the samovar and all the silver until they shined as though they had never been used, and she devoted the rest of her time to baking very special pastries. The flurry of activity heightened my own sense of excitement. "A real prince," I thought, as I imagined a princely figure in royal robes, just like the pictures in my books.

On the day the prince was to visit, I sat quietly waiting for the doorbell to ring, refusing to move so that I might displace neither a bow nor a button. At long last the bell rang and a tall, dark, handsome man with a small, neat mustache entered. He wore a dark suit and a white stiff-collared shirt. He and Mother embraced warmly and exchanged greetings in French. Then Mother turned toward me and said, continuing in French, "Umberto, this is my daughter, Anastasia Vasilievna."

I was very surprised. That was the first time Mother had introduced me as "Anastasia Vasilievna" rather than Asinka, and it made me feel a foot taller. With all of Baroness Andersen's past criticisms in mind, I performed my very best curtsy and greeted the prince in French as he bowed gallantly in response, taking my hand and gently kissing my fingertips. I thought that I would faint.

The conversation was entirely in French as the three of us sat before the gleaming samovar, and Kristina appeared with her delicious pastries. I sat like a statue, speaking only when I was spoken to, as Mother and her friend reminisced about her visit to his family a long time before, occasionally breaking into Italian with a laugh. I watched closely and decided that he was as handsome as a prince should be, although disappointed that he dressed the same as everyone else. As he prepared to leave, he bowed again, but this time he kissed me on the cheek.

"Anastasia, you are a very lovely young lady," he said as I curtsied. "You make me wish that I was twenty-five years younger."

After dinner that evening I asked permission to play my phonograph.

Father had given it to me a year earlier, but I was allowed to play it only on special occasions. I had a small collection of records, including Russian songs by Alexander Vertinsky, then the rage among Russian émigrés, Beniamino Gigli, the Italian opera tenor, Tino Rossi, a popular Italian tenor, and even Spike Jones's "Cocktails for Two." I went to my room and played records by Tino Rossi singing Neapolitan love songs and dreamed of princes and palaces. After all, this was the first time a handsome man, a prince at that, had kissed my hand *and* my cheek.

THREE

War Clouds

The following day Mother entered the living room where I was seated, still dreaming of having been kissed by a *real prince*. She sat on a chair and announced that she had several things to tell me.

"First, Mrs. Ivanovich will be here tomorrow to take measurements and start sewing your new school uniforms. We have only a few weeks to get ready for school."

Mrs. Ivanovich was a very talented seamstress who made all our clothes. Mother, Aunt 'Lyena, and I never purchased clothes in a store.

Suddenly Mother began to cough. Just for an instant, I noticed what I thought were small flecks of blood on her handkerchief before she quickly moved it out of sight.

"Next, Volodia and Zhora have increased their university courses and will no longer be able to tutor you. I have found a very nice older English lady, Madame Spencer, who will come each day. She will teach English language, including grammar, as well as English literature and customs. You have done very well with foreign languages, but I think it is important now for you to strengthen your English language skills. You remember how important fluency in foreign languages is."

"Yes, Mama," I replied, thinking only of Gymnasia and my new uniform.

"Very well, and please remind Kristina that Madame Ivanovich will be here tomorrow morning."

Kristina's smile and blue eyes lit the kitchen as I ran for my usual hug and began to jabber excitedly about my new school and uniform.

"Kristina," I exclaimed in a rush, "can you believe it? I'm starting Gymnasia in just a few weeks. Have you seen Trécha Zhénska? It is so beautiful. And right across the street from Russkii Dom. And the uniforms are absolutely beautiful. I can't wait. Oh, I almost forgot. Mother asked me to remind you that Madame Ivanovich will be here tomorrow for my new uniform fitting."

"Hush," she laughed, hugging me tightly. "I haven't forgotten. Now you have a lot to do to get ready. Also, I think your Papa might have some news for you. Go and get washed and ready for dinner. Perhaps you should rest a bit before the guests arrive."

More news from Papa? I wondered for a moment what it might be, but soon forgot about it.

Aunt Lyalya joined us for dinner that evening, along with General Nazimov, Aunt Nadia, Kolya, and Yura. General Skorodumov was not present, and Father led the conversation.

"Well, we have some news for you all. We have purchased a very nice house in Dedinye and expect to move there quite soon. The land is a little higher in elevation, and it will be away from the traffic and crowding here in the city. The air is much fresher among trees and gardens, and I think it will be much better for Marusha. We hope it will ease her cough."

Everyone seemed very pleased by the news, but I was alarmed. Judging by the general reaction, they had known that my parents were considering a move, but the news caught me by surprise. Dedinye was a wooded, residential district, a suburb of Belgrade.

"But, Papa," I asked uncharacteristically, "what about Trécha Zhénska? I'm to start there in a few weeks."

All eyes turned toward me and then toward Father. Suddenly I realized that it was the first time I had ever spoken at the table without first being addressed. Father's look and tone put me at ease right away.

"Well, Asinka, Mother and I have discussed that, and we have decided that you are ready for a little extra responsibility. You will need to take a trolley every day to and from school. Do you think you will be able to manage?"

"Oh, yes, Papa. I'm sure that there will be no problems."

Father smiled in response as my mind raced—not only Gymnasia, not only Trécha Zhénska, but trolley rides all the way to Dedinye every day!

"Also," Father continued, "we have purchased some land in Yaintse, not much, but enough to build a small house and have a large garden. The political situation is worsening, and it will be a pleasant refuge."

The conversation continued excitedly before changing to political speculation, as my mind began to wander and race with dreams of Gymnasia, beautiful uniforms, and long, wonderful trolley rides.

Early the next morning Father led us to Yaintse to see the land that he and Mother had purchased. Yaintse was at that time a tiny farming village, located a short distance from Belgrade—a long but pleasant walk from the end of one of the trolley lines.

Our land was on the main road atop a small hill. A large garden area had been tilled where rows of vegetables were to be planted on each side of a wide center path already lined with dwarf fruit trees. The path led uphill, starting next to a farmhouse on the main road. A well had been started and already looked very deep. From back of our land, at the crest of the hill immediately behind and a little above the spot where the house was to be built, one could see the rooftops of Belgrade. A huge cornfield began just over the crest of the hill, bordered on the right by the local cemetery and a dark, mysterious forest.

"Well, Marusha, what do you think?" Father asked. "It's a pleasant spot, and the air is good. We already have the garden in, and the well is being dug. The house will be small, but I think we can make it comfortable. It is close to the city, but a safe distance away."

"Yes," Mother replied, "it is a pretty spot, but it seems such a big project."

"Perhaps not," Father said, "in view of current developments."

Father's response left me wondering what he meant by "current developments." Years later, I would marvel at the apparent wisdom of my parents, especially Father, and at the steps they took to try to protect us and many of our friends from the potential ravages of political uncertainty and war. I would enter Gymnasia in just a few weeks, but world political developments were something I never gave a thought to.

Within a few days Mrs. Ivanovich brought my beautiful new uniforms. The beret, socks, and shoes had already been purchased, and the arrival of the uniforms heightened my excitement. Mother, however, now began to cough violently, and I was certain that I noticed spots of blood on her handkerchief. She soon felt very weak and refused to eat anything. Father became alarmed and decided that she must go to a sanitarium in Switzerland. An excellent doctor there was an old friend of Mother's, and she and Father had great faith in his expertise. They planned to leave in just two days. It was a very confusing time for me.

Sadly for both Mother and me, my parents never explained to me the length and seriousness of Mother's illness and that her constant concern about contagion made her always keep me at arm's length. At just ten years old I simply failed to understand, and that failure began to build a wall between us that we would never bridge. I was heartbroken. I simply could not understand why their departure couldn't be postponed just a few days until school started or at least to go with me to register and to meet the headmistress before the official start of school. I was so excited about entering Gymnasia and wanted desperately for Mother to see me off that first day in my new uniform.

On the morning they left for Switzerland, Father hugged me tightly. Mother looked weak and very sad, but I was not allowed to hug or kiss her or even to come close to her. I waved sadly, tears flowing down my cheeks as they drove away, waving through the rear window of the taxi. The next morning, August 30, Uncle Borya appeared unexpectedly to take me to register at Trécha Zhénska. I dressed in my new uniform, and Kristina braided my hair, put my beret on my head, and announced that I was ready to go. Uncle Borya and I went to the main office to register and to meet the headmistress, who then introduced me to my new homeroom teacher, Miss Ljubica Visnic. I liked her immediately. She looked me over carefully, adjusted my beret, and nodded approval.

"Welcome to Trécha Zhénska, Anastasia. I think we shall get along splendidly, but you must always remember that it is an honor to wear the uniform of Trécha Zhénska. You must always behave like a lady."

"Yes, Miss Visnic."

At home I changed back into my regular clothes and hung my uniform out where I could see it. Looking at it on Friday morning I felt very grown-up but suddenly very sad and alone. My large porcelain doll sat on a chair looking back at me. I had named her Matryona when I received her, but I had never played with her much, and now I felt that she too was part of my past.

In my solitude my mind began to wander, wondering at the things spoken of around the dinner table—things I had not asked about. Germany had absorbed Austria and a part of Czechoslovakia, and I remembered Father saying that it would not be long before other Eastern European countries followed. I wondered what it was like to be at war.

I remembered that lovely little nun in Hopovo. I wondered if this was the "despair" that she had spoken of and wished that I could speak to her and visit the grotto. I looked around the room, my eyes misting as they settled on Matryona staring blankly back at me.

"Matryona," I sighed, "tell me that everything will be all right."

I reached to touch her cheek, and at the feel of the ice-cold porcelain, a shudder ran through my body. It felt just like the lady in the casket so long before, the feel of death itself. I ran from my room and practically flew into Kristina's room where I found her listening to the news on the radio. I buried my face in her warm bosom and began to cry with deep, jerky sobs as she held me tight, trying to hush me and concentrate on the news.

September 1, 1939: Nazi Germany invaded Poland, introducing something called Blitzkrieg (Lightning War), beginning World War II.

"Oh my little one, it does not look good, not good at all."

"What is it, Kristina? Are we going to have a war?"

"It isn't anything for you to worry about," she replied, lovingly mussing my hair. "Germany has invaded Poland, but Poland is very far away. Everything will be just fine here in Yugoslavia. Besides, your life is just beginning. You just look forward to your first year in that beautiful new school."

Sleep was slow in coming that night as I tried to picture what an invasion was, if it was the same as war, and if it would mean death for many soldiers.

The following day, Aunt 'Lyena and I went to evening church services to find the church filled to overflowing. Our priest said that we should all light extra candles and pray for the people of Poland and all the peoples of Europe.

September 3, 1939: England, obligated by treaty, declared war on Germany in response to the German invasion of Poland. France, similarly obligated, followed with its own declaration of war on Germany.

We had a very quiet dinner the next evening—just Aunt 'Lyena, Uncle Borya, and I. After dinner, Borya turned the radio on to hear the latest news.

"German panzer units are amassed at the outskirts of Warsaw," the announcer was saying. "The Red Army is continuing its advance on Poland from the east."

With a sigh, Borya reached to turn the radio off.

"Uncle Borya," I asked, "aren't German troops in Rumania already?"

"Rumania, Bulgaria, Czechoslovakia . . . "

"But that's so close to us. And aren't they in Albania as well?"

"Well, Italian troops are in Albania, but they are German allies, so one can say that, yes, the Germans are there, too."

"But . . . but that means they are all around us. Are we going to be in the war, too?"

"Well, aaall Euurooope is at waaar. Engggland declaared war oon Germaaany just this mooorning," Aunt 'Lyena said.

"Yes, Elyena Petrovna, it does look like all of Europe is at war. It's just a matter of time before we start to feel it."

"Uncle Borya, will Father come back before the war starts here. It will start here, won't it?"

"Yes, Asya, your father will come back soon. There is no way to know if the war will spread to Belgrade. But you shouldn't worry about the war. You have your whole life ahead of you. You're going to be so busy with Gymnasia."

His thoughts drifted off, but I didn't pursue it. I didn't want any more worries cluttering my mind than I already had. Will Father really come home soon? Will we have a war? What happens when nations are at war?

By Monday morning, September 4, the news had dampened my enthusiasm for Gymnasia. Miss Visnic explained that we were to remain in our homeroom for all sessions and that there would be a ten-minute break between classes. Our teachers would come to our homeroom, and all subjects would be taught there except for religion. Orthodox, Muslims, and Catholics would each report to a particular religion classroom, where they would be joined by girls of their faith from all other homerooms for religion class. She gave a lengthy speech about the conduct code we were to follow at all times, whether on school grounds or elsewhere, and reminded us that we were not to wear our uniforms without our berets.

"You are to behave as young ladies at all times," she concluded "and you are to remember that it is a *privilege* to be a student here at Trécha Zhénska Králitse Maria. You have the floor plans of the school in your packets and may now familiarize yourselves with the premises. Your classes will begin in the morning, and your schedule of class periods is included in your packet."

The girl seated next to me was at least a head taller, and we exchanged faint smiles. I noticed two smaller girls across the aisle. We exited the room two at a time to disperse. I joined the two smaller girls walking together to explore the building.

"Hello, my name is Asya."

"I'm Ljubica, and this is Jovanka. Are your parents going to pick you up, Asya?"

"No, they're in Switzerland. I'm going to walk home."

"Where do you live?"

"On Dr. Kester Street."

"We live only a few blocks from you. Let's walk together."

We went back to our homeroom, gathered our books, and left the school. Our route took us past the Palace and the Royal Gardens. The flowers were exceptionally bright under the blue autumn sky.

"Were you born in Belgrade, Asya?"

"Yes, and you?"

"Yes, but we aren't going to stay here forever. We're going to become big movie stars and travel all over the world. We're cousins," Ljubica said, "and my father makes movies."

"Movie stars? That would be exciting. I've never thought about what I want to become. My parents want me to go to the Sorbonne and study and study."

"But you have to speak French to go to the Sorbonne, you know."

"Oh, I already speak French, and German and English too. Well, I'm not too good in English yet, but I'm getting better."

"Let's speak only French outside of school, starting now," they said in unison.

The three of us switched to French, speaking louder than usual and happily giggling at the puzzled glances of people as they passed us. Ljubica stopped a man and asked in French for directions to Dr. Kester Street. The poor man struggled hard to understand and to give directions in Serbian that we could grasp. We thanked him very graciously and suppressed our giggles. We turned the corner, pulled off our berets, and collapsed on a bench in loud laughter.

Suddenly we stopped and looked at each other, becoming serious as we remembered Miss Visnic's admonition about our berets and her instruction "to always behave in a ladylike manner."

We looked around sheepishly to be sure no one was watching us. As we parted at Dr. Kester Street, we promised each other solemnly that we would *always* behave in a ladylike manner. There would be at least one other day of youthful exuberance in Gymnasia, and those two days have remained fondly in my memory.

I went to my room to begin looking over all my new textbooks—history of Serbia and the Balkans, geography, mathematics, Greek mythology, biology, and literature—six plus notebooks for each. No wonder my briefcase was so heavy, and I was to receive my religion text and notebook the following day.

I began to wonder how long each day was to be. I would attend classes each day from 8:00 a.m. to 3:50 p.m. with a lunch break. French and German were offered from 4:00 to 4:50 each day. I had been blocked from taking them because I was so advanced, but my language tutoring would begin as soon as I arrived home. Then, I realized, there would be two to three hours of homework to complete. I looked at Matryona, my big porcelain doll.

"You're lucky," I said. "You have all the time in the world to do nothing."

It seemed so strange to me that I had never played with her but lately found myself speaking to her.

"I wonder what Mama is doing right now, Matryona, and if she is feeling better."

I felt ashamed, remembering a recent lunch conversation with Lyalya.

"Mother just cares for her horses," I had said. "I think she cares more for her horses than she does for people."

"No, Asya, that isn't true," Lyalya had answered, reaching to cover my hand with hers on the table. "Your mother is a very caring person, always thinking of and caring for others. You should try to understand her. She loves solitude. She grew up always with a governess at hand, and her life was always rigidly scheduled, both at home at Kotchubeyevka and at school in Switzerland, with nearly every minute of every day carefully planned for her. The only time she had to herself was when she could ride her horse, always alone, through the steppes around Kotchubeyevka, and she grew to treasure that solitude. I suppose there is a wild streak in her, but it's different from, for instance, my wild streak." She laughed, pausing to light her cigarette in its gold holder.

Father returned from Switzerland in late September. I was in my room studying, with Priska curled around my desk lamp and purring gently, when a knock at the door startled us both. I opened the door to find Father, and Priska, upon seeing him, jumped off the desk and hid under the bed. She still remembered Mother's rules. Father looked tired from his journey.

"Papa, when did you get back? How is Mama?"

"Just now. How are you? Good heavens, Asinka, I do believe you've grown. And you are probably smarter, since it's already your second week of Gymnasia." He hugged me, smiling warmly. "Yes, you are growing. You're not my little puzik any longer.

"Now, you asked about Mama. She has had a very serious operation, and it will take her a long time to get completely well."

"Operation? What kind of operation?"

"Her left lung was removed. It was an acute case of tuberculosis, and the lung could not be saved."

"Will she be able to breathe all right with only one lung?"

"Yes, but she will have to be extra careful not to exert herself. Tell me about school. Do you like all of your teachers?"

"Yes, very much. I like all of my classes, but we have an awful lot to learn."

"I'm sure you'll do fine. I'm just sorry that I wasn't there for orientation and for your first day."

"It's all right, Papa. Uncle Borya was very nice when he took me. Besides, I could have done it by myself."

"Yes, I know. Sometimes I think you are growing up too fast. You're never with children your own age. Even in school you have always been placed with older children. I hope it wasn't a mistake." His thoughts seemed to drift, his blue eyes staring into space as a deep wrinkle appeared between his brows.

"Papa, I love you," I said simply.

He hugged me tightly. "I'm so very proud of you, Anochka. Mama and I love you very much." As he spoke, I felt a warm teardrop land on my head, tickling my scalp as it moved toward my forehead. "I haven't even unpacked yet, and I have to make a quick trip to Dedinye—a few details about the house. I probably won't be back before you go to bed, but we'll talk tomorrow after school. You'd better finish your homework now. Sleep well."

As he gently closed the door, Priska returned from under the bed and curled around the desk lamp again. In bed that night my mind raced— Mother's illness, my growing up "too fast," Father's tear on my head. Life suddenly seemed far more complicated than only a few months earlier. I thought again of my favorite nun in Hopova and wondered if I was being "burdened," as she had said, and if washing my face in the grotto would ease the heaviness I felt in my heart.

FOUR

Childhood Ends

When I returned from school the following day, Father met me at the door with a hug and kiss.

"Asya, Madame Spencer is here. You remember that Mother told you that Madame Spencer would be taking over your tutoring each day. You need to work out a schedule with her."

We walked together into the living room to find Madame Spencer seated on the sofa. A slender woman dressed in a white blouse with a high collar, long green skirt, and laced brown shoes, remained seated as we approached. Her graying hair was tightly tied in a bun, and her eyeglasses, suspended from a chain around her neck, rested on her ample bosom.

"Madame Spencer, this is my daughter, Anastasia. We call her Asya for short."

I curtsied and waited for her to extend her hand. Her hand remained in her lap, and her facial expression remained stony.

"How do you do, Madame Spencer."

"First," she replied, "I am not a 'Madame.' You may call me Miss Spencer or ma'am, and I shall call you Anastasia. Now where are we to study, and what is your school schedule?"

"Well, I'll leave you two ladies alone to work out your schedule," Father said, bowing as he left the room.

I took my school schedule from my briefcase and handed it to her, explaining that we could study here in the living room or in my room.

"I think your room would probably be more suitable, Anastasia."

We walked together to my room to find Priska curled around my desk lamp. As I walked over to the desk to move her, she leaped to the floor and ran from the room rather than just under the bed. Priska, I realized, did not want even to be in the same room with Madame—*Miss* Spencer! A comfortable, upholstered chair, which held Matryona, stood next to my desk, and a straight, wooden chair stood against the wall opposite my bed. I quickly exchanged the two chairs, placing the straight wooden chair next to the desk for Miss Spencer.

"Do you still play with dolls?" Miss Spencer asked.

"I have never played with dolls. Matryona and I just talk," I replied, getting at least a puzzled look in response.

"Well, let's review this schedule now."

She moved her glasses to her eyes and turned her head to look at the schedule. In profile, her thin nose looked even more pointed, and the tight bun in the back allowed a strand of gray hair to hang down to her shoulder and looked funny. I suppressed a smile as I watched her and felt a bit easier.

"Hmm, you arrive home each day about 4:00?"

"Yes, usually a little after 4:00."

"So if we meet from 5:00 to 6:30 every day, that would work. You don't have much time for homework, do you?"

"My bedtime is at 9:00 now, so there will be plenty of time for homework."

"You do understand that we will concentrate primarily on grammar. You will have grammatical exercises to do daily, and you will, of course, speak English with your parents."

"Yes, ma'am."

"Was your mother educated in England? She speaks such perfect English."

"Mother was educated in Lausanne."

"Well, if you just speak with your mother in English and do the grammar with me, you should thoroughly learn the language. Your father, of course, well, he does have a very strong Slavic accent."

I smiled in spite of myself. Poor Papa, no matter how hard he tried, whether he spoke in French, German, English, or even Serbian, he sounded unmistakably Russian.

"Very well then, since this is Friday, I shall leave now. We shall begin our studies on Monday at 5:00 p.m."

Miss Spencer rose, smoothed her skirt, removed her glasses, tucked the errant strand of hair back into her bun, raised her nose as if to sample the air, and, nodding to me, said, "Cheerio."

"Good day, ma'am," I replied.

"You are absolutely correct, Anastasia. A 'good day' is more appropriate. So then, good day to you."

I escorted her from the room, showed her to the front door, and ran to Kristina in the kitchen.

"Oh, Kristina, she has a witch's nose, and I think she really is a witch. Do you know that she didn't smile once? Even Priska ran away as soon as she saw her."

"I'm sure she's not a witch. She is probably very nice once you get to know her."

"But, Kristina, my day will end with *her* from now on—from 5:00 to 6:30 every day."

"Maybe you can start practicing the piano when she leaves. That way it will end with music. Besides, you haven't practiced in a long time."

"You should be glad. It wasn't music, just banging the same notes over and over. I hate that, too."

"My, my, you sure hate a lot of things today. What's the matter?"

She stopped whatever she was doing, sat down, and drew me to her, stroking my hair, and hugging me. Kristina's warmth and hugs were always comforting.

"My stomach hurts," I said. "Maybe that's why I hate everything."

"Where does it hurt?"

I pointed just below my ribcage.

"I'll fix some chamomile tea, and it will be all better."

The tea helped, and I went back to my room to look over my notebooks.

My homework was minimal and was quickly finished. I started to return to the living room, when I heard what sounded like sobs and sniffling from Aunt 'Lyena's room. I knocked on her door and, when she opened it, could see that she had been crying.

"May I come in?"

She smoothed her bed, and as we sat down, I put my arms around her.

"What's wrong, Aunt 'Lyena?"

She removed her glasses and wiped her tears, trying hard not to sob again.

"It's our faaaaamily. Your mother is soooo ill, your father so fillllled with wooorries and aaaalways gone . . . the war, and nooow we have a strange woooman raising you."

"Aunt 'Lyena, Mama will get better, and Papa is already home. And Miss Spencer isn't raising me, just giving me English lessons for an hour and a half."

"Poor Asinka. I shooouldn't haave toooold you all thiiis. Youuu aaare still a chiiild. Yooou have groooown soooo serious, but yoou shouldn't thiiink of waar. Juust tryyy toooo stay a chiiild as loong aaas youuu can."

We embraced and kissed, both crying as the sound of the doorbell interrupted us. We wiped each other's tears and embraced again as I left to answer the doorbell. Father had been seated in the living room and had already opened the door to admit Uncle Borya.

Borya settled in a chair as Father poured a glass of wine for each of them and began to discuss Mother's operation and her progress.

"Borya, you'll stay for dinner, of course," Father said. "Asya, I want to know how you like Madame Spencer. You can tell us all about it at dinner."

"Madame Spencer told me not to address her as "Madame" but as Miss Spencer or just ma'am."

"Well, that is more appropriate . . . and we have to talk about Dedinye."

"Borya," Father continued, "you know that we will be moving soon. Asinka, you're going to like it very much. It has a beautiful garden and a giant oak tree that's perfect for climbing. There is a fishpond on the terrace, and the whole house is covered with ivy. The air is so pure. It will be good for Mama."

"Won't it be much further from school for Asya?" Borya asked.

"Well, yes, it will probably take her thirty minutes."

"Will I be riding the trolley every day, Papa?"

"Yes, and it's a beautiful ride because the trolley goes through the woods, and the walk from the trolley to the house is also through some woods."

"I think I'm going to like that."

"What about the place in Yaintse?" Borya asked. "Are you planning to start building there?"

"Yes, we are, but it's on hold for a while. I want to wait and see how Marusha does when she comes home for Christmas. In the meantime, I think Dedinye will be good for her."

"When are we moving, Papa?"

"As soon as I can arrange everything. Perhaps in a few weeks."

Aunt 'Lyena sat listening but taking no part in the conversation. I noticed that she shook her head sadly in disapproval several times, but she remained silent throughout the meal.

"May I be excused, Papa? I'm tired, and I still want to look over my notes for school."

Once in my room, I quickly undressed. The water for my bath was already heating, and I bathed quickly, anxious to get into bed with time to think. I dreaded the thought of moving from Dr. Kester Street. It was the only home I had ever known, and I loved everything about it—the stenciled walls, the high ceilings, and wide french doors, the courtyards and the Italian street singers who seemed to appear two or three times each week. I had always been protected from change, and that was ending.

Word reached Father that the general he had served with had passed away, and he invited our regular friends to dinner in remembrance. The conversation turned as usual to the current conflict, and everyone grew silent and attentive as General Skorodumov spoke.

"What I can't reconcile is how any nation, particularly an intelligent, civilized nation like Germany, could endure an alliance with the Hooligans. I fought the Germans at the front in 1914 until I was wounded and unable to continue, but it was a fight between gentlemen based on principle. The Bolsheviks haven't an ounce of civic responsibility among them—no morals, no decency, no religious values!"

"I think what attracts other nations to them is their strength—just the vastness of the land itself and the enormous population." said General Nazimov.

"Perhaps like a small, frail boy makes a friend of a bully," Aunt Nadia added. "The bully may not have much going for him except for his size, but that would impress other boys who might pick on the frail one."

"I'm afraid it's not as simple as that," responded Skorodumov. "I'm afraid that someone has been boiling a kettle and not watching the fire. That kettle will boil over. I'm just thankful I have no children to worry about. You must be worried sick with two boys in the Cadet Academy."

"Certainly, I'm worried, but my boys aren't going anyplace to fight, war or no war."

"You are wrong," said her husband forcefully. "It is the duty of every man to defend his country in time of war. It's a matter of honor."

"But just look at what it has done to all you 'honorable' men," Aunt Nadia retorted. "You have no country. Your families have been killed off. We live in exile, dangling on a string, not knowing what tomorrow may bring. And you want our sons to go out and fight?"

"That's a chance every man must take. His honor is at stake."

"Oh, I just can't talk to you. You'll always be a general in your heart and in your mind, but they are my sons, too!"

Father noticed that the conversation between the Nazimovs had become heated, and he interrupted to propose a toast—his usual strategy for calming things.

"Let's drink to Maria's health, her speedy recovery, and her return home. I'm beginning to feel like a bachelor, and it's time for her to return and put the reins to me."

Everyone laughed, and the topic shifted from war to the relaxed conversation common among old and good friends. That was the last dinner on Dr. Kester Street with our friends.

One day in late October as the days were growing shorter, I returned from school to find Kristina busily filling boxes with pots and pans. I went from room to room only to find boxes already packed everywhere I looked. I rushed to Father and Mother's room to find her wardrobe empty, the wonderful smell of her perfume almost completely gone, and boxes neatly packed and stacked. The thought of leaving the house, the street, and the neighborhood that I loved and knew so well filled me with a sadness I had never felt before. Father told me that the move would be complete the following day and that he would meet me at school the next day for the first trolley trip to our new home.

FIVE

The Move to Dedinye

The following day Father was waiting just outside Trécha Zhénska, and we walked together to the trolley stop. Because of Mother's illness, this was the first time I would have an opportunity to see our new home or to take the trolley trip that was to become routine for me. We boarded a trolley at a stop quite close to Trécha Zhénska, and after about a fifteen-minute ride reached the outskirts of the city. There the trolley continued for about another ten or fifteen minutes through a parklike setting. It was simply beautiful. Birches, chestnuts, hazelnuts, and other varieties of trees were changing to autumn colors now in late October, and flowering shrubs and wildflowers filled the landscape on both sides of the track with no buildings in sight.

When we stepped off the trolley, Father pointed out two ways to walk to our new house: the regular paved road that went around the continuation of the wooded section we had just come through, or a pathway through the wooded section. The pathway was a short-cut to Shenoyna Street, through trees, shrubs, and wildflowers, with benches spaced along the way.

The house was located almost at the end of Shenoyna Street, adjacent to the Royal Estate, the White Palace, Prince Paul's residence until Prince Peter matured to ascend the throne. The Estate stood at the corner where

Shenoyna ended, intersected by another street, and was surrounded by a stone wall perhaps eight or ten feet high, which also formed the division between our land and the Royal Estate.

The stone wall of the Estate was built along the left property line of our land. A wrought iron fence crossed the front of our lot and continued up the right side and across the rear. The land was sloped, and the yard had been built in broad, terraced levels, the first about two feet above street level, the second about two feet higher. Both of these terraces held raised, brick flower beds that served as a retaining wall for the next level and were filled with bright chrysanthemums now in spectacular full color. The second terrace also held a fish pond with bright goldfish, a lovely gazebo, and the ancient oak tree that Father had told me would be perfect for climbing. The house itself seemed to form a third terrace, as the same brick planters had been built across the full width of the front of the house. The house and grounds were completely isolated, unlike our home on Dr. Kester Street.

The main entrance was reached by a wide flagstone walk and steps that rose from street level to each terrace and continued to a front porch extending across the front of the house. The new home had three bedrooms, two bathrooms, and the living room to the right as the home was entered; a dining room, kitchen, and Kristina's room to the left, and a central hall, interrupted by the entry foyer but connecting to all rooms, completed the main floor. Just past the door to Kristina's room, at the end of the central hallway, steps led down to a finished basement and Kristina's bathroom, or up to a very pleasant sunroom, which had large windows across three full sides. From the sunroom we could see over the stone wall that bordered the Royal Estate. The Palace could not be seen, but the gardens and grounds were lovely to view.

The furniture had all been put in place, but there were boxes everywhere waiting to be unpacked. Dear Kristina, she knew how I dreaded moving, and as I entered my new room I found that it had been all fixed up. Matryona was sitting in her usual chair, and all my clothes and books had been placed the same way I had them arranged at Dr. Kester Street. I hope I had the presence of mind to thank her.

Kristina fixed a very simple dinner of cold cuts, bread, and milk. Father and I went out to the front porch after dinner. The evening air was quite chilly but fresh and clean.

"Well, Anochka, do you think you are going to like it here?"

"Yes, Papa, I'm sure I will. It's very pretty and so very quiet. I think both Mama and Aunt 'Lyena will like that."

"Well, I think it will be very good for Mama. Dedinye is elevated, and we are surrounded by trees. The air is much fresher. I know the fresh air will be better for her and make it easier for her to breathe. At least I hope so."

"When will she be able to come home?"

"If everything goes well, I am going back to Switzerland to bring her to spend Christmas with us."

"Will she be staying home then?"

"No, the doctor didn't even want to let her come home for Christmas, but he thinks that if she stays no more than a week or two it will be good for her. He thinks that by the end of May she should be strong enough to remain at home with us."

I looked at Father, who was clearly worried. His eyes filled with tears as he put his arm around my shoulders.

"Come, Asinka, let's sit on the steps for a while. You're not cold, are you?"

"No, Papa," I replied, but I snuggled close to him in the chill evening air. We heard a train whistle somewhere in the distance. It was getting dark, and stars were beginning to appear.

"The stars look brighter here than on Dr. Kester."

"Yes, they are. There are no city lights to obstruct them. But my star is always bright. You are my starlight *and* my sunlight." Father hugged me and kissed the top of my head, brushing away his tears with the back of his hand.

"Oh, Papa, I love you so much."

"We should go inside, Anochka. It's getting cold and late. You have to get up earlier tomorrow morning. Everything is new to you. You don't know how long it will take to get to school from here."

"Oh, I know my way, Papa. I'll take the short-cut, the way we came today. It'll be fun."

"You're a good girl, Asya, already so mature, so self-sufficient. I never have to worry about you."

Back inside I stopped in Aunt 'Lyena's room. Although boxes remained on the floor, waiting to be unpacked, she had made certain that the corner shelf which held her icon and a small oil lamp had been put up. The flickering light of the oil lamp gave the whole room a soft, warm glow. Her Bible was lying open on her night table, next to the lamp. She had already been reading it. Her bed had been turned down and was ready for the night.

"Aunt 'Lyena," I asked, "when did you get the shelf put up?"

"As soooon as I entered myyy roooom. Thaaat's the mooost important thing. Yoooou should maaaake aaaa place for God as sooon as you ennnter the room. Isn't your Iiiiicon uuuup yet?"

"No, I guess they didn't have time to do it."

"How saaaad. People expect God to be there foooor them at aaaall times, and yet they doooon't have tiiiime to light a lamp for Him or puuut up an icon."

"I'm sure everybody was just so busy with boxes and furniture."

"Oh, Anochka, I hoooope that wheeen you grow up yoooou will nevvver forget to put God firrrrst and foooooremost in your liiiife."

I put both arms around Aunt 'Lyena and hugged her as tightly as I dared.

"I won't, Aunt 'Lyena, I promise. And I'll always remember what you have taught me—that my life is in God's hands and that He will always cradle me in His hands as long as I live according to his teachings."

"I hoooope so, Asinka. I hoooope so, my dear, and I'll alwaaaays pray for you and remiiind God that yoooou are sooo young and that he neeeeeds to hold yoooou securely in His haaaands."

"I love you, Aunt 'Lyena." We hugged, and I closed her door behind me.

It took about a week for the house to be placed in good order, but each day it looked cozier. The paintings were hung on the walls, and the rugs placed on the floors. Father purchased a new Persian carpet that covered almost the entire living room floor. The colors—dark red, blue, green, and beige—added so much warmth to the room. The french doors faced west, and the long white curtains and dark green drapes came alive in a light evening breeze and the rays of the setting sun. I walked into the room on the first day that the house was finished and noticed that Mother's grand piano had the lid down. I put it up, sat on the stool, and suddenly wished with all my heart that I could play as well as Mother. "Well," I thought, "someday I'll continue practicing, but for now . . . " The doorbell rang, and I glanced at my watch. It was 4:55 pm. I knew that it was Miss Spencer, and I went to open the door and to welcome her to our new home.

I don't know if it was my mellow mood, thinking of Mother and the beauty of the new living room, but as the lesson progressed, I was surprised that I no longer objected to drilling the *th* sound. Maybe I had grown wiser and decided that it was silly to resist her insistence on correct pronunciation. After all, I realized, that was the whole point of her lessons. Beginning early in my first year of Gymnasia, just about this time, I also made a conscious decision not to curtsy before anyone. That too had become childish. Instead I bowed my head very slightly when greeting an adult. I think attending the first year of Gymnasia made me feel much older and more mature.

The house was finally cleared of all the boxes, and everything looked as though we had always lived there. It was homier than our home on Dr. Kester. It was simpler to maintain an even heat, which would be good for Mother, although we all agreed that the radiators were a bit ugly and sometimes noisy. Priska arched her back and hissed several times at the strange noise coming from the radiators, but in a week or two she would learn to ignore it.

Life in Dedinye gradually became pleasantly routine. Unfortunately, our friends did not stop as often as before. It was far less convenient for most of them than Dr. Kester Street had been. Only Uncle Borya seemed to be in our home in Dedinye as often as he was at Dr. Kester. Triska would have been lost without him.

Father planned to leave on December 21 to bring Mother home. He went through the house several times to be absolutely sure that everything was as near perfect as he could make it.

"Asinka, do you think the house is all right? Is there anything else we should do to make it presentable for Mother?"

"No, Papa. Maybe some flowers would look nice, especially on her dresser."

"Oh, yes. Let's not forget. When Kristina goes to the market, she should get fresh flowers."

"When will you be back, Papa?"

"We should be back on the 26th."

"Oh, good, then you'll have time to get a Christmas tree when you return, and I'll be starting my vacation from school. We'll have almost two weeks to prepare, and maybe I can start working on decorations before you even get home."

"Too bad we won't have a big tree," Papa said. "The ceilings are much lower here and the rooms are not as large." He was looking around as he spoke and his voice trailed off, sounding almost apologetic, as though he were trying to explain to Mother why we would have only a small tree.

"Papa, it doesn't matter if we have a smaller tree."

"I know, I know. I just want everything to be pleasant and happy for her."

Papa walked to the french doors in the living room and stood for a moment looking out at the view of the front yard, and the wooded area beyond, across Shenoyna Street. He opened one of the doors, filling the room with the now brisk evening air.

"Oh, yes," he said, "I forgot to tell you. Borya will come tomorrow, and he'll be bringing a little black Scotty puppy. I was supposed to pick him up today, but I was too busy. I hope you'll like him. Mother always liked little Scotties. Well, goodnight. I'll be gone by the time you are up tomorrow."

Once in bed that night, Priska next to my legs purring and performing her nightly grooming, I laid awake thinking of how Father had tried so hard to make everything perfect for Mother's return. He loved her very much. She had been through so much in her life, and all her illnesses must have been very hard on both of them.

Strange, I thought. Mother is so very pretty, poised, a perfect lady in every respect . . . so athletic, yet she has contracted so many illnesses, while Aunt 'Lyena, who is so very plain in appearance, and so unathletic, so frail, seems never to have had a sick day in her life. Still she has the most beautiful soul I could imagine. Surely, God must have His reasons for arranging things the way He does. Maybe someday His plan will be clear.

My thoughts were interrupted as Priska began shaking the whole bed by intensively grooming herself.

"In a couple of days, Priska," I said, stroking her, "you'll have to scoot under the bed. Remember, Mother does not like you sleeping with me." Her gentle purring put me to sleep right away.

I had just returned from school the following day and started to work on some homework when the doorbell rang. Kristina opened the door, and Uncle Borya entered. He took the puppy from under his coat and placed him on the floor. The puppy immediately ran all over the house, sniffing everywhere. Kristina did not look happy about it. She wanted the house to be immaculate.

Suddenly we heard a piercing yelp, followed by hissing and a loud meow. The puppy was trying to run toward us while Priska was blocking his way, standing with her back arched and her hair standing up all over. Borya grabbed Priska and placed her on his lap, and the dog ran under the piano, still yelping. Kristina, mumbling to herself, went to get her new Hoover, convinced that the entire house was now full of dog hair.

The following few days were hectic for Kristina, as she baked and cleaned the house and kept peace between Priska and Scotty, the puppy's unofficial name while waiting for Mother to return and give him a proper name. It seemed as though her new Hoover was on before I left for school and still in use when I came home. Uncle Borya teased her.

"Kristina, you are going to wear out the new rug with that noisy machine. All the threads and colors will get pulled out."

"We moved here so that Madame would have fresh air. Well, what good does the fresh air on the outside do if the inside is full of dog hair?"

She sounded grumpy, but I think she had begun to enjoy the convenience of her new Hoover.

The day before Mother came home, Kristina must have bought out a whole flower shop. When I left for school the following morning, she had already placed fresh flowers everywhere. She kept Scotty locked in her room, afraid that Priska and he would get in a fight and knock down the vases.

I couldn't concentrate in school. I ran from the trolley stop, but as I approached the house, I slowed and almost tiptoed, afraid to disturb Mother. As I put my foot on the first step, she was there at the door to greet me. I ran up the steps and, without thinking, hugged her tightly until I felt her stiffen. I relaxed my grip, snuggling my head against her, realizing,

"Oh, that beautiful scent. Yes, Mother is really back." She gently embraced me, kissing the top of my head.

"You have grown, my little one." She spoke in French, then quickly changed to English. "Oh, I forgot. No more French, just English, right?" she added with a bright smile.

"Oh, Mama, it's so good to see you. How do you feel? Do you hurt? Was it very bad? Are you able to breathe all right with just one lung? Did you see the lung they removed? What did they do with it?"

"Oh, my, so many questions all in one breath. Your mother is getting dizzy just trying to remember all your questions," Father said in Russian, holding Mother's hand gently as we moved into the living room where she could sit down.

"Now," Mother began, "it does hurt just a little. No, it did not hurt during the operation since I was under ether, which was the worst part because I was so sick from the ether following the surgery. No, I did not see the lung, and I don't know what they did with it. Any other questions?"

She looked at me with that beautiful smile. I noticed now that she was very pale, her dark eyes even darker because of her pallor. Even her beautiful hand, now resting on my leg, looked pale and thin.

"Miss Spencer has done a good job. Your English has come along beautifully. Do you have a lesson this evening?"

"No," Papa interjected. "I told Miss Spencer that you would be coming home and that you and Asya would need some time together. And besides, you'll be speaking English with her."

"Oh, that's wonderful, Papa."

"Do I sense a slight dislike for Miss Spencer?" Mother asked.

"No, Mama, I like her fine. She has really helped me a lot. I think it's just that she never smiles."

"It's just the way of the English. They often come across as so very formal and dry."

We heard the samovar "sishing" in the dining room as Kristina brought in a tray of tea and pastries with a glass of milk for me. Aunt 'Lyena followed Kristina to join us for tea.

"Yoooou should reaaally have milk, toooo, Marusha," she said, looking at Mother with deep concern.

"I will, 'Lyena, but it seems that was all I had in the sanitarium—four times a day. The tea is a welcome change. Have you seen Sonya lately? How are she and Sergei doing?"

"Poooor Sooonya is driiinking even moooore than before. She is sooo cooonceeerned that the waaar may spread heeere to Belgrade. Offf course, thaaat could be juuust an exxxxcuse, too."

"I'm sure she is worried about the war spreading. Everyone is," Mother replied. "In Switzerland they too think Germany is unstoppable, that Germany is like an octopus, reaching for prey in all directions."

"Welll, we juuust haaave tooo praay haaarder."

"Don't you remember how hard you and I prayed when we were girls, and here we are, parents, country, all we had, gone."

"Yeeess, buuut wee haaave muuch to be thaankfuuul fooor. We aaare aaalive, and youuu haaave yoour own faaamily nooow, God muuust haaave had reeeasooons for uuus to go throoouuugh whaaat we did when weee were yooooung girls."

"Oh 'Lyena, I love you, You're such an optimist."

"Nooot an oooptimmiiist, Marusha deear. I juuust haaave faith iiin God and iiin his wisdoom and gooodness."

Mother rose and turned to kiss and embrace me, saying that she was tired and needed to rest a bit. Papa quickly moved to take her arm and went with her to their room. I went off to my own room to begin my homework.

I was overjoyed that Mother was home. She was so much more affectionate than her usual self. But she looked so pale, even more serious than usual, and I worried that all the talk about war again would sadden her and delay her recovery. I sat at my desk, poring over an open school book, but could not concentrate. I found myself again wondering what war was like.

Father had told me that he and his men often sat for days in wet, cold trenches waiting for an enemy attack. That they, in turn, had stormed enemy trenches, bayonets fixed, guns firing all about them as soldiers on both sides were mortally wounded or killed outright, neither side having time to bury their dead as they pursued the enemy or tried to escape an attack themselves. Is that how it would be with us? I wondered. But we have no guns. Would we have to dig trenches? Suddenly I felt very cold and moved to open the radiator valve all the way. The radiator clanked, bringing heat into the room, and I hurried to finish my homework to have as much time as possible free to be with Mother during vacation.

Over the next several days it was wonderful to walk through the house catching the faint scent of Mother's perfume in the air. It gave me a secure feeling. Everything was going to be all right. The lid was raised on the piano, and the soft music of Chopin and Schubert, Beethoven and Brahms filled the house. The only hint of trouble was when Mother went to the stables to check on her horses. She told us that she could not understand why Abdul acted up when she tried to ride him. Why she wasn't able to control him as she always had? Since she was still a bit weak, she decided to ride the gentle, even-tempered Silva and to let Abdul get a bit "more civilized."

"Maybe he has been cooped up too long," she told Father, who was already concerned about her trying to ride so soon. "But the groom who cares for him told me that he has not been able to control him either. He hasn't been able to ride him, and during the exercise walks Abdul behaves absolutely wildly."

"Well, he is pure Arabian and high-strung, and maybe he just missed you as much as we all did."

"Yes, you're probably right. He'll be fine when I come back to stay. Do you know when that will be?" she asked, looking like a little girl full of hope.

"The doctor said that if you follow his advice closely, he felt certain that the first of May would be a good time for you to return for good."

"Oh, yes, Mama, the first of May would be wonderful. All the trees and flowers will be blooming, and the birds will be singing everywhere. And I'm sure that the spring here in Dedinye will be extra beautiful."

"You know," Mother said, "it often saddened me when in the sanitarium patients spoke of other patients who had died, a number of them in the springtime. Everyone thought that must be such a sad time to die, just when nature comes alive. But I would like to die in springtime, when there is so much fresh beauty to console people."

"Mama, did a lot of people die in the sanitarium?"

"No, not while I was there. But let's not talk about morbid subjects. We should concentrate on making Christmas decorations."

Father had a tree brought to the house the following day, and all of us began making preparations for Orthodox Christmas on January 6. Aunt 'Lyena, Mother, and I began making ring chains out of brightly colored foil paper, and Kristina busied herself baking pastries and preparing kutya, a dish made of honey and poppy seeds, for the holidays. When Mother took a break, the house was filled with the soothing sound of her piano, and 1939 faded away without much notice on my part.

Aunt 'Lyena and I went to evening mass every night during the week before Christmas. Plans had already been made for one of Mother's usual dinners with all of our regular friends a few days after Christmas. It seems that all of them came, all of the "regulars," plus Aunt Nadia and General Nazimov. Kolya and Yura must have been busy with another school function. For some reason which I could not understand, I detected some restraint on the part of everyone. As usual, the conversation was in French, but it seemed subdued. It was the first time that I remember becoming aware of and concerned with the possibility of hostilities reaching Belgrade.

I was still not comfortable joining in the conversation, but I did pay close attention. The countries now mentioned in connection with the war— France, England, Italy, Spain, Greece, and Africa—left me almost dizzy. I pictured the map of Eastern Europe in my mind. All right, I thought, we border Italy, Austria, Hungary, Romania, and Bulgaria and down to the south Albania, Greece. But what do we have to do with these other countries? Why are we so consumed with the threat of war?"

"Asya," Lyalya's voice interrupted my thoughts, "you are so quiet today. How come?"

"I was just thinking."

"You're getting too serious since you started Gymnasia," Lyalya said.

"It wouldn't hurt young people to think of current events and to realize that our lives are changing daily," General Skorodumov interjected.

"But not for a young girl who doesn't yet understand the true meaning of life," Nicolai Fedorovich, the General's brother, said. "Let her live without worrying for a while. Let her go and chase butterflies for now."

"Believe it or not, life is not a theatrical stage. Life is not make-believe. I hope when you finally come down to earth, it won't be with a bang," the General retorted.

Everyone knew the two brothers were getting too serious. They could never see eye-to-eye. Father quickly rose.

"A toast," he said, "to returning to Russia and to all the beautiful women in the world." He looked around, smiling at Mother and the rest of the ladies.

"Thank God, you came up with a sensible toast, Vasya. I was already preparing for a faint," said Lyalya, but now in Russian, raising her wineglass and flashing one of her charming, coquettish smiles, to which all of the men bowed and lifted their glasses.

"Well, I happen to agree with the General," said General Nazimov forcefully. "I fully expect my sons to follow events very carefully and be prepared to defend their country."

"That is absolutely absurd," Aunt Nadia stated emphatically. "Exactly what country would you want them to defend? They are *Russian*. We have no country to defend. We had our chance in 1918, and we lost."

Aunt Nadia looked directly at her husband, who had never acknowledged that he was now just a civilian, an émigré without an army to command or a country to defend.

I noticed Father trying desperately to think up another toast, just as Baroness Andersen spoke up:

"Is there a war? I just want to go home to Russia. I wonder if my servants are waiting for me?"

"Dear Baroness," said Uncle Borya, rising quickly to offer an elegant bow. "Dear Baroness, there is no war in Russia, and I am sure all your servants are waiting with champagne and caviar."

"Well, I hope so, and you, my dear Borya, are cordially invited to my soiree."

"Thank you, Baroness," replied Borya with another bow.

I watched Lyalya as she rolled her eyes, sent a large puff of smoke toward the ceiling, and smiled at the Baroness across the table.

Mother was very quiet and looked relieved when the samovar was placed in the middle of the table and Kristina brought a tray of pastries. The aroma of freshly ground Turkish coffee filled the room as Kristina ground the beans with a long brass grinder, brewed the coffee, and served it in tiny demitasse cups with sugar cubes. I was allowed barely half a cup, just enough to be soaked up in three cubes of sugar. It was very rare that my parents would allow that, and when they did, I felt very special—and quite sophisticated. General Skorodumov almost spoiled it as he watched, shaking his head as he saw me dip the first cube.

"That's not good for you, Asya. It would be better for you to chase butterflies as my brother suggested than to take that poison."

"Oh, leave the girl alone. You're just old and cranky, General. Why don't you go off and form an army someplace," Lyalya stated.

This was the only time I saw Lyalya genuinely aggravated, and she put her arm around my shoulders and kissed my cheek. Her sharp comment would prove sadly prophetic within another year or two. Everyone moved into the living room as the coffee was finished.

"Will you play some Chopin for us, Maria?" the Baroness asked as she plopped onto the couch, her skirts taking up most of it.

"I am very sorry," Mother replied, "but I'm so very tired. Perhaps some other day, Baroness?"

"Well, you too are most welcome at my soiree, and perhaps you can play there."

Lyalya's eyes rolled to follow a large puff of smoke she blew toward the ceiling as she said with a great sigh, "Baroness, let me help you off this couch. It's so soft you'll never get up by yourself."

"And who are you? I don't want to get up just now. Maria is going to play a little Chopin for us."

"No, Baroness, she is going to play at your soiree, remember? And we'll all come and have a wonderful evening. But now we must go."

Wonderful Aunt Lyalya, she saw that Mother was exhausted and made the first effort to get everyone moving. The embraces from each of our friends were almost too much for Mother. She stood holding on to the piano, and in her smile I could see that she was exhausted and relieved that the evening was coming to a close.

That evening was the last formal dinner with all our close friends that I remember—the last time that all of our friends would be gathered together. It wasn't a normally pleasant evening, not the relaxing conversation that everyone was so accustomed to. Everyone had seemed on edge. The war talk was stressful and very frightening. I suddenly wished that it was summer and that I *could* chase butterflies and find a secluded place on cool grass in the woods to lie quietly and watch puffy white clouds form mysterious shapes to enhance my fantasies.

Mother seemed to be looking forward to her return to the sanitarium. Perhaps, I thought, it hadn't been wise for her to come for a visit. She looked very tired and pale. Her first few days at home she had been relaxed and cheerful, but her experience with Abdul had upset her, and the last dinner with our friends had been very trying for her. I believe that all the talk of war upset her terribly. Her memories of Kotchubeyevka, her own experiences, and her concern for her present family added to her distress. The evening before Mother was to leave, she came to my room.

"I wanted to say good-bye now, because you'll be in school when Papa and I leave tomorrow."

As she sat on my bed, Priska lay curled around the lamp on my desk, and I quickly sat at the desk trying to block her view of the cat.

"Sit here, Anochka," she said, patting the bed. "You don't have to hide her."

"Yes, Mama. Do you like the little Scotty that Papa got for us?"

"Yes, but I didn't have a chance to get to know him or even to give him a proper name. Priska doesn't seem too fond of him. I'm not wild about him either, to be truthful. But I don't want to talk about the dog. How are you doing? It hasn't been much fun for you: new school, moving to a new home, and me being away so much."

"I'm fine, Mama. I'm very busy, but I love school. I just miss you."

She put her arms around me, and I snuggled close, inhaling her perfume. How I wanted to just squeeze her hard and kiss her, but she was so frail. She hugged and kissed me. She was so much more affectionate than I remembered her ever being, and I didn't want to let her go.

"I am so very proud of you, Anochka. You are doing so well in school and exceptionally well with your languages. You do remember that knowledge of other languages is very important. I'm not insisting on your piano lessons. You can always pick them up again later. The world is changing fast, and we live in such uncertain times that knowledge of other languages is like a safety net. You'll never go hungry if you are fluent in other languages."

"I remember, Mama. Is that why you learned foreign languages when you were a girl?"

"Well, it was a bit different with me. When I was growing up, young ladies were simply expected to know at least two other languages."

"I wish I could see Kotchubeyevka."

"Someday we might all go back. At least we can hope for that. But we don't know what the future will bring. Right now Europe is in such turmoil. Oh, God, I am so tired. I don't think I could cope very well with another war. Above all, I don't want you to get caught up in a war. Let's just hope and pray that it will all turn out all right."

"Mama, is war really terrible?"

"Yes, it is, but you shouldn't trouble yourself with these thoughts. Let me hug you hard enough to last until we see each other again in May."

As I tried to sleep that night, my mind was racing. This was the first time I felt Mother had really shown love and affection for me—the first time I could remember being permitted to hug and kiss her. The thought that fear of contagion might have forced her to keep me at a distance in the past never occurred to me. She had been so gentle; her eyes had shown so much tenderness, love, and sadness at the same time that I was just grateful.

It was also the first time that Mother allowed me to see her deep concern about the political situation in Europe and the possibility of war extending to us. Just recognizing her concern was worrisome. And why did General Nazimov say that he wanted his sons to defend "our" country? That thought was a bit frightening.

Christmas vacation ended the following day. I submitted the home assignments that I had completed over the break, and when they were returned I found that for the first time five points had been taken off my grade. I had dated the paper December 1939, when I had completed it, instead of January 1940, when it was due.

"Your assignments were done extremely well as usual," Miss Visnic said, "but you did not pay attention to the correct dates. I have noticed, as have other teachers, that you don't seem to be paying attention as well lately. Is anything bothering you?"

Miss Visnic looked concerned but very stern.

"No, nothing is bothering me. I *am* sorry I overlooked the date."

"Is your mother feeling better? When do you expect her to come home to stay?"

"Mother left this morning. We expect her to return in early May."

"It must be very hard on you and your family. I hope that the spring will bring only good news for you. I am sorry about the points, but you know that we demand the highest performance."

"Yes, Miss Visnic, and I'm sorry about the dates."

SIX

Life in Dedinye

Father returned from Switzerland a few days later, and life both at school and at home, as well as my tutoring with Miss Spencer, returned to normal. Our friends stopped by occasionally to inquire about Mother, and Uncle Borya was with us as much as ever. Kristina planted flower seeds in the brick terraces. The weather warmed, and the days grew longer. I enjoyed walking to and from the trolley stop more and more because as I lightly kicked at the leaves looking for beetles, tiny green sprigs began to appear, and it seemed that each day there were more of them.

We made frequent trips to Yaintse to check on the progress there. Father was upset because we had still not found fresh water, and he was delaying the start of construction of the house until water became readily available. Although the well had already been dug quite deep, no water had been reached, and he grew concerned.

Father now seemed to spend more of his evenings at Russkii Dom. He never discussed the reason. It was obvious to me that most of the Russian émigré community gathered nearly every evening for meetings, but the frequency of meetings did not alarm me because the community social life also seemed to be much more active. There seemed to be many more plays, concerts, and ballets, but perhaps because I was now attending

Gymnasia and beginning to mature a bit, or because he felt that the social events would provide some distraction from worrying about Mother, Father simply took me more often.

In any case, I enjoyed each event. When I attended a ballet or concert, I secretly imagined myself a prima ballerina or a concert pianist, and I genuinely regretted that I no longer continued with ballet or piano lessons. I had resisted the piano lessons so much that I had been relieved when Mother stopped pressing me to continue, but I was sorry for that childish foolishness.

In late March, Father was contacted by Mother's doctor to say that because of the worsening political situation, it would be wise to bring Mother home early. Medically, he felt that she was strong enough to return, and being with her family would be beneficial. He was concerned that political developments could cut her off from us, and *that* would be detrimental to her health. Father was concerned about taking her away from the excellent medical care she was receiving but equally worried that German advances might trap her in the middle of the chaos plaguing Europe.

Mother returned to us in the second week of April. When she arrived, the weather was warm, in the low 70s, and spring was bursting everywhere. She was completely relaxed and enjoyed reading in the little gazebo and in the sunroom that overlooked the grounds of the White Palace, where I often joined her. Best of all was the music that was once again heard throughout the house as she resumed her love of the piano.

The only dark spot was early evening. Mother and Father now listened intently to the radio news broadcasts. Only a few days before Mother left the sanitarium, Germany had invaded Norway, Denmark had surrendered to the Germans, and now, in early May, Holland, Belgium, and Luxembourg were in German hands. The dark cloud that hung over Europe was spreading and becoming ever more threatening.

May 10, 1940: In London, British prime minister Neville Chamberlain resigned.

May 22, 1940: In his first speech as prime minister, Winston Churchill told the British House of Commons, "I have nothing to offer but blood, toil, sweat, and tears."

May 26, 1940: Evacuation of British troops from Dunkirk began as hundreds of small, private fishing boats joined the effort to cross the Channel, rescue the troops from the beaches of Dunkirk, and return them safely to England.

Mother's strength returned rapidly, and by late May she was determined to resume visiting the stables and riding. She was relaxed and happy again; however, her personal happiness was soon to be shattered. Father and I went with her on her first trip to the stables. Before even entering the stable we could hear Abdul rearing wildly and making a noise I had never heard before, almost as if he were snarling.

Mother approached him very gently, but he began foaming at the mouth, rearing high and kicking the walls of his stall. I was petrified and ran from the stable. Mother and Father came outside shortly, and soon the Kalmik groom, the only person Mother would trust with her horses, brought Silva out to her, saddled and ready to ride.

When Mother had ridden off, Father called the groom aside.

"The veterinarian has examined Abdul several times now," the groom explained. "He can find nothing physically wrong with him, but I'm no longer able to take him for his regular exercise in the ring or even to enter his stall on most days. No one here at the stables will go near him. Madame must be very cautious around him."

Mother soon returned from riding Silva, but on our return trip home, she was distressed about Abdul.

"You must be very careful, Marusha," Father told her. "You should not even enter his stall. Even the groom is concerned."

She understood Father's concern, but replied, "How can I not ride him? I've loved Abdul since he was a yearling. I might as well stop riding all together. I know he'll come around. He just missed me, as you suggested before. He'll come around."

She went several times to the stable until one day about two weeks later when she returned, pale and badly frightened. The left shoulder of her riding jacket had been completely torn off where Abdul had bitten her. She was holding her riding helmet, which had been trampled.

"He was going to kill me. He wanted to kill me. I know. I felt it."

Mother was in tears as she called the vet to explain what had happened. Her shoulder had been badly bruised and had begun to swell. Father insisted that she see the doctor. Luckily, nothing had been broken, but she had to apply compresses to bring the swelling down. The bruise was terrible to see—green, black, and purple—and spread over her back and chest.

Within a few days the veterinarian visited the house to tell Mother that Abdul had to be destroyed. "He has gone mad, and nothing can be done for him. He now presents a mortal danger to everyone around him."

"How can this be?" Mother asked. "I'm the only person who has ridden and cared for him. I've had him since he was a colt, before he first began his training."

She looked at Father, tears now streaming down her face.

"You have to do something," she pleaded. "You can't let them kill Abdul. Please *do* something."

Father felt helpless. No matter how hard he tried to explain the danger to her life and to others, she could not, or would not, listen to any reasoning. Throughout the night I could hear them talking, Father explaining and consoling, Mother sobbing. The following day when I returned from school, Father told me that Mother had gone to the stables with the vet and that she would stay with Abdul for a couple of days.

"Papa, does Abdul really have to be destroyed?"

"I'm afraid so, Asinka, but I'm most concerned about what it will do to your mother."

When Mother returned, my heart ached for her. She looked absolutely devastated and cried for days. Gradually I learned that she had not allowed anyone to touch Abdul.

"If he must be destroyed, then it is my responsibility, no one else's."

She refused to allow anybody else to come near Abdul. After sitting for hours outside his stall and witnessing his mad and tormented behavior, she finally agreed with the vet. The vet told us that Mother had borrowed his pistol. As she approached the stall, Abdul quieted, his ears moving as though he was listening for the sound of Mother's voice. He approached the gate snorting gently. Mother kissed him, took two steps back, raised the gun, and fired at his head. As Abdul fell, she entered his stall and remained there for hours, inconsolable. The vet and the groom had left her alone in the stall to give her a little private time with her beloved Abdul. Her feelings and affection for the horse were well known throughout the stables.

When I heard the story, I cried. Abdul had always terrified me, but he was such a beautiful animal, and it was very sad to think of his life ended, especially like this. I remembered my trips to the stables with Mother several years earlier, remembered how he had always approached her when the groom brought him out to her, how he always bowed his head just long enough for her to gently rub his forehead before he started rearing and prancing nervously, impatient for Mother to mount and to be off. And I knew that his end had been just like that. He approached and lowered his head just for a few seconds, just long enough to receive one single, fatal bullet from the only human he had ever trusted. It was a terrible picture. I put it out of my mind as quickly as possible, realizing how devastating it must have been for Mother.

Abdul's name was never mentioned again by anyone in the family nor by any of our friends. The sorrow in Mother's eyes was evident and would continue so for weeks. Years later, remembering this event, I would marvel at the inner strength it must have taken for her to act as she did—to refuse to allow anyone else to do what she believed was her responsibility alone but which was certainly the most difficult thing she had ever undertaken. Unfortunately, the event seemed to resurrect Mother's reserve. She began to pull back into herself. The affectionate, caring manner and softness that I had welcomed so much when she returned from the sanitarium slowly disappeared.

Within just a few days, I finished my first year of Gymnasia and received, along with my final grades and report, my coveted Roman Numeral II to be sewn onto my beret for the return to school in the fall. No longer, I realized, would I have to fold the beret just right in order to hide the I, which proclaimed to the world my lowly status as a "beginning student."

June 10, 1940: Italy declared war on France and Britain; Canada declared war on Italy.

June 14, 1940: German troops entered Paris. Germany opened Auschwitz Concentration Camp in occupied Poland.

June 17, 1940: France asked Germany for terms of surrender.

As summer began, I spent most of my time at Gypsy Island, swimming and exploring. I saw Kolya and Yura and many of their schoolmates almost daily. As the summer progressed, Russkii Dom began offering classes in first aid, which I attended with Mother. We all cut and rolled what seemed like miles of bandages and transferred iodine from large bottles into two-ounce bottles. We made up first aid kits of bandages, cotton, gauze, aspirin, iodine, and razor blades.

There was something obviously in the air—not necessarily alarm, but a strong sense of urgency that I could feel but not comprehend. The discussions I heard during first aid classes focused my attention on the concerns for the war that everybody was feeling. Each day there were new broadcasts from the OKW (Oberkommando der Wehrmacht), the official Nazi source for radio news broadcasts. It was the news broadcasts of the OKW and the BBC (British Broadcasting Corporation) that held everyone's attention.

It was impossible to avoid the war concerns that were becoming so widespread. Oddly enough, I had not encountered much discussion of the war in school, but now, during the summer months, it seemed all around me. Of course, the classes and activities at Russkii Dom put me in the company of adults, but even at Gypsy Island, Kolya and Yura and their classmates were more subdued.

July 10, 1940: The Battle of Britain began, as the Royal Air Force mounted a determined, continuing, and successful defense of Britain against systematic German bombing of southern England.

Mother never completely recovered from the loss of Abdul, and she rode Silva much less frequently. She disliked the hot weather, had always suffered from it—perhaps even more since her operation—and she had frequently sought relief from the summer heat by riding Abdul. Father spent most evenings at Russkii Dom, involved in meetings that always seemed to leave him in a somber mood. Mother and I continued to attend first aid classes, and in late summer each family received a first aid kit to be kept in their home. Later that winter Russkii Dom offered gas masks to families. OKW and BBC reports gradually replaced the tranquility and piano music in our home.

One day in late summer, my parents called me in from where I sat reading on the terrace to tell me that I should get all of my English gramophone records together, including my favorite, "Cocktails for Two" by the American band leader Spike Jones. We broke them all into small pieces, and

Father burned them. My Russian, French, German, and Italian records I was allowed to keep.

"Why am I studying so hard to learn English, but cannot keep my English language records?" I asked Father.

"It's very hard to explain. We don't know exactly what lies ahead, but for the moment, we think it's the wisest thing to do. I'm sorry, Asinka. But one day you'll understand."

> August 20, 1940: Prime Minister Winston Churchill spoke to his nation paying tribute to the British Royal Air Force in their success defending Britain from constant German bombing raids to famously say, "Never in the field of human conflict was so much owed by so many to so few."
>
> September 16, 1940: President Franklin D. Roosevelt signed the Selective Training and Service Act, which established the first peacetime military draft in U.S. history.

SEVEN

Adolescence Ends

September 27, 1940: The Tripartite Act, also called the Axis Pact, was signed in Berlin, formalizing an agreement between Germany, Italy, and Japan, committing them to cooperate in efforts to establish a "new order" of things and to assist one another with all political, economic, and military means.

The days were still August hot, and while the evenings were becoming cooler, it was the resumption of classes at Trécha Zhénska in September that heralded the official end of summer vacation for me. I very proudly displayed the II on my beret. What a difference. The previous year I had taken great pains to fold the beret "just so" in order to hide the Roman I. This year I took great pains to be certain there was *no* fold that might in any way obscure the II. It was good to see all the girls in school again. They all seemed quieter, more grown-up— or was it me? I would be forced to recognize, a few weeks hence during a second brief burst of youthful exuberance, that it was not me.

On a lovely, warm day in late October, similar to what I learned many years later would be called Indian Summer in New England, my friends

Ljubica and Jovanka and I left school to walk together to a more distant trolley stop rather than taking the trolley right away on such a beautiful day. We were all so proud that we now had the Roman II on our berets, despite the fact that there were girls who had III or IV on their berets. We decided that they looked much older than we did, anyway.

They did look pretty sophisticated. The oldest girls wore lipstick, and their skirts were longer. I didn't understand why, but the skirts in classes I, II, and III were very short—perhaps two inches above the knee. The skirts for class IV were two inches *below* the knee. So, we reasoned, even if the girls in the lower classes continued to try to hide their roman numerals, the skirt length would give them away.

We seemed to be in a silly mood. Perhaps the warm weather, similar to a spring day, affected us, but as we walked past the Winter Palace, I stopped, looked at the other two girls, and said very seriously.

"Remember your uniforms, girls. We are to behave like Young Ladies both in and out of school at all times."

As if on command, the three of us tossed our briefcases on the sidewalk and snatched off our berets. I tossed mine into the air, jumping high to catch it, as the others tossed their berets as well, the three of us laughing hysterically. As we caught our berets, we put them on backwards, and sat, or rather collapsed, on the foundation wall of the gilded, wrought iron fence in front of the Palace. We parted at a trolley stop, still laughing, feeling pretty good about not being "perfect young ladies."

October 29, 1940: Number 158 was drawn in the lottery for the United States' first peacetime military draft.

Our teachers still did not discuss political events in class. Our religion class was the only exception. The Orthodox priest who conducted the class placed much greater emphasis on the need to "strengthen our faith" during these "troubled times" and to stress that it was our "faith in God" that would carry us through the "rough waters" that lay ahead. I really enjoyed our religion classes. Those classes, Aunt 'Lyena's deep faith, and our regular attendance at Saturday evening vespers and weekly Sunday Mass all combined to give me a greater sense of security. The other girls, however, did seem worried about events taking place all over Europe and about political movements in Belgrade. We gathered under the huge oak in the enclosed courtyard during recesses and talked about what we had heard on the radio and from the discussions of our parents.

November 14, 1940: German bombers, flying across the English Channel, destroyed most of Coventry, England.

November 15, 1940: In the United States, 75,000 men were called to serve in the armed forces under the first peacetime draft in U.S. history.

Father stayed extremely busy throughout the autumn trying to get all the materials ready to start construction of the house in Yaintse. Although the well had now been dug very deep, they still had not reached water, and that weighed on his mind and added to his worries as work started on the foundations. There was a sense of urgency as Father, several friends, and some local workers from Yaintse worked every day on the house. I think I knew instinctively that Father's sense of urgency stemmed from his concern about the war and political events, but I didn't make a conscious connection.

Mother had started to make wonderful progress when she first returned from the sanitarium, but she had changed since her loss of Abdul. I knew how very much she loved Abdul, but I had no idea how to help her. She had become withdrawn, and the warmth and affection I had cherished was gone. She didn't even seem to find the same pleasure she always had in playing the piano.

I know now that she too was concerned about the war and political events, but that was the kind of thing I always ascribed to Father, not to Mother. She was, however, very pleased with my accomplishments, particularly my language skills. I found it much easier now to speak English and German, at times forgetting myself in school and answering in German or English instead of Serbian.

November 26, 1940: The Jews of Warsaw were ordered from their homes and forced to live in a walled ghetto.

One exceptionally warm evening in December, Father and Mother were sitting on the terrace conversing. I sat next to an open window in the living room studying, and their voices drifted through the window clearly as I heard my name in their conversation.

"Aren't you proud of Asinka?" Mother asked. "She is doing so very well in school and with her languages. Her English and German have absolutely no trace of accent."

"Yes, dear, she is doing exceptionally well, but . . ."

"But what? Is there anything wrong?"

I saw Father take her hand and kiss it. "I'm just so afraid that somewhere along the way she could lose her identity. You know . . . you know I want her always to remember that she is our daughter . . . that she is Russian. That is so important."

"Important to you?"

"Yes." His yes sounded as though there were more that he wanted to say, and after kissing Mother's hand again, with great tenderness in his voice, he continued:

"You see, our future, once more, is so uncertain. The plans we had for her may never come true. I just wonder if, instead of concentrating on language skills, social graces, and all of that, if we should have given her some practical guide. You know, something down to earth, like cooking, peeling potatoes. Wouldn't that have been better for her?"

There was an apologetic tone in his voice, as though he didn't want to say it but felt he had to.

"That's absurd," Mother replied. "You well know that languages and social graces are very important. Besides, if we do have war, it's not going to last. Things will get back to normal, and we may even get back to Russia. Wherever we are, she'll be totally prepared for an intellectual and social life."

"Perhaps you're right," Father sighed. "She can always pick up the practical side of life later on."

The night air was getting chilly, and they rose to come into the house. I quickly closed the window so they wouldn't suspect I had overheard their conversation. When I had returned to my room, I thought about what I had heard.

Why or how could I "lose my identity"? All my life Father had reminded me that I was Russian. Whenever he praised me, he always said, "Well, you are my daughter and you are a Russian," which was always why I was "so smart" or "so brave" or "so pretty." Whatever the occasion, success was always attributed to the fact that I was a Russian. As for cooking and peeling potatoes, well, I'd never thought of that. Besides, we had Kristina. They mentioned that the war wouldn't last forever. So they, too, were expecting war. They had talked about going back to Russia, and I wondered what Russia would be like. Father had always said that the Soviets were Bolshevik "Hooligans." Well, maybe they were talking about after the "Hooligans" were gone. But where would they go? They too were Russian.

Suddenly I wondered why my mind was always clogged with unanswered questions. I wished that it was summer again and that I could find a nice secluded meadow to just lie down in and watch fluffy white clouds form castles and imaginary creatures in the hot, summer sky. Perhaps while looking at them I would be able to figure out this confusing world.

One morning just after the Christmas holidays in January 1941, I awoke to find the house unusually quiet and went to find Kristina in the kitchen.

"Here little one—your cocoa and toast."

"Must I, Kristina? I really don't like cocoa anymore. Besides, it's for little children."

"Oh ho, so the big Gymnasia student is all grown-up, eh?"

"No, Kristina, but I'm not a child any longer."

"Well, drink it anyway. It's good for you and will help your bones to develop and grow strong."

"Kristina, is it hard to cook and peel potatoes and such?"

"No. Once you learn how to do things in the kitchen, it's very easy. Why?"

"Well, I heard Papa . . . Oh, please don't tell him I overheard him. I heard him saying that I might be better off if I had learned how to cook and peel potatoes instead of languages and curtsying. Do you think I would be better off?"

"Everything in life has its time and place, my little one. When the time comes, you'll have plenty of time to learn these things. For now, you shouldn't worry your little head about it. And finish your cocoa."

"That's what everybody tells me. 'Don't worry your pretty little head about it.' And yet my head is full of things that I 'shouldn't worry about.'"

Kristina came and hugged me. She mussed my hair, and I could feel tears starting, but I held them back.

"Life is full of puzzles and questions, my little one. I wish I could make it easier, but you are still a child, and I hope and pray that you'll still have a few years to remain a child. I wish I could help you to 'unclog' your mind. But you know, even I am still looking for the answers to many questions."

She gave me another big hug and said that she had to get on with her work, but as she walked away I saw tears in her eyes.

My classes at Trécha Zhénska and Miss Spencer's tutoring kept me busier than ever, and the school year was passing quickly. When I returned from school one day at the end of winter, I found a beautiful new dress lying on my bed. It was very thin white wool. The top had a sailor suit collar with a navy blue striped border and a navy blue tie held together by a golden ring with small pearls, and the skirt was white with tiny pleats. I ran breathlessly into the living room where Mother and Father sat drinking tea.

"This is beautiful. Thank you so much. When did you get it?"

"It was supposed to be ready a long time ago," Mother said, "but Mrs. Ivanovich has been ill, and it took her much longer than usual. Did you try it on?"

"No. May I now?"

"Of course. Isn't your 'Free Day' coming up soon? You can wear it then."

"Yes, Mama. That would be perfect."

All the girls looked forward to our Free Day when once a month we could wear a dress of our choice instead of our uniform. As I turned to run back to my room, Father stopped me.

"Asya, before you go, we want you to look at something. Perhaps we should talk a bit."

As he spoke, he handed me something. I could see that it was a photograph, and as I looked at it, I realized that it was of me—both feet off the ground, one arm stretched high over my head, tossing my beret in the air in front of the fence at the Palace. Ljubica and Jovanka were watching me and laughing. I was mortified! A family friend had seen me walking along the street with my two schoolmates, decided that a snapshot would be a perfect present for my parents, and, as luck would have it, snapped the picture at the very moment my beret was tossed.

"Do you remember, Asya, when you were starting Gymnasia and we talked—when I told you that the girls at Trécha Zhénska were older and already behaving like young ladies, and that you must also begin to act as a young lady?" Mother asked.

"Yes, Mama."

"Well," Father added, "perhaps you need to think a bit about that and what you might do to ensure your proper behavior."

"Yes, Papa."

The subject was never mentioned again, but how I've wished over the years that I still had that photograph.

The following Sunday, after Mass, we went to Yaintse, and I was surprised to see that the frame of the house was already up. Its location was very pretty. Standing in the front, one could see the entire village of Yaintse, with its farms and meadows. Directly below our lot was a farmhouse, and a wide pathway led up the hill from the farmhouse yard to our house. A dirt road led from the highway up the small hill and passed the rear edge of our property as it led to the village cemetery and a wooded area. Our house overlooked the highway, which continued from Belgrade to Mt. Avala, about ten miles away.

Our land sloped up behind the house. Part of the slope to one side was a rock and clay ledge that rose to about the level of the windowsills of the house. Between the house and the ledge a shallow cellar—like space had been excavated which was to be roofed over to hold garden tools and to serve as storage for vegetables. At the top of the slope behind the house, the gravel road leading to the cemetery separated our land from a gentle slope down the other side. A large cornfield began at the edge of the road and extended down the slope, bordered on one side by thick woods, a meadow on another side. Beyond the cornfield one could see the road that led from Mt. Avala, winding through fields and woods toward the rooftops of Belgrade.

"It's very pretty here, Papa. Are we going to have water?

"I don't know. We first have to finish the house and then start on the well again. I just don't know how deep we have to dig."

"But where will we get water for drinking, for cooking, for bathing?"

"I've spoken with Mirko, the farmer below us. He has said that we're welcome to all the water we need from his well."

"That means that we won't have a bathroom either," said Mother, looking alarmed and dismayed.

"We'll have a bathroom in the house, of course, but we won't be able to use it until we strike water in the well," Father replied quickly, taking Mother's hand to kiss it.

"How will we go to the bathroom, Papa?"

"We're going to build an outhouse. I'm going to put a window in it so we'll have a pretty view, too." Father smiled broadly, trying to sound upbeat and amusing. But it brought only a deep frown to Mother's face.

"An outhouse, Papa. Oh, how primitive. Why don't we just continue with the well until we reach water, and then build the house?"

"Because, Asinka, it's very important that we have the house ready as soon as possible. Wouldn't you like to come out here on weekends and explore the woods and the countryside?"

"I guess so." The thought did have lots of appeal. I had already discovered that it was great fun to lie down and roll down the hill on the shorter grass beside the cornfield. Mostly, though, I simply found quiet places in the tall grass of adjoining meadows to lie, watching clouds and inventing stories to explain their changing shapes. Why Father wanted the house "ready as soon as possible" failed to raise my curiosity.

Hmm, an outhouse. I'd never used an outhouse, but it might be interesting. I liked being outside. But poor Mother. I just could not picture her in an outhouse.

In late February Miss Spencer asked to meet with Mother and me together after my regular lesson. She said that my knowledge of English was quite sufficient, and that since Mother spoke English with no trace of accent and would be speaking English with me daily, there was no need to continue with her tutoring. More important, she explained, political developments were such that she felt she would be needed at home in England.

I was delighted. That meant I would have more free time, a luxury I hadn't enjoyed for a very long time. Miss Spencer turned to me with a warm smile to add, "Now, Miss Asya, if you just remember to put your tongue between your teeth for your *th* sounds, and don't roll your Rs, you will do just fine. Oh, yes, and don't call English ladies 'Madame.'"

"Yes, Miss Spencer. I'll remember."

We wished her a safe journey. War between Britain and Germany was raging.

One day that spring, Father found me in my room and joined me to explain that we were to have a house guest. Close friends of his and Mother's had been killed in an accident, and they had left an orphaned daughter. Her name was Aljona, and Father was to bring her home the following day. I don't remember much about Aljona, except that she was a very sweet little girl, about eight. Her father had served with Father during the Russian Revolution. My parents wanted to take her in, but I think that their concern for the international situation and the fact that their own plans were changing caused them to change their minds.

She shared my room with me, but was with us for only about a week. As the possibility of war breaking out became more ominous, the people in charge of the orphanage at Russkii Dom decided to send all the children to the Russian émigré community in Paris, where they would be safely out of the way of possible hostilities. Aljona went with them, and we sadly kissed each other good-bye as she returned to Russkii Dom. Poor, sad little Aljona was to have a far greater impact on my life than either of us could possibly have guessed at the time.

Although I was unaware of the changes already under way, the world and I had reached the end of our adolescence. By the beginning of March 1941, Belgrade was beset with protests, general unrest, and demonstrations. Germany had requested "free passage" through Yugoslavian territory to reach Greece and North Africa and for better access to the oil fields in Romania. The regent, Prince Paul, who ruled in young Prince Peter's stead, felt he had little choice given the strength of Germany and its determination to reach its objectives. The Serbs, however, were bitterly opposed to allowing German troops to pass through Yugoslavia, and a charged atmosphere of unrest hung over the city.

There was widespread nervous anticipation that something was about to happen, but no one seemed to know exactly what— or when. Classes continued at Trécha Zhénska at their usual pace. Although all the girls clearly felt the electric charge that seemed to pervade everything in our city, politics were still never discussed in class.

Our "Free Day" was scheduled for the first week in March, and I was looking forward to wearing my new dress. By now I had modeled it at least half a dozen times for Kristina, and she had convinced me (as if I needed convincing) that it was really beautiful. When the big day arrived, I didn't even want to sit down to eat breakfast, afraid to ruin the pleats.

"You had better sit down and have your breakfast correctly," Kristina scolded lightly. "Those pleats will not wrinkle, but you might spill your cocoa standing up."

"Oh, Kristina, must I have cocoa? I have a bit of a stomachache."

"Drink your cocoa. It will be good for your stomachache."

There was no use arguing. I finished breakfast, drank my cocoa, and off I went.

It was always nice to see the other girls in their different dresses. We all seemed "different" on our Free Day, probably because we all felt more relaxed, uninhibited without our uniforms. My stomach was bothering me, cramping, but I was sure it was due to the cocoa and to my excitement over my gorgeous new outfit. All the girls thought it looked very smart, and I had received many compliments on it.

That afternoon our religion class started as usual with a prayer. Since it was getting close to Easter, we were covering the time of the Crucifixion. The priest called on me to go to the board and point out the location of Golgotha on a map of ancient Jerusalem. Of course, I knew its location, and I boldly marched to the front of the room where the map hung and took the pointer the priest handed me. As I walked to the board I heard tiny snickering behind me, but thought nothing of it. I pointed out the location of Golgotha and turned to return to my seat, when I suddenly felt the priest's hand on my shoulder.

"We are going to have a two-minute recess. Please remain in your seats."

His hand never left my shoulder as he gently pointed me toward the exit, walking behind me and steering me ahead.

"Father, did I do something wrong? Where are we going?"

"No, Asya, nothing is wrong," he said calmly.

We walked to the nurse's office, and he opened the door and whispered something to the nurse.

"Father, how did you know that my stomach hurts?"

He patted me on the head, saying that the nurse would take care of me, as he turned and walked back to our classroom.

The nurse smiled as she said, "I'll go to your classroom to get your briefcase and books. Why don't you go and use the bathroom."

"But, Nurse, I still have one more class to go. I don't want my books, and I don't need the bathroom."

"Do you know why Father brought you here?"

"No, I hadn't told him about my stomachache. And besides, it doesn't hurt anymore."

Without a word, she took my hand and led me to a full-length mirror in a dressing room, lifting the back of my skirt so that I could see it in the mirror.

"Oh, no, I hate her. I told her I didn't want that awful cocoa anymore. Oh, look at my beautiful white skirt."

Tears streamed down my face. I was furious. I went to the bathroom and found the same stains on my slip and panties.

"I want to go home," I told the nurse. "Now maybe she'll believe that the cocoa makes me sick."

The nurse brought my books to me. She found one of her nurse's smocks, put it on me, and found a belt somewhere.

"There, this will cover your skirt, and we'll make it shorter with the belt."

She adjusted the smock, fluffing up the upper part, tightened the belt, handed me my books, and sent me home. On the trolley I wondered why the girls had snickered. They could have said something. And why didn't the priest say something when he took me to the nurse's office? Is it a sin to drink so much cocoa that it just comes out of you? Well, if it's a sin, I'm certainly guilty, and he will certainly preach about it and tell me so at confession. Now I was missing my gym class. Oh, well, I couldn't jump the horses anyway. My stomach was cramping again.

I jumped off the trolley at my stop and rushed home, not even stopping to look for new buds on the shrubs as I usually did. I almost ran, undoing the nurse's smock as I rushed up the steps to the front door.

"My little one, you're home so early. Why?" Kristina said as I entered the kitchen.

I dropped my books on the table and the nurse's smock on the floor, turning my back toward her and holding up my skirt.

"Do you see this, Kristina? And this is my brand-new dress. Do you believe me now? Do you understand why I don't ever, ever want to see another cup of cocoa as long as I live?"

"Oh, my God. You poor child, I'm so sorry. Here, let me help you. Let's go into the bathroom. You can wash and give me the dress."

I had to change everything, of course, feeling frustrated because I was sure it wouldn't have happened if she had only listened to me about her "daily cocoa." I washed, but as I put on fresh underwear, it happened again. There seemed to be no end to the cocoa.

"May I come in?" Kristina knocked lightly at the door.

"Yes, Kristina."

"Why don't you come to my room. It's quite private so we can talk, and there is still plenty of time for me to fix dinner."

We went to Kristina's room to sit on her bed where she looked deep into my eyes, stroking my hair, wondering where to begin.

"First of all, I promise that I will never make you drink cocoa again. All right?"

I nodded my head, now feeling guilty because I had been so cross. After all, she was always wonderful to me.

"Now, the stain on your dress isn't cocoa. It's blood."

"Blood?" I asked in a panic. What had I done? I hadn't cut myself or anything. It must be serious, I thought, looking desperately at Kristina.

"Yes, blood. It's very normal. You are a normal, healthy girl. When we reach a certain age, our system, our body, tells us that we are ready for a change—a change from girlhood to womanhood."

"And will I always have this now every day of my life?"

"No, it comes only once each month for a few days, and it only stops when a woman is blessed with a child. It is God's way of telling us that we can have a child."

"So I'm not sick or anything because I'm bleeding?"

"No, it's all very normal, and it's called menstruation."

"Did you ever have a child, Kristina?"

"No, I never married."

"Oh, so you have to be married to have a baby?"

"Yes. Well, no . . . well, yes, you have to be married so that the baby will have a mother and a father. That's what makes a family."

Kristina shifted, uncomfortably I thought, then began to explain proper hygiene to me: how to be prepared for the next period and what to do. That night in bed, I had so many new questions on top of worrying about probable war, worrying that Mother would get sick again, that Father wouldn't find water in Yaintse. And now this.

I got up and went to the wardrobe where our first aid kits were, the ugly gas mask staring at me from the floor. We each had one. Father had said he would show me how to put it on—what for, I wondered—something else to worry about. I didn't sleep well that night and was very tired the next morning, almost falling asleep on the trolley ride to school. All day, the other girls asked why I had left school early. They had all guessed, but wanted to hear it from me. Now, I found, we all had something in common, and I began to feel quite grown-up as a result—almost all the other girls were three or four years older than I, and it felt good to know that we had something in common.

My classroom experience returned to normal immediately after my latest bout with growing up. Now, however, although the subjects of war and political developments still were not raised in classes, they began to dominate the conversations during recess in the courtyard. By the second week in March it was difficult not to be aware of something happening all around us. The city was extremely restless. Everywhere I walked, I saw groups of men huddled together in what were obviously serious conversations.

Mother and Father both became very nervous about me going to and from school, and I was given strict instructions to come directly home immediately after school. Passengers on the trolley who normally greeted me did so no longer. Everyone seemed preoccupied.

One evening, after I had finished my homework, I returned to join my parents. As I approached the living room, I heard Mother say, "Oh, I forgot to tell you. Asinka is no longer a child. Our little Asinka is now a young woman. My God, it makes me feel so old."

"Oh, when did that happen? Did she tell you? How did you find out? Isn't it a bit early? She is only twelve years old."

"It happened a few days ago. She didn't tell me. Kristina did. Apparently it started in school, and Asya came home early. I suppose it is a bit early for her. I was trying to remember, and I may have been a year older when I started. But I don't think it's unusual."

"Well, who explained things to her? It must have been quite a shock."

"Kristina explained everything to her. I suppose it was a bit of a shock, but I'm sure she was able to cope with it very well."

Mother never mentioned the subject to me, and when I told her a few days later that my new sailor suit had been "mussed up" and that Kristina was trying to clean it, she never asked how it had gotten soiled. She simply replied that she was sure that Kristina would do her best to clean it. I could never bring myself to raise the subject with her. I found it embarrassing, and I'm sure Mother felt the same. Still, it saddened me deeply that she hadn't been the one to explain things to me—that we did not seem to be close enough to discuss "personal" things— and I think it added to future problems between us. I remember telling myself that if I ever had a daughter, I would be sure to tell her in advance.

Father organized a group of friends to work on the house at Yaintse, and the next time I saw it, the roof was up and closed in and ready for the roof tiles, and the doors and windows had been installed. The windows looked a little odd—they were framed to place them about eighteen inches out from the wall. They would eventually be at the outside of the wide mud-brick exterior wall, which was still to be built. The floors were still bare earth. Father explained that he was having difficulty obtaining the lumber required to frame and install the new floors. A lot had been accomplished, and it now looked like a house, at least from the outside.

At home in Dedinye, a radio was turned on every hour, and at Yaintse Mother constantly checked the radio at the police chief's office to listen to the latest news. Each German OKW announcement gave an account of their daily victories in several countries. Local news broadcasts from Radio Belgrade provided news of Prince Paul and his efforts to negotiate with Germany.

It was rumored throughout Belgrade that Germany had given assurances that they would not go through Yugoslavia to reach Greece, but would respect the sovereignty and integrity of Yugoslavia at all times. Father did not believe this. Militarily, he said, Germany would benefit from free transit across our country, and he and our friends continued to worry.

Father constantly checked our first aid supplies, making sure that we all remembered where the gas masks were and that we all knew how to put them on and use them. He not only worked continuously on the house at Yaintse, but attended organizational meetings each night at Russkii Dom. The émigré community drew up plans on where to meet and how to keep everyone informed of developments, changing plans, and the whereabouts of everyone in the event of hostilities.

The next time we went to Yaintse, I found that all interior walls had been built and painted. There was a large living room, a large kitchen, and two bedrooms. Aunt 'Lyena and I would share one of the bedrooms. Furniture—beds, chairs, tables—all had been brought by friends and placed on the dirt floors. Pots, pans, linens, and dishes had been brought as well and were piled on top of the tables. It seemed so strange that all this furniture would be brought and placed in the house when the floors still had not been installed.

EIGHT

War Comes to Belgrade

News flashes were heard constantly, growing worse and more worrisome by the hour. The population of Belgrade divided into political factions. Some favored at least limited cooperation with Nazi Germany to avoid being drawn into the larger conflict, some favored joining the Axis Pact as the best way to mollify German belligerence, while others violently opposed *any* cooperation with the Nazis. The Regent, Prince Paul, was out of the country trying to come to some agreement with Germany as Adolf Hitler raged.

Father insisted that I was to wait at school until either he or one of our friends arrived to accompany me home. I had, in fact, begun to feel uneasy going to and from school. Groups of men were seen demonstrating against the possibility of cooperating with Germany. Most of the serious demonstrations took place in the government sector of the city, around Skupshtina, near our old neighborhood on Dr. Kester Street. The demonstrations in the area of Trécha Zhénska tended to be small and short-lived, but I was nervous seeing any group of men gathered and talking among themselves.

On March 25 everything began to change rapidly and in frightening ways. Yielding to pressure, Yugoslavia became the next nation to join the

Tripartite Act, or Axis Pact, when Prince Paul signed for Yugoslavia at a ceremony in Berlin on March 25, 1941. The agreement was specifically designed to allow free passage for German troops moving through Yugoslavia to attack Greece.

It had not been easy for Hitler to gain the cooperation of Yugoslavia. Prince Paul was sharply aware of the strong anti-German feelings held by his subjects, particularly the majority Serb population. Whatever pressure induced him to sign, the next day he was overthrown in a military coup d'état. On March 27, 1941, the eighteen-year-old heir to the throne, Prince Peter II, was declared king. The city of Belgrade was placed under a blackout order, and everyone was issued lapel buttons that glowed in the dark.

Father went to Yaintse almost every day, but had been unable to find the materials or the help needed to install and finish the floors. Everyone was preoccupied with recent political shifts and developments and their own preparations. In school, for the first time, many of the teachers were short-tempered.

The only thing that seemed indifferent to everything that was happening was nature itself. The weather was warm with a slight breeze, and every day tender new leaves began to cover the tree and shrub branches. Every place I looked in the terraces at home, green shoots were poking above the ground, and I knew that they would soon have bright flowers showing. The sky seemed almost a magic blue, and the bird song that filled the air in Dedinye sounded sweeter and more intense than I remembered it. I wondered why people didn't react to the spring in the same way, why they seemed oblivious to the new life that was appearing all around us. And I remember telling myself that I would be different when I grew up.

At the end of the school day on Monday, March 31, we were told that, due to the unsettled conditions in Belgrade, we would not have school for the next few days. An announcement would be made on the radio telling us when classes would resume. Miss Visnic wished us all well.

"I'm sure this will take only a few days. Before you leave, remember that this does not mean that you are on vacation. You are to study at home, of course, even more now that you don't have to come to school. You have your assignments, and I'll see you all back here in a few days."

That evening at dinner, Father suggested that we all go to Yaintse for the few days that school would be closed. Kristina was concerned about her family and wanted to go to Ljubljana and check on them. While she was gone, we could all "relax" in Yaintse.

When we arrived in Yaintse, I was surprised by the appearance of the house. It looked very pretty at the top of the hill. The exterior had been painted and was very white. The window and door frames had all been painted brick red to match the roof tiles. The dwarf fruit trees lining the walkway that sloped up to the house were beginning to blossom, and the vegetables were all up and a bright, light green.

Mother must have been pleased and briefly happy as we walked up to the house, but dismayed when we entered. Inside the floors had not been installed, and the bathroom had nothing in it—an empty room with a dirt floor and a window. Furniture lay about haphazardly. Nothing matched, of course, and there were far more mattresses than beds. The kitchen table and the coal-burning stove were piled high with dishes, pots, and pans. The kitchen cabinets had not yet been hung.

The exterior mud-brick walls were very thick, and the windows had been set at the outside of the walls so that there was a very deep interior sill at each window—about two feet deep, which I thought would be a nice place for plants.

Aunt 'Lyena and I gathered linens and began to make up the beds in the two bedrooms. Mother and Father were in their room when I went in to make up their beds. Mother was crying, and Father was stroking her hair.

"It will be all right. We'll only stay for a couple of days. The farmer down the hill will fix us some food for this evening."

"But I *can't* use the outhouse. I can't even wash. Oh, I really don't care about food."

"Don't you remember when they put you in prison? You and 'Lyena shared a cell with six or eight other women much of the time, and you had only a hole in a corner of the cell."

"Oh, but how can you compare? I was only seventeen then, and besides, your squad came and rescued us. It's so much more hopeless now."

Father had a look of total helplessness as he stroked her hair and wiped her tears, asking her to have faith in him, that he would make things better.

"Mama, can I do anything?"

I felt uneasy because I had entered in the middle of their discussion.

"No, no, Anochka, I'm just so sorry that you are probably going to go through the same hell that I did. But, no, you're even younger than I was." She turned to Father, and now crying hard pointed to me as she continued. "Do you realize that she's just a child? Is she going to have a life like we had during the revolution?"

Papa reached for me and pulled me down to sit next to them, his own tears flowing as he struggled to speak.

"I promise and I swear that nothing is going to happen to my girls," he said, embracing both Mother and me. "I know that God will protect us all, and besides, we'll have the house fixed up. This is only for a couple of days. And maybe if Hitler decides he has to go through Yugoslavia, he'll just go through and they'll be gone as fast as they came."

"Yes," sobbed Mother. "But this is how it started before the revolution in Russia."

"Oh, Marusha, that's altogether different. It was the "Hooligans" who started the unrest, who instigated the uprisings. Here we are dealing with highly intelligent people from a civilized country. They want passage. Let them."

Father didn't sound at all convincing, but Mother dried her tears. I went outside to let my parents have a few moments to themselves and to clear my head.

I couldn't sleep that night, and I went outside, wondering how it felt to be in London now that the Germans were bombing continuously. They were not only all around us but in Africa as well. I could not understand why Hitler wanted Africa. And what was happening to all the animals? Were the elephants and lions being bombed, too? Nothing made sense to me. I could not understand why Hitler wanted other countries. Germany already had everything that other countries had. There were so many questions on my mind. Nothing made sense to me.

Father had said that God would take care of us. But I wondered if God knew what was going on, and if so, if he really cared. God, I thought, must be on Hitler's side, helping him to conquer all these other countries. I looked up at the heavenly canopy of bright stars and suddenly felt I had sinned by questioning and doubting God. I would have to tell our priest that at confession next Saturday. I returned to my room and bed feeling guilty and ashamed.

We returned home to Dedinye on Thursday, April 3, and it felt luxurious to walk on parquet and carpeted floors and to take a long, hot bath. We had bought fresh milk, meats, and cheese from the farmer in Yaintse, and after a light, late supper we all collapsed into our beds.

Father went to Russkii Dom the following day, giving me instructions not to leave the house under any circumstances. He was gone nearly the entire day, and when he returned he told Aunt 'Lyena that she should not go to church for vespers the following evening. The city was extremely tense. Sunday would be Palm Sunday, he reminded us, and we would all go to church together.

Kristina had not returned from Ljubljana yet and was not expected until Monday. Father and I fixed a light supper on Saturday evening, and we all ate in the dining room by candlelight, the drapes tightly drawn because of the blackout order. It was really rather pleasant, reminding me of our candlelight dinners on Dr. Kester Street. We had turned the radio off while eating because the news continued to be worrisome with nothing new.

"I have made some arrangements with the Poltoratskys," Father said. "Now I'm not saying that it will become necessary, but should the situation change in any way, Sergei will come here to fetch us."

"Where to, Papa?"

"To Yaintse. He and Sonya could stay with us there. And I have told friends at Russkii Dom to feel free to come and stay with us if need be."

"Is that why so many brought mattresses and things? So that they can stay with us, Papa?"

"Yes, Asya, but that's not to say they will. It's only if there is trouble."

"What kind of trouble?"

"Well, it looks like the Germans will go through Belgrade, and we all hope and pray that it will be without any trouble or any bloodshed."

"Weee shooooould have gooone to vespers!" Aunt 'Lyena complained.

"'Lyena, the trolleys are not running, and there is a total blackout in the city. It's absurd to venture out, and Sergei has things he needs to tend to. I didn't feel we could impose on him for a ride with so much going on. You can pray right here, and we will all go to church together for Palm Sunday services."

Aunt 'Lyena looked defeated. I could tell she didn't agree with Father.

"What should we pray for?" I asked uncharacteristically. "God isn't listening to us. He's on Hitler's side."

The minute I said it, I was sorry, as three pairs of eyes turned toward me in shock and total disbelief at what they had just heard.

"God does not take sides, Asinka," said Father softly. "It is not God that causes the misery in the world. It is people's lack of faith in God that is the cause."

"I know, Papa. I'm sorry I said that, but I just get so confused."

Father embraced me and Aunt 'Lyena and brought us to the couch to sit with Mother. All four of us sat on the couch crying—each of us, I believe, for a different reason. I, because I was truly ashamed of what I had said; Aunt 'Lyena, I believe, because she felt she had failed at making my faith as strong as it should have been; Mother, because she could see the future she had hoped to build for me slowly falling apart; and Father, because as the head of our small family he felt helpless against events that were disrupting not only our lives but lives throughout Belgrade and all of Europe.

Father and I went to the kitchen to fix a pot of tea. When we returned, I witnessed something I had never seen before. Mother and Aunt 'Lyena sat on the couch with their arms around each other, crying. I had never seen the two sisters even engaged in a real conversation before. Their relationship always seemed formal.

Mother never had the patience to listen to Aunt 'Lyena's difficult, drawn-out speech and always made sure that they didn't get into a lengthy conversation. Aunt 'Lyena, on the other hand, was critical of Mother's casual approach to church and to religion, always trying not to comment on it. I am positive they loved each other deeply, but they seemed to lack the ability to express their feelings. It made me happy to see them in an embrace.

I kissed my family goodnight and went to my room to say my prayers and go to bed. I asked God to forgive me that night for saying that He was on Hitler's side. And I prayed very hard for our family and friends. I knew everything was going to be all right.

Dawn was just breaking when I was awakened by loud thunder. I jumped out of bed to rush and close the window. Strangely, there was no rain, not even any clouds. Yet there it was again—very loud, continuous thunder and a high-pitched scream. There were no clouds. I couldn't figure out what it was. I ran to the living room to look in the other direction and collided with Father.

"Quickly, Asinka," Father said. "Put your clothes on, grab a few extra clothes, get your toothbrush, and . . . oh, I don't know . . . just throw some things together. Is Elyena up?

"'Lyena, 'Lyena," he called out loudly.

Papa ran from room to room, all the while pulling on his socks, his shoes, his shirt. Everybody was up now and doing the same.

"Papa, what is it? What is happening? Why are we running? Why the clothes?"

"We are being bombed, Asya. It's very serious. Hurry now."

> April 6, 1941: Palm Sunday. German bombers based in Romania began bombing Belgrade without warning, beginning just before dawn. The bombing continued for three full days and nights.

Father and Mother were both pale, fear reflecting in their eyes. Aunt 'Lyena was kneeling in prayer by the couch, and Mother was beginning to cry.

"Don't worry," Papa said. "I made all the arrangements, remember? Sergei and Sonya should be here soon."

Now the thunderous explosions and screaming became louder. It sounded as though hundreds of airplanes were roaring high above. Suddenly a burning, dusty smell reached us. Belgrade was on fire. Papa turned the radio on. We heard only silence and a bit of static. No news reports. Nothing.

"They must have hit the station for Radio Belgrade," Father said.

The noise grew louder, and the sky was filled with airplanes. We heard a loud screech of tires and frantic horn blowing.

"Hurry, hurry now! He's here. Grab what you can," Papa called as he tried to move everyone toward the door. "Are all the windows closed? Oh, never mind. Let's run."

Uncle Sergei's taxi already had three people in it besides Sonya and himself. The four of us squeezed in. I sat on Aunt Sonya's lap in front, next to another woman, while Mother sat on Father's lap in the back seat next to Aunt 'Lyena and another couple. Four in the front and five in the back, and we drove off.

"How is it out there, Sergei?" Father asked.

"Awful, just awful. So many dead already. The streets are blocked with debris, and there are bodies everywhere. Belgrade is burning. They seem to have bombed the north side most heavily."

We pulled onto another street, and suddenly there was silence. No explosions, and the planes had disappeared.

"What's happening? Why is it so quiet? Is it all over?" asked Mother, anxiously looking out the window.

Sergei drove as fast as the engine would allow. The streets we first passed through seemed untouched. However, people were everywhere, carrying small bundles and running, as cars sped through the streets in every direction.

"Do you think the bombing has stopped?" Mother asked again. "Maybe they wanted to destroy a specific target and it's all over."

"No," answered Sergei. "I think they are just refueling in Romania and will be back soon. The buildings we saw destroyed had no military value at all. They are shops and homes in areas of the city that could have no—"

"How about east of the city center where you are?" Father interrupted. "Any serious damage there? Was your place hit?"

"We are all right, but there is a long beltlike area from the north to the east side of the city that has heavy damage. I had to make several detours to get through it because of bomb damage and debris. But ambulances were already there tending to the wounded."

"Uncle Sergei," I asked, "are there many dead people?"

"Yes, child. I'm afraid quite a few."

We were driving along a street I did not recognize, the houses on one side a mass of rubble spreading out to the street. No people were seen, even though the houses on the other side seemed in good shape. The trees on the heavily damaged side were lying down or simply gone, while on the other side they had only lost large branches, which hung down, broken but still full of spring buds.

The area we were driving through began to look familiar to me, and I realized we were coming close to the Avala-Belgrade Highway, which would take us out to Yaintse. Suddenly the rumble of aircraft engines began again.

"Hurry, Sergei," Aunt Sonya cried out, tears in her eyes as she put her arm around Sergei's shoulders. "Please, dear God, don't let it happen again."

Just then I heard that screaming again and felt a sharp pain in my ears as the car rocked.

"Papa," I cried, "it's an earthquake."

Suddenly I heard a terrible explosion. I leaned over from Sonya's lap and saw a building collapsing. Sergei sped away as fast as possible. It felt to me as though we were flying instead of driving.

"Papa, my ears hurt. Was that an earthquake?"

"No, Asinka, it's pressure from the explosion. Sergei, will we make it through? Please hurry."

"But what's that terrible screaming?"

"I'm not sure, Asinka. It's probably the whistle of the bombs as they fall."

German dive bombers were fitted with sirens attached to the wings that would spin and emit a terrifying, high-pitched scream as they dived to drop their bombs. Their purpose was only to foster terror among the people being attacked.

I looked back over my parents' heads at the area we had just left. The street was now obscured in a large cloud of smoke and dust. Within minutes we turned onto the main Avala-Belgrade Highway. I knew that it would be only a short drive then.

The sound of the explosions behind us grew less loud, less urgent. The sun was now up, and the contrast was astounding. Everything looked as it had always looked to me: cows peacefully grazing in roadside fields, the trees that light, early spring green, the sky a brilliant light blue with puffy white clouds, their progress measured by their shadows crossing the meadows.

The highway, however, was full of cars, and both sides of the highway were lined with people clutching bundles or suitcases, headed nowhere, just escaping the horrors of the bombing. When we arrived, we left the car by the farm below and walked up the slope to the house carrying whatever we each had grabbed to take with us from home. Father and Sergei stopped to talk to Mirko, the farmer, who wanted to know what was happening in Belgrade.

As we reached the house, I saw a group of people I recognized from church or Russkii Dom, waiting to be let into the house. I put down the things I was carrying by the front door and ran to the top of the rise behind the house to look across the cornfield. The sky over Belgrade was filled with war planes, the rumble of their engines now constant. I could clearly hear the explosions and that terrifying scream as the planes dove to drop their bombs.

The people standing in front of the house now gathered on the ridge all around me to view the horror. Most were crying, wondering aloud how many had already died in the city.

The planes just kept coming in wave after wave, as far as I could see, high above, flying like flocks of migrating birds. I looked toward the path to see more people coming toward the house, each carrying bundles or suitcases.

"Papa, are we going to get bombed, too?"

"I don't think so. They just want to destroy Belgrade."

"But why Belgrade?"

"It's war," he said wearily, walking away from me. Father looked pale, wide-eyed, barely acknowledging the people around him.

NINE

The Destruction of Belgrade

I watched the spectacle over Belgrade for only a minute or two, unable to comprehend what I was seeing. As the smoke from growing fires within the city rose steadily higher, I turned and walked slowly down the small slope to the house. Inside I found people setting out mattresses, pillows, and blankets. Everywhere I looked there were pots, pans, suitcases, and bundles lying on the dirt floor or piled on whatever furniture was handy.

As worried voices and crying throughout the house overcame me, I rose and walked to the cemetery and then to the woods beyond. The woods were dark, densely shaded by the thick trees, muffling the noise from the highway and the house.

How strange that the birds keep singing in spite of all the chaos, I thought. So this is what war is like—my city is burning and people are dying. Those who are alive, like those now in the house, are crying, wringing their hands, talking to no one in particular, and staring in total disbelief and shock.

I tried to picture exactly what the day was like for the people back in the city, but could not. I had experienced only about one hour of the surprise bombing, but except for awakening to the "thunder" of exploding bombs, and the terrifying experience as we drove to escape the city, I had no way to picture the destruction that I knew was taking place. I wanted to talk to someone, wanted someone to tell me that everything would be all right again. I wanted Papa to explain why they were destroying Belgrade, not just to hear him say, "It's war." I wanted to know what would be coming next.

I walked back to the house, unable to understand how everything could have changed so suddenly. Only last night as I said my prayers at bedtime, I had been so sure that God had heard me and that everything was going to be all right. Well, I thought, maybe it is all right. We are all still alive.

Aunt 'Lyena and Sonya were walking toward the cemetery; I wondered if Aunt Sonya had her flask of vodka in her huge purse. Much of their very close friendship stemmed, I knew, from Aunt 'Lyena's ability to be completely nonjudgmental about Sonya's drinking problem and sympathetically trying only to strengthen Sonya.

I wondered where Lyalya was and smiled in spite of myself. Would she faint at the sight of this multitude, or just puff on her gold cigarette holder, fluttering those beautiful eyes at the crowd? She couldn't possibly walk on this gravel in those high, high heels.

I hoped Uncle Borya was at our home in Dedinye. It was comforting to think of him rubbing Priska's ears to calm her. Then suddenly I realized I was thinking of completely unimportant things. What did anything matter now? People were dying in Belgrade. I walked slowly back to the house.

Sometime in midafternoon, the planes disappeared and the sound of explosions grew very far apart. As the lull became apparent, everyone grew quiet, all wondering, Is it over? Is it finally over?

The same question reflected in pale, exhausted faces all around the yard. As an hour passed with no planes in the sky, many of the people who had crowded into the house and yard began to gather their bundles and prepare to return to Belgrade, concerned about property or friends who had remained in the city. As another hour passed with no planes in sight, people began to leave. Those who remained seemed somewhat relieved. The departure of some encouraged all to believe that perhaps the worst was over, that soon we could all return. They began to rummage through the bundles or suitcases they had brought, looking for something, anything, that might help them relax now that the opportunity was here. Someone went down to the farmer's well carrying buckets for fresh water. It was peacefully quiet, and I walked up the rise behind the house.

The sun would soon set, off in the west where the horizon was clear. On the other side of the highway below, farmers were beginning to round up their cows and sheep, and the sound of cowbells could be faintly heard. In the new silence, the bird song seemed louder, more beautiful. Aunt 'Lyena and Sonya were walking slowly toward me, returning from the cemetery, each with an arm around the other. I wondered if Aunt 'Lyena had been praying for Sergei?

"Aunt Sonya, is Uncle Sergei coming back?" I asked as they came close.

"Knowing Sergei, he is probably digging in the rubble and taking the injured to doctors or the hospital in his cab. I don't know where he is."

"I'll say a prayer for him tonight, Aunt Sonya."

"Yes, Asya, please do. Your Aunt Elyena has been praying for us all. But I'm afraid God can't hear anything above those dreadful planes and the explosions."

Aunt 'Lyena embraced her, assuring her that God can and does hear all our prayers as they both wept. I walked back up the rise behind the house to look across the cornfield toward Belgrade. In the dusk, the outlines of the taller buildings of Belgrade were visible through a smoky haze, a smoky cloud rising high over the city. I looked hard at the sight and could see a pink haze forming the lower part of the cloud. It was quiet. Even the birds seemed to be settling for the evening. A light April breeze sprang up to replace the warmth of the sun, and as a slight chill started, I returned to the house.

Inside, everyone had begun to prepare their mattresses, pillows, and blankets for the night. Aunt Sonya would take my bed. I had been happy to give it up because I knew how much comfort she brought to Aunt 'Lyena. I knew I would find a place. Cold, fresh water had been brought from the farm below. The top of the wood stove had been cleared, and tea was brewing. Fresh eggs, sausages, and ham had been purchased from the farmer, and the cooking food began to smell good.

People began to relax, sitting wherever they could find a chair or something to sit on. Those relaxed enough to eat had just finished when the muffled drone of aircraft engines was heard again. The house was silent for a moment, a shocked silence registering on the faces of everyone as they realized that the planes were returning. The first attack had taken place at dawn, when the first light enabled the war planes to easily locate their targets. The fires that now burned continuously allowed the planes to locate their targets in the dead of night and continue the attack twenty-four hours a day.

I went outside and ran up the slope to look across the cornfield again, others from the house following. The pink haze at the bottom of the black cloud over Belgrade now looked orange as the blackness of the night deepened. As I watched, the flash of explosions began again, hundreds of explosions, and the black cloud that hung over the city turned red. Belgrade was burning. Aunt 'Lyena was wrong. God did not hear her prayers. What about those poor people in the city? They must have prayed, too. Why would God allow this horror to go on?

The village below was in total darkness. Muffled voices could be heard from the highway. People were still fleeing Belgrade. Cars were occasionally heard, driving at a snail's pace because they could not use their headlights. One by one, everybody returned to the house, resigned to the continuing, distant horror.

Inside, a kerosene lamp was lit and the wick turned down as far as it would go. Blankets were hung over all the windows. The dim light from the lamp cast moving shadows of people and objects, creating an eerie mood on top of the already dismal atmosphere. Everyone sat in silence, counting the explosions that were now continuous, at regular, short intervals. There seemed to be no pause. I don't think anyone slept that night. Some dozed at best. Morning came. Everyone looked exhausted. Fresh water was brought up from the farmer's well and people began to dip washcloths and wash their faces.

"It's still going on?" someone asked, really more a statement.

"Yes," someone answered, "all night long. It never stopped."

I went outside to find my parents already sitting on the bench in front.

"Good morning, Mama."

"Good morning, Asya. Where did you sleep? Or did you?"

"No. I curled up on a windowsill in the kitchen, but I didn't sleep."

"Have you had something to eat?" Father asked.

"Just a piece of bread, Papa."

"That's not enough, Asinka," Mother added. "Do we have anything to eat in the house?"

"Yes," Father answered wearily, his mind a million miles away. "We bought food from the farmer, and all of our friends brought food with them."

The sun was now rising in the east. We couldn't see much from the top of the slope except for planes and the ever-present black cloud of smoke hanging over the city. The red glow of the fires disappeared in the bright sunlight, but the drone of aircraft engines and the continuing sound of explosions was a constant reminder that the bombing continued.

It was Monday, April 7, I remembered, wondering why I had thought of the day and date. The spring sun felt warm, but I was chilly because I was so very tired. Moving in order to warm up, I walked down between the fruit trees, reaching the farmer's house just as they were bringing in the morning eggs.

"Ah, good morning, Asya," said Jovanka. "Were you able to sleep with all that noise? Or did you have any room to sleep? Your house is so full of people."

"I don't think anyone slept, Jovanka. I know I didn't."

"Come on in the house. You're so pale. I'll fix you a cup of warm milk. We just finished milking our cows."

Her kitchen smelled of freshly baked bread and a pot of hot milk rested on the stove. A plate of smoked ham stood on the table.

"Come, sit. There is your milk. Have some bread and help yourself to the ham. It's from our own pigs."

The warm milk felt soothing going down, but I couldn't eat anything. I was just too tired, so very tired. I felt something warm covering me. Suddenly I sat up, looking around, trying to understand where I was. I was on a daybed in Jovanka's kitchen, a soft blanket covering me. Jovanka stood by the stove, mixing something in a very large pot.

"I'm so sorry, Jovanka, I must have fallen asleep. How did I get to the bed?"

"My husband, Mirko, put you on the bed. You fell asleep at the table. Now you look much better, rested. But you must eat."

Jovanka put a cup of warm milk in front of me, and I helped myself to some bread and the fresh butter on the table.

"They are still bombing, aren't they?"

"Yes, they have never stopped. I am just a farmer's wife, you know. I went to school for only four years, but I bet you I am a lot smarter than those people in governments. How can anyone be so godless and evil as to kill so many people, people they don't even know?" She continued stirring her pot, but now with fast, jerky movements. "They will all burn in hell for that. God will see to it."

"Maybe there is no God now. Maybe the devil has taken His place."

"Oh, don't say that, Asya. You know there is a God. He is just teaching us a lesson. We all have to repent our sins and be good again."

"My Aunt 'Lyena believes that, too. She keeps praying and praying."

"So she should. We all should. Do you pray, Asya?"

"Yes, every night and sometimes during the day."

"That's good. Now let me fix you something to eat."

"Oh, no. No, thank you. I've got to go back to the house. My gosh." I looked at the clock, shocked to see it was already 12:15. "Thank you for the bed and the milk. I'll see you later when I come for water."

As I walked up between the dwarf trees, I realized that the bombing had never ceased. We seemed to be getting used to the constant drone of aircraft engines, the continuous sound of explosions, and that terrible screaming sound. I noticed several people on the dirt road that led from the highway and divided our land from the cornfield, and as they approached the house they were bombarded with questions:

"How did you all get here? What's happening in Belgrade? Is anyone left alive?"

They reported that the highway had not been hit, but that Belgrade was a smoldering ruin. They had started out very early that morning, between bombing runs, and had to crawl over or between piles of rubble, since the streets were blocked with debris. Bodies were seen everywhere, placed close to the street awaiting identification, while those still alive tried to find shelter in bombed-out buildings. Ambulances were everywhere, but they were little help at night, since they couldn't use their lights. I saw the Nazimovs among the newcomers and ran toward them.

"Aunt Nadia, where are Kolya and Yura?"

"They stayed behind, trying to help out, digging people out from the rubble, some dead, some barely alive. Oh, it is so gruesome. It's a real hell, a burning hell."

All the people that were arriving were wide-eyed, disheveled, some obviously in shock. Almost all of them were crying, praying, and cursing the Germans—some cursing God. Aunt Sonya rushed out to inquire about Sergei.

"Have you seen him? Why didn't he come with you?"

"We saw him, but only from a distance. He was clearing rubble, trying to dig out those still alive and taking them someplace in his cab."

Sonya quickly crossed herself, thanking God that Sergei was all right. Nobody knew anything about other friends or acquaintances. The city apparently had collapsed into complete chaos. They reported that in the central part of the city there wasn't a street left undamaged. Whole city blocks had been leveled. And still the bombing continued. Along the highway an endless stream of cars, now mixed with horses, wagons, people walking, and Yugoslavian military vehicles, all headed south, away from Belgrade. The second day of continuous bombing was slowly coming to a close.

In Yaintse, the sunset was as beautiful as the day before. The cows, bellies fat from grazing all day, slowly moved toward the farms, and a few farmers could be seen herding in their sheep, the animals all looking peaceful and content, unaware of the human tragedy all around them. There hadn't even been any clouds for the past two days—with the exception of the black cloud that hung over Belgrade. As evening darkened into night, I knew the cloud over Belgrade would turn from black to orange to red. It was as if God were mocking us.

Why doesn't God send a rain storm to block visibility? He must be on the German side, I thought again. It's much easier for them to find Belgrade on a sunny day, and the rain would help control all the fires. At night the city is in flames to serve as a beacon to guide them back in spite of the blackout. I knew I shouldn't think that way. Father had told me that God would protect us. But what about other people? Why should we be protected while others die? Is God really taking sides? I was so very tired, tired of thinking, tired of seeking answers, and so confused.

Inside the house, the windows were being covered as the kerosene lamp was lit, its wick again lowered all the way. The eyes of the people looked hollow, their faces pale, their shadows on the white walls enormous, mysterious.

By now there was almost no space left in the house. Mattresses had been placed along all of the walls and in any available space in the bedrooms. I found a blanket and climbed up on the kitchen windowsill again. The sill just large enough for me to curl up on.

I dozed off, the drone of airplanes and the distant explosions by now sounds I had grown used to. I think the continuing sound actually helped me to fall asleep for a couple of hours. I awoke with my body aching from curling in one position, unable to turn or stretch my legs out. Everyone else must have been sleeping—the sound of gentle snoring contrasting with the sound of explosions. The kitchen window faced the slope in the rear of the house, and as I sat up and looked out, I could see a small, dim, red glow at the top of the rise that I knew was Belgrade burning.

I sat there thinking about the people who remained in the city, wondering if everybody was dead by now or badly hurt. If they were lying there hurt, injured, was there anybody to help them? But how could anyone help when the bombs kept falling? Someone coughed and stirred somewhere, and I quickly lay back down, pretending to sleep. I didn't want to talk to anyone. I wondered if Kolya and Yura were still trying to get people out from beneath the ruins and if they could see anything in the dark. But the fires would probably light the way for them. Were they still alive? Oh God, I prayed, please keep them safe.

The next morning, I was the first one up, and I carefully stepped around mattresses to slip out and go down to the farmer for water. I brought a towel with me and washed my face in the icy cold water at the well. The sun was up when I got back to the house, and so were most of the people as I brought the fresh water in. I knew it was refreshing to dip a washcloth in the cold water and wash your face, and everybody seemed to appreciate my bringing water so early in the morning. Someone had boiled eggs, and we each had an egg and a piece of bread with a little tea.

When I went back outside, I saw Mother and Father walking down the path toward the police station. They knew the police chief and had received permission to use the bathroom at the station. They carried a couple of towels, and I knew that Mother could not face another day without a bath. People seemed to have become placid, immersed in their own thoughts and resigned to what was taking place. The planes continued, each formation arriving just as the preceding squadron had dropped their bombs and circled to return to their base.

It was now Tuesday, April 8, and the black cloud climbed still higher over Belgrade. It was the third day of continuous bombing around the clock. We had no radio, though there was probably no need for one. Radio Belgrade surely had not resumed broadcasting since Sunday morning. Yugoslavian armored vehicles kept moving on the highway, and there was a steady stream of people walking, now in both directions, something I would see often over the next four years and never understand.

I went for a long walk in the woods past the cemetery. I found the path that I had seen a few weeks earlier from the top of the cornfield, and I was certain it was a short-cut to Belgrade. I didn't follow the path, but I could see the winding highway below, and the path led over the hills cutting the distance to the city almost in half. One day, I promised myself, I would take that path all the way to Belgrade—once the bombing was over.

About 2 p.m., Mirko and Jovanka walked up the hill carrying two enormous pots of chicken stew and several loaves of fresh-baked bread. The house suddenly came alive as the smell of the food circulated. Everyone crowded around the two large pots, peeking in before they rushed off to find a bowl. It was delicious, and everyone was soon ready for a nap. I found an unoccupied mattress and laid down to snuggle into a blanket. It felt so good to be stretched out horizontally.

When I awakened, the sun was already low in the west. Mother and Father were sitting together on my windowsill in the kitchen, speaking in low voices.

"Is this the first time you've been able to sleep on a mattress?"

"Yes, Papa."

"I'm so sorry that we just don't have enough room for everybody. I should have started building much sooner . . . at least to have gotten the floors installed."

"Papa, nobody knew they were going to bomb Belgrade. I'm sure everyone is very happy just to have a place to come to."

"Yes, well, I hope so. I wonder what's going to happen now. How long will the bombing continue? Probably when they are certain there is nothing left to bomb."

"Asya, you should go to the police station and have a bath," Mother said with a vacant stare.

"I wonder where my sons are," Aunt Nadia said as she entered the kitchen with General Nazimov.

"Maybe we should go into the city to look for them. Maybe they have joined the Yugoslav army," said her husband, twirling his mustache with a faraway look in his eyes.

"You have the damned army on your brain. Look where it's gotten you. General-bah. So what good did it do you? Or you?" she added, pointing at Father.

"I don't know what's worse. To have young sons or a young daughter in these times. The worries are the same, I suppose," Mother said, looking at me with a frown wrinkling her brow. She sighed deeply and grasped Father's hand.

I rose to go outside. Their conversation upset me, made me feel that I was contributing to their worries just by "being."

"Asya, why don't you take the pots back to the farmer's house before it gets dark. And don't stay too long," said Aunt Nadia, moving to hand me the pots. I took them from her and started down to the farmhouse below, grumbling to myself as I went. "Why does it have to be me, and why should *she* tell me 'don't stay'?"

Jovanka and her husband were in the kitchen, lighting the kerosene lamps for the evening and drawing the curtains shut.

"Thank you so much for the chicken stew. It was delicious. Everybody enjoyed it very much."

"Well, they were your father's chickens," replied Jovanka. "I just thought you might as well eat some of them."

"Did you have to kill the chickens yourself?"

"Sure. You just twist their necks a few times and snap it," she said, turning her hand in a circular motion to show me how it was done. I smiled, glad that Lyalya wasn't there. She would have fainted dead away, without even a murmur, picturing the poor chicken. Yugoslav armored vehicles were steadily moving in a column right outside their windows.

"Up at our house we can't hear the trucks this clearly."

"Yes," said Mirko, "I do wonder where they're all going. Well, as long as it's our army, I don't mind. Is Belgrade still burning? We haven't been up to the cornfield since last night."

"Yes, you can still see the red cloud above it," I answered, amazed that they seemed so much calmer than my parents and the others. They were so busy with their animals and with plowing and seeding their fields that they hadn't had time even to go to the cornfield to look toward Belgrade. I realized that our house was so full of crying and hand-wringing because there they had nothing to do but worry.

"I'd better get back now," I said.

"Are you hungry? Why not stay and have some supper with us. You should eat more. You are too skinny," said Jovanka, squeezing my shoulder and stroking my face.

"No, no, thank you," I said with a smile as I headed for the door. "I'm really full."

"Then God be with you in your dreams, Asya. I'll see you tomorrow. Good night."

I thanked them both again as I went out. The sun had just set, the last pale pink and purple in the sky hurrying to the western horizon before the dark blanket of night took over. The stars were not yet visible, but the steady drone of aircraft continued. Before going into the house, I went up to the edge of the cornfield for a last look. The orange cloud still hung over the city, showing flashes of explosions as bombs continued to fall. As I watched, the night blackened and the orange became a dark, angry red.

When I entered the house, I found it much brighter than usual. The windows had all been covered, and the wick in the oil lamp in the kitchen had been turned up all the way. Aunt 'Lyena and Aunt Sonya sat together at the kitchen table, reading the Bible.

"Asinka!" Aunt 'Lyena looked up at me sternly for the first time in my life. Her eyes through her thick lenses looked enormous, and the shadows of her jerky movements loomed huge on the white walls. "Weee haaaven't been to church fooor two weeks noooow, and yoooou haven't been to cooonfessssion. You shoooould read the Biiiible and pray exxxxtra hard."

"I know, Aunt 'Lyena."

"Knoooowing and doooooing are twoo diiifferent things. If you knoooow it, then yoooou should dooo it."

"Elyena," Mother said as she entered the room, "why don't you leave Asya alone. She is going through a lot of misery right now, and she doesn't need to carry guilt on top of everything else."

That was the only time I ever heard Mother speak harshly to Aunt 'Lyena—and in my defense at that! Father came into the kitchen just then, arriving at just the right moment as usual. He took the Bible from Aunt 'Lyena and sat down at the table.

"Elyena is right. We could all benefit from reading a passage or two. It will do us all good."

The kitchen filled as everyone crowded in to hear Father as he read from the Bible. He chose the Gospel of St. Luke, chapter 4, the Temptation of Christ. Listening to these passages again, I was sure that Hitler had signed a pact with the Devil, for he was well on his way to devouring the world. Or was Hitler himself Satan?

Father closed the Bible and handed it back to Aunt 'Lyena. There was complete silence in the room, as everyone was immersed in their own thoughts. Somehow Father's choice of passages to read had struck a chord with everyone. Aunt Sonya rose silently and began to brew a pot of tea, and someone placed a plate of Zwiebacks on the table. The tea was soothing, and soon everyone was dispersing with washcloths and toothbrushes in hand to wash for the night.

Around 11 p.m. the lamp wicks were turned down to their lowest, the blanket was removed from the kitchen window, and I arranged my windowsill for the night. I curled up facing the window so that I could watch the twinkling stars and drifted slowly off to sleep. Suddenly, I sat up, unable to understand what was happening. It sounded as though someone had turned off a very noisy, static-filled radio. There was total silence. My ears were filled with a "sishing" noise, as if I held a seashell against my ear to hear the sound of the sea. The sound was gone, but the constant noise that had lasted for three days and nights was still in my head. I sat up on the windowsill and pressed my hands against my ears, shaking my head. It was dead still. I crept outside, and there were no warplanes, no explosions. I called from outside at the top of my voice, "Papa, Papa! They're gone. Listen! They're gone. The war is over."

How little did I understand then about war! Papa and all the others were outside now, faces turned toward the starry sky as they all strained to hear something. The night was silent, almost eerie, as we moved up to look over the cornfield. The red cloud still hung over Belgrade. The city was still burning.

"Maybe they used all their bombs. Maybe they'll be back soon with another load," someone ventured.

"Maybe there is nothing left in Belgrade. Maybe everybody is either dead or injured, and that's why they stopped," someone responded.

Nobody slept the rest of that night. The silence was deafening. People wandered about in a daze, everyone wondering what was to come now. What would be next? We had become accustomed to three days and nights of bombing. But now there was this dreadful, unexplained silence.

TEN

Invasion

As the first rays of the sun lit the eastern sky on Wednesday, April 9, I took a bucket and started down to get water from the farmhouse well. Mirko had taken his cows to the lush green pasture across the highway, and Jovanka was busy feeding the pigs and chickens. Jovanka had planted a small flower garden surrounded by a short, white picket fence between the highway and the well, and early spring flowers were already beginning to bud. I walked to the well and brought up the water to empty into my bucket. I loved the creaky sound that was made as I turned the crank to raise the well bucket.

"Good morning, Asya," Jovanka called as she moved back toward the house. "Come and have some breakfast with us."

"Good morning, Jovanka." She had a warm, friendly smile as I joined her.

"Do your parents allow you to have coffee?"

"Yes, I've had coffee before," I replied, fibbing. The only time I was permitted to have coffee was to dip a sugar cube into the very thick, strong Turkish coffee we had at home. I wondered what General Skorodumov would say if he heard me.

"Come, sit down," she said as Mirko joined us. The three of us said grace, and she poured three cups of coffee, leaving mine less than half-full and placing a pitcher of warm milk in the center of the table. The milk, just brought from the barn, was still steaming and half cream. I filled my cup with the rich milk, added a bit of sugar, and thought the "coffee" delicious.

Jovanka served eggs, ham, freshly baked hot biscuits, and preserves.

"Eat, eat." said Mirko, as huge amounts of food disappeared from his plate.

"Mirko, do you think there will be more bombing?" I asked, watching in amazement at how quickly he was eating.

"To tell you the truth," he answered between bites, "I have no time to listen to the bombs or think about it. You know, the spring is the busiest time for us. Plowing and seeding, making sausages, hams. But I hope the Germans will get here and get the hell out to wherever they are going."

"It must be fun to have a farm," I said, not knowing how to continue the conversation about the Germans.

"It's a healthy life. At least you see the results of your labor."

"Well, I think I'd better be going. They're waiting for the water by now up at our house. Thank you for breakfast. I'll see you later in the day, Jovanka."

Back at our house, everyone was outside, looking up at the sky from time to time, afraid to believe that the bombing had finally ended, that the warplanes would not be back at any minute.

"Ah, fresh water. I'm so thirsty," Aunt Nadia said, dipping a large ladle into the water and pouring it into a glass. "Do the farmers know anything?"

"No, they didn't know anything. They are so busy with their animals and spring planting."

Father gave me a warm hug as I joined him and Mother on the bench in front of the house.

"Papa, can we go back to Belgrade now that the bombing has ended?"

"No, Asinka. Mother and I were just discussing that. We think we should stay here for another day or two to see what's going to happen next."

Most of the people staying with us came out of the house, stretched, and wandered off to take a walk.

By midday there was some confidence that the bombing had ended, but more of our friends from Russkii Dom began to arrive because of loss or damage to their city property. Thankfully, some of those staying with us decided to return to the city, making room for the newcomers. The new arrivals brought terrible news. The city was now "nothing but a smoking ruin." They had no idea who had survived, whole streets were blocked by debris from collapsed buildings, ambulances were everywhere trying to help people, and the parks served as temporary morgues, with the dead placed on the sidewalk for access and identification. They reported that both Kolya and Yura were helping to dig people from the rubble.

I left to walk through the cemetery to the woods to try to picture what I had just heard. All the wide, beautiful streets now were nothing but rubble with bodies covering the sidewalks under the beautiful chestnut trees. I could not imagine Belgrade looking like that—*my* Belgrade. I could no longer hold back the tears. I had been so sure that if I prayed hard enough, God would protect us. But hadn't all the dead people prayed also? Why would God allow so many people to die?

I wished that I was back in Hopova again, and as I remembered that lovely little nun who had helped me with my scrapes and bruises, I wondered if she was praying, if the nuns were all frightened, too. Gradually I became aware of the sounds around me: birds pushing aside dead leaves to peck for worms or bugs, their mates singing high in the trees, a woodpecker hammering loudly. A few vehicles drove down the highway, then a few more before the stillness returned.

When I returned to the house late that afternoon, everyone was still talking about the devastation of Belgrade. Aunt Nadia and General Nazimov decided to stay with us for another few days. They had been very worried about Kolya and Yura, but now that they knew they were all right, they decided to stay put. That way the boys would know where to find them. The city was apparently in total chaos, with survivors desperately searching for family members and friends. I was glad that we were in Yaintse. I could not imagine my beautiful Belgrade in ruins.

As the sun began to set, I went into the house to find Aunt 'Lyena and Aunt Sonya already straining their eyes to read the Bible by the pale light of the kerosene lamp. Father and Mother came in from outside and looked for a place to sit. Both of them looked tired and worried—older, I thought. Their bedroom had two single beds, the same as the smaller bedroom

Aunt 'Lyena and I shared, but their room now had six people. I don't know how they both fit in a single bed, but another couple occupied the other single bed, and a third couple slept on a mattress that had been placed on the dirt floor between the beds.

Mother caught sight of me and smiled faintly.

"There you are. We haven't seen you all day. Were you down at the farmer's house?"

"Yes, only for a little while. I was walking in the woods."

"You haven't eaten a thing today. You need to have something in your stomach," Father said as he put a kettle on for tea.

The hot cup of tea felt good going down and helped me to relax. I still felt a little dizzy, and took my blanket to curl up on the windowsill. I was so glad that nobody cluttered my windowsill. They all knew that it was now my "bed." As night settled in, the windows were covered with a blanket and the lamp light grew brighter, casting a soft light everywhere except right next to it on the table, where it was bright enough for Aunt 'Lyena to read by.

I almost felt cozy, either from the hot tea or the soft lamp light. I was tired and sleepy, and the voices around me became almost whispers. When it had grown dark, and the kerosene lamps were turned to their lowest, a loud, frantic pounding at the door broke the silence. Everyone sat up on their mattresses, chairs, or cots, panic filling their eyes. Father suddenly entered the room with his finger to his lips.

"All of you stay where you are. Don't say a word."

All eyes were fixed on the door. As Father unlocked it, he was pushed back by a man who slammed the door behind him. The man was naked except for his undershorts, and he stared like a frightened animal, his eyes wide.

"Please, can you give me some clothes? It's all over. Soldiers are running in every direction. I just want to get home to my family."

Father stood between him and the rest of us and questioned him:

"Who are you? Where do you come from, and where are your clothes?"

"I'm a Yugoslavian soldier. The Germans have crossed the border and are in Yugoslavia. Our army is scattered everywhere. I threw my uniform in your well. All I want is to get to my family."

The first wave of German bombers had knocked out Radio Belgrade, as well as most telephone connections and radio transmission towers. Communication between Yugoslavian military units and Central Command had been lost.

He looked terribly frightened, tears in his eyes. Father left him for just a moment and returned with a pair of his trousers, a shirt, and a light sweater.

"Here, put these on. Are you hungry?"

"Thank you, no. I'm not hungry. I just want to get to my family."

He pulled on the trousers and finished dressing while still standing, then quickly grabbed Father's hand and kissed it.

"God bless you, sir. God bless you all." He ran out of the house and disappeared into the night.

A sigh of relief came from everyone—everyone except General Nazimov, who looked at Father sternly and said, "You are an officer of the tsar. You know that this man is a deserter, and you know the punishment for desertion."

"For God's sake! This is not the Russian army, and besides, we are no longer in the army!" Father replied, obviously annoyed by the remark, "All this man wanted was to get to his family and see to their safety. The war is over for the Yugoslavian army."

The General lit his pipe and, between puffs, looked at Father sternly again and said, "Once an officer, always an officer. War or no war."

"For heaven's sake," interrupted Aunt Nadia. "An officer should also be a compassionate human being. I wish you would get it through your head that you are no longer in the army, no longer a damned general. The tsar is dead. Russia is dead. For once just try to be a human being."

By then the sleepiness had left everyone. We sat there thinking about the frightened soldier, hoping he would get home to his family. And everyone wondered just how far away the German army was. Would they occupy Belgrade, or just go through as they had originally said?

In the very early morning on April 10, I was awakened by a slight tremor of the window. I sat up, but could not hear anything, yet there was something. I turned slightly and touched the window pane. Yes, there was a slight vibration. There wasn't any accompanying noise. Had the bombing resumed? No, it was a constant light vibration. An earthquake? Everyone seemed to be fast asleep, and I quietly put my dress on and moved to open the door. The night was black. I couldn't see anything except the stars, but there was a distant, persistent low rumble I could not identify. Aunt Nadia came out, still half asleep, pulling on her bathrobe.

"You heard something, too?"

"Yes, what is it?" I asked.

Slowly now, one by one, the others were rousing, coming outside and straining to identify the rumble.

"What time is it?" someone asked.

"Almost 5 a.m. The sun will be up soon."

It was very dark, as it always is just before dawn. I went back inside because of the chill, sat on my windowsill, and wondered what the new day would bring. What could the rumble be? Gradually, everyone else came back inside. Nobody seemed alarmed, just puzzled as they returned to their beds to try to get a little more sleep, and I drifted back to sleep as well.

Soon I was awakened again, this time by a very loud rumble and shaking of the window pane. It was light outside. The sun was already above the trees. I sat up and realized that I had not taken my dress off when we came inside. It was now 7:30. I rushed outside to find the highway below crowded with an endless line of huge tanks, the noise from them now much louder than the bombers. They resembled giant steel caterpillars moving slowly, coming from the direction of Mt. Avala and moving toward Belgrade, crushing the asphalt beneath them.

"Oh, my God. The Germans are here. What's going to happen now?" said Aunt Nadia as she emerged pulling on her bathrobe. The others followed, sleepy eyes quickly widening to reflect fear.

"How many of them are there? The highway is filled with tanks as far as you can see," someone said. Others stood wringing their hands and looking at the highway in disbelief.

"I don't know why everybody is in such a panic," said Father. "After all, we are not being invaded by the "Hooligans," the Bolsheviks. This is a highly intelligent nation with morals and integrity."

"Is it moral to take one country after another, leaving death and destruction all along the way?" demanded Sonya, who was obviously very frightened. Not knowing where Sergei was, she was beginning to fear the worst, especially now in the midst of an enemy invasion.

"Asya, dear, there isn't a drop of water in the bucket," said Aunt Nadia. "We haven't even brushed our teeth, and we have no water for tea."

I looked down at the highway and saw the tanks moving at a slow steady pace from the direction of Mt. Avala toward Belgrade. I could hear German soldiers speaking. It sounded as if they were at the well. With the bucket in my hand I hesitated, wishing someone else would go. But everyone simply stood there staring in the direction of the well.

"All right, I'll go and get the water."

As I started down the path toward Jovanka's house, I could hear the soldiers talking below. They were not angry voices; I even heard light laughter. I walked close to the shrubbery at the bottom of the path and hid behind a large bush close to the well. I could see a huge tank in the yard, close to the well. Jovanka's flower garden and its little white picket fence had been destroyed by the tank.

Two soldiers in black uniforms holding guns sat on top of the tank. The huge cannon mounted on the tank pointed at the highway. The tank was as high as the farmhouse. Two other soldiers were at the well. They wore black trousers that looked like riding breeches tucked into shiny black boots. Their black shirts or tunics were lying on the ground as they washed at the well.

I suddenly realized that I hadn't had a bath in almost a week. "God," I thought, "I haven't changed my dress in a week. I've even slept in it a couple of nights. I wonder why Mother hasn't complained about my appearance."

I remained crouching there behind the bush, trying to think of what would happen when I went to the well, trying to plan exactly what to do and how to act and asking myself, "Am I afraid? Yes, a little. Should I speak to the soldiers? No, I won't. I don't want them to know that I speak German. But will they shoot me? I haven't seen Mirko or Jovanka. Have they been shot?" No, I reasoned, there has been no gunfire. "No, I mustn't be afraid," I told myself.

Suddenly I remembered my appendix operation a few years before, and Father looking into my eyes as he said, "Remember, you are my daughter and you are a Russian, and we Russians are never afraid of anything," and how I had jerked my hand from the nurse's grasp to climb up on the operating table by myself to show the world my bravery, that I "was a Russian." That little flashback gave me whatever courage I needed, and I stood to walk out from behind the bush.

As I approached the well I was stunned by the appearance of the soldiers. They were tall, blond, and lanky. They were now putting their tunics on, and as I came closer I could see a silver skull on their caps. The tunics were jet black and matched the breeches. One collar had a silver skull to match the one on the cap, and on the other side the collar had a stylized silver ss. I realized that this must be one of the ss Panzer Divisions that we had heard so much about on the radio. As I drew near the well, the soldiers moved off and wandered around the tank.

The highway was crowded with other tanks that kept moving slowly toward Belgrade. Mirko came out of the house with a large box that he carried to the tank and handed to one of the soldiers. The soldier looked into the box and said in German, "Ah, it's a beautiful ham. We'll eat well tonight. Thank you." Mirko turned without a word—I don't think he understood German—and returned to the house. As Mirko reached his house, I finished filling my bucket and started back up to our house.

"Have you talked to them? Are they in the city already? Where are our soldiers? Why didn't they fight?" The questions seemed to come from everywhere at once.

"I didn't speak to them; I just tried to listen to what they were saying. They weren't mean to me. They didn't even speak to me."

The whole village had come to life by then. Soldiers seemed to be everywhere, rifles menacingly at the ready. Two soldiers soon came to the house, and Mother spoke to them, as polite as she had been to everyone all her life.

"We need to search through the house," one of them said, "and we may need quarters."

"You may certainly search, but the house is already filled, as you will see for yourself." Mother replied.

"Do you all speak such perfect German?" the soldier asked as Mother led him into the house. "Are you German, perhaps?"

"Heavens, no," Mother replied with a small pout, a curious mix of pride and distaste on her face. "We are Russian."

This early in the progress of the war, Germany still honored an alliance with Soviet Russia, and her answer may have unwittingly won us a brief reprieve.

"Well, I do see that the house is quite full, but we will be establishing a temporary watch post behind the house. I see that the whole village is in view from here."

"That you may do," Mother said, as though her permission mattered.

The two soldiers left, but returned in only a few minutes with more soldiers that moved a lot of equipment to the ridge behind the house. In what seemed no time at all a tower of sorts was being erected, while the two who had inspected our house remained in our yard.

"Have your troops reached Belgrade yet?" Father asked.

"Today Belgrade, tomorrow Athens, then ... " one of them responded with a shrug and a smile. "You know what the Fuehrer said—'Heute gehört uns Deutschland, morgen die ganze Welt.' So we're on our way."

"How long are you going to stay here?" Father asked.

"What do you mean 'how long'? This all belongs to Germany now. We're here to stay."

The soldier's words were followed by an awkward silence.

"Is this your daughter?" the other soldier asked, looking now more closely at me. "She is very blonde. I was going to say she looked German until I noticed those black eyes. Do you speak German?" he asked, turning to me. I ignored the question and moved toward Father, to stand close and partly behind him. I had extremely light blonde hair, and this was the first of several times that I would be mistaken for being German.

The tower was erected very quickly, and the two soldiers left the yard to take their posts in the tower. Later that morning a soldier came to the house with a handbill that announced a curfew. Everyone was to be inside by 4:00 p.m. daily. Violators would be shot. By midafternoon, lookout posts had been set up all around the village.

That afternoon, as we sat inside the house, a sudden rumbling noise accompanied violent shaking as dishes clattered and a loud crash was heard at the front wall. Frightened, I rushed out to see a huge tank lumbering past the house. The tank had effectively destroyed the gravel road that led to the cornfield at the top of the hill and had damaged our house. A section of the mud brick exterior wall had cracked and partly collapsed beneath one of the front windows.

Two tanks patrolled the highway constantly, and occasional gunshots were heard. The Germans set up their headquarters in the villa that had served both as home to the local police chief and as the police station. I never saw the local police chief again.

Aunt Nadia and General Nazimov changed their minds about staying. The appearance of the Germans increased Aunt Nadia's concern for Kolya and Yura. The boys would now be encountering German patrols constantly, and she was adamant that they return immediately to be closer to them. They left early the following morning.

The confusion that had engulfed our family with the bombing and invasion was replaced in just a few days with at least a semblance of order. Father, horrified to realize that I was wandering alone through the village, told me that this was far too dangerous and gave strict orders that I was to stay only around the house. I remember feeling like a trapped animal. I longed for something, but did not know what, and I needed someone to talk to. I wondered if the bombing had destroyed Trécha Zhénska, if my teachers were alive. And I thought often of Kristina. Every day I prayed that she would come back to us.

Father's strength and determination to maintain an air of normalcy, coupled with my restriction to our house and yard, insulated me from the chaos surrounding us, but not completely. Our house had a good view of the highway and the German military vehicles that moved constantly toward Belgrade, crowding the road as far as we could see. German troops searched throughout the farms and took all the food they could find.

About four days after the arrival of the invasion force, Father announced that the three of us would return to the city the following morning to try to resume our lives. Aunt 'Lyena was to remain at the house in Yaintse, and Aunt Sonya would remain with her to provide help and companionship. Early next morning Aunt 'Lyena walked with us to the path that led down to the highway. She didn't seem to mind staying behind in Yaintse, and we embraced warmly.

As the three of us reached the highway, just the thought of the long, long trek ahead of us began to tire me. Tanks, motorcycles, and military trucks moved steadily along the highway, their occupants shouting sometimes friendly, sometimes insulting remarks. I didn't understand how they could feel superior because they had destroyed our city and killed so many people who had been unable to defend themselves. God *must* be on their side, I told myself, because He had let it all happen. My feet began to ache, and I felt as though I could not take another step.

Military trucks and motorcycles sped past us so closely that they seemed to almost touch my skirt, and I began to wish that one of them would run over me so that I could just forget everything and leave it all behind. I don't know how Mother found the strength to walk as far as we had come. As we reached the outskirts of Belgrade, I looked up to see an ancient, dilapidated truck, lacking a windshield, coming slowly toward us. It stopped just in front of us on the other side of the road, and Yura and Kolya jumped out.

"Now this is what I call timing," Kolya exclaimed. "I just stole this truck." He paused to correct himself as he noticed the stern look on Father's face. "I mean I just borrowed it from an empty, bombed out garage. Come on, get in. I was on my way to pick you all up. Your house is standing. In fact, Shenoyna Street and your whole neighborhood escaped damage. They," he motioned toward the German trucks speeding past, "must have preserved the nicest sections for themselves." Kolya was joking, but his remark would prove prophetic in another year or so.

Yura jumped into the rear and helped Mother climb in, and I sat in front between Father and Kolya as he turned the truck around to head into the city. Black smoke still hung over the central area.

"Really, Asya," Kolya began. "I drove by your house, and it hasn't been touched. Your school has some damage. One wing of Trécha Zhénska was hit, but the rest of it seems fine."

"What about your house, Kolya? Has there been any damage there?" Father asked.

"One bomb fell just in front of the house and broke some windows. Some of the doors are jammed, but the house is still livable. One terrible thing is that there are so many bombs that didn't explode. They're a real danger because they are hidden. There's no telling where they are. A couple of them exploded right near the garage where I got this truck.

"This was the only truck still intact when I got there. As soon as I bring you home, I'm going to return it. Oh, guess who is back?"

"Back where?" I asked.

"At your house. Kristina. She came back two days ago. She knew you were all right since the house was undamaged. She knows that I went to rescue you, milady," he said bowing comically.

The news that Kristina had returned and was waiting for us at home made everything else seem less terrible. I had prayed so often that she would come back to us that I was convinced that God had answered my prayers and was watching over us. Suddenly Kolya swerved, the truck almost running into a pile of debris in front of us.

"Kolya, we've come through a lot and we're all still in one piece, so let's try to stay that way," Father said, smiling at him.

"Besides," I added, "it would hurt my ego something terrible to be killed in a raggedy old truck like this."

We both burst out laughing—the laughter bringing relief.

"You know, Kolya," I said thoughtfully, "sometimes I think that this is all just a bad dream. That tomorrow when I wake up I'll still see the beautiful streets, all the chestnut trees and fountains, and all the buildings standing just as I remember them."

"Yes, it would be nice if it were only a dream," he answered wistfully.

Kolya had to stay alert for standing water that might hide a bomb crater and to make frequent detours because the streets were blocked with debris or furniture that people tried to salvage. At almost every turn, people milled like ants about the ruins of buildings that had been their homes just a few days before, crying as they dug, trying to salvage anything that might be left. Covered bodies lay on the sidewalk, close to the curb, awaiting identification and removal. Just ahead of us, two torn and bloody bodies were being carried to the street, and I quickly turned my face away.

"Kolya," I asked, "what is that terrible sweet odor? It's almost sickening."

"That's the dead that are still buried in the rubble. That sweet smell is from decaying bodies."

It was an odor that would remain in my nostrils and that I would encounter many times in the next few years.

"My God! Haven't they found all the poor dead ones yet?"

"No, they are finding them all the time. Why, it will take weeks to dig out all the bodies, and the dumb curfew slows up everything."

"They have a curfew here in the city, too?"

"And how! The Germans are shooting us down like flies. The city is under martial law. If someone is on the streets after curfew, they don't ask questions. They just shoot."

"Careful, Kolya," Father cautioned, just before an unexploded bomb blew up immediately in front of the truck on the driver's side. Kolya swerved and managed to safely stop the truck. But blood was running down the side of his head.

"Kolya, Kolya, are you badly hurt?" I cried, pulling out a handkerchief to begin wiping blood from his ear and face as he slumped slowly forward on the steering wheel.

"Papa, Papa, Kolya has been hurt!"

Papa was out and over to the driver's side in a second, examining the wound. "It looks like shrapnel just above his ear." He pushed Kolya to the center and took the wheel of the truck. "We have to find a doctor or a hospital."

Father sped through the streets to a hospital he knew was close by, only to find it guarded by German soldiers who turned us away. He sped to another only to meet the same response.

"Hold his head and press that hankie on the wound," he said. "I'll find a doctor someplace."

I moved Kolya's head to rest on my shoulder and looked in horror as blood dripped down over my blouse and skirt. "Hurry, Papa. He'll die."

"Russkii Dom!" Father exclaimed. "They always have a doctor or at least a nurse on hand for the children in the orphanage."

Papa drove so fast through the streets that I was afraid the old truck would turn over. We reached the orphanage in what must have been only minutes but seemed like hours. Papa blew the horn as we stopped, and the sound of the old horn brought back that curious "memory," or dream, just as it always did. A nurse rushed out at the sound.

"Is someone hurt?" she called.

"Yes. Quickly," Papa said, lifting Kolya from the seat.

Mother, distraught because of Kolya's wound, remained in the truck with Yura as we brought Kolya inside. Father carried him to a room where the nurse could examine him. I waited outside the room, looking down the hallway, and walked toward an old nurse seated at a desk outside one of the offices.

"Where are all the children?"

"When we heard that the war was threatening, we made arrangements to send all the children to Switzerland and then on to Paris."

I had forgotten that.

"Have they already arrived?" I asked, thinking of Aljona, remembering that she had been sent to Paris on the same train.

"We don't know. We haven't been able to get any information."

As Belgrade became embroiled in disputes between Nationalist Serbs and those who wanted to cooperate with the Nazi request for free transit through Yugoslavia, and as the threat of hostilities grew, the Russkii Dom Orphanage placed all the children on a train bound for Paris and the Russian émigré community there. The train was rerouted because of unexpected hostility and then stopped by the Soviet army. All the children were identified as Russian, taken from the train, and sent to the Soviet Union.

Papa came out to the hallway smiling broadly. "He's all right. There wasn't any shrapnel. It just grazed his head, and we fixed him up. He'll be fine."

I entered the room and found Kolya lying on a small steel bed with no mattress, a smile on his face.

"Now you're gazing upon a real war hero, wounded in the line of duty. I just hope you appreciate the sacrifice," Kolya said with a serious look, barely able to suppress his smile.

"Oh, lie still or you'll be a dead hero," I said, leaning over to look at the bandage.

"You look mortally wounded yourself," he said, looking at my blood-spattered blouse and skirt. "Did I make all this mess?"

"Yes, your brains were all dripping out. Oh, how grizzly," I said. "I never knew I could have such thoughts."

"How do you like my bed?" he asked, pointing at the bare springs. "Isn't this the very best?"

"How long are you going to be a gentleman of leisure?" I replied, smiling.

"The nurse said that if your father can drive that truck like a Rolls-Royce, with as little jolting as possible, I can leave now."

Papa returned to the room, and together we helped him out to the truck and into the front seat. Off the bed and walking, Kolya seemed weak and tired. I sat in front with Kolya's head again resting on my sticky, blood-stained shoulder, as Papa drove slowly off, carefully avoiding any bumps that might jostle Kolya.

"Kolya," he said, "you and Yura had better stay at our house tonight, and I'll get a message to your father."

April 17, 1941: The Kingdom of Yugoslavia formally surrendered to the armed forces of Nazi Germany.

ELEVEN ·

Occupation

Many streets were blocked, and Father drove cautiously because of Kolya and heavy damage in so many areas. But as we reached Dedinye and turned into Shenoyna Street, I could see that Kolya had been right. The trees were all in splendid bloom, birds providing the only sound. The street showed no trace of damage or war. We stopped in front of the house, and everything looked as though we were just returning from a normal weekend in Yaintse.

As I opened the gate and began to walk toward the house, Kristina ran out and embraced me.

"Oh, my dear girl. How I've prayed for your safety. Oh, how I've missed you. How are you? You look so pale and thin—and, I must say, dirty. You have blood all over you, even in your hair. Are you hurt?"

"No, Kristina, I'm fine. Kolya was hurt, but he's fine now, too. How have you been? Is your sister all right? Are you going to stay with us now? I missed you so very much," I replied, kissing her and hugging her tightly. The warmth and comfort of her hug made me feel safe and secure again.

"Kristina," Mother said after embracing her, "do we have any food in the house? We might have more people than usual. And I'm so dirty. I've got to have a bath."

We all went into the house to find everything just as it had been when we left in such haste, and I rushed to look at my room. How silly all the stuffed animals and dolls looked to me at that point—how completely useless and pointless. I went into the bathroom and quickly filled the tub, looking forward to clean clothes.

With my hair still damp, but braided and wound round my head, I dressed quickly and went into Aunt 'Lyena's room where Kolya would stay.

"My, my, a princess out of some fairyland, come to honor the wounded hero," he joked.

"No, just clean. I think someone is going to take care of you, too. I think Kristina is going to make you a bath, and you can lie in some warm water and soak."

"Do I really smell that bad?"

"Well, violets in the woods do have a more appealing aroma." We both smiled as Father came in.

"Kolya, can I help you up? I took Yura home, and he'll tell your father you are spending the night here. Your tub is ready, and we're going to get you all fixed up. You, young lady, go and see if you can help Kristina. There's a whole herd of us to be taken care of."

"Yes, Papa," I answered, leaving for the kitchen.

When dinner was ready, I went to call my parents and found them seated in the living room.

"Mama," I asked, "may I eat in the room with Kolya? He's all alone, and I'd like to keep him company."

Mother looked to Father for an answer. "Go ahead. You young folks should talk together. We're old and boring," he said.

After the warm bath and clean clothes, Kristina's cooking tasted even better than usual. Kolya obviously enjoyed it.

"Asya, do you ever kiss your mother?" Kolya asked unexpectedly when we had finished eating.

"I try, but each time I'm pushed gently aside because of her lipstick or her hair, I guess, or perhaps because she has a headache . . . something . . . I don't know. She changed so much after her operation. Mama was so very affectionate when she first came home from the sanitarium, but she has been changing back since Abdul died. You know, Aunt 'Lyalya once told me that Mother was taught to always hold her emotions in check, to be very reserved. Maybe that's the reason. What a strange question. Why?"

"Oh, I just wondered. You seem so warm and affectionate with Kristina and your father, but you seem never to talk to your mother."

"Well, I guess we just don't have much to say to each other, except for language practice. I love Papa. I think he's wonderful. You know, I think he was the one who wanted a child, not Mama. I love Mama, too, but . . . "

"Oh, poor, poor Asya," said Kolya, teasingly.

"I'm not poor. I'm very happy . . . sometimes, I guess. Anyway, only idiots are happy all the time. Don't you know that?"

"So in order to prove that you're not an idiot, you reserve the right to be sad, gloomy, and very serious at times?"

"Well, aren't you that way, too, sometimes? Or are you a happy idiot?"

"No," he replied, growing very serious. "I'm very happy, and I have great plans for the future. I want to get away from here as soon as this war is over and build a life far away from the memories my father longs for. When I talk to him about this, he gets terribly angry and tells me that I'm not being a patriot, that I don't love my country and my ancestors. But he doesn't understand that I don't know anything about the things he feels so strongly about.

"I was born *here*. Sure, I'm proud that I'm Russian, but what does that mean? An Englishman is proud to be English, and a German is proud to be German. I guess I'll just never get along with my father on this point. You know, Asya, we're really the children of emigrants, people who fled because they could no longer fight an evil they felt had taken over their own country. But I can't feel the same things. I can't feel the same patriotism. Maybe if I had been a general in the tsar's army, then I'd treasure the experience and long to return. But we—you and I—we were born here."

"I'm not sure I was born here," I interrupted.

"Where were you born?"

"I'm not sure. You know, Kolya, sometimes I think that I was adopted. I have this strange memory—at least I think it's a memory. It's very confusing." I told him about the automobile horn and the memory it always provoked, and swore him to silence. "So you see I'm not sure who I am or where I came from."

Kolya smiled warmly, thoughtfully, and then said, "Perhaps you are really a little princess out of some fairy land."

"Or an old witch disguised as a princess. Well, you should get some rest, and I want to say goodnight to Kristina. Goodnight, Kolya."

Kristina's hugs were as warm and comforting as always and made me feel secure in spite of the events of the past several days. I was home at last. It had been a long and frightening day, and blessed sleep was not long in coming.

Over the next few days Father's determination to return some measure of normalcy to our lives did help. The same attempt was made throughout the city, and at the end of April we learned that Trécha Zhénska would resume classes the first Monday in May.

I looked forward to returning to school, but classes were limited to half-day sessions, and the empty seats of classmates injured or killed in the bombardment or who had left the city made it impossible to study. We learned that two of our teachers had been killed. The headmistress's attempts to resume everything as before failed, of course, as did our teachers'.

Nothing seemed organized as classes became student-teacher discussions about the war, the friends we had all known and lost, the beautiful city now resembling a ghost town with blocks of ruins, and the danger of buried, unexploded bombs. Still, talking about these things, though painful, seemed to help all of us. They helped me to realize how fortunate our own family had been. And they helped all of us deal with the frightening uncertainty of military occupation. The social fabric of Belgrade had simply ceased to exist for all of us in about four days, replaced with the fear and uncertainty of martial law.

In a few weeks the curfew was extended until 6:00 p.m., but the rules continued just as strict as before. In fact, German occupation forces faced constant resistance from the civilian population. The fiercely independent Serbs shot and killed many German soldiers from windows after the curfew hour. The Germans retaliated, of course, dragging people from their homes to face immediate execution. Depending on the rank of the German who had been killed, a certain number of people from the same street were simply rounded up and shot. Young, old, women, children—it didn't seem to matter as long as some evil Nazi quota for retaliation was met without delay.

Many of our acquaintances had been killed or badly injured during the bombing, many still dying, perhaps because of injuries or the psychological difficulty of living under the occupation. Whatever the reason, Mother's inner strength and commitment to helping others would become a source of tension between us that would eventually deepen beyond reconciliation.

Mother began attending funerals almost as soon as we had returned from Yaintse. She wanted me to accompany her on what seemed to me to be daily trips to the church for services for yet another acquaintance. I went willingly, at least at first, but I steadfastly refused to accompany her as she approached the casket to kiss the face of the corpse in a final farewell, when the person had been a particularly close acquaintance, the memory of my childhood experience still fresh in my mind. Mother seemed to understand and never made an effort even to encourage me, but as the funerals continued, I became more and more depressed at the thought of accompanying her. I began to make excuses, and eventually I simply refused all together. Mother tried to explain to me how important it was to accept personal responsibility for consoling and helping one's friends. Her reasoned arguments made no difference. I simply wanted nothing more to do with death, and I did not believe my attendance to be necessary.

Time lost all importance for me. Classes, such as they were, continued for several weeks until one Monday morning, nearly at the end of the school year in 1941. As I neared the school, I saw German military trucks crowded into the courtyard. The school windows were open, clothing and various articles hanging from many of them. The ground around the building was littered with books and broken furniture.

German soldiers stood about in groups as I approached. Two guards flanked the entrance as I stopped and looked around, puzzled at the scene.

"Yes?" one of the guards addressed me in German. "What is it that you want?"

"This is my school. What has happened to it?"

"Well, well. This must have been a good school if they taught you to speak German as well as you do."

"I spoke German before I started school," I replied, chin held high.

An officer leaned from a first floor window to find out what the discussion was about, and the guard quickly froze at attention.

"Yes, young lady? What are you looking for?" the officer asked.

"I don't understand what has happened to my school."

"Well, go home and be happy. There is no more school. This building is now quarters for German soldiers. Was this a school for girls?"

"Yes," I replied, chin held even higher in my best imitation of Mother in a conversation she found distasteful.

"We will soon open German schools, and you may continue your education in the traditions of the Third Reich."

"How amusing," I replied loudly as I turned to walk away. It was my first face-to-face encounter with German soldiers, and I was very proud of myself. I thought of Father and his stories about building a strong foundation, and I decided that my foundations were fine.

With school canceled, my day was free, and I walked about the streets of Belgrade, at first unable to recognize many areas. So much of the centuries-old beauty I loved had been destroyed, so many innocent people killed. Rumors were that over seven thousand people had been killed in the three-day bombing horror. I came to the park where Kristina let me play as a little girl before we went to shop in the market across the street.

The park hadn't changed much. Only one bomb crater was visible, but buildings all around the park had been badly damaged. There were people in the park, even a few small children playing in the sandboxes. I wondered about our home on Dr. Kester Street, but quickly put it out of my mind. I loved that home so much that I resolved never to go there, never to allow myself even to think of its possible destruction.

I found a bench in the shade and sat down. Sitting there, I made up my mind that from then on I would try to walk through the city every day, determined to impress it on my mind, in my memory, to be sure that I remembered everything about it before the Germans changed it.

A man, a Serb civilian, walked by slowly, turned around, and came back to ask if he might sit on the bench. I didn't answer, but moved to the end of the bench and leaned back, closing my eyes. There was a refreshing light breeze in the shade. I wondered why the man had chosen this bench with so many empty ones around, and I opened my eyes to look at him. A newspaper covering his lap shook and rattled, his hands under the newspaper, and he turned toward me as he lifted the newspaper to expose himself.

I sprang to my feet and began to run, run as fast as I could. I must have run for several blocks when I reached the edge of another small park and sat on the grass, exhausted, frightened, and crying. I heard footsteps and glanced up to see an elderly German officer approaching, a wide red stripe on his trousers, his car and driver following closely at the curb.

"What is the matter, little lady?" he asked in German, but in a gentle voice.

"Nothing. Nothing is wrong. I just want to get home," I answered in German.

"Where do you live? Are you in trouble? I have my car here. May I take you home?"

I looked up at him for the first time. He had a kindly face, gray hair visible under his cap. He looked like a nice man.

"Yes, please."

He helped me to my feet, and I gathered my books. We walked to the curb, and his driver held the door for us.

"You look so very frightened. Have any of our soldiers been annoying you?"

"No, no." I was unable to speak about the incident in the park. "No. Please just take me home."

"You know, my home is near Munich, and I have a daughter just about your age. In fact, she has long blonde braids, too," he said gently, his smile putting me a bit more at ease as I gave the driver directions

"Is she here with you?"

"No, she's back home. I hope this will all be over soon so that I can go back to her—back to my family."

The car pulled to a stop in front of our house, and I got out, turning to thank him.

"Thank you very much for bringing me home. Won't you please come in so that my Papa can thank you, too?"

"No, thank you, but we are not allowed to enter civilian homes. Good-bye, young lady."

"Good-bye, and thank you again," I said, turning to run to the house.

Kolya had stopped by to visit and was reading in the living room when I burst in. Mother and Father were not at home, nor Aunt 'Lyena, but I heard Kristina in the kitchen.

"What's the matter?" Kolya asked. "I thought I heard a car outside."

"Yes." I ran past him to the kitchen to find Kristina.

"Kristina, Kristina," I cried, embracing her and crying as I blurted out the story of what had happened. "It was terrible. There must be something wrong with that man—that growth . . . "

"Asya, dear," she began, stroking my head, "men are different than girls, you know. Oh, you probably don't know. You see, that's how we tell the difference between a man and a woman. It was criminal of him to do what he did. You should have gone to the police, and they would have arrested him immediately. But as for the appearance . . . that was normal."

I was shocked, my eyes as big as saucers at her words. I knew that men didn't have breasts like women, but it had never occurred to me that there were other differences. I went to my room to wash my tear-swollen face and returned to find Kolya still immersed in his book. I couldn't bear to look at him.

"Asya, how are you?" he asked. "Did you have school today? Our classes have been canceled. The university was taken over by the Germans a few days ago. I guess there will be no more classes for me for a while."

"No, we didn't have classes either. Trécha Zhénska was taken over today, too."

"Well, no school means we can pile up on Gypsy Island and just let the world go by."

I remained silent. The thought of being on the beach with Kolya or any other boy sickened me. Even the thought of Father made me sick.

"Let's go outside," Kolya said, "and sit under the tree and dream."

"No," I answered shortly. "It's too hot."

"But it's cool in the shade."

"Oh, please shut up," I snapped, remembering what had just happened in the shade.

"Hey, what's going on? Do you miss school so much that it makes you bad-tempered? Don't worry, it'll open again soon." Kolya smiled. "What's the matter, Asya? You're so tense. Has something happened?"

I remained silent, and Kolya shook his head and rose to go out and sit under the tree to read. In a few minutes I heard voices and went to the window to see Kristina sitting with him and talking. In just a moment Kolya came back into the house.

"Asya, why don't we just walk around the garden a bit?"

"All right."

"I know what happened in the park today. Kristina told me everything. It's such a terrible way of finding out. Sooner or later you would find out, of course, but I'm so sorry that it happened this way. The world is full of bad people. I'm so sorry it happened in such a cruel way. I wish I had been there to beat his brains out."

I looked at Kolya, remembering his head wound and the talk we had. I thought again how nice he had become, suddenly surprised to realize this was the same boy who had taken coins from my bank as a bribe to play games only a few years earlier. I was just twelve years old, and Kolya had not yet turned seventeen. We had grown together and had both matured rapidly over the past few months. I had never paid any attention to him, and now I felt that we had become friends. Somehow this terrible war had brought us together, given us a chance to know each other better.

"Are we friends again, Asya?"

"Yes."

"Then let's go to the beach tomorrow and see what the murky old Danube looks like. What do you say?"

"I'll ask Papa. I'm sure he'll let me go as long as I don't go alone."

The next morning my period started, and when we arrived at the beach I remained dressed in spite of the heat. Kolya jumped into the water immediately.

"Hey," he called, "are you going to bake until you're crisp and then jump in the water?"

"I'm not going in the water today," I said, feeling a blush come over my face.

While Kolya was swimming, my thoughts kept drifting back to the frightening event in the park. I could not reconcile the two apparent extremes I had experienced: the man on the bench, a Serb, a fellow Yugoslavian, who had frightened me and acted so disgustingly, and the German officer, one of the "merciless invaders" responsible for the death and destruction now all around us, but who had been so kind and gentlemanly. It would not be the last time I found myself trying to understand and reconcile the differences in people.

Kolya came out of the water and sat next to me without saying a word except to suggest that I put on a wide hat because of the sun. We talked briefly between his trips to the water to swim. He never asked why I wasn't swimming, but probably thought it was due to the episode in the park. He knew how much I loved to swim—how I was always the first one in even when the water was icy cold—and I was terribly embarrassed wondering if he understood. I would never have an opportunity to ask him.

Kolya came to the house the following morning to ask if I would like to go to Kalamegdon for the day. Uncle Borya was talking to Mother and Father when I returned home that afternoon.

"Where have you been, Asinka?" Mother asked.

"At Kalamegdon, looking at the animals and walking."

"Did you go alone?"

"No, Mama, Kolya and I went together. There were lots of people. It was more crowded than usual, but we didn't see any friends, perhaps because it was so hot." I was surprised. Mother had never asked about my activities before, and it puzzled me.

Borya stayed for dinner as usual, and I excused myself as we finished, going to my room to study. Although school had ceased, Mother insisted that I continue reading in both German and English each evening. After Borya had left, Mother knocked and came into my room to sit on the bed.

"Asya, dear, when was the last time you had your period?"

"Yesterday and today."

"Are you sure?"

"Why, Mama, how could I not be sure of something like that?"

"All right," she said with a gentle smile. "Goodnight, dear, and sleep well."

I lay on my bed for a long time, wondering why Mother had suddenly developed this interest. She had never before even indicated that she knew that my period had started, had never mentioned anything to me. I could hear Kristina still cleaning up in the kitchen, and I went to ask if she had any idea why Mother had seemed so interested.

"Well, there are so many troops in town . . . and you and Kolya have been seeing a lot of each other lately . . . and . . . I suppose that she is a little worried."

"Worried about what?" I asked impatiently. "What could troops and Kolya possibly have to do with me having my period or not?"

"Come on," Kristina said gently. "Let's go to my room, and I'll try to explain."

I sat on the bed, wide-eyed, awaiting the explanation from Kristina.

"You see, dear, your period is a sign that you are passing from childhood to womanhood." She paused, grasping for words. Obviously uncomfortable, she began again, only to pause again.

"All right, Kristina, so now that my period has started, I'm no longer a child. Sometimes it seems to me that I was never a child. Besides, you told me all of this before, remember? What I want to know is just what troops and Kolya have to do with all this?"

"Oh, dear. You see, God has made us in such a way that when we no longer have our period, then it's usually a sign that God loves us and that He has chosen us to have a baby."

Kristina paused again, uncertain of how to continue; not knowing how well any of it sounded, she looked at me rather helplessly. By then, of course, I was more puzzled than ever.

"Is that true, Kristina? If God loves us, then He sends us a sign? He terminates our period, and that way we know He is going to give us a baby?"

I was thunderstruck. Deep in thought, remembering when I had seen women who were fat and that Mama had said were going to have a baby.

"Will I get fat, too? I hate to be fat. You mean when my period stops, I'm going to get fat and have a baby?"

"Yes." Kristina shifted uncomfortably, realizing that she had confused me completely without really explaining anything. "Well, let's not think about all this now. When the time comes, you'll find out a lot of things, but in the meantime you just forget about everything."

Dear Kristina, my confidante, my substitute mother. She hurried from the room, leaving me mystified. If God loves you very much, I reasoned, then He chooses you to have a baby . . . and to let you know, he stops your period. Well, that sounds all right, I think. I fell asleep still wondering what any of this had to do with troops and Kolya.

June 22, 1941: Operation Barbarossa began as German troops crossed the border and launched a full-scale invasion of the Soviet Union, breaking the Soviet-German nonaggression pact without warning.

July 20, 1941: Prime Minister Winston Churchill began his famous "V for Victory" campaign during a radio broadcast heard in the countries of Europe already involved in the war. The first four notes of Beethoven's Fifth Symphony are a tonal representation of three dots and a dash—Morse code for V—and always introduced the news broadcast of the BBC. The sign was quickly picked up by the Allied countries of Europe.

My unfortunate event in the park did not reduce my determination to walk through Belgrade as much as possible, and each time Mother left to attend a funeral I took the trolley into the city center. I made sure that I was not in a position to be alone with any strangers, staying only in areas that had many civilians, and leaving if other people began to leave. The German army had taken over many of the buildings for various purposes, but they hadn't changed anything. I simply wandered about the city, careful to avoid any contact with the soldiers who were seen almost everywhere.

August 30, 1941: German forces began the siege of Stalingrad.
September 6, 1941: Germany issued an order requiring all Jews over the age of six in Germany and all Nazi-occupied countries to wear the Star of David on their arm.

The next few months flew by. I turned thirteen, and on my Name Day that year Mother gave me a small icon to be placed on my night table, next to my bed. Autumn turned quickly into winter without any sense of the passage of time, at least for me.

December 7, 1941: The Empire of Japan suddenly, without warning and without a declaration of war, attacked the United States at sunrise as wave after wave of Japanese carrier-based planes bombed the U.S. Navy fleet lying at anchor at Pearl Harbor in the Hawaiian Islands.
December 8, 1941: The United States declared war on Japan.

Without the regularity of school and church and family dinners, time simply seemed to stop for me, to be replaced with endless boredom. Mother continued the language calendar, but French was eliminated, and English became the language of the day three days each week. Mother insisted that English and German were the languages I was to concentrate on.

I read a French book that winter, surprised that I had forgotten so much. Mother's efforts however, seemed to reawaken my eagerness to learn, and I read voraciously in German and English. When Mother spoke English, she sounded exactly like Miss Spencer, and I looked forward to practicing with her.

> December 11, 1941: Germany and Italy declared war on the United States, and the United States quickly reciprocated.
>
> January 20, 1942: A small group of men in Berlin sat down at a meeting which had been called by Reinhard Heydrich, head of the Nazi Security Service and Security Police. The meeting was held at a large villa that overlooked Lake Wannsee, and this has since been called the Wannsee Conference.
>
> A memorandum to all SS officers sent by Heydrich five days after the conference was headed "Final Solution of the Jewish Question" and stated that "all preparatory work is completed." Following this conference, the whole Nazi apparatus, particularly the SS, became involved in the systematic killing of European Jews. Historians still debate the real importance of the conference. Most historians agree that the mass killing of Jews had been set in motion by Hitler himself months earlier.

In March 1942, the German occupation announced that a branch of Munich University would soon open in Belgrade and that all German-speaking people with an appropriate scholastic background were encouraged to attend the Deutsche Wissenschaft Akademie—München (the German Academy of Higher Studies—Munich).

My parents decided that I should enroll, and I readily agreed. In fact, I would have looked forward to anything that offered an opportunity to learn and that promised a break in the boredom that had settled on me with the occupation. My enrollment, however, was postponed, as our family began a downward spiral from which it would never recover.

One bright morning, Mother sat at the piano playing one of her favorite pieces. It had become my favorite as well, and I sat on the floor, my knees drawn up and my hands clasped around them, leaning against one of the legs of the piano with my eyes closed, completely lost in the soft passages of Schubert's Serenade.

Suddenly someone pounded on the front door. Father motioned for Mother and me to remain seated as he rose to answer the door.

"Sir," a German officer said as he brushed past Father, "this house has been requisitioned. It is now the property of the Third Reich. It will be returned to you when the Reich has no further need of it, but you are to vacate the premises immediately."

The officer handed Father a piece of paper, as a soldier who accompanied him pasted a large sign across the front door— "*Beschlagnahmt.*" We tried desperately to gather a few things together. The officer held up one hand to stop the activity and addressed us.

"You are to take only those personal toilet articles and clothing which you can carry. And you are to leave immediately."

Mother faced him, now almost in tears.

"Do you realize that my father shipped most of these things to Switzerland even before the Russian Revolution? It took us years to gather everything together and to make a new home here. And now you want us to just get out? What kind of people are you? What assurance do we have that when you leave, all these things will still be here?"

"None, Madame," he replied with utmost politeness. "But my orders are that you are to leave the premises immediately with only those personal articles which you can carry."

No reasoning, no pleading, no tears—nothing helped. Aunt 'Lyena begged without success to take the stamp collection she had begun so many years before at Kotchubeyevka and which filled a large album. We simply walked out with a change of clothing and the few toilet articles— soap, toothbrush, comb, etc. —that we were able to grab; out to the street where Father tried to console Mother and Aunt 'Lyena, and to assure us that everything would work out—we would all be fine, we would manage. But his customary "Everything is in order" rang hollow.

We walked to the trolley line to get the next trolley into Belgrade where Father stopped to speak to an acquaintance—someone he knew from his associations at Russkii Dom—where he obtained the key to a vacant apartment. The owners were out of the city temporarily, and we would be able to stay in the apartment for about two weeks. Long enough, Father assured everyone, to find more permanent housing. The apartment was small, but clean and orderly. Aunt 'Lyena voiced the only concern when she complained gently that there was not even one icon to be found in any of the rooms.

Father's time was spent trying to find a place for us to live. At the end of our two weeks, he announced that there simply wasn't a vacant apartment to be found and that we would move the next day to stay at the house in Yaintse until something could be found in the city.

Father was permitting acquaintances from Russkii Dom, whose homes had been damaged by the intensive bombing, to use the house at Yaintse until they found other accommodations in the city. When we arrived, I found that three couples were occupying space in the living room, and two other couples were in the "attic," an unfinished place below the rafters where a rough floor had been laid, reached from a ladder in the living room. I gave my bed to Kristina and again curled up on my windowsill.

We were not as crowded as we had been during the bombing of Belgrade. The house was large enough to accommodate all of us without undue stress, and everyone made the best of the situation. I continued practicing English with Mother, studying, and reading—rereading—the books we had brought to Yaintse.

A few soldiers remained to occupy the police station. However, most of the Germans had long ago moved on to Belgrade, and I felt secure enough to resume at least short walks through the village. By May, the fields had been planted and green sprouts were everywhere in view. The small meadow adjacent to the house was lush with spring flowers, and if the house began to feel crowded, I could spend hours lying in a quiet spot watching fluffy clouds, building dreams from them. Those hours allowed me to completely forget the war and the difficulties of the occupation.

I was content in Yaintse, but the time wore heavily on my parents. Without her piano and her friends to talk to, Mother grew depressed and more and more irritable. With the police chief gone, and the station now used as the local occupation office, Mother no longer had access to the bathroom and running water, which had helped to make Yaintse at least tolerable for her. The farm couple below us, Mirko and Jovanka, did not have inside plumbing, nor did most of the village. Father, concerned for us all, rose early each morning to leave for Belgrade and continue searching for a suitable apartment. By the end of May he had found a place, and we all looked forward to returning to something closer to a private family life.

TWELVE

Jovan

June 10, 1942: In Lidiče, Czechoslovakia, the Gestapo massacred 175 men and leveled the village in retaliation for the killing of a Nazi officer. Reinhard Heydrich, infamous for his persecution of Jews, had been wounded in a grenade attack on his car on May 27 and died on June 4.

In the first week of June 1942 we moved to an apartment that Father had found on Kralia Milutina Street, not far from the central plaza of Belgrade. It was a convenient location and a pleasant place. It even housed a piano that Mother would be able to play. Two separate rooms had been rented to two men, but they never interacted with us. We had three bedrooms, a bathroom, and a small sitting room, and in the beginning Mother seemed to be quite content, almost happy again. While we no longer entertained or had guests for dinner, our friends often dropped in to have tea and whatever Kristina had to offer. Aunt Lyalya stopped by regularly, and Uncle Borya continued to be a fixture.

We spent weekends in Yaintse, and in the city Mother, Aunt 'Lyena, and I began daily visits to a large hospital some distance from the apartment. We went first to visit friends who had been hospitalized due to illness or injury, and then, seeing a need, to read letters, newspapers, or even books to anyone who asked. Soon, however, Mother became more withdrawn. Aunt 'Lyena had changed little, but she also seemed unable to help. I asked only once if she knew what was wrong.

"Aunt 'Lyena, what's bothering Mama? I know things are not as nice, but we're all well and together."

"It isn't aaaaanything speeecial, dear. It's ooour situation, our faaamily. Eveeerything is faaaling aaapaaart." She began to cry. The question upset poor Aunt 'Lyena so much that I could never bring myself to ask again about Mother.

I don't think Father ever worked at a regular job since leaving the army at the end of the revolution. Throughout my childhood, both Mother and Father were simply together, unless Mother was at the stables and/or Father at Russkii Dom. We were not wealthy by any means, but there was never any apparent concern for expenses. Looking back, I believe that Mother's parents had established an account in Switzerland that would accommodate her education expenses, personal needs, travel, etc., probably sufficient to include anticipated university expenses, and that she was able to access the account once settled in Belgrade. Access to the account may have been stopped by the invasion and occupation, or perhaps the funds had been depleted by the purchase of our home in Dedinye pending the sale of our home on Dr. Kester Street, which had been delayed by the war.

Family finances were never discussed or shared with me, but in 1942 Father took a job at the Hotel Excelsior as night auditor, and he began to change—subjected to pressures I could not imagine. When at home, he also seemed preoccupied, worried about something, and at the time I thought it must be Mother's well-being that concerned him. Father and I always had a close relationship, and finding him alone and looking worried, I tried to cheer him as I never could with Mother.

"What's wrong, Papa?" I often asked, kissing his cheek as I put an arm around his shoulders. "You look so worried."

"It's nothing, Asinka. Life—just life," he always answered. He would smile as his face softened at least for a little while, but the easy conversation I had become accustomed to didn't follow anymore. Father was becoming distant. Worry began to deepen the lines on his face. I had to interrupt his distant, often sad expression, and felt that I was intruding, that he preferred or perhaps needed to be left alone with his thoughts.

One bright, sunny morning in September 1942 I decided to leave the hospital and spend the day in Koshutnjak. I walked the few blocks to the trolley line, boarded a car, and found a seat next to a window. At the Koshutnjak stop I jumped out of the trolley, stopping for a moment to take in all the beauty of the green fields and the autumn colors just beginning to appear on the trees. It was just as I knew it would be. A fast running brook separated the trolley line from the park and wooded areas, and I walked down the bank to the brook to watch the colorful leaves being carried away. I jumped across the brook to walk through the woods, to a meadow that I knew had a perfect view of the valley below.

One side of the meadow had more flowers, and I found a nice spot to lie down, burying my face and braids in the thick, sweet grass. It was cool and peaceful, the only sounds the singing of birds and the occasional trolley bell. Lying in the grass, home, the city, the occupation, and our family all seemed remote. It was so easy to relax—to watch the clouds move about in the blue sky and let my imagination build dreams from them. Soon it grew chilly, and I returned the way I had come, boarding the trolley car when it arrived and taking the only seat available, next to an old man. The sun was getting low in the sky, and I shivered a little.

"Are you cold? Would you like to have my jacket?" The old man next to me smiled sadly as he held his jacket to offer it. "It's an old jacket, but it's the only one I have. I'm afraid it smells of onions and garlic. I'm a cook up at the German canteen."

"Oh, yes, thank you very much. I am very cold," I answered, smiling gratefully.

"Here, let me put it around your shoulders."

"Thank you" I said, moving my braids out of the way. "It feels so good, and it smells good, too. I didn't realize I was hungry until I smelled your jacket."

"Here," he said, carefully opening a red kerchief he had tied into a bundle. "I have some dark bread, and I also . . . " he looked around, continuing in a whisper, "I also have a couple of sausages that I snatched from the kitchen. Here, let's share it, and I'll have my supper right here instead of in my hole in the ground."

The dark bread and the sausages lying on the red kerchief looked and smelled so good . . .

"Come on," he said, "have some. I'll break the bread. It's a little tough, but it's good bread."

I held out both hands waiting for him to break the bread and eyed the sausage with anticipation.

"Here we go—half for you and half for me—and take a sausage. I rubbed the skin with garlic to make it taste richer."

I bit into the bread and the sausage, and a warm feeling spread inside me. "Oh, that is so-o-o good. Thank you."

"The bread is good, and the sausage is mild. The Germans have good bread. They claim they have good sausages, but I like the smell and flavor of garlic on mine. Do you like garlic?"

"Yes, it's delicious."

"Where do you live?"

"Oh, we live close to the center of town. We used to live in Dedinye, but that area was taken over long ago. Where do you live?"

"I live close to the center of town as well. And by the way, my name is Jovan."

"My name is Asya, Jovan. You are lucky that your house survived the bombing."

"Well, I really live in the basement of my house. I managed to salvage a stove from the house, and an old couch and two chairs. I even have barrels of marinated cucumbers and cabbage and green tomatoes. Funny, you know they weren't damaged at all, but the house is gone."

"Do you live by yourself?"

"Yes . . . well, physically I'm alone, but each night I try to pretend that the upstairs is still standing and that Dusha has just sent me to the basement to fetch some marinated tomatoes. Dusha is my wife . . . she was killed . . . and a neighbor that was visiting was killed at the same time. It was during a lull in the German bombing when we thought it was over. And you won't believe it, but Dusha had just sent me to the basement for something when the bomb struck. It was as if God had sent all the thunder in the heavens down at once. The basement shook, and piles of stuff began to come down, shelves and boxes . . . and the barrels just stood there, didn't even move . . . and then complete darkness. I had something very heavy lying on my left side and my arm . . . it was badly broken and never healed right." He picked up his left arm and let it fall motionless again.

"I crawled through a window and then saw the ruins that had been our house. I could hear sirens, and there were people all around me. Someone asked where Dusha was, but I couldn't speak. I just pointed toward the house. I laid there while they were digging. I saw our chairs flying down, broken furniture, pots . . . I tried to get up but fell down again feeling a terrible pain through my body. I just focused my eyes on the men who were digging. They found Dusha . . . she was all broken up, one leg so badly torn . . . " He broke into sobs, unable to continue.

"Please," I said, my own eyes now filling. "You shouldn't tell me anymore. I'm sorry I asked."

Jovan took the red kerchief that had held the bread and sausage and wiped his tears with it, leaving bread crumbs on his brows and cheeks. He blew his nose.

"I'm sorry I broke down. This kerchief comes in handy. First I carry food in it, and then I blow my nose in it," he said with a chuckle. "I must remember to wash it tonight. It is my food basket, and I'll be lost without it tomorrow."

Jovan smiled sadly, showing uneven teeth partially covered by his long gray mustache. He straightened in his seat, rolling the mustache between his thumb and forefinger as he continued.

"Dusha and I had a good life. We have two children who left us seven years ago. Both of them are married and now live with their own families in Argentina. My son has a farm, a small one, but it's his own. There's nothing like having a piece of ground of your own. A piece of land is almost indestructible, even if bombs fall on it. Those holes could be patched up, and in a couple of springs, with lots of love and care, it will bear again.

"My daughter is married, too, and lives only a few kilometers from her brother. I might go there someday, once we're allowed to move freely. I won't be in their way. I'll just put all my love for Dusha and the children into the ground and watch things grow." He faded off a bit, deep in his memories. "We always wanted to go to Argentina after the children left, but each year I said to Dusha that we should wait until we had enough money so that we wouldn't be a burden to our children. With each spring her heart sang with new hope that maybe this year we would go. And each spring her hopes were dampened by my foolish decision to wait. Poor Dusha. Do you think she forgave me?"

"I'm sure she had nothing to forgive. You must have loved each other very much."

"But do you think it would be fair for me to go to Argentina without her?"

"I know that Dusha would want you to go just as soon as it is possible."

"But she will never have the chance . . . "

"Our priest told us that when our loved ones die, they go to heaven, and from there they can always see you, and in turn, you can always feel them in your heart."

"I wish I could have so much faith in what my priest tells me. He told me practically the same thing." He smiled and added jokingly, "They all must have the same speeches ready for everybody. Oh, this is almost my stop. Say, you said there were five of you at home. Why don't you get off with me. I live only a few steps from the trolley stop, and I'll give you some marinated tomatoes and cucumbers. What do you say? Do you think your people will like that? I'll never be able to eat it all."

"All right," I said. "I'd like that."

We got off the streetcar together, almost in front of the ruin that was now a home to lonely old Jovan. Concrete steps led down to the entry to the basement.

"We have no electricity anymore, of course, but I keep a candle here by the door." he said, standing before the bomb-wracked door that led to the basement that was now his home.

I stood behind him, waiting for him to light the candle, and then followed him down more broken stairs.

"Here, my child, give me your hand," he said, moving carefully down the steps. "One must know these stairs. There, here we are."

Jovan set the candle down on a chair that stood next to four huge barrels. Tall, uneven shadows fell across the floor as the old man lit a second candle. A sofa stood in one corner neatly made into a bed. A kerosene stove stood between the bed and the barrels. A rope strung above the stove and fastened to the beams with huge rusty nails was hung with socks and a red kerchief, a mate to the one that had held the bread and sausages.

Boxes had been stacked along the walls. The floor was earthen and very damp. A tiny table and two small wooden chairs stood next to the bed. A crucifix and a framed photograph stood on one of the chairs, propped against a large piece of lace that hung over the back of the chair, and I bent to look at the photograph.

"Oh, I found this after the bombing. The glass was broken, but the picture wasn't damaged, and the crucifix still hung on one of the walls that had not collapsed. This lace is part of the curtains Dusha made for our bedroom. It's so beautiful. See, this is my Dusha," he said tenderly.

I looked at the pleasant, full face of a woman with dark hair pulled back in a bun and a smile that lit up large, dark eyes—a warm, pleasant face.

"She must have been a very good wife and mother."

"Oh yes, my Dusha lived just for the children and me. You know, we never had any disagreements—any serious ones. I married her when she was only sixteen, and to me she never changed. She will always be my beloved of sixteen."

He placed the photograph gently back on the chair next to his bed before continuing.

"Here now, I have plenty of pots, so I'll give you this one. And I'll just fill it up with some cucumbers and tomatoes. You know, my Dusha was a very good cook. She always prepared food for winter, and our basement was always full of food. I had some smoked meat and fish here, too, but when I came back from Dusha's grave one day all my meat and fish were gone. There are many hungry people, you know. So . . . whoever took it I hope it helped to ease their hunger. That's why I'm a cook now. At least this way I won't go hungry." He busied himself filling the pot with the vegetables. "Well, there we are. Now I had better take you back to the trolley and make sure you get on all right. Do you live far from your stop?"

"No, less than two blocks. It's a very short walk."

"All right, my child, let me get my candle, and I'll take you now."

The basement fell silent in complete darkness as I looked back from the door at the top of the stairs. Here, I thought, was a man's life, past and future, in this one damp, lonely hole. This terrible war—these poor innocent people—what had this man or his wife ever done to Germany?

"Oh, I hate Germans. I hate wars," I exclaimed.

"That's something almost every generation has to go through, my child. Oh, some are lucky enough to escape the gruesome details. But let us hope and pray that this will bring an end to all wars and that at least you young people will have a chance to build a normal life. Look, I see your streetcar coming. God be with you. May you have a better future, and may all your dreams come true someday."

I stepped up on the trolley car and turned as he handed me the pot he carried. The car was nearly empty, and I found a seat near the front next to a window. As I looked out, the old man was waving, and I felt tears streaming down my face. Jovan brought home to me more than anything that had happened up to that point, the tragedy that had overtaken Belgrade. I was so preoccupied with thoughts of Jovan and his wife and children that I almost missed my stop, and I stepped from the streetcar leaving a trail of marinated air behind me.

I walked a bit more slowly than usual. The sun had set, and the streets were beginning to darken as I approached our apartment. Many of the windows flickered with candlelight. It looked very warm and cozy—romantic, I thought, remembering the candle-lit family dinners and our friends of just a few years before. But the warmth I knew was gone, and I no longer rushed to enter.

I went through the entry hall to the kitchen, gave the vegetables to Kristina, who was delighted, and entered the small sitting room to find Uncle Borya, Aunt 'Lyena, my parents, and the Poltoratskys, who had dropped in for a visit. As I entered the sitting room, Uncle Borya jokingly said, "My, my, don't we smell like a princess this evening, straight from the Arabian Nights."

"You do smell like garlic, Asya," Mother added. "Where have you been all day?"

"Oh, I took the trolley to Koshutnjak and walked in the park and woods for a while. And I did eat some sausage and bread with an old man in the trolley on the way home."

"What old man?"

"I don't know his name. Just Jovan. He lives in a basement on M Street."

"So you know where he lives, but you don't even know his name."

"Oh, Mama, he's just a poor old man. He lives like a dog in a hole underneath what used to be his house."

"Well, don't you think we live like dogs now, too?"

"No, I think we are all still pretty lucky."

"Lucky? Look at you. You have two dresses left to your name. I have practically nothing. Everything is gone—all of our things. The clothes we are wearing are going to rot away from our bodies, and there isn't any place to buy anything either . . . even if we could afford it."

"Mama, you have always told me that family and friends are the real treasures of life, not things."

I looked around to find Uncle Borya, who could always add a touch of cheer, but he looked embarrassed and averted his eyes. Father too seemed not to know what to say. It was the first time I had openly disagreed with Mother, and I think it shocked everyone present, me included. I regretted it instantly, as a look came over Mother's face showing that she remembered saying that to me several years before.

I excused myself and went to my room to read and to get ready for bed. Years later, reliving the Nazi occupation of Belgrade, I would begin to understand—to understand that when she was seventeen, Mother's world of great wealth and privilege had suddenly collapsed into the chaos and desperate privation of a different war, to understand that after twenty years of struggle, the world she and Father had built together had collapsed again and that this time the collapse affected her own daughter, to understand the enormous financial insecurity she must have felt on top of everything else. But at that time I did not understand; I simply resolved to spend as much time as possible away from the depressing atmosphere of home.

My behavior, of course, made the situation at home even worse. I knew that my wandering alone throughout the city worried Mother and added to her depression, but she had shut me out completely. I could not bear to be alone with her or to accompany her to what by then seemed daily funerals. I longed to rush and embrace her, to be embraced, but could not bear the rejection I had come to expect. As if to emphasize the growing division between us, Mother came to my room one day when I returned from Gypsy Island.

"When was the last time you had your period, Asya?"

"Oh, Mama," I answered wearily. "I don't know. Maybe two months ago. Why? What difference does that make?"

"Tomorrow you are to stay home. You need to see the doctor," was her sharp response.

The following morning, both parents accompanied me to our regular doctor's office for my first gynecological examination. No one, not even the doctor, made an attempt to explain what was to take place, and it was, of course, a particularly humiliating experience. When the exam was finished, the doctor left me with the nurse and went to speak with my parents. I could hear the conversation through the open door.

"I don't understand why you are concerned, Maria Petrovna. Your daughter is 'intact.' Why did you insist on this exam?"

"Well, she told me that she has not menstruated for several months."

"That isn't unusual. Many young women have the same experience during these times, probably due to the stress of the occupation, bombing, complete disruption of their lives. And for children of Asya's age, the problems are compounded. Her normal cycle will probably return once this terrible war is over. You should explain to her why she had to go through this exam."

I did not hear a response from either Mother or Father, and as I finished dressing, the doctor returned.

"Asya, I want to see you again tomorrow. I think I should explain some things to you about today. Do you think you could come back to see me about 11:00 a.m.?"

Already wondering what "intact" meant, I readily agreed. The following morning I returned to the doctor's office, this time alone, and received a complete biology lesson, enhanced by charts and illustrations. I finally understood what poor Kristina had tried to tell me and why she had been embarrassed. The experience left me better informed, but it drove yet another wedge between Mother and me. Why, I wondered sadly, had she not explained this to me?

The following week, when I turned fourteen, Father told me quietly that we would be moving in a few days. He still steadfastly refused ever to discuss finances within my hearing, and I did not understand his apparent embarrassment. His usual "Everything is in order—no need for concern" was not at all convincing, but I tried to act as though there were indeed no need for concern.

"Asinka," he continued gently, his hand on my shoulder, "Mama is very upset because of the occupation, so very worried about many things. Please try to help her . . . to spend some time with her."

"Papa, I try, but she always waves me away. She has just shut me out."

The next week Father led us to an old garage in Belgrade—an automobile repair complex—closed since the beginning of the German occupation. We entered through wooden doors built to accommodate trucks, to find a very large, open area with a high roof covering repair stalls.

Father closed and barred the wooden doors and showed us a regular-sized door built into one of the large doors, which could be locked and through which we would enter. The central repair area was surrounded by a narrow, one-story part of the building that had been divided into separate rooms originally meant for various business purposes—toilets for customers and mechanics, and several rooms that formerly held parts and supplies.

On one side of the open repair area we found the three connected rooms which were to be our home and which adjoined the former main office of the garage. One room, apparently a former waiting room for customers, held some old office furniture, a couch, a desk, a couple of extra chairs, and a small two-burner kerosene stove. Two large windows viewed the repair area, and a rusted iron cot lacking a mattress stood in one corner. A toilet and sink occupied a closet in another corner of this main room. Two other small rooms each held a rusty old iron bed without a mattress.

Father located mattresses someplace, and we settled in to make the best of it—Mother and Father in one "bedroom," Aunt 'Lyena and I in the other, and Kristina on the couch in the adjoining main office area. Aunt 'Lyena prepared to settle on a mattress on the floor, but I insisted that I would prefer the floor and that she must take the bed. The next day, it was decided that Aunt 'Lyena should move to the house in Yaintse.

The day after we took her to Yaintse, I returned from a short walk to find that Kristina had left. She had chosen to slip away while I was gone because she knew that neither of us could bear to say good-bye. Mother told me that she had returned to her family in Slovenia, since there was so little room and since she was no longer needed as before. Kristina's departure filled me with overwhelming sadness, but I would soon miss her more than even I thought possible.

The first few weeks in the garage must have had a terribly depressing effect on my parents, but I took it in stride. The garage itself and the repair area smelled strongly of automobile grease and oil and gasoline—smells that were new to me—and I found it very exciting to explore the cars and trucks that stood about in various stages of repair when the invasion had halted everything.

No kerosene was available to us or to anyone else at that time in Belgrade, and the weather was growing colder. Mother had changed a great deal since the start of the war. So had Father. When we moved to the garage complex he stopped working, concerned about leaving Mother and me alone in the garage at night. Without electricity we had to rely on carbide lamps for light, and they had to be dismantled and cleaned after each use. The mess, but mostly the horrible smell when they were cleaned, was something I didn't think would ever leave my senses.

The hospital that Mother and I had started visiting was only about a block away. Mother joined me again in visiting the sick, and our daily visits kept us both occupied. By the third week, however, the reality of our situation began to wear on her. Our new living quarters did not provide even the illusion of a home, of course. In early November Mother began to complain about the garage and to suffer from constant headaches. She spent more and more time at von Der Nonne's riding academy, tending Silva, frequently spending the night. Father was gone all day, usually returning just after dark, just at dinnertime.

The weather was still quite warm, and I went swimming at Gypsy Island as often as possible. Perhaps as a result, I became deathly ill. I came home from an afternoon at Gypsy Island feeling very weak and hot. I went to my room to lie down and stretched my hand to touch the coolness of the concrete floor. I awoke for a few moments to see Mother looking at me with concern and Father looking beside himself with worry as he applied a cool cloth to my forehead.

"She's burning up with fever," I heard him say before drifting off again.

Father contacted our doctor, who came to the garage that evening.

"Vasilii Metrofan'ich," the doctor said when he had examined me, "your daughter is very ill. She has a very high temperature that we must bring down right away. She has pleurisy, and the concrete floors here aggravate her condition. She is badly underweight, and I suspect that she is anemic, though we would need a few tests to be sure. The temperature we can deal with without difficulty, but as for the rest . . . These times are harder on children, you know. They become discouraged and saddened, and everything is magnified."

I heard Father start to respond, but I drifted off into sleep or semiconsciousness again without understanding. Children, of course, are often far more resilient than adults believe them to be. By the following morning the fever had broken, but I remained so weak that I had to remain in bed for several days. My chest hurt so badly I could not draw a deep breath. Father hovered about me when he was home. He looked so worried that I tried desperately to get better for his sake.

Mother remained at home with me while I struggled to recover, but it seemed to me that when she was not quietly weeping and even more distant than before, she was angry and vindictive.

"How could you be so irresponsible? How could you do this to us? Running around Belgrade without a sweater when the weather is chilly. And swimming in November! Now we have additional worries—and more expense for medicines."

I wanted desperately to be well enough to resume my walks and trolley rides through Belgrade, but instead I grew weaker and began to be withdrawn and distant myself. Father was both attentive and affectionate. When he was at home he tried again and again to rouse me, to cheer me up, with his old Gogol-Mogul eggnog.

"Here we are, Asinka. Gogol-Mogul," he said. "Just like the old days on Dr. Kester Street, only better. Now drink it all down. We have to get some weight on you. You've gotten so skinny you can't even make a puzik for me anymore."

His remark brought back a special memory and made both of us smile warmly. As a child of perhaps four or five, as I walked about in our home on Dr. Kester Street, Mother, always concerned about my posture, would watch me and gently say, "Hold your head erect, Anochka, shoulders back and straight. And pull your tummy in. It should be flat." I would always correct myself for Mother, but as I left the room, I would pout and shamefully push my small stomach out as far as I could. If I encountered Father in the next room, he would always smile broadly, saying, "Ah, ha, my little Puzik" (a Russian diminutive for 'fat, little belly') as he snapped his finger against my belly, and I giggled as I pulled it in and rushed for a quick hug.

"Thank you, Papa. It is good, and I wish we were all back on Dr. Kester Street."

Father's eggnogs did the trick, at least partially. I was much stronger physically by the following week, but couldn't shake the sadness and silence I had slipped into, and Father's concern deepened. I don't know how he arranged it, but on a warm sunny morning in November he happily told me that he had spoken to the German officers who had requisitioned our home in Dedinye and had received permission for me to spend the day on the sun porch.

The house looked exactly the same except for the German staff car in front. The yard was just as lovely. The flowers were few and faded with the onset of fall, but the trees were still colorful and bright, and the light in the autumn was rather special. As we approached the door, Father explained the ground rules for my visit.

"Now remember, Asinka, the Colonel was very good to allow you to spend the day, but you can't go through the house or even to your room since everything is occupied by the officers now. You can only stay on the sun porch. But it's a beautiful day, and you will be able to rest quietly."

"Yes, Papa. I'm sure it will be nice."

Father rang the bell, and an officer let us into the house. Father went with me, through the kitchen, past the door to Kristina's room, and up the few steps to the sun porch.

"Ah," he said, "it is so beautiful up here. Now you rest, and I'll be back to pick you up this afternoon."

Father settled me on a chaise lounge facing the windows that the sun streamed through, and we embraced and kissed good-bye as he left. It did seem to work. I was fondly remembering the good times we had enjoyed in the house when suddenly the sound of gunfire very close by startled me. I moved quietly to the windows that looked over the wall into the grounds of the White Palace to see what looked like fresh graves being dug close to the wall, and a group of German soldiers with rifles lined up facing the wall. I didn't want to see anymore or even to think about what I knew must be executions taking place so close to me, and I returned to lie down.

I heard the sound of rifle fire twice more before the sound of voices faded, and I tried very hard to think only of Kristina and Aunt 'Lyena. I fell asleep, and sometime in midafternoon I felt a sharp sting on my left foot and moved quickly to slap at a large, green fly that had come through the open windows. I laid back down and, in the silence and warm breeze, drifted back to sleep for about an hour. When I awoke, my foot was throbbing and badly swollen.

By the time Father arrived to pick me up, the swelling had increased and spread higher on my leg, and it was difficult to walk or even to stand.

"What's the matter with your leg? What happened to your ankle?"

"I don't know, Papa. A fly bit me when I was asleep."

I had to lean heavily on Father to hobble back to the trolley stop and return to the garage. Mother looked on unsympathetically as Father placed compresses on my ankle to try to bring the swelling down. She seemed to be thinking that no matter what they did I was still a problem, and I resolved even more to get away from home as soon as possible. The following day the doctor returned to see me, this time to lance the bite, the source of the swelling, and to provide more medicine.

"I think she'll be fine. The fly had probably landed on some rotted food or meat, and the bite was infectious. It was the beginning of blood poisoning. She has a slight temperature, but I believe we have caught everything in time, and she'll probably be fine in a day or two."

I didn't tell him about the rifle fire and the graves, and I never told my parents. I don't know why. Perhaps I thought they would not believe me. But even if they did, they would only have worried and fretted about it— more worries brought on somehow by me. I had recently heard rumors that our Orthodox priests had been hung by their beards in a central plaza of Belgrade. Thank God I never saw anything like that, but the rumors added to my depression.

The following day I started to hobble about in the garage, and within another day or two I began to take short walks as my strength slowly returned. Mother cautioned me and complained, but more gently now. I could see real concern in her eyes for the first time in a long while and the sweet sadness I remembered from before the invasion. I wanted so much to rush and kiss her, hug her tightly, but the memories of being pushed gently away so often always stopped me.

As my strength returned over the next week or so, I gradually increased the length of my walks and my time away from home. Mother's disapproval increased with the length of my walks, and one day I returned after sunset to find both Mother and Father waiting for me.

"Where have you been all day?" Mother asked.

"Oh, just walking. Mostly in the parks, but I went to the old market where the big fish tanks used to be."

"Sit down, Asinka," Father said. "We need to have a talk. You know Mama and I are concerned because of the occupation and because you are spending so much time alone. We think you need to get back to studying."

"I do wish that Trécha Zhénska was still open, Papa. I miss school very much."

"Well, Mama and I have been thinking about it, and you probably remember that the Germans have opened a branch of Munich University here in Belgrade. I have spoken to the people at the Akademie about you, and they agree that you are qualified to enroll. Mama and I think it would be good for you to get back to a little organized study again. What do you think?"

"Oh, yes, Papa. That sounds wonderful. When do the classes begin?"

"The next term starts the first week in January, so there isn't too much time. You will need to register in the next week or two. Mama and I are glad to see that you want to get back to studying. Now, young lady, I want you to stay close to home, both here and in Yaintse, until school starts, so that Mama won't have to worry so about you. Agreed?"

"Oh, yes. But there's nothing to worry about. I just go to Topcider and Koshutnjak and some of the other parks. And the people I meet are always very nice."

"I know, Asinka, but Mama worries because of the soldiers."

December 2, 1942: The first self-sustaining nuclear reaction was demonstrated at the University of Chicago.

December passed quickly, and the first week of January 1943 I began spending my days at the Deutsche Wissenschaft Akademie—München. The German Academy of Higher Studies—Munich was really a business school designed simply to train proficient office personnel to meet the needs of the Nazi occupation bureaucracy.

The classes were German shorthand and typing, light bookkeeping, economics, and a "social studies according to the Reich" class, nothing that required any home study. I thought of the German shorthand courses as learning a new and different language, and I excelled in all of the classes. The classes were interesting but not challenging, and my attendance didn't curtail my wandering. I simply walked after classes until nearly dark before returning home. Mother wasn't concerned because she thought I was in school or studying. On the days we spent in Yaintse, I wandered throughout Belgrade after classes, usually catching a late streetcar to Yaintse, arriving at the house just as darkness fell.

I returned from my classes earlier than usual one day in April 1943. There didn't appear to be anyone at home, and I thought that Mother was probably at the stables. I started to leave again to take a short walk, when I thought I heard a noise from the room my parents used as a bedroom. I went to the door to investigate and found Father sitting on the edge of the bed, his head in his hands. He had obviously been crying, and he looked up as I entered.

"Papa, what's wrong?"

"It's nothing in particular, Asinka." He answered, trying to hide the fact that he had been crying. "These are very difficult times, and our family just seems to be disintegrating. 'Lyena off in Yaintse all the time, Mama more and more upset all the time and so often away at the stables. Since Kristina had to leave, no one is ever at home. We are never together as a family anymore, and I don't seem to be able to do anything to help. And I'm worried about Mama. She has had to go through so much in her life."

I sat down next to Father on the edge of the bed and stroked his hair.

"Poor Papa," I said, remembering the words he so often used to reassure me. "That's life, I guess, just life. Everything will be in order again soon. We're going to be fine. You'll see."

I placed one arm around his shoulders and kissed his cheek as I so often did. Father turned and embraced me, kissed my cheek, and seemed to be fighting tears. He kissed me again, then again, but this time on the lips—hard. Something was wrong! His eyes were glassy, glazed.

I was suddenly frightened and didn't know how to respond, how to get away. Father seemed a stranger, unrecognizable. As he tried to kiss me again, I managed to get my hands together against his chest, close to his throat, and as his hand brushed my breast I screamed and pushed against his chest with all my strength. Father tumbled to the floor, and I jumped to my feet terribly frightened.

As Father sprawled on the floor looking dazed and disoriented, I ran sobbing from the garage and onto the street, now beginning to darken. I was truly frightened for the first time in my life. My links to security had been cut one by one over the past two years, but the firm anchor that Father always represented was suddenly gone, disintegrated in an instant. I ran headlong down one street after another in a panic, without any awareness of where I was or where I was headed. I paused for a moment to try to catch my breath and to stop sobbing, trying to think of where I could go, when I saw old Jovan's basement across the street.

I ran down the few steps leading to the door of the old man's basement and knocked loudly. There was no answer. Jovan had not returned from work yet. I sank down next to the door, crying.

For the first time in my life I was truly frightened—terrified. And I was terrified of Father, my last source of security! I tried to plan an escape route if he appeared and to think of where I could go. I cowered by the door for what seemed hours, until it was almost completely dark. Finally Jovan arrived at the top of the steps, looking down at me in amazement.

"What's wrong? What has happened, my child?"

"Nothing has happened, Jovan," I answered, drying my eyes.

"Come in, come in. I'll make us a cup of tea, and you can tell me what's bothering you. Remember the stairs now. Be careful."

I followed the light from the old man's candle down the broken stairs to the basement. His wife's photograph was still propped against the back of the chair resting on the piece of lace curtain that he was so proud of. He busied himself with starting the stove and putting a kettle of water on to boil.

"Now, my child, something has you very upset. Would you like to tell me about it?"

"Nothing, Jovan," I answered, now beginning to regain some composure. "There has just been some trouble at home. My mother is away for the night, and I'm afraid to be home alone. Could I stay here with you just for tonight?"

"Well, yes, of course you can. But don't you think that I should go and tell someone where you are, or maybe leave a note explaining?"

"No, there's no need. There is no one there tonight."

"Well, let's drink our tea while it's hot and have a piece of bread, and then we'll rig up someplace for you to sleep."

The tea was hot and strong, the bread substantial and tough. The combination helped me to begin to relax. Dear old Jovan kept up a steady monologue while we finished the tea and while he moved boxes and blankets to provide a place for me at the other end of his basement. He hung one old blanket from a beam next to the boxes to provide me a measure of privacy. He talked continuously about his wife and children and their lives before the destruction of Belgrade, pausing from time to time to see if I wished to say anything.

I did not, of course. Nor did I understand or even hear much of what he said. But the steady, calm tone of his voice was comforting, reassuring, and brought me at least an illusion of security. As the candle burned low, Jovan gently remarked that he had to be up early for work and that it was time to sleep. I climbed on top of my boxes as we said goodnight, and I heard him shuffle to his bed, his couch, at the other end of the basement. He extinguished the candle, and in the pitch-dark of the basement, I listened as the old man recited his prayers.

"Heavenly Father, you know that my troubles are past and that I now pray only to join you and Dusha. But these are terrible times. So I ask that you please watch over my little friend Asya and her family and that you keep her safe and guide her always. Amen."

Jovan's simple words reminded me of Aunt 'Lyena, and I wondered at how much they seemed to have in common. She was from a privileged background but broken in body and stripped of so much material wealth, while he was from a far simpler background but stripped of everything he held dear, yet they shared a deep abiding faith that maintained and strengthened them far more than anyone else I knew. And I remembered the little nun and the grotto at Hopovo. And I knew that I was beginning to understand despair.

I did not sleep that night, of course. I went over and over the few minutes with my father, thinking that I was mistaken. I could neither understand nor forget the vacant, glassy expression in his eyes. That man had not been Papa but a terrifying stranger. No one had ever behaved this way before. Sex was still a complete mystery to me, still a rather frightening unknown, and my father had been the one person I could trust.

A sexual meaning in what had happened eluded me until I suddenly remembered my visit and conversation with the doctor a few months earlier, and I became even more frightened. I relived every moment of my short life, and all the happy times we had shared as a family, and finally I remembered the sound of that old automobile horn and the memory it always evoked. I reasoned carefully that the horn must be a real memory and that my real parents had left me someplace never to return. I decided that I must have been adopted. There could be no other explanation.

I longed desperately for Kristina and the comfort she always provided, but try as I might, I could not imagine a conversation with her—could not even think of the words to describe what had happened and how I felt. Dear Aunt 'Lyena would have been destroyed by the knowledge, and Mother's quiet reserve, now conveniently explained by my decision that I must have been adopted, had always made it impossible for us to discuss highly personal matters. The strain of the occupation had worn so heavily on her that I simply brushed away any thought of confiding in her now. And I decided I could not run away. The world we lived in offered no haven, no avenue of relative safety.

In a strange way, perhaps because of the terrible times we lived in, the way I rationalized the event actually strengthened me at a time I needed it most. Since the onset of the Nazi occupation of Belgrade, I had been steadily growing more independent and self-confident—mature in so many ways far beyond my fourteen years. Mother's quiet reserve and aloofness had begun to erect barriers between us years before. The simple, absolute trust I had always placed in my father, however, and my complete reliance on his strength and judgment were now replaced with fear. That fear, however, was accompanied by a fierce determination to survive. I reasoned that since my father had always been so strong and protective, I could still rely on him as long as I was very careful. I must, I decided, continue to rely on my parents for shelter and food, but no longer for emotional support or moral guidance. And I must never, never let Aunt 'Lyena learn what had happened.

As the first light of dawn began to brighten the basement, I heard old Jovan stirring, and I slid from the top of my boxes, slipped on my shoes, and greeted him. I found him in the brightest corner preparing to shave, and I busied myself with making tea and slicing some of the remaining bread. We exchanged brief pleasantries over breakfast, and I followed him up the broken stairs and into the bright sunshine of a new day. I walked with him to the trolley stop, and he turned as the trolley approached.

"Well, good-bye, Asya. You seem much better than you did last evening. But remember that you can come back to see me anytime. God be with you."

"Thank you, Jovan. Everything is going to be fine, but I'll come back to see you."

As the old man boarded the trolley, I turned to cross the street and enter the park on the other side. That was the last time I ever saw dear old Jovan. I was filled with a fresh resolve, but I wasn't quite ready to face home yet. I moved from bench to bench, from one grassy area to the next, trying to imagine every situation I might face and trying to plan how to avoid ever again being alone with Father. In midafternoon, I turned and began to walk slowly toward home. I wanted to arrive home before he did.

THIRTEEN

Kolya

I approached the garage slowly, stopped just inside the entry doors, and waited until I saw Mother. I was determined never again to enter unless I was certain Mother was home.

"Hello, Asya. You're home early today. No extra studying?" she said pleasantly.

"No, Mama. Nothing special."

Mother had apparently spent the night at the stables and was not aware of my own absence. I sat on the sofa next to her and was reading when I noticed my father approaching through the garage repair area.

"Hello, everyone. Marusha, you're back. It's nice to see my two girls together. How are things at the stable? How's Silva getting along?"

I remained silent, pretending to be absorbed in reading, as he and Mother greeted each other, and he began to prepare something to eat. At dinner Mother seemed much calmer and more relaxed as she often was after a day at the stables. She chatted briefly about Silva and her day, explaining that she had ridden a bit too long and, afraid that she had missed the last trolley, decided to spend the night there. I avoided eye contact with Father, but it was clear that he was also avoiding my eyes, that he was upset by his actions.

That night as I lay in bed, I once again went over everything that had happened and thought about our dinner together. Father had avoided speaking to me. He was clearly uneasy, but Mother hadn't noticed any change. His manner and conversation with Mother appeared normal. It was only my observation that he avoided my eyes and did not speak directly to me that enabled me to relax a bit. It seemed clear to me that he was ashamed of the way he had acted. I had begun to convince myself that I was mistaken, that I had misinterpreted what had taken place, but his behavior now made it clear that he was trying to cover up and put the incident behind him. And it was clear to me that I was not mistaken. I would never again be able to look at his eyes without remembering that vacant expression, and I was now determined to avoid being alone with him.

I continued to practice English with Mother each day. I was by this time fluent in four languages—Russian, Serbo-Croatian, German, and English—and still had a good command of French. Old Church Slavonic, the language of the Bible which I read fluently, of course, was not a "spoken" language. I was completely confident in my ability with languages and my pronunciation. I used English only at home because of the occupation, but knew that my ability matched Mother's and that she sounded exactly like Miss Spencer.

The last few days of classes were devoted to final exams, which I passed with exceptionally high grades. The Akademie also tested the language ability of graduates, and I elected to be tested in Russian, German, and Serbo-Croatian, passing with no difficulty. I was asked by the instructor if I knew any other languages, and replied simply, "No." Upon completion of the classes and testing, I was awarded both a Certificate of Completion for the regular business school and a Certificate of Modern Languages, which indicated fluency in three languages. Accompanying the two certificates was a brief letter listing the certificates awarded, language ability, and the address of the labor office where graduates were expected to register.

"Wonderful, Asya," Mother said when she reviewed the Certificate of Modern Languages. "Always remember that you can never know too many languages. The more languages you know, the more opportunity you will have. You will *never* be hungry if you know foreign languages."

At the end of June I reported to the labor office, where the clerk informed me that I was eligible to work as a translator/interpreter in one of the offices of the German occupation forces. As I left the building "Uncle" Max Zengovitz approached, impressively strutting in his brown cap and uniform, swastika proudly displayed on his arm. Max Zengovitz's parents had emigrated from Germany to settle on a farm in Ukraine and had become quite prosperous before the Russian Revolution. Max had grown up in Ukraine, where he met and married Aunt Olga, a cousin or close friend of Mother's. They had emigrated to Yugoslavia at the same time my parents did and had a daughter, Tanya, who was a year or two older than me.

They had never been guests in our home, but Mother visited often with Olga to reminisce about the summers they had spent together while school-girls. I had met them frequently at social functions at Russkii Dom, where Max worked on several programs with Father and where they were devoted and patriotic Russians. The day after the fall of Belgrade, Max declared himself a devoted and patriotic German.

He joined the occupation forces and strutted about in a pillbox cap and brown uniform, with black leather belts, one that crossed his chest, and a red and black armband that displayed the Nazi swastika. His daughter joined the Hitler Youth movement and had been sent to attend school in Germany. Max approached with his arm raised in a Nazi salute, saying, "Heil, Hitler." I was relieved when he didn't stop as I continued walking, responding simply "good morning" in Serbian.

The terror that had gripped everyone in the first few months of the occupation began to ease with the lifting of the curfew and gradual reopen-ing of shops and restaurants throughout the city. Over the last eighteen months, fear and uncertainty had been replaced by apathy and boredom. Although isolated Serb resistance never stopped within Belgrade, most of the population had resigned themselves to the reality of Nazi occupa-tion, sustained by an unshakable belief that it, too, would pass.

By June 1943, however, the atmosphere in the city was beginning to change. Slowly, almost imperceptibly, the nervousness and guarded con-versation was returning. I did not understand what was happening, but the tide of war was turning slowly but steadily against the Nazis. German forces were now retreating from the Soviet army on several fronts, and

Tito's Yugoslav Partisans were gaining control of many areas within our own country.

Following the invasion, Radio Belgrade had been renamed Radio Lili Marlene, an arm of the official Nazi broadcast system. The haunting strains of the popular German song "Lili Marlene" introduced the periodic official news releases of the OKW. However, the famous four notes of Beethoven's Fifth Symphony introducing BBC news broadcasts, although heard clandestinely, gave everyone a lift. Somehow my parents, and all other adults, always had the latest news of Nazi retreats and defeats, Allied advances, and Partisan victories. Rumors of an expected Allied landing in Europe, including American forces, were spreading.

I was determined to avoid my father as much as possible, and that meant avoiding home. With the increasing heat of the summer, I began to venture back into Belgrade even while staying at Yaintse in order to go to Gypsy Island, and while staying in Belgrade I went every day to swim. Mother began to voice her concern about my behavior to the other people staying at the house in Yaintse, and I soon felt alienated from everyone. Poor, sweet Kolya was unwittingly about to become a complicating factor.

By late July Kolya began to appear at the beach, occasionally with a friend, but most often alone, looking pensively across the river, lost in thought. The ranks of the Russian boys who had been his constant companions had been thinning for over a year, and it is strange to realize that at the time this never raised my curiosity.

At first, when alone, Kolya would join me for an hour or so sitting on the beach in idle conversation about the impact of the war on the city and the lives of everyone we knew. Kolya had changed. We all had, of course, but the change in Kolya seemed profound in ways I could not fathom. He had always been a serious boy, quite the opposite of his brother, Yura, but he had matured and grown much more thoughtful. There seemed to be a part of him that he would not, or could not, reveal—some inner turmoil that he struggled with. I understood his inability to speak freely about his thoughts, because I could never bring myself to speak openly to anyone about my feelings toward my parents.

Gradually that summer, we met more frequently at Gypsy Island. Kolya became for me the big brother that many girls wish for. I felt safe when I was with him and looked forward eagerly to our time together. We spent hours that summer talking about books we had read, music we loved, and our dreams and plans for the future, without ever mentioning the reality of the war, the occupation, or our families. It was, I think, an idyllic friendship in the most unlikely circumstances—one that probably would never have developed under normal circumstances, considering the difference in our ages.

By the end of July, the summer heat was intolerable, and I spent nearly every day at the island swimming, often meeting Kolya. In early August, Kolya was more troubled than usual and slowly began to talk about his unhappiness, his certainty that his parents did not understand him, and his conviction that all his dreams for the future were being shattered. We stayed longer than usual that day, often running into the water to cool down. In late afternoon the skies darkened suddenly, and we remained in the water as a driving, wonderfully cooling rain started.

I don't know how long we remained enjoying the rain, but as suddenly as the rain had started, a ferocious thunderstorm appeared. As the lightning began to strike closer to the river with frightening intensity, Kolya yelled, "Asya, we should leave. The lightening is dangerous."

I ran behind him toward the cabanas, where we found that everything had been locked up, and someone had placed our clothes out on the steps. Gathering our clothes, now completely soaked, we ran toward some trees but found no real shelter. The sun was setting by the time the rain began to slow, and we had to put our street clothes on over our bathing suits and head for home. The air temperature dropped quickly in the wake of the storm, and a strong, cold wind blew. I shivered, chilled to the bone, and thought about the long trolley ride home, thankful we were not staying at Yaintse that day.

Kolya remained on the trolley as usual when we reached my stop. We said good-bye, and I stepped from the trolley into the same cold wind. It was now past dark, much later than I usually arrived home, and by the time I walked the two or three blocks to the garage I was shivering. Mother and Father were sitting in the adjoining office that sometimes doubled as a "parlor," talking with friends who were visiting, and Mother came to the door as I passed on my way to our rooms. She stood in the doorway and looked at me with an expression of absolute disgust, ignoring the wet clothes and shivering.

"Where have you been?" she demanded. "You're behaving like a dirty little prostitute." She then slapped me sharply across the face several times. "Get to your room and go to bed."

I ran to my room in tears, shocked at Mother's reaction and at being struck for the first time in my life. I sat on my bed, crying and shivering, trying to understand what had caused Mother to act as she had. I knew that she was increasingly upset by my wandering throughout the city, worried even more since the classes had ended and my time was completely unaccounted for. But her reaction was a complete shock.

I cried bitterly, wondering why Mama thought I was acting "like a dirty little prostitute." I knew that I hadn't done anything wrong. I had been swimming with Kolya and his family for as long as I could remember, and Kolya was like my brother. It wasn't our fault that the rain started and our clothes became soaked.

Trying to understand Mama's words and the shame they made me feel, I remembered my encounter with the man in the park a couple of years earlier. Suddenly I felt terribly dirty, and I undressed and went to the bathroom sink to fill it with water and begin a sponge bath. The mirror over the sink revealed tiny young breasts, no larger than walnuts but in my mind so terribly obvious even when fully dressed. I thought about the strange glances that I had begun to notice from men, glances I had never seen before and which unnerved me. I saw quite clearly that the tiny waist I had longed for a few years before was now pronounced. I remembered the scene in church when I had fainted after binding my waist with a rope to imitate Mother's waist, and now I no longer wanted it.

I cried, wishing with all my heart that I could remain a child, wondering why my body had to change. I wondered if Kolya had noticed the changes taking place in my body, and I resolved then and there never to go swimming with him again, never again to even visit Gypsy Island. So many times I had tried to bind my breasts tightly before putting on my dress, but the binding would always slip and was so uncomfortable. I was ashamed of what I saw in the mirror, and I finished my sponge bath, carefully trying not to touch my breasts. I slipped into my nightgown and into bed, still shivering, crying, and with Mama's words "like a dirty little prostitute" still ringing in my ears, I fell asleep.

I awoke early the following morning and wanted to dress and leave before my parents arose. My whole body, especially my chest, ached, and there was a buzzing in my ears. As I got out of bed I grew terribly dizzy and lost my balance. I lay down on the bed to rest for a few minutes before going for a walk and awoke to the sound of Mother's voice.

"I think Asya is ill again. She has been sleeping since I arrived home about two hours ago."

I felt a hand touch my forehead and opened my eyes to see Father's face twisting with concern.

"God save us," he said. "She's burning with fever. Try to bring her fever down while I go and try to find the doctor."

I heard Mother respond, but my head seemed to fill with a buzzing sound again, and I drifted off without understanding her words. The doctor arrived and shook his head as he diagnosed pneumonia, gave me some pills, and left instructions for my care. Kolya's mother, Aunt Nadia, a trained nurse, spent the next several days nursing me back to health.

Mother's reaction to my late arrival and the slap she had delivered shocked me into realizing just how much my recent behavior was upsetting her. In spite of that, I could not bring myself to tell her what was bothering me—about the "problem" with Father. I grew increasingly despondent over the next several weeks, refusing to speak to my parents except to answer them briefly, not because of any animosity, but simply from lack of will to converse. I no longer felt a sense of place or purpose. Left alone, I chewed my fingernails until there were no nails left. I had always taken great care with my hands, trying to make them appear as beautiful as Mother's. But nothing seemed to matter now.

After about two weeks, I had recovered enough to begin taking walks again, but no longer the full day adventures to Koshutnjak or Topcider or to Gypsy Island. I would never return to Gypsy Island. I worked at the hospital and took short walks in the central area of Belgrade. I visited the market and the shopkeepers I had known since schooldays, and walked through the small parks close to the garage, careful to return before dark, but still waiting to be sure that Mother was home before entering the garage. I saw Kolya on just four of those walks during late summer and early autumn of 1943, each time quite by chance, each of us walking alone. Three of those meetings are vivid memories.

One exceptionally hot day in late August, I had found a shady bench in a park quite close to the garage. I sat there, eyes closed and thinking of nothing when I heard a familiar voice.

"Hello, Asya. Mind if I sit down?

"Kolya. Hi, how are you?"

"No, how are you? My mother told me you were pretty sick. That you developed pneumonia after that last day swimming when it rained."

"Yes. I'm better now, but I was pretty sick, and I guess I upset everyone. You know, Kolya, Mama was furious when I got home so late that day. She slapped me, really hard, for the first time in my life. She said that I was 'acting like a dirty little prostitute.' I still don't understand why she did that. But I don't go swimming anymore. I'll never go to Gypsy Island again."

Kolya didn't answer for several seconds, and I looked at him to see his face reflecting deep sadness. I felt secure with him. I knew without ever thinking about it that we could talk about anything without ridicule or dismissal and in complete confidence.

"My mother didn't tell me that, Asya. I'm so sorry. You know, everyone has changed so much since the occupation. Even you and I are so very different. You used to be smiling all the time, but that last day on the beach is the first time I remember either of us smiling or laughing in a long, long time.

"Everyone has changed so much. Our parents must worry about things that we, especially you, can't begin to guess. We know now that over 17,000 people died in just the three-day German bombing of Belgrade, not the 7,000 that we had first heard, and people are still dying from unexploded bombs, now even from Partisan attacks and allied air raids. Someday this war will end, but I don't think anything will ever be the same. I guess I should be doing something to help." Kolya paused thoughtfully for a moment.

"Say," he said, changing the subject, "are you still waiting for your Italian to come along? You know the city is full of Italian troops now, too."

"Yes, I know."

"Do you still think they're romantic?"

"Yes, but it doesn't seem to matter anymore. I haven't thought about anything like that for such a long time."

"Still," Kolya continued as though something were on his mind, "you remember how you always talked about how romantic, how gentle you thought the Italians were. If that is true, then how could they have joined forces with Hitler and the Germans?"

It was apparent that Kolya was bothered by something, but I could not guess what it was. For some time now, when Kolya and I met, we talked as equals despite the difference in our ages. Looking back, it is clear that this was the result of the conditions we found ourselves in, but at the time it was perfectly natural, and neither of us gave it any thought. In this conversation, however, I could not guess what Kolya was driving at.

"Well," I answered, "if you think about it, there's a dramatic difference between the two occupation patrols. The Germans never crack a smile. They're all business, and everyone is quiet when they are nearby, but the Italians are always smiling and usually singing, and everyone is at ease when their patrols go past. It seems that most of them carry a mandolin instead of a rifle. Haven't you heard the beautiful music that fills some parts of the city? The music, especially the singing, is so beautiful that sometimes you can even forget the sound of Nazi boots on patrol."

"Yes, you're right. Maybe it's just Mussolini who's insane, and the people don't want to fight. They certainly don't look like warriors. Maybe they were drafted and are only doing what they believe is their duty to their country. I guess everyone has to follow his own conscience." Kolya paused and smiled as he continued lightly, "So you haven't changed your mind about the Italians?"

"Never," I answered, smiling. "Mine will come along someday—if I should live that long."

"What if he doesn't, and you have to settle for a Russian?"

"Never," I laughed. "I'll just find me a wandering Gypsy."

Kolya grew quiet, pensive again.

"Asya," he asked seriously, "have you ever kissed a boy?"

"No," I responded feeling a blush starting, "but a man kissed *me* once."

"Who?" Kolya asked with a slight frown.

"You, you silly goat. You sure have a short memory. Or you kiss so many girls that you just can't remember them all."

"Oh, that. That was nothing, just a kiss on the forehead. I mean really kissed."

"What is 'really' kissed? You mean on the mouth?"

"Yes."

"Oh, well, no. Someone tried once, but I ran away in time. Besides, he smelled of tobacco and horses."

"You don't mean your Mama's friend?"

"Yes, but I never told anyone," I replied. Nor, I knew, would I ever be able to tell anyone about Father.

"Why not, Asya? You know old men like that can be very dangerous."

"You know Mama. I've never been able to speak to her about many things, let alone something like that. I'm glad now that I didn't ever tell her. Have you forgotten how she was when I got home late from the beach soaking wet? Besides, it didn't seem so serious."

"This war has turned everything upside down." Kolya sighed deeply. "But parents demand too much. Perhaps they feel guilty about their own behavior, and that's why they fail to understand their children."

"Aren't all married people the same?"

"I hope not. Or else this is one man who will remain a bachelor."

"Oh, Italians are different."

"Not again!" He laughed. "You and your Italians."

We parted, heading in different directions. Our meeting ended on such a light note that I forgot about it until events would bring its meaning into sharper focus for me. I saw Kolya three times in the next few weeks. The next time he was walking on the other side of the street as I exited a park. I waved and called, but he continued walking with his head down, lost in his thoughts. Then in mid-September I saw him sitting alone on a park bench and walked over to join him.

"I haven't seen you in a while. Have you been swimming at the island?"

"Oh, Asya, hi. No, I haven't been to the island since you and I got caught in the rain that day. It isn't the same anymore. All my friends from school are gone—most of them anyway. What about you? What have you been doing?"

"I still work as a volunteer in the hospital, but not much else. I don't take the long walks that I used to. I haven't been to Koshutnjak in a long time. I don't feel as easy about walking anymore. Everything seems so tense now."

"I know, I don't think the war is going as well for Germany as it was a few months ago. They seem to be tightening up the occupation here in the city, too. Asya," he continued after a pause, "have you heard about this General Vlasov who is supposed to be fighting against the Bolsheviks alongside the German army?"

Andrei Andreyevich Vlasov distinguished himself in the Soviet army and rose through the ranks to be promoted to major general in 1940. When he was commanding the Soviet Second Shock Army at the battle of Stalingrad, his army was surrounded by the Germans and all taken prisoner. While in captivity, Vlasov volunteered to form an army of captured Soviet soldiers to fight with the Germans to liberate Russia from the Bolsheviks. Although the Germans issued Russian Liberation Army patches and attracted volunteers from among captured Soviet soldiers and Russian émigrés in Nazi-occupied countries of Europe, Vlasov himself was never permitted to command them. He was captured by Soviet forces on May 12, 1945, and executed by the Soviet Union on August 1, 1946.

"Yes, I think everyone has."

"Well, I understand that a lot of the Russians here in Belgrade have joined up. They seem to have a lot of faith in him."

"Well, Papa doesn't!" I replied emphatically. "Papa said that if a man has reached the rank of general in the Russian army, even as a Bolshevik, even as one of the "Hooligans," he couldn't possibly betray his own country. He doesn't think Vlasov can be trusted, and he doesn't trust the Germans anyway. Besides, he couldn't possibly put on a German uniform and fight against his own country at a time like this. Papa would *never* volunteer. He would gladly volunteer, even give his life if the tsar were still alive, but he mistrusts anyone else. Besides, he could never bring himself to wear a German uniform."

"I thought that one of your close friends had become an influential Nazi here in town?"

"You mean Uncle Max. He and Aunt Olga used to be dear friends, especially of Mama's. All these years he was a devoted Russian who worked with Papa on projects at Russkii Dom. But when the occupation started, he remembered his name was German and that his family had emigrated from Germany. Now he struts around in a brown uniform with a swastika on his arm. Maybe it's unfair to be critical of him. Maybe he's only doing what he thinks is best for his family. But no one else we know has done anything like that."

"What do your parents think about it?"

"I don't know. We haven't seen them in a long time. I understand their daughter has joined the Hitler Jugend and is attending school someplace in Germany."

"Opportunists," Kolya said quietly.

"Yes, I suppose that's a nice way to put it. What about you, Kolya? Would you ever consider joining Vlasov's army?"

"No, certainly not, but . . . well, you know how my father feels. We talk about it a lot. He says that as a Russian it's my duty to do my best to try and liberate Russia from the Bolsheviks. I guess we'll never see eye to eye."

We sat in silence for a moment or two before I decided to start for home. I left Kolya alone with his thoughts there in the park. I had grown accustomed to thinking of Kolya as the wisest person I knew. He always had a thoughtful answer to every question I posed, regardless of the subject. Now his apparent confusion about whatever was bothering him upset me.

Then, one day in early October, as I left the hospital to walk home, I noticed a German soldier walking in the same direction on the opposite side of the street. I saw from the corner of my eye that he crossed to my side and began to walk faster as the sound of his boots drew closer. I began to worry that he was trying to catch up to me when I heard a familiar Russian voice at my shoulder.

"Hello, mind if I walk you home?"

I turned toward the soldier in disbelief, shock registering in my voice as I spoke. "Kolya. God save us! What are you doing in that uniform?"

"Well," he smiled, "you know—like father, like son. The old General finally laid down the law, saying that this is my chance to fulfill a patriotic duty."

"What does your mother say to all of this?"

"Well, I was surprised, but she finally agrees with Father," he said, adding with a light laugh. "They always wanted me to go to Russia someday."

"When do you leave? How long will you be gone?"

"I'm leaving for camp tomorrow. They have waived a lot because of my graduation from the Cadet Corps, but I still go through a short training camp. Just a few weeks, I think. Then I'm hoping to be assigned to Vlasov, but I've been assured of going to Russia."

We had stopped to talk just short of the garage. Kolya said that he had to hurry to an appointment and could not walk the rest of the way with me. I think he was not yet ready for my father to see him in his uniform. He knew how opposed Father was. Kolya turned to walk back in the direction of the hospital, and I continued the few yards to the garage entrance. I did not mention meeting Kolya to my parents that evening, and the subject of his enlistment did not come up for some time.

My birthday passed without notice. I remember thinking about it briefly, thinking that at fifteen I should be completing Gymnasia and consider myself a "young adult." But I certainly didn't feel any different. At dinner about a week later Father mentioned Kolya's enlistment.

"Asya, you may have heard that Kolya has joined the Wehrmacht and that he hopes to be assigned to General Vlasov. He is to leave in a few days, and his parents are having a small party as a farewell for him on Friday evening."

"Will we go to say good-bye?"

"Yes, of course. Kolya and Yura have been like members of our own family since even before you were born."

His voice was gentle, but it was clear that he did not approve. His shoulders sagged as he spoke. It was the first time I remember noticing that. The light and mirth in his wonderful blue eyes had dimmed long before. I looked at him much more objectively since our "encounter" a few months earlier. I still longed for the old Papa who had filled my life with so much love and joy, but I would never again experience an unguarded moment with him.

I looked at Mama seated next to him, still as beautiful as ever, though no longer dressed as nicely. I watched her closely, remembering all the happy times in the house on Dr. Kester Street. I remembered watching adoringly as she played the piano and wondered now how she could play a Chopin nocturne or a Beethoven bagatelle with so much feeling and beauty, yet seem so cold and distant. I longed to rush and embrace her as we sat there, but could not bring myself to move. Something I did not understand had grown up between us. Watching her, I remembered one of the phrases she had always admonished me with: "Asya, if you don't study and do well in school, you'll end up just like Kristina." That always caught me off guard. I thought that Kristina was wonderful—warm and loving and kind—and that being like her would be just what I wanted. I came to realize, of course, that Mother wasn't criticizing those qualities but expected me to be more accomplished.

On Friday evening, we dressed as nicely as possible with what was left of our clothes and boarded a trolley for the ride to the Nazimovs' home. Father admonished that we would not stay very long. He was so strongly opposed to Kolya's action. By the time we arrived, the home was already filled with people, all of whom I knew by sight but not well, including two of Kolya's friends from the Cadet Academy with their parents. The group began singing Russian folk songs, and as a toast followed each song, their enthusiasm grew.

The toasting changed, quickly it seemed to me, from good wishes for Kolya to more somber, tearful toasts to Russia, her freedom from the "Hooligans," and fervent wishes that soon "Mother Russia" would be free.

I watched from a corner, and as the room filled with smoke and sadness, I moved to the door to go out into the quiet of the evening. I thought that everyone had forgotten Kolya and the reason for their gathering. As I reached the front yard, the door was closed a second time, and I looked to see Kolya following. He looked very sad, as though he did not himself understand what he was doing in uniform.

"You don't want to go, do you, Kolya?"

"No, not really."

"Then why go?"

"Oh," he replied softly, "I guess it's to please my father. I think he is reliving his own life through me. But he doesn't seem to understand. Everything is very different now, different from his days as a young officer in St. Petersburg. They faced combat during the revolution, of course, but for the most part their military duty consisted of beautiful uniforms, gay parties, reckless living, and adoring women melting before them. I think that's what he wants for me."

"You could hardly call this a glamorous life."

"Yes. If I'm lucky enough to get as far as Russia, I'll be traveling from one foxhole to another, and my nights will be spent lying awake trying to make sure I'm not in the way of a bullet. But Papa is getting old, and for his oldest son to refuse to serve would hurt his pride and break his heart."

"Oh, Kolya, I wish you were not going."

"Well, I'll be back soon, and then maybe we'll be able to finish our education and begin to make something of our own lives. Besides, I want to be the best man. Where will the wedding take place? Rome? Will the pope conduct the ceremony?" he teased.

"No," I pouted. "Probably at the foot of some ruins. Maybe I'll even run away to escape all this." I answered, pointing toward the noisy apartment.

Somewhere in the distance the faint sound of a tenor was accompanied by the strumming of a mandolin.

"See," I smiled, "he's out there someplace, my Romeo."

The door to the apartment opened, and strains of Russian music spilled into the yard, overcoming the tenor.

"Kolya, Kolya, our boy, we're drinking to your happiness and to victory and success in Russia. May you be the one to lead us all back home again," someone shouted.

Kolya walked back into the apartment. As he entered, his father repeated a toast.

"To Kolya, who has filled my heart with pride, and who goes now to open the path for all of us to return to Mother Russia."

I remained outside listening, sitting on the grass. I listened as Kolya thanked everyone, saying that he would do his best to make his father—all of them—proud, as he said good-bye and came back outside.

"I still have a few things to take care of before we leave, Asya, so I'd better get going."

"Not so soon, Kolya. Will we see each other again before you leave?"

"No. Tomorrow there are preparations and formalities that will take up the whole day, and we leave early the following morning."

"Do you know if any other of our Russian boys are leaving?"

"Yes, there are a couple of my friends from school. They seem to go just to escape their families and the situation here. You know how it is."

"Oh, Kolya, I wish I were old enough to just leave. I can't stand it at home anymore—or at Yaintse or anyplace. All of the Russians are so depressed one day and then hysterically happy the next. They seem to live in their own closed little world. I know that they have gone through so much in their lives, fleeing Russia, living here and there without belonging anyplace, but I'm so confused. Kolya, please don't go. My life will be so empty if you're gone. You've become the only friend I have, the only person I feel I can talk to about so many things. Please don't go."

"Well, I don't think I'll be gone too long, and maybe I can help in Russia. Besides," he added lightly, "I don't think they would let me change my mind now. Let's hope that when I do return, things will be back to normal. Good-bye, Asya. Be a good girl, and don't trust any man. Stay as sweet as you are. Maybe I'll come back and try to compete with that mythical Italian."

Kolya bent and kissed my cheek. As I raised my face to look directly at him, my eyes filled with tears. Kolya held my wet face in both hands and bent to gently kiss my lips. Unconsciously I turned and kissed his cheek again.

"See what I mean," Kolya smiled. "Don't trust *any* man. I'm sorry. I shouldn't have done that. But you're such a sweet girl. Good-bye, Asya."

Kolya returned to open the door to the apartment and shout a final good-bye to everyone, as I sat back down on the grass and rested my head on my knees again, crying bitterly. I heard Kolya's footsteps behind me once again and felt his fingers brush my hair before he disappeared into the night, in the direction of the tenor, still heard faintly. I prayed, for the first time in a long time, asking God to watch over Kolya, to keep him safe and to bring an end to this terrible war. In only a few moments Papa touched my shoulder. "Time to go home, Asya."

We walked to the trolley stop in silence. I walked next to Mother. Father broke the silence as the streetcar stopped before us.

"That boy has no business in the army. He doesn't have the temperament, but God be with him. I think it will finish General Nazimov if anything happens to him."

I fell asleep that night crying and praying for Kolya's safe return. I cried not for Kolya but for myself and the loneliness I was beginning to feel so strongly. I had come to think of Kolya as wise and strong and gentle. He had become my last link to the happy, carefree days of childhood, someone with whom to share the laughter of childhood memories, but who could be relied upon to thoughtfully discuss the stresses of growing up amid the ruin of the war. Even though I had not seen him frequently, I had always felt that he was there if I needed someone to talk to, and his leaving left a void I could not imagine anyone else filling. From Kolya's departure in late October 1943 until final liberation in April 1945, the events of the war and its effects on me tumbled one after the other in a jumble of sadness, excitement, and tragedy.

In mid-December Father again did something that, in later years, I would admire as sound planning, although his judgment would ultimately prove tragic. He announced to the friends staying at Yaintse that they would soon have to make other living arrangements, that he wanted to find someone who would stay at the house to look after Aunt 'Lyena, and that he wanted someone from the Serbian population whom he could be certain would be able to remain indefinitely.

Father was clearly planning for something, but I did not even recognize his planning and could certainly not guess what it was. I wondered again why we didn't move to Yaintse, but knowing how Mother would have suffered, I decided that Father must be making the right decision.

December 24, 1943: President Roosevelt appointed General Dwight D. Eisenhower to become supreme commander of Allied forces in preparation for something soon to be known as Operation Overlord, the Allied invasion of Nazi-held Europe.

As if to put a final touch to a terrible year, in late December Aunt Nadia received word that Kolya had been killed in action someplace on the Eastern Front, not three months after enlisting and before his twentieth birthday. I never heard where or how he had been killed, but I don't believe he ever made it to Russia. He was probably buried where he fell. The news added to the depths of my own depression. From that day until final liberation, I simply drifted from one day to the next, existing without feeling anything, without really living. Father had been right. General Nazimov never recovered from the news, but I would yet confront him with what I felt was his lack of understanding and concern for Kolya.

When the news reached us, we went to visit and express our sympathies to his parents. Aunt Nadia was, of course, totally distraught. General Nazimov trotted behind her, his head lowered, forehead covered in deep wrinkles, and mumbling over and over, "He's gone . . . he's gone . . ."

"Well, that should make you very proud. He died in Russia, the Russia you love so much," I suddenly burst out, tears streaming down my face.

"Asya, that's enough. You mind your own business. Leave the room," said Mother.

"Of course! Asya, be quiet. Asya, go to your room. Asya, you must behave like a lady. I no longer have a room to go to," I answered loudly. "And why must I always remain silent? I'm human, too. I have feelings like you. Perhaps more than you, any of you. You, all of you, just sit around feeling sorry for yourselves, dreaming of some glorious past.

"Don't you see the blood and death all around you? Don't you think that everyone else who did not flee Russia under such terrible circumstances has also gone through hell, is still going through hell? What do you all see when you walk down the streets? Have you forgotten all the dead bodies of all ages dug out of the ruins? *Serb* bodies! And that wasn't enough! From some stupid pride and misplaced patriotism, you—" Now almost shouting, I turned to face Kolya's father. "You sent your son to die like a dog on some land he had no love for. What have you accomplished? Is his death going to give you a ticket back to Russia? Have you already packed? They probably couldn't find his body in one piece. Oh, this rotten, stinking world. But still, it's 'Asya, be quiet. Asya, leave the room.' No, I will not be silent." I collapsed in tears into a chair.

"You must forgive her," Mother said softly, shocked and embarrassed and apologizing to General Nazimov. "She is in that 'awkward' stage that young ladies go through."

"She may be young," the General replied sadly, "but I believe she has spoken the truth. Oh, God, we do live in our own dreams—in the past, ignoring the present—and the present is so terrible. At least we have our youth to look back on. But young people like Asya and Kolya and Yura have never really had a chance to live, and the past few years have been misery, more so for them than for us, years of bloodshed, killing, occupation."

"Yes, but at least they have . . ." Mother apologized softly. "Well, Kolya no longer . . . but at least she has her best years ahead of her, whereas . . . what can the future hold for me . . . for us?"

I couldn't stand it any longer. I rose slowly and left without saying good-bye to anyone. I walked to the trolley line to take the next trolley back to the garage. Our visit to General Nazimov's home was never mentioned again.

FOURTEEN

Roach Manor

January 16, 1944: General Dwight D. Eisenhower took command at Supreme Headquarters Allied Expeditionary Forces.

Kolya's death closed forever the door to my childhood, and I did not believe that things could get any worse. Of course, they did. Since I made sure that I arrived home early, Mother and I were getting along much better. We had not grown closer, but we each tried to avoid anything that might flare into disagreement.

March 6, 1944: U.S. heavy bombers conducted the first bombing raid on Berlin.

Mother still worked at the hospital when we were not in Yaintse and when she was not busy comforting someone. Russian boys who had joined the Russian Liberation Army in the Wehrmacht under the grand illusion of defeating Bolshevism and had been wounded in combat were now occasionally sent to the hospital, and Mother felt a special compassion for them. She never discussed it, but perhaps they all reminded her of Kolya.

One day in April 1944 we returned from Yaintse early in the morning and went directly to the hospital without stopping at our rooms in the garage. A major Allied air attack had taken place while we were away, and Mother was concerned that we might be particularly needed. New civilian casualties were indeed being brought into the hospital. We had worked for a few hours when Mother, tired, came to find me and to suggest that we go home. As we approached the garage, it was obvious that something was wrong.

> April 16 and 17, 1944: American bombers from the 15th Air Force based in Foggia, Italy, flying at high altitude, carried out carpet-bombing raids on Belgrade. German military casualties were placed at 18, civilian casualties at 1,160.

Both big wooden doors had been knocked down down. As we stepped across the doors, Mother looked to the left and stifled a scream as she raised her hand to her mouth. The entire section of the garage that had housed the customer restrooms and storage rooms was gone. Where it had stood, there was now a large crater, filled with water that poured from a broken pipe. A body was floating in the water, bobbing slowly in the turbulence.

Father appeared, and I watched as he scrambled down the side of the crater, suddenly stopping to cross himself.

"My God, it's Makharov. He's dead! Poor Makharov."

Makharov was a friend of Father's from Russkii Dom. I never learned the cause of the explosion or why Mr. Makharov had the misfortune to be there. The water supply and sewage connections for the section of the garage that we lived in were now in question. The water was still running in our rooms, but Father began to look for another apartment the following day, and we boiled all water before using it. We moved within two weeks of the explosion, and the move would mark the beginning of what would become the darkest period of the occupation for me—for all of us.

The new "apartment" that Father found was on a major thoroughfare of Belgrade. Even in my deepening depression I hated it so much that I no longer remember the name of the street. It was a "garden-level" apartment, entered by walking down about six steps to the front door—really a basement. When we opened the door the first time to walk in, the walls and floors seemed to move as roaches, thousands, tens of thousands scurried hurriedly in every direction. I would not have believed that many roaches could have existed in all of Belgrade.

Father obtained a container of disinfectant someplace and something to act as an insecticide, and he and I began to wash down the walls and floors in an effort to control the infestation. I started to sit on the bed and saw something move—bedbugs hiding in the seams at the edge of the mattress! Father also obtained some kerosene, and we dragged the iron bed frames and springs out and into a pit that he dug in the back of the building, poured kerosene all over them, and set them afire. We used old toothbrushes soaked in kerosene to scrub all the seams in the mattresses.

If any of us had escaped depression until then, our new living quarters were enough to ensure its debilitating effect. We all hated the apartment. I named it Roach Manor the moment we walked in, and so it has remained in my mind all these years. There was just one small bedroom. I had a cot in the living room. The windowsills were just above eye level for me and offered a view of the ankles and lower calves of passers-by.

The only good thing was that it was early spring; the worst summer heat was still months off. Poor Mother would truly suffer through our time in Roach Manor—Father as well—and his old "Everything is in order" was no longer heard.

I thanked God for the house at Yaintse then. We were able to stay there while we tried to clean Roach Manor. Within another week or two, Father announced that he had found someone responsible enough to move in and ensure that Aunt 'Lyena would have companionship and be cared for. In May 1944 Father introduced Mr. Chuchurovic, who was to move into the house at Yaintse with his wife.

Mr. Chuchurovic was the teacher at the elementary school in Yaintse. I think classes had been suspended during the war. The Chuchurovics had lost their home and had time on their hands. They seemed the ideal solution to Father, being well educated, native Serbs who wanted to remain in the village permanently. Mr. Chuchurovic was of average height, slim, and dark and perhaps in his late thirties.

I don't remember his wife at all, but they moved in with Aunt 'Lyena within days of the time I was introduced to them. When they moved in, of course, it ended our ability to stay there overnight, and I was sorry that I lost that time with Aunt 'Lyena. I would continue to visit on daytrips, most often alone, but it was sometimes difficult to speak with her. She spent most of her time in the local church, and I would usually just wait for her to return.

During that spring, Aunt 'Lyena began to be very sad. Her faith had always helped her to maintain a positive outlook, but that seemed to be fading—not her faith, but her ability to remain hopeful. One visit late that spring is an indelible memory. Aunt 'Lyena was in the chapel when I arrived, and I waited until she returned, and we sat together on the bench in front of the house.

"Aunt 'Lyena, you seem a little sad. Do you need anything? Do you have enough to eat? Is the new couple nice to you?"

"Iiiii'm fine, Aaaaasinka. I stiiiill have myyy bed, aaand I spend moooost of the day in the chaaaapel in the village, aaasking God to care for aaall of us. You know, I'm juuuust no use to aaanyooone anymore."

I could not bear to see Aunt 'Lyena, of all people, depressed. It was she who had taken me to church and confession each week and taught me all that was "good" in the world. It was she who tucked me in each night and read me bedtime stories. I remembered when, in Gymnasia, I had made excuses to avoid going to church with her because I wanted to read or to do something unimportant. I couldn't stop tears from forming, and I did not want her to see them. I kissed her good-bye and promised to return in a day or two.

June 6, 1944: D-Day/Operation Overlord. Allied forces, crossing the English Channel, landed in force at Normandy, France, to begin the invasion of Nazi-occupied Europe. By evening Allied casualties had passed 10,000, but 150,000 men were ashore and moving inland.

A few days later, on another visit to Yaintse, no one was at home, and I sat on the bench to wait for Aunt 'Lyena. Mr. Chuchurovic returned to the house and joined me on the bench with a friendly hello.

"How is Aunt 'Lyena doing, Mr. Chuchurovic? Is she eating enough? Does she need anything?"

Something in my question or manner—something—upset him, and his eyes seemed to burn as he responded.

"You know, people of your class should have everything taken from them and given to the less fortunate."

"Mr. Chuchurovic, this house belongs to my parents," I replied, wide-eyed, "and you know that we now live much more poorly than you do here in Yaintse. You have much more comfort than we."

"Nevertheless, someday, someday the time will come when you will not even be allowed that much. This house belongs to your parents now, but the day is coming when everything will belong to the poor and needy, you will see, and your kind will adorn the trees in the city with your heads hanging down in the gutters."

He frightened me badly, of course. His diatribe was, I think, typical of the Communist fervor that swept much of Europe in the 1930s, but I had never heard anything like it before. In a moment, Aunt 'Lyena returned and we embraced as she joined us on the bench. Mr. Chuchurovic again seemed normal and remained to chat as Aunt 'Lyena and I talked briefly until I rose to return to the city. At home I tried to talk to Father.

"Papa, I went to Yaintse again today to visit Aunt 'Lyena. She seems fine, but I don't think Mr. Chuchurovic is taking very good care of her. I'm not sure he's very trustworthy."

"No, Asya, you're wrong. We were lucky to find Mr. and Mrs. Chuchurovic. They are well educated, kind people. Mother and I are both very happy that we have found them. They will take good care of Aunt 'Lyena."

"Yes, Papa, but—"

"No, Asya, I have a lot of faith in Mr. Chuchurovic. He's a good man." Father interrupted, his jaw set.

The subject was closed. I simply avoided Mr. Chuchurovic on subsequent trips to visit Aunt 'Lyena, although I was able to see her only a few more times. Partisan attacks on German forces were drawing closer to Belgrade. In August, trolley service to Yaintse was discontinued.

I grew increasingly despondent , and Roach Manor just added to my deepening apathy. My fingernails, chewed to nubs, almost disappeared, and I continued to lose weight. I remember one day when, quite out of the ordinary, I felt hungry, really hungry, for the first time. I went to the kitchen and opened the drawer that we used as a breadbox, to find the loaf of bread covered with roaches, and I simply brushed them off, cut a slice of bread, and began to eat it.

The air attack that took place in mid-April had started a continuing wave of smaller attacks. Belgrade was bombed by the Allies in April, May,

June, and July, and groups of Partisans were regularly attacking German troops and installations and drawing ever closer to Belgrade. The Avala-Belgrade highway, which passed through Yaintse in front of our house, was the scene of frequent attacks on German vehicles.

As summer advanced, the heat throughout the city, especially in our apartment, grew to be intolerable. Father, noticing how depressed I had become, sat with me one afternoon and told me that he thought I needed something constructive to do. It never occurred to me, but he was again planning ahead.

"You need to keep busy, Asinka. It's important to keep up your spirits. I spoke to Uncle Max, and he introduced me to the Colonel in charge at German Luftwaffe headquarters. I told the Colonel about your graduation from the Deutsche Wissenschaft Akademie, and he says that he can offer you a small job, a few hours each day. Would you like that?"

The following day Father and I went to German Luftwaffe headquarters where he introduced me to the Colonel. I no longer remember his name, but he was a man in his mid-fifties with graying hair and a gentle face. He had pictures of his family on his desk—his son a captain in a tank corps and married, and his wife, who I thought looked like a lady of great charm and grace. I remained for the day, and he assigned me some routine typing or filing. It was better than staying in Roach Manor.

Over the next few weeks I didn't do anything except to act as interpreter for the Colonel, who did not understand any Serbian. His contact with native Serbs was limited, but I felt I was at least a little help to the civilians. I also did some light typing when the military assistants in the office were busy. I never received any pay for working at the offices; I didn't do much, but it does seem curious in remembering that.

August 4, 1944: Nazi police raided a building in Amsterdam and arrested eight people, including Anne Frank.

I continued working at headquarters two or three days a week, and it became obvious that the Germans were preparing for something. I soon began to work almost daily. My duties were to take papers that had been removed from endless filing cabinets, pack them neatly in boxes, and label the boxes with file numbers. It never occurred to me at the time, but they were clearly preparing for retreat.

One day in late August, when I was sitting listlessly in the living room at Roach Manor, I heard very heavy truck traffic. I went outside to watch as an endless convoy of German military vehicles drove past slowly, frequently stopping because of congestion. A smaller truck stopped directly in front of me, and my eyes met those of a very young German soldier sitting alone in the back of the truck. He smiled and motioned for me to approach.

"Do you speak German?" he asked.

"Yes, a little."

He introduced himself as Hermann Zahn, from Dresden, and I told him my name. I asked if he would like a glass of water, but he declined, saying that they were forbidden to accept food or drink from civilians.

"Can you come a bit closer? I have something I would like to give you." He looked almost my own age. As I stepped closer, he reached somewhere behind him in the truck bed and stretched his arm to hand me something.

"Oh, I can't accept this. It's a very nice camera."

"Please, Fraulein," he said sincerely. "I have enjoyed using it. I have taken a great many pictures. But now it would please me very much to give it to you. In the future, I would like to think of *you* using the camera. I don't think I will have any further use for it. You see?" he said as he removed a blanket to reveal his trousers neatly folded over two stumps at about mid-thigh.

Just at that moment, the convoy started to move again, and I could do nothing except to say thank you, tears rolling down my cheeks as we waved good-bye. What could that boy possibly have seen in me that prompted his action? His gift was a Leica 35mm camera, and it would help me later. God bless him. I hope he reached his home safely.

The convoys of German vehicles continued almost daily, it seemed, as they retreated back toward Germany. The packing of file cabinets at headquarters continued through the balance of August. As I left for work one day, Mother mentioned that she wanted to visit Aunt Nadia, Kolya's mother, and might not be at home when I returned. Not long after I arrived at work, the air raid sirens began, and everyone headed for the basement shelters.

Although we did not know it at the time, on September 1, 1944, the Allies launched Operation Rat Week, a coordinated land-air attack that brought Allied air power and an infant Yugoslavian air force together to support a major push by Yugoslavian Partisans, to be joined by Soviet army units as they steadily advanced on Belgrade. I think the intense bombing was the opening salvo of Rat Week. The bombing seemed to continue forever and was much more intense than anything up to that point. When the all-clear sounded, I left work, expecting that the trolley lines would not be running and that I might have a long walk home.

As I passed the street where Kolya and his family lived, I remembered that Mother had said she might visit Aunt Nadia. Worried, I hurried to the Nazimovs' house, and as I drew near I saw that it had been destroyed. I ran toward what was only a couple of half-walls at the rear and on one side of a smoking pile of debris.

I climbed up on the rubble and began moving boards, furniture, whatever was in front of me, without any idea of what I was doing, when one of the remaining walls tumbled down. Suddenly my eyes filled with dust particles swirling from the collapsing wall. I had to stop, unable to see anything, now realizing that my legs were badly scratched, my fingers bleeding, my dress torn, and my feet sore from stepping on broken glass with shoes that had long since surrendered anything resembling a real sole. I simply sat on the rubble pile crying, when I heard voices and looked up. Several people were running toward me carrying shovels and an axe and a first aid kit—people I recognized from Russkii Dom.

"Is someone beneath the house?" asked a voice.

"I don't know," I cried. "This is the way I found it. Have you seen Mama or Papa?"

"No, when the alarm sounded we went into our basement. We knew that one of them hit very close. We would have come sooner, but we haven't heard the all-clear. I think we are still under a red alert."

"Oh, please do something. Maybe they're in the basement. It's a very strong basement. Maybe you can get in from the back."

It appeared that the bomb or bombs struck toward the front of the house. There was much less debris in the rear, and a crater in the front yard was filling with water. The newcomers moved to the rear, digging at the debris and removing as much as possible. Someone said, "You shouldn't do anything. Go and wash your hands in that crater, and my wife will fix your cuts."

The water looked very dirty, but I had to wash them. As I finished, a woman put iodine on them, and the sting brought tears to my eyes. I sat on the grass, pulled my shoes off, and began to pull small pieces of glass from my feet, wash them, and wince as more iodine was applied. I stood in my bare feet, watching and saying a prayer. It was growing dark by then, and someone lit a carbide lamp casting a bluish light over everything, making the ruins even more disheartening.

"I hear something," someone shouted from the rear of the house. "Yes, one window is almost cleared. Pass me a lamp, somebody. Is anybody there? Are you all right?"

"Yes, just some bruises and small cuts. But we're fine."

I listened, desperately trying to recognize Mama or Papa's voice, when I heard Mother call from behind me.

"Asya! Thank God, you're all right."

I turned just as she embraced me.

"We have been at the headquarters building looking for you. We were so afraid. Then I remembered that I had told you I would be going to visit Aunt Nadia. But she doesn't live here anymore, not since she and General Nazimov separated after Kolya was killed. Are you all right?"

"Yes, Mama, I was so afraid you were under the rubble," I said, now crying. I had never heard that the Nazimovs had separated.

"Never look for me in that," Mother answered, shuddering and pointing at the rubble pile. "I would *never* go into a basement. I hate the feeling. If I have to die, it will be out in the open or in my own home, but never in a basement. Let me look at you. You are all scratched and cut. Oh, Anochka, I've been praying we would have another chance to let you know how much we love you. Papa and I have been looking everywhere."

"Please don't cry," I said, pressing my head against her. Even here in the midst of all this ruin, she smelled so good. Maybe the scent was my imagination, but for just an instant, I was back on Dr. Kester Street, sitting next to her and looking at the family album. As I looked around, I saw Aunt Nadia and Yura standing close to the rubble. Apparently they had come with Mother, to look for me.

"Is everybody out?" someone asked.

"Yes, thank God, everyone seems to be okay," another answered.

"The General? Where is General Nazimov?" asked one of the people from the basement. "Has anyone seen the General?"

"No," someone answered. "He was sitting in the parlor drinking when the alarm sounded. I told him to take his bottle if he wished but to get to the basement. I don't remember seeing him downstairs, but it was so dark I could have missed him."

"Good God," someone added. "If he was upstairs, he's done for."

"Let's remove some of the rubble above. Maybe he didn't go to the basement. Maybe he's trapped upstairs."

It was an empty statement. The men returned to start removing rubble, but unhurriedly. If he was there, there was no need to hurry. What seemed like hours later they found him. General Nazimov sat crumpled in a corner with a bottle in his hand, wearing his uniform tunic, white cloth protruding from the place on his chest where his medals had been ripped off, the medals now held tightly in his dead hand, a terrible gash in the back of his head. I looked at that old, tormented face and thought that he looked childish—a big smudge on his nose and his hair all mussed up. This once proud general had finished his life. However glamorous once, or however pathetic toward the end, it was finished. I hoped he was with Kolya.

I couldn't cry anymore. I had cried so much that my eyes simply dried up. I looked around at Mama and Papa and the others. Life meant so very much . . . and yet so very little. All of them tried hard to preserve memories. How they cherished the past, yet how helpless they seemed in the present, and how quickly everything could be destroyed.

"Your daughter is half frozen," said one of the women who had been helping. "Why don't you all come to my house. It's a mess, but we can make some hot tea."

"What are we going to do with the General?" someone asked.

"Cover his body. There's nothing to do until morning. Then we can try to give him a proper burial," someone responded.

I glanced once more at the ruin, saying a silent good-bye to General Nazimov, then turned and walked away with the others, holding Mama's arm and limping slightly from the cuts on my feet. We walked about a block to the woman's home, and I remember how good the warmth of the house felt as we waited for tea to brew. Once again I was reminded of Serbian hospitality as bread and hot tea was offered. No matter how little a Serbian family might have, inside their homes, they offered warm hospitality and shared whatever they had. I noticed the woman looking at me, and she left for a moment, returning with a dress and a pair of shoes.

"Here," she said to me, "try these on. Your dress is all torn, and those shoes won't even get you home. I have no need of these things. They belonged to my daughter."

"Where is your daughter?"

"She is dead. My mother and my daughter shared the same birthday, and I always tried to give them a nice party together. The day before the party, in order to prepare everything, I sent her to spend the night with her grandmother. The next morning the German bombing began. It took forever to dig them out. The terrible thing was that if we had been able to get to them sooner, they might be alive. Mother's house was very small and was behind a very high apartment building that received a direct hit and collapsed directly on top of her house. They weren't even hurt. When we found them, they were just sitting together."

The woman had a face of stone. She showed not a trace of emotion when she talked about it. I didn't know how to behave. If she had been in tears, I could have embraced her, tried to comfort her. But she showed no emotion at all.

"You know," she continued, "it's better that they are both dead. God only knows what awaits us. What kind of future could I promise her now? Mother was old. She had lived her life. But my daughter was so pretty, such a good girl, so many plans for the future. Maybe some of them will come true for her in the next world. You know, I strongly believe that *this* is hell. This is hell, and God did not want her to go through hell, so he simply took her." Her voice dropped to almost a whisper as emotion began to overcome her, and a faint smile appeared on her face. "Now," she continued, recovering, "you go and change into some dry clothes . . . and try on those shoes."

We spent the rest of the night there. It was almost dawn anyway, and we simply dozed in a chair or on the floor. The distant boom of artillery could be heard now, a long way off, according to Father, but still worrisome. In the morning Mother and Father, relieved to learn that the trolleys were running, returned to Roach Manor, and I went to Luftwaffe headquarters to work, with shoes that almost fit, soles with only tiny holes, and a dress that was miraculously without tears or patches.

When I reached the headquarters building, it was clear that there was more activity, and entering the office I found everyone much busier than usual. I was assigned the task of carrying papers from the office to the courtyard, where soldiers burned them in huge oil drums, continuously feeding the flames. The boom of artillery grew louder and more frequent each day.

A week later, Father sat down to speak to me.

"Asya," he began very seriously, "I have learned that the Germans will leave Belgrade in the very near future. If that information is correct, and I believe that it is, they will be the first to leave the city, and they will no doubt have adequate transportation and food. I'm certain they will have to head for Germany through Vienna.

"I want you to memorize an address in Vienna—almost in Wiener Neustadt—just outside the city. If we should be separated for any reason, this address will be our meeting place. This is Countess von Holzen, a very old friend of Mother's. When you were a very little girl, we visited her twice. You probably don't remember her, but she knows you, and she knows that we would use her home as a meeting place in the event of any emergency." Father told me the address, and I began to repeat it, to be certain I memorized it.

"Also, Mama and I have given Uncle Max and Aunt Olga a box to keep for you. If anything happens to us, you should find Max and Olga. The box contains a few things like Mama's family album with your baby pictures, mementoes, and a few pieces of Mama's jewelry that you have always liked."

"But, Papa," I interrupted, "I thought you were no longer friends with them. That they had become 'German.'"

"Yes," Father sighed, "but Mama and Olga have been close for many, many years, and Olga offered to help us leave Belgrade. Since they have become 'German' now, the box will be much safer with them. War is a funny thing, Asya. You often can't tell friends from enemies during war. Max is probably doing only what he feels is best for his family. Well, enough of that. Remember, you must find Max, and you must always remember how much Mama and I love you. We always have, but I think we tried too hard to give you material things and advantages instead of the closeness we all need."

Father sighed again before continuing. "Mama's idea was that manners and education were the most important things we could give you, and it's too late now to do anything about it. After the Sorbonne we hoped you would find the right young man. Kolya was supposed to have been him, but we were never too serious about that. He just always seemed such a nice boy with such high hopes and plans."

Father paused, sadly remembering Kolya. I could not understand the differences I saw in him—so thoughtful and wise and reliable, and those expressionless eyes that day in the garage.

"But life is unpredictable," he began anew, "like a small sail boat on a sunny summer day. The weather is moody and can quickly turn the ocean into a fury, tossing the boat every which way and driving it toward a rocky shore. Sometimes the boat will sink, but usually it will make it, a bit battered but repairable. Always remember to keep your foundation, your faith and principles strong. Do you understand what I'm trying to say, Asinka?"

"Yes, Papa. I think so," I answered, then, out of nowhere, I asked, "Papa, when you and Mama were married, did you love her?"

I have no idea what prompted me to ask such a question at that time, and Father was silent. Finally, with a frown wrinkling his forehead and his eyebrows looking even bushier than usual, he said, "I love her very much now. Whether or not I loved her then, when we married, is hard to say. The situation was very similar to the present one. Everything was in chaos with the revolution raging toward completion. You know about her parents, your grandparents, and how she was thrown into jail . . . and what a terrible jail. She was very young—both of us were—but she was so pretty. Pretty and spoiled and defenseless! She really clung to me for protection. And you know about our flight to Constantinople and China and then to Belgrade.

"No, I don't think I loved her. We were both so very young, unable really to understand love, both completely alone, surrounded by tragedy and disaster. But I am certain that I love her now, more than anything. She is so terribly independent, and yet at times she acts like a completely helpless little girl. She has a big heart, a very generous heart. It's such a shame that you and she have never grown close."

Father leaned over, kissed my forehead, and left the room as I remained to ponder what he had said.

September 1944: Anne Frank and her family were transported to the concentration camp at Auschwitz.

The frenzied pace of packing and destroying papers at headquarters continued, and at the beginning of October, with the booming artillery sounding as though it were at the gates of Belgrade, Father came into the living room at Roach Manor and again said that he had something important to tell me.

"Asya, you remember our talk a week or so ago? The time to leave is here. I have spoken to the Colonel you've been working for at headquarters, and he has agreed to take you as far as Vienna. When you go to work tomorrow, you will have to stay there. The Colonel and his staff will leave tomorrow night or early the next morning. Do you remember the address of Countess von Holzen?"

"Yes, Papa," I replied, repeating the address for him.

"Good. Then tonight you'll have to pack a few things to take with you. When you go to work tomorrow, they will not allow you to leave the offices."

"But, Papa, what about you and Mama? Aren't you coming, too?"

"No, it's a military train, and they won't let us go with them. Mama and I will come to the office to say good-bye before you leave. We will be driving to Vienna. I've found some old trucks that we have been fixing up. Some other couples from Russkii Dom have been helping and are going with us, and we will meet you in Vienna. Now, tell me again the Countess's address."

I repeated it. Satisfied, he left and I started putting things into a pillowcase. I packed the camera that the German boy had given me a few weeks earlier. As I packed—a dress, a small jacket, and a change of underwear—I started to cry, my emotions ranging from terrible sadness at leaving Mama and Papa to a curious mix of excitement and fright at the prospect of being "on my own" at fifteen years old, even for the day or two I thought it would take to reach Vienna.

The following morning, I left for headquarters carrying my pillowcase. The periodic boom of artillery sounded closer, but less frequent that morning. At the office I found the barrels still burning—papers still being brought out to feed the flames.

"Good morning, Miss Popova. Don't forget that you cannot leave today."

"Yes, Colonel. Father told me."

There was really nothing to do that day. I carried a few more papers out to be burned, amazed at the ashes that stood in piles where the barrels had been emptied. As they loaded the last boxes, the room cleared and the Colonel called me to his office, where I found another officer.

"Miss Popova, this is Lieutenant von Staate. Lieutenant, Miss Popova. You have seen her in the office. She has worked for the past few weeks as my translator. I have given her parents my word that we would see her safely to Vienna. You are to stay with her on the train and do your best to see that she arrives safely."

"Of course, Colonel," the lieutenant replied as he turned to bow slightly and extend his hand. I had seen him in the office, but had never had occasion to speak with him. He excused himself and left the office as the Colonel turned to me.

"Lieutenant von Staate is a very nice young man. Try to stay close to him during the trip. He will know what to do in case of any trouble."

"Thank you, Colonel."

I left the office and looked out of a hallway window. People scurried in both directions out on the streets. Someone came and found me in the hallway and told me that there were people to see me in the front courtyard.

Mother and Father stood at the iron fence, at the gate, but were not allowed to enter, and I ran to the gate.

"Here, Asya," Father said as I reached the gate. "These are a few things I think you forgot. Put them in your pillowcase."

"Thank you, Papa," I said as I took the small package through the fence.

"Now, tell me the Countess's address again."

I repeated the address, and as he nodded, I turned to Mother, surprised again to see tears welling in her eyes. "Mama, don't cry. In only a few days we'll be in Vienna," I said as we embraced as well as we could through the iron bars.

"I know, Asinka," she replied as she removed two rings and the gold watch she was wearing and a brooch I had always admired, and handed them to me.

"Don't wear these. Pack them, maybe tie them around your neck. They can be traded for food if you are delayed."

"Yes, Mama," I replied, tears now rolling down both our cheeks.

The air raid alarm sounded again, and a bomb exploded. Not close, but we could not tell if planes might be heading toward us.

"You should get back inside the building, Asya. Mother and I should try to get to a shelter. We'll see you in Vienna in a few days."

"Yes, Papa," I said and began to run to the building entry. When I turned to wave a final good-bye, they were already gone.

An air raid alarm went off as I reentered the building, but no one moved toward the basement shelter. I went back to the hallway window to see a few people out on the street still hurrying toward shelter, and then I returned to the office, now almost empty as darkness fell outside.

I sat at a desk. One soldier remained at another of the desks completing something, and the Colonel was still busy in his office. I suddenly felt very hungry and went to knock at the Colonel's door to ask if I could get something to eat. The Colonel looked up from his desk and smiled, as he answered, "No, I'm afraid our kitchen was closed right after lunch, and all the cooks have been dismissed and sent home. But you could run across the street and get something there."

"I don't have any money."

"Oh, I can help with that. Your papa left a little money with me just for things like that." He smiled and handed me some money.

"But I thought you told me I couldn't leave?"

"Yes, but I meant not to go far—like home or someplace. But this is just across the street, and you'll still have time to get something. In fact, now that we're talking about it, I'm a bit hungry myself. I'll go with you," he said, as he reached for his cap.

We walked across the street to a tiny restaurant that catered mainly to German troops because of their location. I had not been inside a restaurant since the first bombing of Belgrade, what seemed a lifetime ago. So much had changed. As we entered, the proprietor stared at me with a poisonous look, mumbling in Serbian that I should be ashamed and that my "hours were numbered." I was devastated. My appetite immediately disappeared, and I ordered just a cup of tea.

"What's the matter? I thought you were hungry," said the Colonel.

"Not really, I guess."

"What did this man say to you?" he asked, gesturing toward the proprietor. "It seems you suddenly lost your appetite after his mumbling."

"He just said that he hoped we would be able to finish eating before the air raid alarms sounded, and I guess the thought of sitting in the basement again spoiled my appetite."

The proprietor was watching carefully, and as we left he extended his hand to say that he was sorry, that he was wrong. Evidently he understood German. As we left the restaurant, the Colonel looked at me, puzzled. "Do you know this man?"

"No."

"Well, he seemed very friendly just now, shaking your hand."

"No," I answered, "he just said that he hoped his cooking wasn't the reason I didn't eat, and that the next time he would have something good on the menu."

"I'm afraid there won't be a next time. We will be leaving very soon now."

We returned to the office—my appetite gone—and I sat at a desk with nothing to do but wait. I folded my arms on the desk and laid my head on them. I think I may have started to doze, when the Colonel's voice roused me.

"Time to go, Miss Popova. Hurry now."

FIFTEEN

Farewell, My Belgrade

The streets through which we were racing were all dark. It must have been about midnight. The ruins looked even more menacing with small fires burning throughout the city. The boom and flash of artillery in the distance made the scene even more frightening.

I could hear the crack of rifle fire. I guessed it was Serbs, firing wildly at the Germans finally retreating from Belgrade. I could not recognize the streets we were driving through. The only familiar sight was my last look at the silhouette of Kalamegdon. The old fortress looked majestic lit by the flash of explosions, either bombs or artillery.

Since the beginning of Rat Week on September 1, Soviet forces and Yugoslav Partisans had pushed toward Belgrade. They passed Mt. Avala and were within ten miles of Belgrade by October 1. The artillery and rifle fire I heard as we were rushing to Zemun may have heralded the arrival of their advance units entering the city.

"Colonel, where are we going?"

"We are going through Hungary, and if we're lucky we shall reach Vienna in just a few days. There is a military train waiting for us. At least it should be waiting. We will board here in Belgrade, and the train will stop on the other side of the river to load equipment and troops."

The night air was chilly, and a cold drizzle was falling when the truck stopped beside a train. The Colonel jumped out, hurried me along to the waiting train, and helped me up to reach the step. I followed him into a passenger car occupied by only a few soldiers. The train lurched forward immediately, clearly waiting only for the Colonel to board. It took just a few minutes to reach the next stop, Zemun.

"All right, Miss Popova," the Colonel said as the train began pulling to a stop. "We will be here for some time loading men and equipment, and there should be hot coffee on the platform. If we get separated, we should meet at the coffee station. Take your things with you because we may be on a different car when we get back on."

"Yes, Colonel. Thank you."

The Colonel helped me down from the step, into the same cold drizzle that had been falling when we boarded. The whole area was a mass of confusion. A table under the eaves of the tiny station house held a large open kettle filled with steaming hot coffee, a dipper hooked at the side of the kettle. I walked toward the table with the Colonel, confused and a bit frightened, and poured a dipper of coffee into one of the mugs, holding it with both hands, grateful for the warmth it offered. The faces around me were all soldiers, looking haggard and bewildered, as though they were no more sure of what was ahead than I.

Trucks, tanks, and field guns were strung along the other side of the tracks waiting to be loaded onto flatcars. Freight cars stood empty beyond the flatcars, the whole, chaotic scene lit by floodlights. I thought I could hear the occasional distant boom of artillery, but none of the soldiers around me showed any concern or indication of hearing it.

Civilians held back by armed soldiers stood beyond the equipment, their meager belongings flung across their backs or lying on the ground at their feet. Stuffed burlap sacks, baskets, pillowcases, small suitcases tied with a bit of rope, even a small wagon could be seen. A seething group of people, women with small, screaming children, old people looking exhausted and frightened, waited in the rain for a chance to rush for a place on the train.

Brisk military commands could be heard over all the noise, accompanied by the click of German heels saluting. No one in the military seemed at all concerned with the milling mass of refugees waiting to board. As the last of the military personnel began to board, I heard my name.

"Miss Popova," the Colonel called loudly, motioning me to rush and follow him.

I ran to follow him, and he helped me to jump into the train. I stumbled as he brushed past me and turned to grab a handrail by the door. When I turned back, the entrance to the car was blocked by other soldiers, and the Colonel had disappeared.

The train lurched suddenly backward and then began to slowly move forward. The lower half of the door was closed and locked into place, and I stood at the open upper half looking along the platform, now crowded with civilians rushing to find a place. None were allowed on the passenger cars. They ran toward the rear of the train trying to jump into one of the open freight cars as it moved along, gathering speed.

The platform was covered with sacks and packages, discarded as people jumped into the open freight cars, others running after the open doors with their arms outstretched in a last attempt to jump on. Perhaps the freight cars were included as part of the train to accommodate desperate civilians, but German efficiency, or disregard for the plight of civilians, would not let the train wait for them to board. The train just kept gathering speed, as the platform and those left behind became smaller and smaller.

I stood by the open upper half of the door, holding my pillowcase in one hand and the handrail with the other, with terrible chills going through me. I didn't know which way the Colonel had gone, and I was afraid to move through the group of soldiers between me and the door to the car. The night was cold, clearing, and moonlit, and unidentifiable shapes rushed past. I stood there, shivering, when the train whistle blew sharply and startled me. Somebody grabbed my arm, and I looked up to see Lieutenant von Staate.

"It's better to be stuffed in here. At least you get to stay alive," he said, closing the upper door. "Don't you know how dangerous it is to stand by the open door?"

"I was holding on."

"It's not a matter of holding on. The train is being shot at."

I didn't answer; my thoughts were back in Belgrade, wondering about

Mother and Father and whether they had left for Vienna, whether I would ever again see my beloved Belgrade. I stood leaning against the closed door now, beginning to warm up a little and thankful that the Lieutenant had closed it.

"Where are we?" I heard someone ask.

"We're heading north toward the Hungarian border," another voice answered.

"Come with me, Miss Popova," the Lieutenant said, taking my arm lightly. "The Colonel has a seat in this car."

I looked around as I followed him through the aisle. The car was filled to capacity with a mix of soldiers and officers, some playing cards, some writing letters, others just staring out the window as the train rushed through the night. I felt so strange, so uneasy and out of place as the only girl among all these military men. As we made our way along the aisle, I saw the Colonel ahead of us, leaning over to look out of the partially opened window.

"Come on, Miss Popova, there's plenty of room," he said when he saw us.

I sat next to him and smiled up at the Lieutenant.

"I'm sure there is room for the three of us," I said, moving closer to the Colonel.

"Are your parents already in Vienna?" the Lieutenant asked as he sat down.

"No, they are still in Belgrade."

"When we get to Vienna, do you have a place to go?"

"Yes, we have some friends in Vienna, and I'm to meet my parents at their home."

"Well, you are very young to be taking such a trip alone, especially with all these men."

"I'm not afraid," I answered, looking closely at him for the first time. He was not any older than Kolya, I thought, about twenty, very handsome with dark hair and dark blue eyes. He looked up, saw me looking at him, and smiled, and I looked away quickly, feeling my face start to blush. By this time in the war, I was undernourished, skinny, with lifeless hair, and I was embarrassed at the Lieutenant's attention. The Colonel's head had fallen forward, and he began to snore lightly.

"Is he a friend of the family?" he asked, nodding toward the Colonel.

"No, I was working in the office as his translator, and Papa asked him to take me across the border. He thought it would be the safest way to get out of the country."

"Oh, are you German?"

"No, we are Russians."

"I was almost sent to Russia, but, luckily I guess, I got caught in the confusion on the way. I came from Salonika to get my final orders in Belgrade when all this started. That was only a week ago."

"You are very lucky. A good friend of mine was killed in Russia."

"Oh, do you have German friends?"

"No, he was a Russian volunteer." I did not want to think about Kolya and what had happened to him. The Lieutenant's accent sounded Austrian, and I quickly asked, "Where are you from?"

"I'm from Graz."

"Oh, then you are not German. You're Austrian."

The Lieutenant shifted in his seat and cleared his throat.

"Well, I was born in Austria, but we are all German now."

"Well, I think that's silly," I said, not understanding what was behind his apparent unease. "If you are Austrian, then you're Austrian. Just because Austria was absorbed by Germany doesn't mean you're suddenly German. It would be like me saying that I am German because we are now occupied by Germany."

The Lieutenant looked very uncomfortable and shifted his feet. "We became German by choice. There's a big difference."

Exhausted, I had drifted off to sleep when the train suddenly slowed to a stop. The Colonel, awakened by the halt of the train, raised his head.

"What is it now?"

"I'll go and find out, Colonel," the Lieutenant said as he rose and walked toward the end of the car.

The Colonel leaned toward the window to look out. The moon had almost set, and the sky looked especially dark. He raised the window, and the sudden rush of cold fresh air felt good entering the smoky railcar. I looked out at the tracks to see that a lot of the soldiers were outside and that many of the civilians from the freight cars were also out looking around, wondering what was happening.

The Lieutenant, accompanied by a sergeant, returned to report that a bridge just ahead had suffered minor damage that would require a short delay. The Colonel rose and moved toward the exit. I was afraid to get too far from the Colonel, and I followed the three men as we exited to stand next to the tracks.

"Damn," the Colonel swore again. "How long are we going to be stuck here?"

"The bridge should be repaired shortly, sir."

"Do you know exactly where we are, Sergeant?"

"No, sir."

"Do you know anything?"

"No, sir!" The sergeant stood rigidly at attention.

Suddenly a plane appeared, diving toward the stalled train. Someone yelled, "Everyone down," and the Lieutenant grabbed my arm and threw me to the ground."Quickly," he said, "under the train," as the sound of bullets striking the train and the ground was heard, and the German guns mounted on the flat cars began to return fire. I could hear cries. Apparently someone had been hit. The plane made two more runs at the train, firing each time, and on the third run I heard a penetrating whistle followed immediately by a loud explosion. My eyes were closed. I was afraid to move or even to breathe.

"Are you all right?" The question startled me, and I opened my eyes to see the Lieutenant next to me, both of us lying between the tracks beneath the train.

"Yes, I am. What was that?"

"I think they just shot the plane down."

"What if the train starts to move? We're right on the tracks."

"Just look around you. Remember all the people lined up alongside the train? Well, they're all under the train now. Even the General is under the train. You don't think we would run over the General, do you?" he asked, smiling.

I shifted my weight, wriggling to place my chest and hips on the cross ties to avoid the sharp stones between them.

"How long are we going to be here? The tracks are hard, and the ground is so cold and wet."

"It's almost daylight, and we won't be attacked during the day. At least I don't think so."

The stones between the cross ties were cutting my chest, and I wriggled more to get the cross ties beneath my ribcage.

"You are very pretty, even with those smudges all over your face," the Lieutenant said in a whisper.

"How can you see? It's still dark."

"The smudges are darker."

I thought how strange it was that as a group these people were so ferocious, heartless, and brutal, but individually many were very pleasant. I closed my eyes, longing for Belgrade, fighting tears, and wishing that when I opened my eyes I would find that this was all a nightmare and that I would be back on that hill building castles out of fluffy white clouds.

"I can see those smudges better now. It's almost daylight." The Lieutenant's voice broke the silence.

"Oh, yes, it is much brighter," I answered, lifting my head to look around. "The sun should be up very soon. Are you married, Lieutenant?"

"No, I was attending the music conservatory when I was drafted. Somebody decided it was more important to listen to the whistles of bombs and bullets than to study Mozart and Bach."

"I suppose that if one is a real musical genius, he could compose a symphony out of the sounds of war: bullets, bombs, and the cries of people."

"Perhaps, but why not compose something beautiful, something full of light, color, and laughter?"

"If you can find such things," I sighed, "but I haven't heard or seen such pretty things lately. For a long time now it seems all I've heard are moans and explosions."

"Someday there will be laughter and gaiety again."

"Perhaps you're right. The beauty is not gone. Flowers, birds, the sounds of water, the wind . . . it's all still around us. But the cries and explosions overpower the whisper of pines and bird songs. I suppose that's life. When you combine the beauty and the ugliness and mix them all up, somehow it becomes life. I wonder why people must have ugliness around them in order to live?"

"Perhaps the ugliness makes one appreciate the beauty."

"And the beauty makes one despise the ugliness," I concluded with a sigh. "I guess it does make some sense."

"This is the first time I have ever carried on a philosophical discussion with a pretty young lady while lying under a train with the cross ties cutting me in two," the Lieutenant said as he inched himself out from under the train. "I think you can come out now. It seems to be all clear, and almost everybody else is out."

I crawled over the rail, still feeling the cross ties and rocks under my ribcage, and stood stretching, every inch of me hurting. "I think the train did run over me. I'm just too tired to know the difference."

"No, young lady, I can assure you that you are still in one piece."

I blushed and quickly looked around, noticing for the first time the wooded areas, fields, and tiny farmhouses with red roofs and white fences. Everything looked so peaceful that for a moment one could forget that a war was going on. Somewhere a rooster crowed as the first rays of the sun began to light the fields. The air smelled so fresh and clean that it helped dispel thoughts of the war. I think this was our second day of travel, and I wished I could find some water to wash my face. Even drinking water was a restricted luxury on this trip. I looked around again, hoping for a little brook or stream someplace and walked down from the rail bed into a field. I could see a young woman, obviously from the train, bent low as if washing, and ran toward her.

"Good morning. You have found some water," I said.

"Yes, look how clear it is. It's good enough to drink."

I tied my braids together on top of my head and knelt down, scooping the ice cold water into my palms and splashing it over my face." Oh, it felt so good. Almost as good as a bath, I thought, trying to remember how long it had been since I had a hot bath. I realized I couldn't even remember how long it had been. Hot water and soap had become luxuries. Good soap had long been a thing of the past, and we had been very happy to get strong, brown soap from Yaintse.

"Why are we stopping here, do you know?" asked the woman, cradling a small, sleeping child in her arms.

"I think a bridge is out or something. We should be moving again soon."

"I wonder if I would have enough time to run to that farmhouse and try to get some milk for the baby and a little food or fruit."

"I'll go and ask someone."

I ran back to the train and almost bumped into the Lieutenant.

"Do you know how long we will be here?" I asked.

"It looks like still a half-day's work. I'm not an engineer, but the bridge looks badly damaged."

I ran back to the brook and told the woman what I had learned. She immediately got up and began to walk toward a small farmhouse at the other edge of the field.

"Has the lady had her morning bath yet?" The Lieutenant's voice surprised me. He had followed me back to the brook.

"Oh, sure, fancy oils and everything."

"Too bad," he said, smiling and looking at a bar of soap in his hand. "I was going to offer you this soap that I brought from Salonika. But, of course, it could never compete with fancy oils." He paused, looked at me, and asked, "What is your name?"

"'Wandering stranger.' And yours?"

"'Protector of wandering strangers,' of course."

"Such unusual names we both have," I said, dipping my hands back into the brook to splash my face.

"Please, take the soap. It's too perfumed for me. I hope you will like it."

I took the soap from his hand and thanked him as he returned to the train. I wondered if I would dare to wash my hair with the soap, too. My hair was so dirty, covered with soot and dust from the train. I undid my braids, and lowered my whole head into the clear stream as the icy water sent chills down my spine. I soaped my hair vigorously, repeating it three times until the hair was squeaky and even smelled pleasant.

Suddenly I remembered that I didn't have a towel or comb with me, and I wondered if Father had put a comb in the small package he had brought of things I had "forgotten." I didn't have any idea where the Colonel was, and my pillowcase was with his briefcase. I got up, putting the soap in the pocket of my dress, and holding my hair with both hands, my head bent to try to keep the icy cold water from dripping down my back, I scrambled back up to the tracks to try to find the Colonel.

"Well, it's moments like this that one should have a camera, moments that should be kept forever." The Lieutenant's voice sounded teasingly in front of me.

"Oh, please. Can't you find me a rag or a towel?"

"If you would just lift your head a bit, you would see that your 'protector' is way ahead of you." He laughed, throwing a towel over my head.

"Oh, that's better. It's so cold."

"Why, you have blonde hair. I thought you were a gray-haired, middle-aged lady. What a pleasant surprise."

"Well, could you find the Colonel for the old lady?"

"What do you want the old crank for?"

"He has my pillowcase."

"Your pillowcase? I thought you knew him only slightly, as his interpreter. How does he happen to have your pillowcase?"

"Oh, please. I didn't have a suitcase when we left, and I packed my things in a pillowcase."

The Lieutenant laughed and turned to run toward the train and jump up onto the flat car. I could see the Colonel trying to tune his car radio to get some news—without much luck, judging from the expression on his face. When the Lieutenant handed me the pillowcase, I rummaged through it to get Father's package and found my comb. Thank you, Papa, I thought, turning to walk back to the stream. I sat on a rock and combed and dried my hair. The Lieutenant sat opposite me on the bank, dipping a stick in the water.

"Yes," he said suddenly, "now I can see why all those sailors wrecked their ships."

"Where? What ships?"

"See that one?" he said, pointing to a stick in the water. "That's all that's left of a once beautiful ship."

"What in the world are you talking about?"

"The Lorelei on the Rhine. That's what she used to do. Sit on a rock and comb her hair."

"Well, she must have been very stupid," I interrupted, "because it's uncomfortable to sit on a hard rock and try to comb your hair."

We both burst out laughing happily.

"I haven't smiled or laughed in a very long time," he said quietly.

"Neither have I," I said, sadly remembering the day Kolya and I had said the same thing.

"Well, now that you have properly washed your hands, how would you like a superb breakfast?"

"Consisting of what? Leaves?"

The Lieutenant reached into his jacket and brought out a loaf of black bread and some chocolate.

"Where did you find chocolate?"

"It is rations. All the Afrika Corp men had this as a standard ration. It's supposed to give you strength. Here, I have lots more back in my duffel bag."

We ate the dry black bread and chocolate, and drank the water from the stream. I braided my hair and felt 100 percent better. Despite the fact that I didn't know where I was going or when I would get there, I felt pretty good. I closed my eyes, dreaming that there was no war and that this was a young man who was madly in love with me and was courting me. I imagined that he could sing superbly and that he was indeed Italian.

"Do you like Italians?" I asked.

"What a question, out of the blue and in the middle of nowhere. I should, and I do. My mother is half Italian, her father was Italian, and my grandmother was Austrian. Why?"

"Because I'm going to marry an Italian."

"Oh, where is he?"

"I don't know."

"Well, how are you going to marry him if you don't even know where he is?"

"Oh, I'll find him."

"Well, if he really loves you, he should try to find you."

"Oh, he doesn't even know that I'm alive."

"Why don't you let him know?"

"Well, I haven't found him yet. You don't understand. I don't know who he is or where he is. All I know is that someday I will marry an Italian."

"Why an Italian?"

"Because they make such beautiful music. They have such tender, touching operas, and they seem to be so terribly friendly and happy. They're so different from my own people or the Germans. Even during the occupation there was such a difference between the two. I like them, and I'll find mine someday." I stopped to listen. "What is that?"

"What?" the Lieutenant asked. "Oh, yes, I hear it now. It's a plane again."

In seconds the plane was flying at treetop level above the train, strafing, the stillness shattered by the sound of the screaming plane and its guns. It disappeared almost as fast as it had appeared. The Lieutenant and I jumped to run toward the train, afraid it might start moving.

The bridge repairs had been completed, and the train sounded one shrill whistle and gave a big jolt just as we reached it. The Lieutenant, holding my pillowcase, ran to the flat car where the Colonel had been, and I jumped into the first freight car. I looked back to see people who had been left behind again, running to try to catch the train, but just falling farther and farther behind.

"My wife! My wife is still by the stream. I can't leave her behind," cried a man behind me.

As I watched, he jumped from the car and began rolling down toward the field. Someone inside threw out a sack that apparently belonged to them. I couldn't see whether or not the man got up after jumping. All I could see was the sack lying there at the side of the tracks. I looked around, and my heart felt as if it were being crushed.

There were at least fifty people of all ages in the freight car. Children with dirty faces and flimsy clothing were crying, their mothers trying to comfort them; other children were lying on the cold floor with only a bit of straw beneath them; old people stood all about me, their tired faces indicating that they didn't really understand why they were on the train or where they were going.

"Do you know where we're headed?" someone asked. I was the newcomer in the car, and they hoped I had information.

"We are going through Hungary and then on to Vienna." My answer started a chain of questions and statements throughout the group as they moved about and began to sit on the floor.

"I hope we stop in Hungary. I have relatives there," one said hopefully.

"Why bother with Hungary? The Germans are there, and the Soviets and Partisans will be there soon."

"Where else? To Germany?"

"Well, Vienna isn't Germany. It's Austria."

"You mean it used to be Austria. The dragon has lashed its fiery tongue across that country, too. It's Germany, all right. Do you know what will await us in Germany? Camps! Dirt, filth, and certain death. The Germans are confiscating food from every country they've entered in order to keep their troops fed. I heard there isn't much standing in Germany now either. But, of course, they deserve it."

"You should be quiet, or we could wind up in a camp before we ever get to Vienna. You never know who's sitting next to you," said a woman clutching a small child to her breast and looking all around, her dark eyes searching everyone's face, as though trying to catch an enemy.

"I hope King Peter is well and will be back when we are able to go home," someone said.

"Hah! King Peter. He sure got cold feet and ran when the Germans came. The Partisans are the ones who are fighting for our Yugoslavia," another responded.

Soon the whole car was shouting and arguing—some for the king, others against the king and for the Partisans. I looked at the angry faces all around me, growing angrier with each statement, and became frightened. I didn't understand or care about this king vs. Partisan argument. The real enemy was the Germans. Surely these people knew that.

Suddenly a fist fight broke out between two men. More joined in as the children and some of the women began to cry and scream. The doors to the car were open. I was afraid that I might get pushed out, and I crawled to a corner as far away from the fighting as I could get. A man grabbed a large cast-iron pan and swung it to strike another's head. Blood ran down the face of the man hit, and he struggled to keep his balance as a woman screamed, "Watch out, watch out!" I saw the cast-iron pan start to swing again, when a piercing scream froze everyone in position. A woman on the other side of the car bent, sobbing over a small, bloody bundle on the floor.

"Oh, God! My baby, my baby! What have you done? My baby is dead!"

The man who had been hit with the pan stood over the woman, his arms outstretched to her, blood from his head now covering one eye, his voice cracking.

"Forgive me, forgive me. I didn't see the baby. I just felt a crunch and . . . oh God, what have I done?" He looked down at the baby, realizing that he had stepped on its skull. Then he said to the man who had hit him, still holding the pan, "Kill me! Just kill me! I can't live with this. Just kill me."

The drama unfolding inside that freight car held everyone spellbound, and no one noticed the sound of another plane diving low to begin a strafing run. I huddled in my corner, covering my ears, trying to block the penetrating whistles accompanying the bullets slamming into the train. The attack seemed to be over in an instant, as the train screeched and jolted to a stop.

I peeked through a crack in the wall and saw that we had stopped in the middle of a field, the tracks leading toward a wooded area ahead. Not a house or farm was visible, just meadow, forest, and a small stream. Harsh German voices were heard outside, as the sound of planes approaching again added to the confusion and terror. A stern command was heard at the side of the open car.

"Everybody out of the train. Now! Heraus! Heraus!"

The soldier waved his rifle toward the door of the car, then ran toward the next car just as another plane screamed low over the train and a bullet slammed into him. As he fell, his rifle discharged, striking one of the people jumping from the car.

People began to jump from the train wildly, throwing themselves under the train for cover. I jumped from the train, ran to the ditch beside the rail bed, and lay there trying to burrow into the ground, shaking from fright.

I looked around to see people running to the field and falling like boards. I couldn't tell if they fell to take cover or if they had been hit. I don't know how long I lay there. Probably just seconds, although it seemed forever. When I looked up, I saw the Lieutenant running along the train and looking under it.

"I'm here," I called. He looked toward the sound of my voice, saw me, and ran to jump into the ditch next to me, all out of breath.

"Thank God you're all right. We have orders to set up our guns and try to stop the air attack. I think the Luftwaffe has planes on the way to help. We are very close to the border, but the train is on its last legs. If we can stop any further damage to the train, they think we can make it. Hungarians are friendly toward us."

"Lots of people would be friendly if you hadn't taken their country, food, and everything else."

"It looks like the war is on its last legs, too," he said, ignoring my outburst. "Perhaps I shouldn't say this, as an officer, but common sense tells me it can't last much longer."

"You asked for it," I said sharply, fighting tears. "I'm sorry, I didn't mean you personally. But your maniac Hitler has caused so much bloodshed and destruction throughout all of Europe. So many people have already lost their lives."

"As a friend, wandering stranger," he said softly, "I would advise you not to say anything like that in front of other Germans. If you do, your life could be short."

"I may not even live beyond the next ten minutes."

"Well, God might have mercy on both of us. We may yet come out of this madness alive. Look, the Luftwaffe has sent at least one fighter to help."

"I thought you didn't believe in God—that most of you gave up God for Hitler," I said bitterly.

"I had a long battle within myself, trying to decide whether or not there was a God. I had my doubts. If there really was a God, I could not believe that he had permitted this terrible war, that he could have blinded so many German people, allowing them to deny Him and embrace Hitler. But God has given the world sunrise and mountains and so much beauty in nature, and He has given people the gifts of writing books and composing beautiful music to describe those things. And all those things will still be there when Hitler has gone. No, I'm certain God is watching. Perhaps he just turned his head away, toward nature instead of man, to see if man can teach himself the things He has been trying to teach us . . . if the horrors we are causing to each other will finally teach us."

"Before the occupation," I answered, "I was very sure that God was watching over everything. I used to see Him daily in so many things—in flowers, in stars, the birds, or the moon, even in some people. But then my thoughts began to work beyond blind belief, and I began to doubt, to ask questions without ever finding answers, and now, lying here in this ditch, I begin to doubt again. Did you see the baby with the crushed skull in the freight car I was riding in?"

"No, the car was empty when I went to look for you. What baby? What happened?"

"Oh, the men began to argue, some for the king, others for the Partisans, and a fight broke out. During the fight one of the men lost his balance and stomped on the baby's head. It happened so fast that the mother didn't have a chance to pick up the baby, or maybe she had been pushed out of the way during the fighting. At any rate, the baby is dead, the mother is half crazy with grief, and the men are all broken up. See, again, don't you think that God could have protected this helpless little creature?"

"Maybe this was the best way out for the baby," the Lieutenant answered softly, "considering what could lie ahead."

A plane screamed overhead, and I heard bullets thudding into the ground all around us, smashing into the rail cars. The Lieutenant and I both lay burrowed as close to the ground as we could get. My face was pressed against the cold ground, and I didn't dare to raise it. The screaming sound of the planes above us and the sound of German guns on the train now firing rapidly was terrifying. I heard a terrible whistle, followed by an explosion, then another, and then it grew silent.

"What now?" I asked as I raised my head.

"I think it's all over. I think they shot two planes down. Come on, it's safe to get up now. Wait here until I find out what is happening."

I stood and looked around. It was eerily still now that the attack had ended. Black smoke was rising from the field beyond two trees only about a hundred meters from where I stood, and the burning tail of a plane could be seen. The Lieutenant returned to say the train had suffered only minor damage and that we would be moving again in about thirty minutes.

I looked toward the smoke rising from the trees. A couple of civilians were walking toward it, and I decided to go and look myself. I hurried across the field to stand close to the plane. The fuselage was completely burned off the frame, and there was no identifying insignia. I walked to the front of the plane and was horrified to see the burned skeleton of the pilot still sitting in the cockpit. Nothing was left of the plane except the frame and the skeleton. One arm rested on the edge of the cockpit frame. Inside the cockpit was only the arm bones attached to the rest of the skeleton, but on the outside of the frame, the forearm and hand were intact. The hand looking almost alive. Even the uniform cuff was unburned. As I looked, I could see a wedding ring on the hand, and I started to cry, wondering if his wife would now have children to raise alone. I turned quickly and ran back to the train, arriving just as soldiers were ordering everyone back on board.

I saw the Lieutenant waving at me. I ran toward him, and he helped me to jump into one of the passenger cars. I turned to look back along the tracks and saw many of the civilians trying to catch the train, many still running from the field. As the running figures became smaller and smaller, I covered my face and started to cry again.

"God, what are you doing? Those poor people might be hurt or wounded. Why don't we wait?" I sobbed, starting to lean out the door.

"There is nothing we can do." The Lieutenant grabbed my arm, leading me into the car, "This is a war. We almost missed the train ourselves. Didn't you see the bodies of the German soldiers lying along the tracks? They wouldn't even wait to pick *them* up. Here, please sit down and be quiet. Do you smoke?"

"No, thank you," I said, drying my eyes as an officer appeared to demand, "What is this young woman doing here?"

The Lieutenant jumped to salute and to explain. "This is Miss Popova, sir. She was the translator in our Belgrade offices, and my Colonel promised her father that we would take her to Vienna. He has ordered me to see her safely through the trip, sir."

"That's fine, Lieutenant, but the passenger cars are reserved for military personnel. No civilians are permitted, so you will have to carry out your orders in other sections of the train," the officer said curtly.

"Yes, sir," the Lieutenant responded and took my arm to lead me back toward the door. When we reached the passage between cars, he turned to me and said, "I know what we can do. Follow me." He led me through the next car to the flat car that held the Colonel's staff car.

The Lieutenant smiled, bowing as he opened the door of the automobile.

"Here we are, Miss Popova, the first class compartment. We may even get Radio Lili Marlene if the battery isn't dead."

My face and eyes had dried, and it was already dark. The night had come out of nowhere. I stood leaning against the open door of the staff car, the Lieutenant seated in the driver's seat, trying without success to tune the radio. The night was quiet, and the moon just beginning to rise outlined tall pines passing swiftly, looking like tall sentries standing guard over the train.

"We are in Hungary now. Did you see the sign next to the tracks a few kilometers back?"

"No, I didn't."

"Have you ever been to Hungary?"

"No, have you?" I answered, beginning to be very chilly. I climbed into the back seat of the staff car and closed the door. The Lieutenant leaned back against the driver's door and put his feet up on the passenger seat.

"When I was studying at the conservatory, I had an opportunity to go to Budapest several times. It is a beautiful city."

"Belgrade was a beautiful city before you destroyed it," I said, looking at the stars, wondering if they were aware of the terrible destruction going on below them.

"I've told you before, I did not do it," the Lieutenant said softly. "Please don't blame me. If I could, I would bring everyone back to life and restore all the cities."

"Then why do you wear that uniform, a uniform that signifies death and destruction throughout all of Europe?"

"Because if I did not, I would be sitting in a prison right now with little hope of ever getting out. At least this way there is a chance I'll survive, that I will have a chance to finish my studies and to compose music. I have never killed another human being, and I don't intend to. Do you believe me?"

"I do, but you are wearing a uniform that represents death and destruction, and that's hard for me to understand. Oh, I don't know *what* I understand. Let's not talk about it."

"You know, I would like to see you when the war is over," he said after a moment.

"Who knows where we'll be when it's over . . . if it's ever over."

"I don't even know your name, Wandering Stranger Popova?"

"A name is so insignificant now."

"Then you won't tell me your name?"

"No."

"Well, my name is—"

"I don't want to know," I interrupted. "In just a few hours we'll never see each other again. This way when I hear a beautiful symphony I can imagine that you wrote it, not some other von Staate . . . just in case you turn out to be a failure and become a drunken bum instead," I added, smiling.

"You're so realistic. So young and yet so terribly sentimental and romantic. I could compose music right now describing you just as you are," he said, also smiling.

"It would never sell."

"I wouldn't want to sell it. Just to play it for you."

"Now who's being silly and romantic? Besides, I'm tired and getting cold."

I leaned back against the seat, thinking about the day that had just ended. I felt so alone, cold now, yet thankful for the solitude. I wondered again about Belgrade, whether it was under attack, and whether my parents were already in Vienna. I tried to remember the last time I had slept on crisp, clean sheets that Kristina had dried in the sun and how fresh they smelled. The clicking sound of the wheels on the rails was almost hypnotic, and my eyes began to feel so very heavy.

"What do you want to be? What do you want to do when this war is finally over?" The Lieutenant's soft voice roused me.

"What I want . . . what I want is to know what is beyond every mountain. I want to see if there is both a beginning and an end to the rainbow, and to know what people in other lands, faraway lands, believe in, what they dream about. I want to cross every ocean, visit every foreign shore, see if the stars and moon look the same in other lands. I want to find a country that truly believes in peace, where people care only for beauty and nature and love itself and never ask, 'What is your nationality?' and where children know nothing but laughter and beauty. I want to find a place where trees bend in rhythm to the music in the wind, and where soft waves roll gently against the shore. I guess I want both the natural and the impossible at the same time. But right now I wish I had a soft, clean bed and a warm bath . . . and quiet. What do you want?" I asked, yawning.

"I want everything you do, only in triple doses."

"See?" I said, suddenly sitting up straight. "That's what I mean. You're German at heart. It's never enough. 'Today Germany, tomorrow the whole world.'"

I looked at him sheepishly then, trying to see if I had offended him. "I'm truly sorry. I know you don't think or feel that way. I shouldn't have said that."

"It's all right. I know you didn't mean it. It's this terrible situation we find ourselves in. I'm sorry, too, as sorry as you are. Well, since I can't fulfill your immediate wish for a warm bath and clean sheets, allow me to fold my tunic for a pillow," he said, leaning over his seat to place his tunic on the rear seat for me. I put my head on the tunic, moving the scratchy insignia away from my face. I heard the Lieutenant say, "And now my coat," but I heard nothing else.

I opened my eyes because of a light shaking at my shoulder. The sun was shining brightly, and the October air was brisk and fresh. The Lieutenant was leaning over the front seat, shivering, obviously very cold as he said, "Could I have my tunic? I'd like to go back to the front of the train to get us some coffee and maybe something to eat. But we are supposed to always wear our tunics."

"Oh," I said, sitting up. "You must have been freezing. You've given me both your tunic and your coat. I'm so sorry." I tossed my braids behind my shoulders and quickly handed him the tunic and coat.

"No, I don't think I'll need the coat. You may still need it." he said, smiling.

"Where are we? Do you know?"

"We are in Hungary, close to Pecs. That's where this train is supposed to meet another command before proceeding through Budapest to Vienna. Let me go and get some coffee for us," he said, buttoning his tunic—gratefully, I thought—as he started back toward the passenger cars.

I got out of the car and shook his heavy overcoat out in the fresh air. The sun was up and warming, but the October air was brisk, and I put the coat around my shoulders. We were passing slowly through a small village. I looked at the tiny houses, noticing that almost every house had colorful strings of red peppers hanging from the porch ceiling. I could see farmers moving about in the fields, chickens pecking, and a rooster crowing, dogs wagging their tails. How peaceful it looked. One of the farmers waved as the train slowly stopped.

How I wished I could just get off the train and feel human again, to know what the daily chores were to be, to have someone glad just to see me at the beginning of a new day. I felt at that moment as though I had nothing—no home, no definite destination. Nothing, not even the next hour, held any certainty for me. I wondered again if my parents and our friends had made it out of Belgrade, if there was fighting in the streets of the city. The Lieutenant's voice sounded happily behind me.

"Here's our coffee. And a farmer was selling fresh, warm bread. How's that for a perfect breakfast?"

"Oh, it smells delicious. Is it really still warm?"

"Yes, the farmers were very friendly. They greeted the train with smiles."

The Lieutenant broke the fresh loaf in two. It smelled so good that it made me feel weak. "Heavens, I had no idea I was so terribly hungry."

"Oh," he said, "I found out that we will arrive in Peĉs in only another hour or so. In Peĉs we'll be able to have almost everything."

"Yes, you will," I answered. "You have a 'passport,' your uniform, but not me."

"Oh, don't be silly. Didn't the Colonel promise your father that he would be sure you got to Vienna all right?"

"Yes, he did. But I haven't seen the Colonel for the past two or three days. Is he even still alive?"

"Oh, yes, I just spoke to him, and he asked about you. So you see no one is going to leave you behind."

The train started to move slowly forward. Perhaps because the coffee and fresh bread tasted so good, it seemed only minutes before it again slowed to a full stop.

"I think this is Peĉs," said the Lieutenant. "I need to go forward to check with the Colonel."

We seemed to be in a lush valley surrounded by soft hills and meadows. From the flatcar I could see a delightful little village, or small town, and on top of a hill beyond the village, a large building that resembled a castle. The train stopped beside a wide walkway, and the familiar sound of German boots was heard once again as soldiers began to form up on the concrete. Shrill commands and the clicking of German heels filled the air, as everybody disembarked. Only the guns and equipment remained on the train.

The few civilians who had managed to stay throughout the trip now began to disburse, carrying the few meager possessions they had brought. They all looked exhausted, bewildered, like cattle with no idea which direction to head. The military cleared the platform quickly. I got off the train and saw the Colonel looking very important and issuing orders. He didn't show any trace of the long, miserable, hazardous journey. He noticed me standing there and spoke to a sergeant. I looked at the Lieutenant, standing beside the Colonel, but he had assumed the stony expression of a dedicated German air force officer.

The Sergeant approached and spoke to me, and I turned to follow him carrying my dirty pillowcase toward a truck filled with leering soldiers, grinning from ear to ear.

"I wonder what gutter they found this one in?" one said loudly.

"Oh, she probably came in on the train. The Hungarian girls around here sure don't look that dirty," another answered.

The Sergeant I was following spoke up. "I have the Colonel's orders to put this girl in the truck. She arrived with the Yugoslavian train."

"Oh, we thought the Colonel could have done better than that. Well, his tastes will change after a few hours in Pecs," the first soldier said.

"I think all she needs is a bath and some clean clothes. She might even start to look human," another added.

"Nah, none of these foreigners resemble real humans."

I stood there feeling so ashamed, wondering how long I would have to stand there listening to the insults.

"Hey, Sergeant, is she supposed to ride on top with us or up front with the driver?"

"I guess with the driver."

"Too bad. We could have had some fun if she was riding back here," the first soldier added, as they all began to laugh.

I suddenly lost patience, took two steps back, and hurled my pillowcase at the jeering faces on the truck.

"I wish it was filled with bombs. That would really be fun," I said through tears. The sound of a response in German always embarrassed them. The pillowcase hit one of the leering soldiers in the face, who turned beet red and spat in my direction.

"You dirty little swine! How dare you hit a German soldier!"

"I wish it had torn your stupid, ugly face to shreds," I shouted, choking back the tears as I ran from the truck, with the pillowcase flying after me. I grabbed the pillowcase and sat on the ground crying bitterly. I was exhausted, angry, humiliated, and so completely alone and lost.

"Come on, Miss Popova, I'll take you to Peĉs. I know where the Colonel wants you to stay," the Lieutenant said as he picked up my pillowcase. I got up, drying my eyes, and followed him toward the waiting staff car. "I have to drop off the Colonel and another officer in Peĉs, and then I can drive you there."

SIXTEEN

Maria and Rosa

The car pulled to a stop in the village. The Colonel and the other officer got out, waved, and turned to enter a building as we drove away.

"Where are we going?" I asked the Lieutenant.

"Just a few kilometers from the town. I understand it's an old estate of some kind, supposed to be in the middle of the forest, with a natural hot spring that supplies a swimming pool."

"Are you and the Colonel going to stay there?"

"I don't know. Personnel arriving from Belgrade are designated to stay in Peĉs. My orders are simply to bring you and deliver a note from the Colonel to the General. The facility in town is a military billet with no place for females."

We were driving through a thick pine forest, and as the road ended, I thought I had reached the one place on earth that knew no wars, no death. The Lieutenant stopped the car on a circular drive and ran up the steps to enter a large building.

I stepped out of the car and looked around. White marble steps formed a gentle curve as they surrounded the building, and flower gardens followed the curve of the steps. To the left, in front of the building, more marble steps led down between flower beds to a swimming pool, barely visible as steam rose above it. Small green cabins, apparently dressing rooms, stood on the far side of the pool, and just beyond the cabins, dense forest began again. To the left of the pool were a tennis court, riding stables, and a garage. The air smelled of fresh pine mixed with the mineral smell of the natural hot spring.

It was perfectly peaceful. The only sound was the soft creak and whisper of the pines as they swayed in the wind. I turned back to look at the building and its gardens, to see a peacock, its tail feathers vibrating in full spread with the sun highlighting the greens and blues, as two female peacocks followed sedately. I hadn't seen peacocks since my last summer at Hopova, what seemed a lifetime ago.

An elderly woman appeared at the door, motioning for me to come in, and I walked slowly up the marble steps. The woman at the door spoke very poor German. I could not make out what she was saying, and she broke into Hungarian as she motioned again for me to come in. I entered a huge entry hall with walls covered with silk damask wallpaper and a heavy chandelier reflected in a highly polished parquet floor.

The room was round, with a wide free-standing central stairway that imitated the same curve of the walls and rose to a balcony. A huge picture of Hitler occupied one section of wall, below a large flag displaying the Nazi swastika. Faded, empty rectangles flanked the display where other paintings once hung. On the opposite side of the room, large portraits of older men and women in formal attire hung facing the Nazi display, and I wondered if they liked their present company.

I could almost hear the clicking of Nazi heels and picture German officers entering the room, pausing with an arm stiffly raised in salute to the Fuehrer. I looked away from the piercing eyes in the picture and followed the curve of the wall, noticing four doors and wondering what was behind each of them. As I looked around the curve of the room, my eyes suddenly met those of the elderly woman who had called me inside. She had waited patiently as I looked around. She had a beautiful face and gentle eyes, and she held herself erect with great poise as she began to speak in Hungarian.

"I'm sorry," I said in German, "but I don't speak Hungarian. Do you speak French, Russian, Serbian, or perhaps English?"

"No French, Russian, English, or any other barbaric language will be tolerated within these walls," said a stern voice behind me.

I turned to see an elderly German general striding briskly toward us. "I understand that you, young lady, served as a translator in Belgrade."

"Yes."

"Excellent. Now then, do you speak fluent Hungarian?"

"No, I don't."

"You don't! Then what the devil are you doing here?"

"Sir," the Lieutenant said quickly. "My orders are to bring the young lady here. She was employed as a translator in Belgrade, and the Colonel gave his word to her father that he would see her safely to Vienna. I am charged with seeing to her safety."

"Well, Lieutenant, this is not a stopover for civilians. I am in charge here, not your Colonel, who is simply being extended some courtesy since he lost his command in Belgrade." The General turned sharply and strode back in the direction he came from, his shiny boots reflected in the polished floors.

The Lieutenant shrugged helplessly and followed the General, as the elderly woman bent to whisper in my ear in English, "Don't worry. If they won't let you stay here, it will be all right. This is my home, although I now have only two small rooms. My sister lives in Peĉs, and she would love to put you up." Her English was perfect, much better than her German.

"But I don't have any money," I said forlornly, pointing to my pillowcase. "Only a few trinkets Mama let me have in case I got in trouble."

"We don't need any money. You're too young to be in this house anyway."

"Who lives here?"

"General von Stoiber and his staff."

"And you?"

"Yes. After all, it is my home. I talked them into letting me stay. They have treated us pretty decently, and I have no complaints. But you are too young and too pretty to be left alone."

I blushed when she said "pretty," knowing that I hadn't looked in a mirror or had a bath in weeks and that the dress and light jacket I was wearing were wrinkled and dirty and didn't even fit well.

"Oh, I must look terrible. My hair hasn't been washed or combed, and my shoes are falling off my feet. These clothes aren't mine. A kind woman gave them to me because they were her daughter's, and her daughter had been killed."

The elderly lady placed her hand softly on my head, looking gently into my eyes.

"Hush, there's nothing to worry about, poor child. We'll take care of everything," she said, as she left me standing in the middle of the huge entry hall and entered the same door through which the old General had disappeared.

I stood there looking around at the large portraits that hung on the wall, trying to avoid looking at the picture of Hitler with his piercing eyes. Suddenly I felt Hitler and the people in the portraits staring and coming closer and closer. I ran outside, feeling so stupid at being unnerved by the portraits.

I sat on the top marble step and just let the peaceful beauty of the setting unfold before me: the steam rising from the pool, the flowers, and the peacocks, the stillness of the forest, and the gentle swaying and whisper of the pines. I sat on that step and wondered just what I was doing there, in a strange country where I didn't know anyone, didn't even know the language. I wondered what was going to happen next and how I would ever get to Vienna to meet my parents. The trip had been so difficult and dangerous that I began to wonder if Mother had purposely sent me on the train just to get rid of me, just to let me get lost in the confusion of the war.

Torturous thoughts filled my head, questions again without answers. Even worse, I had no one I could talk to about everything. Chills went down my spine, and I felt cold and tired. I rose from the step, picked up my pillowcase, and walked down toward the steaming pool, the warmed air filling my lungs. The sight of the warm water was so inviting. I sat on the first step that led into the pool, and, oh, how I wished that I could shed my dirty clothes and torn shoes and just immerse myself in the water. "But no," I told myself, "I couldn't do that. Well, maybe just my feet?"

I looked all around, as though expecting to see a giant eye staring at me. I hesitated and then untied my shoes. As I looked at them, tears filled my eyes as I realized how terrible I must look. Dirty, torn clothes, shoes in shreds, braids like shaggy, long rattails. How I longed for the wardrobe left behind in Dedinye. I had always had beautiful clothes hand-tailored by Mrs. Ivanovich. Each day a different dress for school, shoes . . . pretty ribbons for my braids . . .

I lowered my head on my knees and felt so sorry for myself. I knew that I was not unattractive, remembering the glances I received at school dances and at events at Russkii Dom. But I just felt so ashamed of the way I looked right then that I wished I could jump into the pool and drown. What does the Lieutenant think of me? I wondered. He is so nice and gentlemanly. He must pity me. Surely he couldn't see anything pretty about me. Not the way I've looked since we met.

I slowly eased one foot into the water, and then the other. I looked around again, but the place was as deserted as when we first arrived. I slowly eased to the next step, and then the third. The water was then above my knees, and I took the last step down into the pool, raising my dress as the water rose to the top of my thighs, just below my panties.

The hot spring water felt wonderful. No, I cannot get my panties and dress wet, I thought. What if that grouchy old general should come out and find me in the pool? He would probably put me in front of a firing squad for stepping into a pool reserved for "superior Aryans." No, surely he wouldn't do that. Or would he? I turned to look toward the house, horrified to see the General standing at the entry. I bent low, hoping the heavy steam would cover me, and walked slowly out of the pool.

"Where in the name of Heaven is she?" he thundered, his voice echoing across the yard and down to the pool.

I quickly picked up my pillowcase, shoes, and socks and ran toward the house, water still dripping from my legs, the dress clinging to my wet thighs. I stood erect, head held high, as though awaiting his command for the execution.

"What the devil were you doing?" he demanded, looking down at me.

"Bathing my feet," I answered, looking directly into his eyes.

"You bathed your feet in my personal pool?" he thundered.

"There was no other place, and the pool looked so warm and inviting."

He cleared his throat a couple of times and then continued, more gently.

"Well, you could at least have taken a bath in the house first, put on a bathing suit, and then gone into the pool."

"I don't have a bathing suit."

"Do you at least have some clean clothes to put on? And look at those raggedy shoes. For heaven's sake, how long has it been since you changed into clean clothes?"

"I don't have any other clothes or any other shoes. The few things I have in my pillowcase are not mine. They were given to me."

"Don't you have anything besides that dirty pillowcase?"

"No, not since you took it all away from me."

"I took something from you?"

"Not you personally. The German army took everything when our home was 'requisitioned.'"

"How is it that you speak such wonderful German? I must say, it is almost too good."

"Despite what you may think," I answered, chin slightly raised as I remembered Mother doing, "we are educated and intelligent. Many of us speak several languages quite fluently."

"Hmm, too bad you don't speak Hungarian. Which brings me to what I came out here to tell you. I have talked to the Colonel, and neither he nor I can use you in our headquarters now. We are in the process of moving to our new post in Vienna, so that leaves you out. We will not require your services any longer."

"But how am I going to get to Vienna? How am I going to live, and where?" I asked, choking back tears. "I can't walk that far, not in these," I added, holding up my raggedy shoes.

"Well," he harrumphed, clearing his throat and coughing slightly, "why don't you come in, and Frau Maria will help you out. She'll figure out something . . . I guess. I don't know why it should be my responsibility. I certainly have enough other problems to be concerned with."

I padded behind him back into the hall, leaving wet footprints on the highly polished parquet. I looked behind me in horror, thinking what Mother would say if I had done this in our home: "Ladies do not ever walk barefooted." I looked back again and smiled, delighted to see that the prints were still there, and then wondered if I was somehow "getting even" with Mama in some strange way.

The elderly lady was just coming out of one of the doors.

"Come, dear," she said. "I have spoken to my sister, and the young officer is going to take you to her home in Pecs. I am sure you will find her very charming."

She put her arm around my waist to lead me upstairs. "Now," she began, "we are going to get you cleaned up. Give me your pillowcase. The first thing to do is get rid of it. It's coming apart at the seams. I have a small suitcase that I have not used since my husband passed away. And then we're going to wash you and your dresses and iron them up."

She turned the pillowcase upside down on the bed to empty it, and out tumbled everything I had in the world—a dress, a wool jacket, two pairs of panties, a comb, a little box containing a brooch with a large aquamarine stone in the middle, a gold Orthodox cross, the gold watch and rings, and the camera from that wounded German boy.

"Is this all you have?" she asked.

"Yes."

"You don't have any more underwear? No shoes or other clothes? Why, you don't even have soap or a toothbrush."

"We lost everything. All of this was given to me by a lady whose daughter had been killed," I said, embarrassed. "Mother gave me the few jewels to trade for food if it became necessary."

"Well, come along," she said, leading me to the bathroom. "I'll take your dresses to Bianca. Bianca is my maid—or rather she's the German maid now. But she has been in my home for the past fifteen years. She'll wash and fix your dresses, and while she is doing that, you can take a bath. There is plenty of soap, and I'll try to find a toothbrush."

I walked into the bathroom. How wonderful it felt just to be inside a real, clean bathroom. The tub was built below floor level. Water constantly flowing from the same mineral spring that supplied the pool kept the tub filled with clean hot water, the mineral odor mixing with the smell of perfumed soap.

Steam rose slowly from the water, and I shed my dirty clothes and slowly stepped down into the tub in anticipation of how good it was going to feel. I just froze, not daring to sit down, afraid it was going to feel too good to be true. I was convinced that no one had ever felt about a bath the way I felt at that moment. I put my arms around myself, lifted one foot above the other, closed my eyes, put my foot back into the water, and slowly lowered myself into the tub. The door opened slightly as Frau Maria took my dirty clothes.

I soaped myself until my skin glowed, then let the warm spring water soak in soothingly. I decided to wash my hair with the same soap that left my skin now feeling radiant, the aroma of the soap filling the pores. I untied my braids and lowered my head into the water. I soaped my head until the hair squeaked, remembering Kristina's smile as she said, "When the hair sings, it's a sign that it's clean." I leaned back and let my hair float around me, forming a circle, luxuriating, wishing I never had to get out of the tub. I was startled by a gentle knock.

"Yes? Who is it?"

Frau Maria's voice came through the door. "May I come in?"

"Just a minute," I answered, drawing my knees up and wrapping my arms around them, trying to cover myself.

"Here are your clothes, dear," she said, laying them across a chair, "and I have found a toothbrush you may have. There is a problem, however. I didn't see any socks or stockings anywhere. Don't you have any more?"

I was so embarrassed. I had several pairs of socks when I left Belgrade, but I had been forced to dispose of them for hygiene purposes. There was no place to buy luxuries like that, and nature didn't wait to be accommodated. Besides, I had no money, and the train hadn't stopped anyplace except forests or fields during the air attacks.

"No, I don't. I don't have any more socks," I said, feeling a blush spreading on my cheeks.

"Have you ever worn silk stockings?"

"Oh, no, Mama would never allow it."

"If you wish, I could let you have some of mine. But it's up to you if you think you should obey Mama's orders."

I thought about it for just an instant, wanting to feel the silk stockings on my clean smooth legs, but knew I couldn't dare.

"No, thank you, it will be all right. It's not so cold outside."

"And there is the question of shoes. All I have is high heels, and they would be too large for you. I hate for you to put your old shoes back on. There's nothing left of them. But maybe when you get to Pécs . . . they have very nice stores, and maybe Rosa, my sister, will help you to get some shoes. This small suitcase will be much better than that old pillowcase. I'll leave it in the other room so that you can pack your things in it, and you can come downstairs when you are ready." And she slipped out as quietly as she had entered.

I hated to leave the warm bath, but got out reluctantly, dried myself, brushed my teeth with real toothpaste for the first time in months, and put on my clothes. Everything was ironed and smelled fresh and clean. I dried my long hair, combed it out, and braided it. I liked to wear either one braid to hang down my back or use two to form a circle on each side of my head. I looked in the mirror, the first I had seen in weeks, and liked what I saw. My cheeks looked rosy, the black eyes even darker now that my hair and face were clean.

"I'm sure glad I don't have blue eyes," I said to my reflection and left the bathroom to walk downstairs.

"Well, she looks like a new girl," the General said. "Why, you are even very pretty. In fact, you remind me of my niece."

Here we go again. They see blonde hair, and they think pure Aryan blood is running through my veins. I looked up as I neared the bottom of the stairs and saw Lieutenant von Staate standing next to the General.

"Well, you do look different, 'wandering stranger.' Are you ready to once again trust your 'protector'?"

"Yes," I answered with a smile. "I guess I'm ready. My suitcase is packed."

"My, my, we are traveling in style. No more pillowcase, but a real suitcase?"

"Nothing but the best for me!" I answered, pointing at my raggedy shoes.

"My sister Rosa knows that you're coming," Frau Maria said. "So when you get there, she'll have everything ready. God be with you, my dear. I hope we will meet again. I almost never leave this house now, so I don't think I'll be going into Pecs. But maybe this nice young man could bring you back again."

We embraced as she wished me farewell, and I thanked her for all her kindness. I walked to the door, glancing once more at the portraits on the wall, thinking to myself, *You're all stuck here with only Hitler to stare at. You can't go anyplace else. But I'm as free as a bird.* I said good-bye to the raspy-voiced General and walked down the steps to the driveway, glancing around for a last look at the peacocks, but they were nowhere to be seen.

The Lieutenant drove slowly through the forest, and I looked back to see steam from the pool rising above the pines. Twilight was just beginning. Pines lining the road looked even taller and darker, the fading light giving them a mysterious look. The forest road began to darken as the sun sank lower, when the car suddenly came to a stop. I looked ahead to see a young deer standing in the middle of the road. It turned its head to look at us, its huge brown eyes staring unafraid. With a jump, it disappeared into the thickness of the forest.

"I wonder if they realize that there is a war raging?" I said, leaning back in my seat.

"I doubt it. We humans are supposed to be superior," the Lieutenant answered. "With all our intelligence we are the fiercest of animals, yet so much good could be done if we used our intelligence correctly. So many wonderful things could be accomplished."

"Are we going on, or are you waiting for the deer to come back?"

"I just hate to leave this peaceful place," he said with a sigh. "I feel my uniform is so out of place in the middle of all this natural beauty."

"It's out of place anywhere. I hate uniforms. I think they deprive a man of his individuality. An army looks like mass-produced factory objects with one name, one purpose, one color, one ultimate end."

"But don't you think that a nation needs an army?"

"What for? My father was a captain in the Russian army during the revolution, and all of our friends were officers as well, two of them generals, and what did they accomplish? As you said a moment ago, the human brain is capable of so many wonderful things, and if used properly, with a goal of universal peace, there wouldn't be any need for armies."

"Perhaps," he said, "but peace is just a cliché. Nobody really cares about it or wants it."

"That's not true. We were a peaceful country. At least we had peace before you came, and after you had taken over the country, why do the German soldiers yell, 'Untermenschen' at everyone? What makes you all think your nation is superior? Just because you are tall and blond and of German descent? Well, I don't mean you personally, of course, when I say blond."

I felt my eyes blazing as I looked at him, feeling hatred toward him, but still feeling attracted to him.

"If I thought you were beneath me, do you think I'd be sitting here talking to you like this?"

"See, that's exactly what I mean," I burst out, sitting up and turning to face him. "Even if I were aware of someone being 'beneath' me, which as far as I'm concerned doesn't exist, but if I thought he was less educated than I, or from a poorer origin, how can I . . . what would give me the right to treat that person with less respect than I would a university professor? Given the right education and opportunity, perhaps this person could have become a professor as well. Why can't all people be given the same opportunity in life? I've heard that in America everyone has the same equal rights, opportunities, and that no matter who you are or where you come from, you are treated the same, that no one regards you as a 'foreigner' or different. I wonder if it's true?"

"Is that why you mastered English, so that you could one day go to America?"

"My parents expected that I would make a trip there after I had finished my education, to see what the country was like."

"Well, aren't you?"

"Are you joking?" I asked hotly. "We're not even supposed to speak the language, let alone think of going there. In fact, my parents made me destroy my American phonograph records just before we were attacked for fear of being labeled spies."

"You must have gone through hell for the past three years."

"Well, we had better times, but I still consider myself lucky, extremely lucky. You should have seen Belgrade after the three days of bombing. It's impossible to imagine unless you have gone through it yourself—" I broke off. "I'd rather not remember."

The Lieutenant edged closer to me and put his arm across the seat behind me. He sat looking at me for a long time, not saying a word. I finally turned my head to look at him, to see his lips coming closer to mine, and when they were almost touching I suddenly turned away.

"Do you really hate me that much?" he asked.

"I don't hate you. I just have too many painful memories. I just can't forget."

"If I weren't wearing this uniform, would you have kissed me?"

I wished he hadn't asked that question, because when our lips were so close I had wondered the same thing. He was quite handsome, and he had been so very considerate throughout the entire trip. We had been lying side-by-side in ditches together, dodging bullets together, watching together as people died, and sitting helplessly as others were left behind in fields or along the tracks.

"You haven't answered my question," he said, searching my face for an answer.

"I know."

"Can't you just close your eyes and forget about the uniform?"

"It's not just the uniform. It's what it stands for, what Germans all believe and how they look upon other people. How little regard Germany has for anyone else."

"And the fact that I'm Austrian doesn't change anything?"

"How can it? You're wearing that uniform. You chose to put it on, and wearing it means that you agree with everything that Germany stands for."

"What makes you think I agree with everything?"

"Well, if you do not, then why in God's name do you just go along with everything?"

"Survival. If I did not—" He broke off, moved away, and turned the key in the ignition. "I'm sorry, I had no right. As you said, I'm a mass-produced factory object, and you are a person who has definitely not lost her ideals, pride, and self-respect. Please stay that way."

"Now you sound like my Papa."

"I wish I had met your parents. They must feel very proud and lucky to have you. Are you the only child?"

"My parents . . ." My thoughts drifted back to Belgrade.

"Yes, your parents. Your mother and father."

"Yes," I replied. "Are we going to be in Pecŝ soon?"

"See the clearing just ahead? That's the turnoff, and from there it should be only about ten minutes."

We rode the rest of the way in silence—my thoughts back in Belgrade, his perhaps back in Graz. He turned off the path and onto a wide road. A few houses began to appear. The town looked very welcoming with its lights coming on, the cool air and fog lending a wintry look.

"It will soon be Christmas," I said.

"Yes, I wonder where I'll be . . . and *if* I will be," the Lieutenant answered, his voice dropping to a whisper.

He pulled the car to a stop in front of a house just at the edge of the town. Only one light appeared to be burning, and we found a note pinned to the side of the door, fortunately written in German. "Be back shortly. Gone to town to get a few things. The door is unlocked. Just go on in. The tea is on. Rosa."

"She must be a very trusting soul," I said.

"I have heard that the people here are extremely friendly and trustworthy, that almost no one ever locks their door."

He opened the door, and we walked through a small but pleasant entry hall, into the kitchen to find the walls decorated with corn and dried peppers. A huge old mud-stove painted snow white was built into a corner. It dominated the room, radiating heat in every direction. Benches had been built to extend from the stove along each wall and were covered with small colorful pillows. A table stood on the left, one of the benches extending from the stove serving as seating on one side. Salt, pepper, sugar, and some home preserves stood in the middle of the table. A bench on the opposite side of the table held more colorful cushions. Starched red-checkered curtains adorned the windows, which flanked a door leading to what I guessed was the garden area.

I sat on the bench opposite the table, leaning against the stove, feeling the soft, pleasant warmth spread over me. The Lieutenant stood for a long time next to the table, looking at me but not saying a word. Then he slowly approached and asked if he could sit next to me. That was something I admired in him. He was extremely polite and gentle; no matter what the circumstances, he never lost his Austrian courtesy.

"This place is so cozy. I could stay here forever," I said.

"Yes, it's very different from that palace her sister lives in. Maria married a well-known German banker and engineer, and God knows what else he was. They were extremely wealthy. The estate is still hers. It is only temporarily rented, but since her marriage to a German banker, she and her sister have not been close. Rosa, I understand, is a pure farm soul. At least that's what I heard back at the estate."

"I'd like to have a kitchen like this when I marry."

"Could you have married me if we had met in Vienna and this war had never happened?"

"Maybe."

"Don't forget, my grandfather was Italian."

"That's why you're so nice . . . in spite of that uniform."

I looked at him then, afraid that he could read my thoughts. I suddenly wished that he would kiss me. I felt a shiver run down my spine in spite of the warmth of the stove next to me. Would I be destroying my ideals, my beliefs, my principles, and my pride if I were to let him kiss me?

"What are you thinking about?"

I felt a warm blush spread over my cheeks and neck, and I glanced away trying to hide my thoughts.

"My name is Hans. Won't you tell me your name?" he asked, almost in a whisper.

"Asya," I answered, also in a whisper.

His face was now inches from mine, and he placed an arm across my shoulders. His arm felt like hot coals, the heat spreading throughout me. "Asya," he whispered, his lips now only an inch away. I suddenly felt weak, helpless, and did not turn away. I closed my eyes as the whole room began to spin. I felt as though I were melting, my head going round and round. My lips parted from sheer weakness as his kiss began to burn all of me. I felt I was on a pink cloud floating away.

My arms were resting on my lap, but now I raised them to embrace him, holding on to this wonderful trip on a cloud, afraid I would fall off if I didn't hold him tightly. I felt as though his lips were an oasis in the middle of a desert, and I tried to get every drop of water, trying to satisfy a sudden terrible thirst. He moved gently away and looked into my eyes. His eyes had filled with tears, and it looked as though at any minute a tear would spill over and run down his cheek. I felt as if I were being gently put down on soft cool moss, delivered from my pink cloud. I leaned back and looked at him in amazement, unable to understand what had made me feel this way.

"I'll never forget this kiss," he said. "Please forgive me. I just couldn't help it. Asya. What a beautiful name. It suits you perfectly. I felt I could compose the most angelic symphony the world has ever heard. Notes exploded in my head with the most brilliant colors. I could have held you forever and just let the whole world go by."

He moved away then, lit a cigarette, and stood staring into space, not saying a word. I sat on the bench, in the same place, not moving, my eyes wide, not believing that a kiss could be so wonderful.

"Are you angry with me?" he asked.

"No, I wanted you to kiss me."

"You've never kissed before, have you?"

"No. Have you?"

"Yes, but it was never anything like this. I don't want you to think I'm preaching, but a kiss like that could lead to a lot of trouble. It was a battle for me to stop."

"Why, what would have happened if we hadn't stopped?"

"Oh, Asya, please don't ask questions like that. I'm sure you know what I'm talking about . . . or do you?"

"I don't know. I'm not sure."

Steps were heard outside the front door, and the Lieutenant, now Hans, went to the door to greet an older lady.

"Ah, I'm sorry I'm late. Have you had some tea?" Rosa asked, laying a basket and several bundles on the table. "You must be Lieutenant von Staate, and this child must be Asya," she said, stretching her arms out to me.

"Yes," I answered as we embraced. "It is so kind of you to let me stay here until I can leave for Vienna." Strange, I thought, that her German was so much better than her sister's, when her sister had been married to a German.

"We'll have something to eat, and then we can look at some things I got. Maria told me your sizes. Oh, please sit down, Lieutenant. You, too, Asya. Just make yourselves at home. I'll be just a minute," she said, taking off her coat and leaving the room.

"She is very nice. So are you, Lieutenant Hans von Staate. I'm very pleased to meet you," I said, smiling.

"It took us a long time to introduce ourselves."

"Yes, but just think. Now I'll be able to look at the programs of famous symphonies being played all over the world and see that the composer is none other than my old friend Lieutenant Hans von Staate."

"It certainly won't be Lieutenant," he said as we both smiled.

"I'm glad you don't wear lipstick," he whispered. "I would have had no time to erase it."

Rosa came back into the kitchen, wearing slippers and tying an apron around her ample waist.

"Now I'll get busy here, and it will only take a minute," she said. "I prepared dinner ahead of time. Nothing fancy. It's just goulash. But the simpler the food, the better it is for you." She looked like a mother hen gathering bits of grain for her chicks.

"Can I help? Can I do something?" I asked.

"No, dear, you just sit down and rest. But maybe the Lieutenant could take this bucket and get some water. You know, we have a well and it's nice to have warm water to wash up in. I have plenty for drinking on the ice blocks," she said, pointing to a small room off the kitchen.

"I'll be happy to," Hans said, taking the bucket and moving toward the back door.

I could hear the bucket being lowered into the well, then the creak of the chain against the wood and the slow squeaking of the wheel as the bucket was raised. I loved sounds like that. They always made me wish that faucets and plumbing and telephones had never been invented.

"Asya," Rosa said, "you know we do have a bathroom. Just never bothered to bring the water into the kitchen. It would take so much away from the beautiful, simple life. There's just something about a well that I love."

"Funny," I said. "I was just thinking the same thing. I love wells and simple things."

"But my sister told me that you are very well educated and grew up in a big city."

"Maybe that's why I adore wells and checkered curtains instead of velvet drapes," I said, remembering Jovanka and Mirko's kitchen in Yaintse.

Rosa brought earthenware dishes with a beautiful hand-painted design to the table, just as Hans walked in and placed a full bucket of water on the stove.

"Here, ladies. I hope it will get warm enough for you to wash up."

"Thank you, young man. Now you just go and sit down, and I'll put some of this goulash in the terrine and we can begin to eat. You know, the air is chilly, and the walk from town and the brisk air made me hungry. And just look at me," she said, putting both hands on her hips. "You'd think there's enough fat inside to keep me going for years. But . . . eating is good for you."

We all sat down on the bench along the wall, Rosa next to the stove, Hans between us.

"Lieutenant, is it all right if we say grace?" Rosa asked.

"Why ask me? This is your home. By all means. Would you allow me to ask the blessing?"

"You? I thought you no longer knew God. I better keep my foolish mouth stuffed with goulash and not try to philosophize," Rosa said with a sheepish smile.

We bent our heads low, as Hans said grace. I don't believe I heard Hans's prayer. I was so touched by the homey atmosphere of Rosa's kitchen and hospitality that I felt a lump in my throat and asked God to make me humble, to help me overcome all the horrors of the war.

"Aren't you going to eat, my dear?" Rosa asked.

"Oh, yes, I'm sorry. I was just talking . . . I mean thinking . . . I mean saying my prayers."

"That's okay, talking. That's the way God wants us to be. Just talk to Him and not recite some prayer that some wise man put in a book. God can understand all languages, all talk if it is sincere."

I took my spoon and began to eat, suddenly feeling that if I didn't start eating quickly, I might drool. How terrible, I thought. This was my first solid meal since our last visit to Yaintse. All of that now seemed so distant; here in this cozy kitchen, life seemed not to have changed for the past hundred years. I glanced at Hans, quickly remembering that the war was very real. This place seemed not to have been touched by it, and I prayed that it never would. I thought of Mother and our friends and looked at Rosa, wondering again at the great differences in people.

"Are you still talking to Him?" asked Hans.

"No," I answered, "I'm enjoying this delicious goulash, and I'm afraid this dress is going to pop."

The meal was finished, and nobody had said more than two words, yet it was the most enjoyable meal I could remember.

"Why don't we do the dishes and let Rosa rest?" I said to Hans.

"Of course."

"Oh, no," Rosa said quickly, "you city folks don't know how to wash dishes when there is no sink and running water." She hustled around the stove, filling a large dish pan with water. She dropped the dishes in the pan, talking continuously, and before anyone could say anything they were washed, dried, and put away on a shelf along the wall, in individual little partitions.

"Now you, young man," Rosa said still smiling, "could empty this water just under the chestnut tree in the back. It's good for the trees to get dishwater."

Hans picked up the dishpan, and I went to open the door for him.

"He sure is a nice young man," Rosa said, "not at all like the rest of them in town, and he is an officer. Sure nice, not at all like the rest of the Germans."

"He's Austrian," I said.

"Ah, what a shame. What a shame that those wonderful Austrian people had to fall under the swastika. I have a lot of Austrian friends. I used to go to Graz every year before the war. They have such beautiful music festivals."

"I was wondering why you spoke such perfect German, but in the Austrian dialect."

"Well, now you know. Good thing I speak it, or else we would have all sat here like dummies. I understand you also speak French, English, Russian, and Serbian. My, my, what a brain."

"No, Rosa, not a brain. My mother wanted me to learn different languages. Now I'm sorry I never learned Hungarian."

"Almost all Hungarians speak some German—maybe not too good, but they get by."

Hans came back in with the empty pan. "The chestnut tree thanks you, Miss Rosa."

We all laughed, feeling warm and comfortable seated by the stove with full stomachs.

"Miss Rosa," Hans began.

"Just plain Rosa."

"Rosa," he continued, "you must excuse me, but we have a curfew. I have to be back at our quarters in Pecs by 10:00 p.m., and it is almost 9:30. I do want to thank you for your wonderful hospitality and for graciously allowing Asya to stay here."

"A young girl doesn't belong up at headquarters, and anyway, I'm glad they didn't want her. She's just a child, and there are so many bad people these days. You just run along. Will you be back tomorrow?"

"I don't know. Someone will be back for Asya, but I'm not sure if it will be me."

"Well, God be with you, and if you can, you come back to see me. You are a fine young man."

"Asya," Hans said, turning to me, "would you walk with me to the car? Would you mind, Rosa?"

"No, no. Asya, go ahead and walk him to the car," Rosa said. She looked sad to see him leave.

We walked out into a cold, clear night. The moon was high above the house, spreading silvery shades everywhere.

"I want to thank you for the wonderful trip we had together. Do you realize we have just formally met? That we traveled all this distance, went through several attacks together, and didn't even know each other's names?"

"I know, but names seem so completely unimportant the way things are."

"I have no idea if we will see each other again. When I get back tonight, my orders might assign me to a different command. If I do have other orders, I know that the Colonel will send someone else to pick you up. I wish I could say something sophisticated. All I can say is that I wish we had met under different circumstances and that this was Vienna during peaceful times. That I could invite you to dinner and introduce you to my mother. What can I say?"

"Don't say anything. Just good-bye and good luck. And God bless you."

"Look, I almost forgot! Your suitcase is here in the car," he said, handing it to me.

"Thank you, Hans."

"I wish you all the luck in the world. If I don't get back tomorrow, and if we should ever meet again, let's hope that it will be after the war. Good-bye." He got into the car, clearly trying not to look back.

I walked slowly into the house, refusing to look back as I heard the car drive slowly away. I found Rosa sitting next to the stove, busily knitting what looked like a sock, and she looked up to say, "That young man is sure a nice person. Not at all like the rest of the Germans in town."

"Yes, but he is still wearing that uniform."

"You don't like them very much, do you?"

"How could I? Have you any idea what they have done to Belgrade?"

"I've heard."

"I can't ever forget the sight of mangled bodies . . . bodies of old people and children . . . parts of bodies sticking through smoldering ruins. Hearing of all the people dragged out to the street in the middle of the night to be shot because someone had shot a German soldier." I covered my eyes and began to cry at remembering. "No, I think I forgot for a short time because I feel so alone, so lost. I just get so tired, so lonely and lost. I'm sorry, Rosa. I don't mean to cry," I said, drying my eyes, "but sometimes I get this big lump in my throat, and I know that I must cry or I'll simply die."

"Your parents are still alive, aren't they?"

"My parents? Yes, they're still alive, or at least I hope they are. When I left, there was such confusion that I really didn't know what was going on. They told me that they would try to get out quickly, and if everything goes well, we will meet in Vienna. We have some good friends there. I don't know where my parents are now. I hope on their way to Vienna."

"Well," Rosa said, "rumors are going around the town that the Germans will pull out of here in just a matter of days. Some say the Russian army is moving toward Hungary. I don't know what is going to happen here in Pecs either. I just hope and pray that whatever happens, there will be no death and bloodshed. Here I am gabbing and keeping you awake. I've fixed your bed, and you can wash up here in the kitchen because it's the only warm room in the house." Rosa left the room, returning in just a minute to hand me soap, towel, and a flannel nightgown. "I'll be back to say good night, dear."

As Rosa left the kitchen, I washed and began to undress, slowly, in anticipation of the snuggly warmth of the flowery flannel nightgown. The nightgown was too big, the sleeves and shoulders were much too large, and it dragged on the floor, but it felt so cozy. I left the kitchen to enter the room where Rosa had prepared a bed for me.

The room was very homey, plain but so very cozy, with hand-woven rugs, windows that reached all the way to the floor, and starched white curtains. Simple pictures hung on a wall: scenes of a field being plowed and a still life with fruit and a pitcher of wine.

A night table stood next to the bed, and an old-fashioned clock ticked loudly. The bed had a simple frame with a spring and a very thin mattress, but on top of the mattress, Rosa had placed several feather-beds, then a fresh white sheet, then several down-filled comforters. As I was admiring and anticipating it, Rosa came to tuck me in with a plain, gentle good night.

As I snuggled down into the bed, I felt like a little bug lost between the fluffy soft feather beds and the layers of soft down-filled comforters. The window was slightly open. Cold, fresh air and a silvery glow from the moon entered the room. I was so terribly tired, but sleep just would not come. I couldn't stop thinking of the experience of my first kiss and the maddening feeling that it had created in me. I wondered if the guilt I felt remembering it was why I had told Rosa about German atrocities in Belgrade.

I did feel guilty about the kiss. But why? Was it an awful sin? Was I losing my self-respect and pride? Would I feel as guilty if my first kiss had come from someone other than a German? Austrian, perhaps, but that uniform . . .

I felt ashamed, not because of the kiss but because of the way it had made me feel and because those feelings had been aroused by a German. But was it so wrong to kiss? Again and again some inner voice whispered, "Not the kiss, but the German . . . not the kiss, but the German."

If this was to have been an "awakening," it was the wrong time, the wrong war, the wrong uniform! I again began to think about the kiss and felt a blush come over me, remembering how weak and listless I had felt when he kissed me. "Oh, God," I prayed, "please make me forget it, and I promise that it will never happen again. Never! Not a German—ever!" and I finally fell sound asleep.

When I next opened my eyes it was to find the room flooded in daylight and a wonderful smell drifting from the kitchen—ham. The starched white curtains moved gently, and the cool morning air was refreshing. The bed was so cozy and warm I didn't want to get up. It had been so long since I had slept in a clean bed, and I even had that delightful bath in the elegant home of Rosa's sister. Oh, what a blissful and restful night it was after I fell asleep. I stretched slowly, not wanting to leave this cozy nest for fear that it might be the last time I could sleep in such a comfortable bed. I stretched slowly again, turning my head toward the night table, to notice with at least mild alarm that it was already 10:00 a.m. Heavens, I should have been up long ago.

I jumped out of bed, and the icy cold floors woke me quickly. I closed the window, stretched again, and ran toward the wonderful smells coming from the kitchen, picking up the hem of the nightgown as it dragged on the floor.

"Good morning, Rosa. I'm sorry I slept so late."

"Young people need sleep," she replied with a cheerful smile. "You are still growing, and sleep is very important. Come now, dear, do you like ham?"

"Ham," I answered. "I have forgotten what it tastes like. The smell is making me almost dizzy."

"A cousin of mine," Rosa began, "lives some thirty kilometers from here in the middle of nowhere. They have a huge farm, and about every other month I hitch up my horse and buggy and go out there to get half a smoked pig. They have a large smokehouse, and it's always full."

"Your cousin is lucky," I said, remembering Jovanka and Mirko. "Our farmers back home have absolutely nothing. Their livestock was the first to go, and each year they are stripped of their crops and have to hide and bury whatever they can to try and keep something for themselves."

"Oh, this blasted war," Rosa said. "So much grief, so much sorrow."

"Can I help with something, Rosa?"

"You could set out a couple of plates and mugs. I shouldn't be eating again. While you were sleeping, I milked my cow and had breakfast. But I'm not young and don't have to worry about my looks. So I'll eat again just to keep you company." she said, smiling sheepishly and wiping her strong hands on her apron.

"The winter will soon be upon us," she observed, biting enthusiastically into a piece of ham.

"In winter the trees look like hungry beggars on the streets. I hate winters," I said, "but not as much as autumn, when it seems the whole world is dying."

"But the autumn is so beautiful."

"Yes, but it's so sad. Maybe the reason everything gets so beautiful is because as nature dies away, God reminds people that we should not forget that spring beauty is ahead. My mother said that she wants to die in spring, when the world is lovely. But I want to die in the autumn, because I want to die with nature. The only difference is that I will not come back."

"My, my, what ghastly thoughts for such a young girl."

"Well, we all have to die sometime, and I would like to think that I could choose the time of year for my death."

"You shouldn't be talking about death. How about if we go into Pečs and see if we can get you a pair of shoes?" Rosa said brightly.

"Oh, that would be wonderful. Oh, that reminds me of something," I said, jumping up from the table. I ran back to my room, opened my suitcase, and took out the camera that terribly wounded German boy had given to me during my last days in Belgrade. I rushed back to hand it to Rosa.

"I don't have any money, Rosa. But could you trade this for shoes and maybe a little money to help pay for the things you got yesterday?"

"Well," Rosa answered, "this is a very nice camera. I think it's worth much more than the shoes and the few things I got yesterday. Are you sure you shouldn't keep it?"

"No, Rosa, I know I'll never use it, and if you can trade it, it will help me to feel that I'm contributing something."

"All right. Now, you know what else I did this morning? There is a wealthy family in the village that has a daughter just about your age. So I went there while you were sleeping and asked the lady if she perhaps had a coat for you because it's starting to get so cold. Just wait and see what I managed to talk her out of, for just a few pounds of ham," Rosa said, smiling happily and rushing from the room.

"Here, look," she said, returning to open a bundle on the table. "There is a pretty coat with a fur collar, a skirt, and a blouse. Here, let's try the coat on." She stood with the coat spread in front of her, a broad, childish smile on her face. "That's why I thought we could go and get you a new pair of shoes to go with the pretty coat."

I smiled and slipped the coat on, a beige wool coat with a brown fur collar, and found that it fit perfectly. It looked new.

"My, don't you look pretty. Here, take it off, and try on the skirt and blouse, and we'll fix your braids. Don't ever cut your braids, Asya."

"Rosa, how can I ever thank you?" I said, feeling tears welling up. "It's so hard to find the right words when you want to express what you feel inside."

"Words don't mean much. Sometimes it's what you don't say that counts. Here, let's fix you all up," Rosa said, hurriedly pushing a tear off her face as her large nose reddened. She nervously adjusted her apron and helped me out of the coat. "Oh, the lady I got the coat from told me that there is a lot of activity in the village. The Germans were loading their trucks and assembling in the square. I wonder if that means they are pulling out."

"Oh, Rosa, maybe we shouldn't go this morning then. Whenever there is a commotion like that, it often means trouble and shooting. I'm afraid."

"Maybe you're right. Let's stay home for a while and see what happens."

I tried on the clothes and decided to wear them—a dark brown skirt and beige blouse, apparently a set. I combed out my hair and braided it into a single braid. "Look, Rosa, I feel like I'm going to a ball."

"You do look so pretty," Rosa said. "But the shoes . . . oh, those shoes. Your toes are sticking out."

"That's all right, Rosa. They will ventilate my feet. God knows when I might get another bath," I said, smiling to cover my sadness at viewing the torn shoes. Oh well, I thought to myself. I have a warm coat and a pretty skirt. Who cares about shoes anyway? I'm glad I'm still alive. But will I ever see Belgrade again? Ever be able to walk through those thick green woods and smell the flowers? Ever get to lie down on the lush moss in Koshutnjak or run through the meadows in Yaintse saying hello to all the cows? Will I ever see Mama and Papa again? Maybe not.

The thought of my parents brought some strange anxiety flooding over me. What if I never see them again? Would that be so bad? Then I will be free, free to do what I want to do, to say what I want to say, to act the way I want to act, to be me and not what they want me to be. Strange, I don't miss my parents. I miss the crooked streets of Belgrade, the old fortress overlooking the Sava and Danube, the woods, the meadows, Gypsy Island, but not Mama and Papa. What is wrong with me? I heard my name being called from far away, off in the distance, or was it here in this room where a strange woman had taken more interest in me than I thought Mother ever had.

"Asya, what's the matter? Are you all right?"

I turned slowly to see Rosa and Hans standing there, staring at me.

"Hans, I thought you would be hundreds of miles away by now."

"You're the one who is far away. I've asked you something several times now, but you didn't answer."

"I'm sorry, Hans. Lieutenant. I was just thinking."

"I'm afraid we have no time for that. We are moving out in less than three hours. This will be your only chance to get to Vienna."

I looked over at Rosa, who was busily packing my suitcase, not even bothering to wipe the tears that ran down her face as she turned toward me.

"May God bless you, my child, and may you find your family in Vienna."

"Oh, Rosa," I said as we embraced, both crying as Hans grabbed the suitcase and hurried to the car. "Thank you for everything, and may God spare you and the people of Peĉs from bloodshed and bombs and . . . and maybe someday when this is all over I can come back again and . . . Rosa, do you think this war will ever end? Oh, Rosa, I'm so afraid. I want to go home, back to Belgrade."

"There, there, we must hope for the best. Now you have to hurry." She freed herself from my embrace, wiping her nose and tears. She gently pushed me toward the gate in the white picket fence and into the car. I caught a final glimpse of Rosa standing by the gate, waving with one hand while she wiped her eyes with her apron as the car sped away.

SEVENTEEN

Hans von Staate

October 18, 1944: The Soviet Army crossed the border into Czechoslovakia, driving the Wehrmacht back toward Germany.

Normally a quiet rail stop, the area was now chaotic. As in Zemun when
we had left Belgrade, a huge urn of coffee was set up at the platform, and
a crowd of officers were milling around it. The roar of engines, the shouting of men, and the rapid movement of both troops and equipment being
loaded was overwhelming.

"Try to stay close to me. If we get separated, we can meet at the coffee
station. I must let the Colonel know we are here," Hans said as he looked
for a familiar insignia among the cars and trucks now lined up for loading.

As we approached the coffee urn, I recognized an elderly officer who
had been on the same train when we left Belgrade. I stood by the wall next
to the urn as Hans spoke to him.

"This young lady was the translator in Belgrade, and the Colonel promised her father that we would see her safely to Vienna, sir."

"I know, Lieutenant," he replied, his raspy, strong voice at odds with
his kindly face. "If there is room, fine. Or she can remain in the staff car
and be on the freight part of the train. I don't care. Do whatever you wish."

"Thank you, sir," Hans responded. The gallant click of his heels seemed louder to me for some reason. It was the never-ending click of German heels and the sound of the soldiers' boots on the cobblestone streets of Belgrade that I had grown to despise. The Streife, the German patrol that walked the streets night and day, had made me hate the sight and sound of boots.

"Come on," Hans said, turning to me. "We can just stay with the car, and they'll load it on the train."

Sitting in the back seat of the car when it was finally loaded, I had a perfect view of the poorly lit station. Troops still milled about on the platform, but all vehicles and equipment were finally loaded. The shouting and the roar of engines had died away. Only the murmur of distant conversations alongside the train could be heard.

"We are almost ready to roll now," Hans said.

"Yes."

"Are you cold? It will be dark soon, and it's already chilly."

"No."

"You have been very quiet all this time. Why?"

"I guess I have nothing to say. I just feel empty, like this station now, all emptied out." I had no idea how to explain to him how I felt: my first kiss and the guilty feelings and conflict that I found so confusing—that it seemed so silly now to address him as "Lieutenant," but that "Hans" felt wrong.

"Well, if all goes well we should reach Vienna in a day or two, and then you will be able to see your parents and friends again," he said gently.

"Yes, if all goes well."

"What could go wrong?"

"You must be joking, Hans . . . Lieutenant. Have you forgotten the horrors we went through on the train from Belgrade? The screams, the planes shooting at us, the killing? Or is that all just daily routine for you?"

"No, I haven't forgotten, and it's not my daily routine."

"I'm sorry, Hans. I don't know why I so often sound like I'm accusing you. I don't mean to sound that way. I really don't."

"I understand, but you shouldn't worry. It's pretty safe on the train, and Austria isn't far away now. Is your coat warm enough, or shall I go and see if I can find a blanket?"

"No, I'm fine. Thank you."

As I looked toward the end of the train, I was again surprised to see civilians, gathered in the fields, waiting to rush for a place on the train. At first, German guards held them back, but now, as the train started moving, people began rushing toward the train, running with bundles and children. I remembered that the Soviet "Hooligans" were closing in and the way I had always heard them described. Perhaps these people were just trying to escape the relentless advance of the Soviets. The train eased from the station, slowly gathering speed.

"You know," Hans said, "if we were in Vienna now, in peacetime, we would just be going into a theater, and later I would take you to a nice restaurant where we would discuss the symphony we had just heard or the ballet we had just seen. I'd look into your eyes and see if I could count the reflection of the chandeliers, and a violin would be playing in the background. There aren't any stars tonight, but if there were, I'd like to see them in your eyes."

"No, the sky is black, the night is black, and there are no soft gypsy melodies, only the sound of the train wheels, and there is nothing in my eyes but blackness."

"I've never seen a girl with such light blonde hair and such dark eyes. They are very pretty."

"Thank you."

He was silent for a long time. I knew he understood that I didn't want to join in conversation. The car wobbled and felt unsteady on top of the flatcar, and I looked out the window, peering into the blackness, the silence broken only by the sound of the wheels, occasionally screeching as the train braked for a curve.

"Oh, I almost forgot," he said, suddenly breaking the silence. "Rosa pushed this bag into my hands as we were leaving. It smells like ham. Are you hungry, Asya?"

"Oh, yes. Dear Rosa. She is the most wonderful person I've ever met. So simple, so very kind."

Hans opened the bag and brought out a large chunk of ham wrapped in a light cloth, some black bread, and two apples. He sliced the ham with his pocket knife and tore the bread apart, handing half of it back to me with a smile.

"It's not exactly the dinner I was talking about, but since we can't go the opera or symphony, I guess it will do."

We ate the ham and bread in silence, deciding to save the apples for later, and he turned to say, "Why don't you lie down on the seat and try to get some sleep. I'll keep watch to be sure the car doesn't fall off the train. I'm just joking," he added quickly. "The car is chained to the train."

I took my coat off, laid down on the seat, and covered myself with the coat, silently thanking Rosa again. The night was very cold and damp, but Hans got out of the car, stretched, and stood there silently. The steady clickety-clack of the wheels was the only sound to break the stillness, except for an occasional harsh German command barely heard from somewhere toward the front of the train. I dozed off, but whether for only a few minutes or an hour or more I don't know. I was awakened by the sound of the car door closing as Hans got back into his seat.

"What in the world am I doing here?" he said, his voice very soft and low. "This is so different from my plans. Music is my whole life, not this horror. How long have guns, bombs, and screams replaced the soft notes of Vienna? What in the name of heaven am I doing here, on top of this broken-down train going God-knows-where? How can I continue wearing this uniform and screaming, 'Heil Hitler' when I hate everything Germany stands for? Dear God, let me never fire a gun at another man, never contribute to the misery sweeping the world. Grant me the opportunity to return to the mountains and music of Austria, to my beloved Graz and Vienna. We're so close to Vienna now. Maybe, dear God, with your help I can stay in Vienna."

The brakes screeched as the train suddenly slowed, jolting him sharply, and he sat up.

"What's happening?" I asked.

"I think we are approaching Budapest. I'll go and make sure. I'll be right back."

I looked around as he left. We were passing an intersection of some kind, and a few buildings began to appear next to the tracks as we moved along very slowly. Hans returned in just a few minutes.

"This is Budapest," he said as he took his place in front again. "We will be in the station in about twenty minutes. We're going to stop to refuel both the train and the vehicles we are carrying, so we will probably be here for one to two hours. Asya, before . . . when the train started to slow suddenly . . . was I talking?"

"Yes. At first I thought you were talking to me, but then I realized you seemed to be just thinking."

"I'm sorry. I guess I was thinking out loud. I don't normally do that."

We traveled then in silence. He was troubled about something. I knew that he was, but I didn't know what to say to help. I was lost in my own thoughts: first remembering Belgrade, then wondering what I would do when we reached Vienna, how I would find Countess von Holzen's address and my parents—then remembering Belgrade again.

We soon slowed to a stop in front of a small building and rail platform. Hans helped me down from the train, and I saw a large bridge right next to the platform.

"Asya, the refueling should go quickly. We should be here for one hour, not more than two at the most. I have to report to the Colonel, and I may have some duties while we are here. If you walk around, please don't go far. The train will leave as soon as the refueling is complete, and it won't wait. I'll come back to stay with you for the rest of the trip. But remember, please be here and ready to reboard right away."

"All right, Hans, I'll be here. I'll be fine. Go ahead."

I watched him walk toward a group of officers as equipment began moving into place next to the engine. I looked toward the bridge, certain that it crossed the Danube, and I was so homesick. I walked out on the bridge to look at the river.

I leaned over the rail looking down at the water, now black with the eastern sky just beginning to lighten, and thought of everything I had lost over the past three years: Dedinye, Yaintse, Dr. Kester Street, Trécha Zhénska, all the friends and family now scattered, and I began to cry.

Watching my tears fall into the Danube below, I realized that they would soon be passing Kalamegdon, and I began to cry even harder. I have no idea of the date as I stood on that bridge—sometime in the second or third week of October 1944. I stood there, flooding the Danube with tears, when I remembered that I should get back to the train. I wiped my eyes and hurried back to the platform just as Hans returned.

The battle to drive the Nazi occupation forces from Belgrade began with Operation Rat Week on September 1, 1944. It continued through the month of September, as Partisan forces continually harassed German units, benefiting from Allied supplies and limited support, progressing steadily toward the city. Units of the Soviet army, approaching from the south, from the direction of Avala, supplied the strength needed to finally push into Belgrade itself. The Soviet army, primarily Ukrainian units, would have passed our house in Yaintse very early in October, as they moved into Belgrade to battle street by street to drive the Germans from the city. I don't know the precise date that the Soviets entered the city, but the battle was terrible until Belgrade fell on October 20. The German army, fighting doggedly, retreated to their last defensive position in Zemun, going north across the last bridge remaining that crossed the Sava. It was the same bridge the truck had to cross as I rode the train to Zemun, a frightened and confused fifteen-year-old, fleeing Belgrade with the Colonel from Luftwaffe headquarters perhaps two weeks earlier.

Fitzroy Maclean's 1949 book *Eastern Approaches* recounts the almost unbelievable twist of fate that enabled the pursuing Soviet units to cross the bridge and to bring the battle to a successful conclusion: German engineers had mined the bridge in order to blow it up as soon as the last of the German units had escaped across it. Across the street from the bridge, a retired schoolteacher watched closely. Thirty-two years earlier, as a soldier in the Balkan war of 1912, he had been decorated for disconnecting the demolition charges from a bridge across which the enemy was retreating, allowing the Serbs to pursue and defeat them. Watching German activities closely, he understood what to do. When the guards were distracted, he crossed the street and calmly disconnected the explosive charges. When the Germans tried to detonate the bridge, the charges failed, and before they could correct the damage the old man had done, the Soviets were across the bridge. The old school teacher was decorated a second time.

"Asya," Hans said, "I'm glad you're right here. The refueling went faster than expected. We can get back on board. We will leave immediately."

We returned to the staff car, and I sat again in the back seat, shivering now from the cold and pulling my coat tighter around me. The train moved slowly along the river toward a rail bridge, and I had another look at my Danube as we crossed in the predawn light.

"Soon," Hans said softly, "we will be in Vienna."

We traveled in silence again. My thoughts, saddened by my look at the Danube, were back in Belgrade, now so far away; his, almost certainly, were lost in Vienna and Austria, now so close.

We were very soon out of Budapest and moving again through fields, with a main road paralleling the tracks. I heard the screech of the wheels as the train suddenly braked, almost throwing me from the seat. The sound, by now familiar, of a plane diving on the train and beginning a strafing run brought both of us sharply alert.

"Quickly," Hans shouted, pulling me from the rear seat and pressing me down on the wet floor of the flatcar. "Just crawl on your stomach, and don't even pick up your head until we get under that large truck in front of us."

We crawled and wriggled like snakes, heading for safety under the truck. Bullets seemed to strike everywhere.

"Pull your feet under the truck, too," he shouted. I pressed against a huge tire, trying to spit out the dirt that had found its way into my mouth. There was an explosion from somewhere in the front of the train. The plane made one more run, but its fire was directed forward, toward the engine, and then it was gone. Rifle fire could be heard in the wooded area adjacent to the track, but died away quickly. The attack had lasted only a few minutes, and now there was an eerie silence.

"What now?"

"Stay here, under the truck, Asya. I'll find out what we are going to do."

Hans crawled out and ran toward the passenger cars. I could see guards running alongside the train, looking for something, perhaps checking for damage. He soon returned.

"Come on out, Asya," he called. "There was minimal damage, but we are close to the Austrian border and the train is going to try to make it. Apparently there were a few Partisans in the woods, but they have been driven away. We can just wait in the car again until we get there. We don't expect any more attacks. That last plane was quite a surprise. They are just going to check the tracks ahead, and that won't take long."

I crawled out and climbed back into the car, cold now because I had left my coat in the car in our rush to get under cover. I shivered in the chill morning air, shrugged into my coat, and leaned back against the seat, pulling the coat tightly around me. Hans sat in the front seat, the door open and his feet on the flatcar as he lit a cigarette. We were both silent, waiting for the train to move, when I heard harsh German commands coming from the section just ahead.

"Off. Everybody off the train," a guard shouted as he walked along the track.

Hans spoke to the guard as he reached the car we were on.

"The tracks ahead have been damaged, Asya," he said when he returned. "We are going to unload all vehicles and form a convoy to proceed. They expect further damage to the tracks between here and the border. We will be delayed a bit, but Austria is only a few kilometers ahead. The convoy should get there in about two hours."

The stillness of the early morning was now replaced by running motors, shouting, and an occasional rifle shot. The guard came past us again, shouting, "Everybody off. No civilians allowed on the trucks. This is a military convoy. No civilians. Positively no refugees."

Hans helped me down off the flatcar and told me to wait while he checked with the Colonel for his orders.

I stood on the grass bank, between the tracks and the road, looking at the chaos all around me. There were soldiers and people everywhere. I watched the utter confusion, growing more frightened and confused myself, as Hans returned.

"I tried to place our car last in the convoy so you could ride with us, but it's a staff car," he said, taking my arm to walk toward the rear of the convoy, "and it has to be in front. The trucks are to follow. I've already talked to the driver of the last truck in the convoy. He's going to load as many refugees as possible, and no one will know they're in it. Come on. I'll come back to check on you at the first stop."

As we approached the rear of the last truck, I could see that it was already filled with women, children, and the very old.

"Remember, Asya, it isn't far to the border. Soon you'll be able to find your family and friends. Who knows, perhaps by then everything will be over and we can make a date for our first opera together. I have to run, but I'll be back at the first stop."

"All right, Hans," I said, as he squeezed my hand and turned to run to the front of the convoy.

I climbed into the open truck with my suitcase, barely finding room to stand at the rear and hold onto a rope at the side. The other people in the truck were expressionless, numb with exhaustion. Some stood, whispering among themselves; others sat with heads resting on drawn-up knees, lulled to sleep by the hum of the motor and the warmth of the bodies around them.

We were traveling through a wooded area. A light fog lay between the trees. The sky looked clear, but it was hard to tell with the light fog. The sun had not fully risen, but its first rays cast a golden orange tint to the fog between the trees—the promise of a lovely day.

"We should be close to Austria by now," someone said.

Suddenly there was an explosion and then another up toward the front of the convoy. The driver slammed on his brakes, throwing everyone toward the front of the truck.

"What is it now? I didn't hear any planes," I heard someone say.

"It was a grenade," I heard a soldier yelling. "They just threw it from the woods. Someone threw a couple of grenades into the convoy."

It was our first stop, and I jumped down from the truck to wait for Hans. As I stood beside the truck, I could see activity and apparent confusion toward the front of the convoy.

"Just push the vehicles off the road. Let's move on," came the same harsh, raspy voice that had become so familiar on the train. "Search the vehicles, remove what can be removed, and let's move on. The border is just ahead."

"Do you know what happened?" I asked the driver of our truck as he returned.

"Partisans, I believe. They threw grenades into the front of the convoy. You better get back in because we're going to start moving again right away."

"All right," I said, climbing back into the truck.

I was sad that Hans hadn't been able to get back to see me, but I knew he had been busy. They were anxious to get across the Austrian border, and there still would be time to thank him and say good-bye. We moved along steadily then, and villages began to appear, and judging from the swastikas and the number of troops, I thought we must be in Austria. Finally the convoy halted in front of a very large building. The driver came around to the rear of the truck to tell us that this was as far as the convoy was going. From here on, everyone was on their own. As I jumped down from the truck, I turned to the driver.

"Have you seen the Lieutenant?"

"Lieutenant von Staate?"

"Yes."

"No, he's probably still up in front reporting to the new command."

I thanked him and began walking toward the front of the convoy, carrying my suitcase. I couldn't see or recognize the car Hans and I had ridden in. They all looked the same.

"Have you seen Lieutenant von Staate?" I asked a young officer near one of the cars.

"Yes," he said, pointing to the first truck. "He's over there."

I thought he must be helping with the activity around the truck. As I began to walk toward the truck, two soldiers came toward me, carrying a stretcher with a body on it.

"Excuse me. Have you seen Lieutenant von Staate?" I asked.

"Yes," one replied, nodding his head toward the truck. "He's right over there."

I looked all around the truck but did not see him. I stood on my tiptoes to peek over the side and into the truck, but could see nothing except two more bodies lying on the truck bed. The two soldiers carrying the stretcher came back to place the stretcher on the street next to the truck. A young soldier handed them a small package.

"These are von Staate's. He's next."

"All right" was the indifferent answer. One of the stretcher bearers put the package on the stretcher, as two men placed a body next to it.

"Oh, no, no! Lieutenant von Staate is dead?" I sobbed. "Please let me see him before you take him away."

I knelt next to the stretcher, to gently touch his face, tears now flowing so much that I couldn't see. I started to wipe my eyes and saw that my hands were bloody from touching his uniform, but there was no mistake. It was Hans. I knelt there, sobbing. You poor, poor soul. You never even made it to Vienna, and you wanted that so much. How could God allow this? He was so full of hope and dreams. His heart was filled with only gentle music. He could have contributed so much once this terrible war is over. I cried uncontrollably, until I felt someone push me gently to the side so that they could remove the stretcher.

"Tears won't help now." Someone took my arm and pulled me to my feet. "It's very sad. He was very young, but he was a good officer." I recognized the same harsh, raspy voice that had issued commands throughout the trip. "Where are you going now?"

"To Vienna."

"But that's much too far to walk, and I don't think the trains are running."

I didn't answer, just watched the soldiers carrying the stretcher into the building.

"I have to go to Vienna to report to my headquarters. Would you like to come along?"

I finally turned to look up into the kind, tired face of an elderly officer. I remembered him from Pećs. It was he who told Hans we could stay with the staff car. But he looked so much older now, so exhausted.

"Yes," I answered, still trying to stop crying. "Thank you."

"You know, I have a daughter, perhaps a bit older than you. They should be still in Stuttgart, but it's been a long time since I have heard from my family. My son was on the Russian front."

"Yes." I answered simply, not caring where his family was. After all, he too was responsible for this terrible bloody war.

"I can't take you into the headquarters building, but you can wait in the car, and I'll have my sergeant bring you something to eat."

"Yes, thank you."

The officer took my arm again and led me toward a staff car parked in front of the building. Someone opened the door and helped me in. I leaned back against the seat and began to sob, tears now rolling down my cheeks— bitter, hot tears. I couldn't stop crying. I didn't know what I was crying about—the violent, sudden loss of a new friend, self-pity, the exhaustion, Belgrade—my Belgrade, now so far away—perhaps the combination. I cried so hard that my eyes became tiny slits that I could no longer see out of. Somebody brought me a glass of water and a pill, and I cried myself to sleep in the back of the car.

When I awoke, it was to the familiar sound of an air raid siren and some-one gently shaking my shoulder.

"Quickly, we just made it. A refugee center is right here, but you had better get into the shelter first."

I looked toward the voice and recognized the kind-faced officer pull-ing at my arm and reaching for my suitcase with the other hand. He handed it to his driver as the three of us began to run.

"Where are we?" I shouted.

"Vienna," the officer answered. "We are at the outskirts of Vienna."

The three of us ran toward the shelter, but I was confused. I must have slept ever since someone gave me that pill. I couldn't understand why we were being bombed if we were in Austria. Who could be bombing the Ger-mans? All this time I must have thought that Germany and Austria were relatively untouched by the war. I found a spot in the shelter and sat down with my suitcase, but didn't see the elderly officer or his sergeant anywhere.

When the all-clear sounded, I walked straight to the refugee center the officer had pointed out. It was a charming old home, and a typically polite Viennese lady greeted me. I told her that I would like to spend the night at the center, and I asked for directions to the Countess's address. She smiled pleasantly and said that the address was just on the outskirts of Vienna, not too far from the shelter, and wouldn't be difficult to find at all. She brought me a cup of tea, a bowl of hot soup, a piece of bread and butter, and a little hand-drawn map with directions to the Countess's address for the morning.

I couldn't get the picture of Hans lying dead on that stretcher out of my mind. My refuge for the night was a cot in the hallway since the house was already filled. Sleep was slow in coming that evening, as I lay there remem-bering Hans von Staate.

The next morning, after a quick cup of coffee, I started off early to find the Countess's home, a very large estate with well-tended gardens sur-rounded by a high wrought-iron fence. I pushed open the gate and walked up the drive to the front entry. A member of the staff answered my knock and informed me that the Countess was residing in Zurich for the dura-tion of the war and that "the estate is now closed."

"Has anyone else inquired for Countess von Holzen or left a message perhaps?"

"No, not that I am aware of," he answered, "but I am not here all the time, so I may have missed someone. Will there be any message? You look tired, Fraulein. Are you hungry?"

"No, thank you," I said sadly, turning to leave.

I walked slowly back to the gate, trying to think what I should do. My parents were not here to meet me. They were God only knows where. I had no money and knew nobody in Vienna. I would have to find a job quickly, and I wondered if I could find work as a translator. But where?

As I went through the gate and closed it, a horse-drawn cart came through what must have been the service gate for the estate. As the old man who was driving the cart got down to close his gate, I walked over to ask directions to Vienna.

"I have just made my last delivery for this morning, Fraulein, and I'm returning to the city center," he said. "If you wish, you can ride on the back of the wagon, and I can take you right to the Ringstrasse."

"Thank you very much," I answered, putting my suitcase on the wagon and hopping up to sit beside it.

I sat at the rear of the open wagon, my back leaning against the rail side, my legs drawn up, my arms folded across my knees, my head resting on my arms, trying to figure out what I would do, how to begin looking for my parents. The cart ride into Vienna took over an hour, giving me time to think things through. It had never occurred to me that I would not find Mama and Papa waiting at the Countess's home. I had never thought about what I would do if I didn't find them. I reviewed the events of the last several weeks, especially my trip from Belgrade to Vienna and everything that had happened along the way—all the danger, death, and tragedy—my first kiss—Hans's death so close to his home and the city of his dreams—Maria and Rosa in Hungary—the dead baby on that freight car—the planes diving and strafing.

I had come through all of that, I realized, and had not only survived but had gotten along very well. Mother and I had grown apart during the last three years of the occupation, and the thought of living with the morose Russian émigré group helped me to decide. No, I would not make any effort to find Mother and Father. That would probably be fruitless anyway. I would find a shelter in Vienna, and they would help me to find a job. After all, I spoke five languages fluently, didn't I? Ironically, it was Mother's words, "You will never go hungry if you know foreign languages," that were ringing in my ears as the cart drew to a stop.

"Here we are, Fraulein," the old driver said. "This is as far as I go, but this is the Ringstrasse. You see the trolley right there? Well, you can get on the trolley, and it will go around the Ringstrasse again and again. You can just keep going around the city center until you decide where you want to get off."

"Thank you very much. Do you perhaps know where a refugee center is located?"

"No, Fraulein, but the trolley conductor should be able to help."

"Thank you again and good-bye," I said, crossing the Ringstrasse to the waiting trolley.

I suddenly remembered that I didn't have any money. Quickly opening my suitcase, I rifled through it to find my student identification card from Belgrade. It had always been good on the trolleys at home. I climbed up on the trolley and showed my card as I approached the conductor, who just waved me past without even glancing at the card. I found a seat next to a window and began to look around at the beautiful city. On the right side of the trolley tracks was a park, on the left, the broad Ringstrasse. Immense homes lined part of the avenue, and other parts were lined with shops, offices, and theaters. Tiny crooked streets and wide boulevards led off the Ringstrasse.

It was just beautiful, with trees, gardens, parks, and theaters. But this city, too, I realized, had suffered and now revealed the gaping wounds of war: ugly ruins, huge holes in the streets and in the parks. But who was doing it here? Belgrade had been destroyed by the Germans, but this? Of course! I realized that the Americans, British, or Russians were bombing here, and their bombs were just as ghastly as those that had fallen on us from German planes, just as cruel and devastating. As the trolley continued its circle around the parks, I kept thinking of my decision not to look for my parents, but to look for a job and begin to make my own way. "After all, I do know several languages." Just as that thought became firmly entrenched in my mind, the air raid sirens began to scream and the trolley braked quickly.

Everyone rose and rushed to exit the trolley, and I followed, carrying my suitcase, bewildered and unsure of where to go. As I stepped down from the trolley, I saw that everyone was running toward what looked like the entrance to the park, toward what I would later learn was a statue of Mozart. For some reason that I have never understood and never will, I turned to the left, away from everyone else, and ran across the Ringstrasse toward the shops and office buildings. I ran quickly, hearing the drone of approaching planes, and just as I placed my foot on the sidewalk, a voice to my left called out, "Asya!" I turned to see one of Mother's friends from Belgrade. "Asya, when did you arrive? Have you seen your parents yet?"

"No."

"They are well. We have been waiting for you. Everyone is staying with old friends right here on Mariahilferstrasse. Come on. Everyone will be so glad to see you."

We hurried into an air raid shelter, as the woman kept up a steady stream of depressing talk, telling me all about the difficulties they faced on the way to Vienna and how happy they had all been to get here. I listened, nodding politely now and then, but feeling trapped, unhappy at being back in the midst of this morose group. I didn't know if I could stand it again, being cooped up with the émigré group, with their depressing atmosphere and what I knew would be endless questions.

How would I even begin to tell them? Did I even want to try? How could I tell them that I had seen a baby crushed to death while its mother screamed in despair, that I had watched soldiers and civilians die before my eyes, that I had received my first kiss from a young German officer and cried bitter, bitter tears over his death? I could already hear the responses. "Well, ladies do not behave that way. Be quiet. You're too young to understand. Speak only when spoken to." No, I didn't think I could face all of that. The woman beside me kept rattling on until the all-clear sounded.

"Well, come on, Asya," she said. "I'll take you to your Mama. All this time she has been wondering where you were."

"Yes," I answered dejectedly.

"Aren't you the lucky one to run into me just like that. You might have spent days looking for your parents. Everything is in such confusion these days. You're thin and pale, and your dress is rather dirty."

"Yes."

We walked less than half a block from where I had stepped off the trolley, to the first large building on Mariahilferstrasse. A single door led into the building, but we entered through a wide arched entry, built to admit automobiles, into a large, paved courtyard. She led me to the first door on the left of the courtyard and into a large room. It had very high ceilings, and very old but still elegant furniture was now occupied by all too familiar faces. Even the smell of the room reminded me of Yaintse when we had been packed in like sardines.

"Everybody, look what I found," the woman exclaimed.

"Asya, my dear. God, you are so thin and pale . . . and you need a bath," someone said.

"Yes."

"Where have you been? When did you arrive? How was the trip? Did you encounter many Partisans on the way? Did the Germans treat you well?" The questions seemed to come from every direction at once. "Oh, but you do need to wash your hair, and that dress, it doesn't even fit well. It can't be yours. Did you go to the Countess's house? You know she's living in Switzerland now? That's what we should have done. Well, it's too late now. Well, we can discuss that later. Well . . . eaten . . . dirty . . . pale . . . dirty . . ."

The room began to spin, and I suddenly cried out, "Stop. Stop it. Just stop it!"

I looked around and saw Mother standing there asking questions with all the rest of them. Good God, I realized, she hadn't even made a move to embrace me.

"Where is Papa?" I asked, looking at her.

"He should be back shortly, dear. He is trying to arrange for us to leave soon. Did you know that the Soviet army is heading for Vienna? That means, of course, that we can't stay here. It would be unthinkable. Papa is trying to arrange for transit into Germany because . . ." and she rattled on.

"How are you, Mother?" I asked, interrupting.

"I'm fine, dear, and you? When was the last time you washed your hair? And look, you have some dried blood on your skirt. Why is your hair such a mess?"

I couldn't stand it. I turned without another word and walked from the room out to the courtyard and closed the door behind me. I sat on a step in the courtyard, with no particular thoughts in my mind. I couldn't cry. I had cried myself dry when Hans had been killed . . . and he was so close to home. Oh, God, I thought, why did I cross the Ringstrasse? Why didn't I follow everyone else into the park?" I would never have run into the "old friend," I realized, and now I felt chained by the gloom that always pervaded the émigré group.

I felt guilty about having let Hans kiss me, about kissing him back, and I didn't want to feel that way. I wished that I had let him kiss me more, instead of sounding so accusatory during the trip from Peĉs to Vienna. And I think I blamed the émigré group for that and for the guilt I felt. I knew that I hadn't done anything wrong, anything to be ashamed of, and I wanted desperately to be free of this group of "friends," free to go where I wanted to go, to do what I wanted to do, and to think what I wanted to think. I could not understand what was happening to me, why I felt the way I did, why I should feel any guilt at all about Hans and my first kiss, why it had made me feel as it did. Why? Why? But there were no answers.

"Asinka, my dear, beautiful Asinka."

I looked up to see Papa rushing toward me, and jumped up from the step to embrace him.

"Papa, dear, dear Papa. I missed you. Please, Papa, let's just go away. I don't want to go back into this house," I said through my tears.

"Now, wait a minute. Let's go to a coffee house just next door. I have enough food stamps so that we can even afford a pastry. Let's just slip away from here and we can talk."

We walked from the courtyard and turned left to a very small coffee house right next door. Over a cup of tea, Father told me how difficult and tricky it was to escape from Belgrade because of the hasty, chaotic retreat of the German army, the advancing Partisans, and the endless difficulties they had encountered along the way.

"What about the rest of our friends? Are they still in Belgrade?"

"Yes, most of them couldn't make it."

"I didn't see Aunt 'Lyena inside."

"No, we left her behind. Mama thought the trip would be too difficult for her. You know her health isn't that good, and Mama thought that it would be too much for us to care for her when we didn't know what we might encounter."

"Too much," I cried. "But how is the poor thing going to make it by herself? She is so helpless. She's Mama's own sister. How could she leave her behind?" Tears rolled down my cheeks, remembering how caring and tender Aunt 'Lyena had always been with me.

"War is a very nasty business, Asinka. People do all sorts of things, unable to clearly decide their next move. So please don't judge Mama too harshly."

"I don't believe she *is* my mother. I'm tired of pretending. Do I have to stay in this awful place with all those 'friends'?"

Father looked on the verge of tears as he answered, "Just for a little while. I made arrangements for some trucks to get us this far, and I think they will carry us further. I had to trade away some more of Mama's jewelry. Well, not everything at least, and don't forget that Uncle Max has a box for you."

He smiled faintly as he continued. "At any rate, we have to move on rather quickly. Soviet troops are advancing toward Vienna, and I won't allow you and Mother to fall into their hands. We'll have to start moving soon . . ." His voice drifted off as he began to think of something.

It was clear that they had been waiting for me, and now there was a rush to get moving, to ensure staying out of the reach of the Soviet army.

"Are all of these people going with us?" I asked.

"But they are our friends."

I didn't answer. Instead, I tried to change the subject.

"Where are we going?"

"We have no firm plans. We have discussed the possibility of going to Magdeburg. It's in the northeastern part of Germany, and there is a Russian émigré community there that formed after the revolution, like Belgrade's. Oh, I almost forgot. Mother and I have discussed it, and we are all to begin spelling our name as "Popoff" with a double *ff* instead of *v* or *va* ending. It is the spelling adopted by many of the Russians who fled the revolution and settled in Paris. Mama and I agreed that it has a certain French sound and may prove useful if we need to claim that we are residents of France, not Yugoslavia. So please remember the new spelling. Now tell me, did you have a difficult time getting to Vienna?"

"No," I replied, thankful that he didn't ask about the details of the trip.

The change in the spelling of our name seemed so silly. It didn't sound

French at all. There was no disguising the fact that we were Russians. What difference could where we were living possibly make anyway? But I didn't say anything, just simply accepted it.

"Well," he said, "I thank God that we are all back together again."

I looked at him then, thinking how gentle and understanding he had always been, wondering what could have caused him to act as he did back in the garage. We finished our tea and a pastry we had shared and walked slowly back to the courtyard. Inside, I avoided speaking unless I was asked a direct question.

Each morning I simply left the house to go for long walks. I learned that the German authorities had issued each member of the group a yellow armband printed with the word *Östarbeiter,* which proclaimed them to be "Eastern Laborers," and that while in Vienna they worked at clearing the rubble from air raids, earning food ration stamps in exchange for the labor.

I believe the place where we were staying was owned by a Russian known to some member of the group, just as Countess von Holzen was to Mother. The group seemed to be in quite good spirits, given the events of the time. They apparently were free to come and go as they wished, reporting for work only when they wished to earn more food stamps. Eventually I would be forced to wear the same armband, but in Vienna I was never questioned. My German was, I knew, accent-free, and I could imitate an Austrian accent. I simply never gave the armband a thought. In fact, I was never stopped or questioned. Required to return each day to a house filled with the same dour Russians I had tried so hard to avoid back home, I found that the time in Vienna seemed to go on forever. At last, although it was only a few days, Father announced that everything was ready for our trip to the north.

On the appointed day, the men in the group left early and returned with six small, beat-up diesel trucks. They were about the size of a modern pickup truck and had open beds with wood slat sides. Odd that I remember the six trucks when I don't remember the number of people in our group. There must have been twelve couples plus me, because I seem to remember that we traveled two couples to a truck. I assume they were the same trucks used on their trip from Belgrade to Vienna, but I don't recall ever asking or hearing it discussed. Everything was loaded into the trucks, and we formed a caravan. Father drove the lead truck.

The trip from Vienna to Magdeburg on today's highways and in a modern automobile should take no more than six or seven hours, but in 1944, in the middle of the war, the trip would take us many days. The trucks were in poor condition and had to be coaxed along slowly, and once we entered Germany, the roads were clogged with traffic. An endless line of refugees moved in both directions, most walking and pulling a wagon with a few possessions on it—old people, young women with children. I remembered seeing the same spectacle in Yaintse during the three-day bombing of Belgrade, and I felt just as sorry for these poor German civilians as I had for the Serbs.

Contrary to the atmosphere in Vienna, the air in every town seemed charged with panic. Allied planes flew high overhead each day, on their way to some distant target. I couldn't hear the sound of bombs, but I knew that the refugees clogging the roads were fleeing them.

Everyone in our caravan had to wear the Östarbeiter yellow armband, and the general attitude of townspeople everywhere was unfriendly, suspicious. There was a special time each day when we Östarbeiters could receive food rations, which took endless hours of standing in line, adding to the length of the trip. Standing in those lines was a special humiliation, as the German nationals passing by shouted insults and harassments. This was a shocking change from Vienna, where people were always friendly and maintained courtesy toward everyone.

We made very slow progress. It was cold, and people took turns sitting in front with the driver. When it rained or snowed, people just huddled together, covering their heads with blankets that soon became wet. The diesel exhaust pipe ran up through a front corner of the truck bed, and I huddled next to it for warmth, happy to let the others huddle under a blanket or to take turns sitting inside so that I wasn't required to talk to them.

One day when it was particularly cold but free of rain or snow, I sat huddled against the exhaust, reviewing the past few weeks of my life. Somewhere during my odyssey from Belgrade to Vienna, my birthday had occurred, and I had turned sixteen. I couldn't guess where or when—I didn't even know the date while I was sitting there in that truck—but I decided that it had been the day I stopped at Rosa's, the day I had received my first kiss. It was, I thought, a perfect birthday present.

How I hated the thought that I had been ashamed and had sounded so accusatory toward Hans. I cried softly, remembering Hans von Staate and his dreams, wondering what beautiful music he might have created; remembering Kolya as well, wondering if he might have designed a bridge both stronger and more beautiful than any known. And I remembered Hermann Zahn, the terribly wounded German boy who had given me the camera, hoping he had made it home.

How many other talented and gentle young men has the world murdered or maimed in its current madness? It would be the last time I thought of Hans or Kolya for many years. For at least the next three years, all my thoughts and energies were to be occupied with survival.

On most nights, we slept in the trucks, but when the refugees on the roads thinned, we occasionally found a farmer who allowed us to sleep in his shed or barn. They may have charged us, but what luxury—soft, warm, sweet-smelling hay, out of the weather. But the trip always resumed in the same misery.

Our caravan approached the town of Halle about one hundred kilometers south of our destination, Magdeburg. The road divided at an intersection, the main road leading north to Magdeburg, one branch to a village called Nordhausen, another leading to the village of Blankenburg am Harz, neither of which we had heard of.

Our caravan was signaled to a stop at a military checkpoint. After checking our papers, a German soldier ordered us to follow him to his headquarters in Halle, and our caravan duly followed his motorcycle. He led us to a large building, a warehouse of some kind, with military vehicles clustered about it, where we were ordered to leave the trucks and enter the warehouse.

Throughout my life, my memory has been extraordinary, almost legendary to many who have known me and to most of the people I have worked with. It was either the result of, or the reason for, my success with learning foreign languages, but to this day I have never been able to remember what took place at that stop in Halle. I remember our group was ordered to stand before the desk of an SS officer, but other than that, the time remains a complete blank. I know that Mother was dramatically affected by whatever took place, and I don't think she ever fully recovered.

Over the years, I have gone over this event again and again, trying to remember what took place and to understand what happened to Mother.

She was a sensitive, talented, intellectual member of a very old aristocracy, accustomed to her position in life and the respect that she had always been accorded from everyone who met her, and I believe that the SS officer who conducted the interview or interrogation in that warehouse was particularly brutal and disrespectful. It must have been a severe shock to her sensibilities on top of everything that had already happened.

I believe that when the group left Belgrade, they must have had some official papers or letter of transit that identified them as exiled Russian émigrés seeking work as "Eastern Laborers" in northern Germany, and that although required to wear the yellow armbands for identification, they were in fact free to travel and to purchase diesel fuel and to obtain food rations. I think they felt themselves "free" people seeking work as refugees, their experiences throughout the journey from Belgrade to beyond Vienna reinforcing that belief.

Once the group entered Germany, however, everything changed rapidly. With our first encounter with an SS officer, we were finally faced with the stark reality of being stateless refugees in the middle of a country and population that had absolutely no regard for any of us or any concern at all for what or who we might have been. I don't know how long we were held at that warehouse, an hour or two at most, but when we left, we followed the road that led to Blankenburg am Harz, not to Magdeburg.

EIGHTEEN

The Labor Camps

We were escorted to Blankenburg am Harz about November 1, 1944. It was very cold. The little village, a resort town nestled in the Harz Mountains, was disarmingly pretty. Contrary to most other towns we had passed through, it appeared untouched by the war. I looked around as we drove, frankly charmed by the pleasant homes and streets of the residential area. But the charm soon gave way to reality.

At the very edge of the town, across the last residential street, a large compound of barracks appeared behind high barbed wire fences, immediately on the other side of the street, and adjacent to other barracks and buildings.

The caravan was halted in front of a building outside the barbed wire enclosure, and we were ordered out of the trucks. The building we stopped in front of was an office of some sort, and a large sign proclaimed "Emil Bentin Contractors."

Our trucks were immediately driven off by German soldiers. We were sprayed with insecticide and then marched to the empty barrack building assigned to us. We found that its construction had been abandoned some time earlier. It had rafters erected, but roof boards covered only half of the building. The doors and windows were simply open holes lacking any glass or doors. Bales of straw were lying on the concrete floor and looked wet.

A smartly uniformed ss officer entered the barrack and ordered everyone to line up, his shiny boots pacing the length of the line as he took all names and ages. He then turned and faced the group, to order everyone to be lined up in front of the barrack in the morning, to report for work. "Six a.m. sharp. There will be no exceptions." He turned without another word and strode from the barrack.

What little shred of dignity Mother had managed to retain after the stop at Halle surely was lost here. The officer's manner left her absolutely speechless. Other women in the group cried, and the men tried to offer comfort and make the best of it. There was no water supply in sight, nor any bathroom facilities. After investigating the grounds, we discovered a well about a hundred meters away and a couple of outhouses that apparently served all of the buildings not enclosed behind the barbed wire. Although I never counted them, my impression was that there were a dozen buildings, all similar, and all complete except for ours. A few of these served as barracks, but most of them, I believe, were used as warehouses or offices.

At the end of the group of buildings where we were located, a narrow wooded area began. Beyond the trees a large camp compound stood behind a tall barbed wire enclosure with lookout towers. I knew it was a concentration camp that housed political prisoners and "undesirables," euphemisms for slave laborers. I had seen enough of them on our journey through Germany.

The men in the group left to gather wood from the nearby wooded area. Upon their return with a few branches, they informed the rest of us that the camp beyond the wooded area was patrolled by German soldiers and dogs. Someone brought a bucket filled with water, and a fire was lit in the pot-bellied stove. Our clothes were damp and dirty, and we had no idea if the water was fit to drink, but nobody worried about such things. It was clear that clean water, food, bed, bath—all those things were now a part of the past as we would try to survive one day at a time. As the fire began to heat the stove, a truck pulled up and the men were called out to organize a food line.

Each member of the group was issued a metal cup and a spoon, and we moved slowly through a line while a soldier dished out soup. It was warm, not hot, and had something floating in it, but no one could figure out what it was. The soup had no taste other than that it obviously had been thickened with flour. It was soon discovered that the things floating in it were lumps of flour—a simple broth with lumps of flour.

Each of us was also given a piece of hard, dark bread. We were told that there would be nothing else, so we had better make the best of it. We were so tired and anxious about the situation we now found ourselves in that there was no grumbling as we tried to "settle in."

Fortunately, the boarded roof extended to just past the stove. A rope was found someplace and strung across the room close to the stove, and people removed their outer clothing, hanging it to dry. Everyone soon took a place around the stove to silently stare at the flicker of flames inside it.

We were too tired to talk or to argue, too tired for the usual round of complaints or criticisms. It was so strange to watch everyone in the barrack take some of the straw and try to make a bed for the night. Slowly, each couple rose to huddle together beneath their blankets, and very soon snoring came from every direction, breaking the silence.

I took some straw and soon lay down close to someone. I laid there for a long time, awake, wondering what was ahead, what kind of future awaited me. I was sure that there were places where people lived normal lives, where young girls dreamed of the future and made plans. Or was there? Was the entire globe at war?

The bits of news we had heard told only of German advances and victories. What was the *real* news? What was true, and what was not? I was certain that Goebbels did not tell the truth in his broadcasts. Or did he? Maybe this was the end of the world. Maybe this was the holocaust that would bring an end to all civilization.

Aunt 'Lyena had told me that God was angry with mankind, that unless people changed their ways, the end would be near. Maybe she was right. But why does the end have to come now? But if the end comes next year or in a hundred, a thousand years, there will always be young girls who will never see another spring. With those terrible thoughts in mind, I slowly drifted into a troubled sleep that first night in the forced labor camp.

The next morning, everyone was awakened by a shrill whistle. The barrack was icy because the stove had gone out long before. Everybody sprang to their feet, not anxiously answering the whistle but because the brisk movements helped their circulation. The same truck that had brought the soup the night before was outside, and everybody grabbed their tin cup and rushed out into the cold November air. Our hands shook as we held the cups. It began to drizzle, and the sky was as gray and unfriendly as the uniformed German soldiers around the truck. The soup was distributed, the same soup as the previous night, with the same flour lumps and with a piece of the same dark bread.

Everyone ate quickly, standing outside, and placed their cups and spoons in their pockets. It was about 5:45 a.m. Everyone lined up on command, was given a shovel, marched a few yards to the side of the road, and was informed that we would be responsible for digging a drainage ditch along the road in front of the compound.

At precisely 6 a.m. a car pulled up and six German soldiers stepped out and spread along the side of the road facing us as we were ordered to begin digging. The soldiers were all dressed warmly, even wearing earmuffs and gloves. Each carried a rifle on a shoulder strap and walked back and forth along the length of the line, one yelling, "Schnell, schnell, das ist nicht eine Erholungsreise" (Hurry, hurry, this is not a vacation trip).

Oh, did any one of us even for a second confuse this whole experience with a vacation trip? We all dug, no conversation. The ground was hard, the drizzle cold, and nobody had gloves. Our noses were dripping, our hands so cold that they quickly became part of the steel shovel, ice cold and with no feeling. In midmorning the drone of aircraft engines overhead was heard, and everyone looked for planes, fearful that the camp might be a target.

"Los, los arbeiten, oder erwartet ihr vielleicht ein packet from Amerikaner?" (Get, get to work, or are you perhaps expecting a package from the Americans?). The guard who said this roared with laughter as he slapped his hands on his sides in order to keep warm. Everyone bent their heads again to continue digging into the frozen ground. I remember thinking that if they were American planes, then clearly Goebbels was a liar.

The days passed slowly, one after another, everyone too exhausted at the end of each work day to do more than gather a few branches, light a fire in the stove, and just sit, each lost in their own little world of broken dreams. In truth, although I didn't know it then, we were quite fortunate to have landed in a backwater of the war and out of the line of fire, at least for the time being. I could not imagine the difficulties faced by young girls in other camps all over German-occupied Europe.

November 1944, Auschwitz: Anne Frank and her sister, Margot, were selected to "survive" as slave laborers and transferred to Bergen-Belsen Concentration Camp.

We had worked for about two weeks on the ditch when the SS officer came at the end of one day to inspect the work. He walked the length of the ditch, turned toward us, and barked that the ditch was too close to the road. It would have to be filled in the following morning and moved about two meters closer to the barracks! Each day passed slowly in the same way. The boredom of the occupation back in Belgrade was nothing compared to this—except, of course, that we all now had the advantage of being too exhausted at the end of each day to dwell on our boredom.

Each day as we worked, a detachment of men dressed in what looked like striped pajamas were marched past our ditch, and I was able to clearly see tattooed numbers on their arms. The weather was often extremely cold, but there was no change in the way they were dressed, and they were obviously very cold. We were forbidden to talk to them, but the men in our group found a way to exchange bits of news, especially if they were halted next to the ditch for a few moments.

We learned that they were Jews, consigned to slave labor, and that they were building an extensive tunnel system that was being used to produce munitions and parts for Nazi war machinery. Each morning these men passed our barrack and ditch on the way to the tunnel, thin, hollow-cheeked, often with long heavy steel pipes carried on the shoulders of groups of six or seven men in the line. Each evening they trudged back past us toward the fenced slave labor compound. They were obviously more restricted and more controlled than we were, yet they always seemed to have new bits of information about the war. Whenever they passed our group, and particularly if they were halted by the ditch for a few minutes, they whispered the latest news to us, and we whispered to them whatever we had heard.

One morning, an SS guard called me out of the ditch and showed me several pairs of boots that he had in his motorcycle side-car. He asked if

I knew how to polish boots, and I looked dumbly at him, pretending, as always, that I didn't understand German. He struggled to make me understand with gestures that he wanted me to polish the boots. Finally, when I was afraid I couldn't hold my laughter any longer, I opened my eyes wide and exclaimed, "Oh, ja, ja."

He visibly relaxed, sighed, and tried to make me understand that he would bring the boots each morning. "Oh, ja, ja," I nodded, as he brought several pairs of boots and polish and put them on the steps to our barrack. From then on, my job was to polish the boots of the ss guards, sitting on the steps to our barrack where I could watch the others as they continued to work on the ditch.

Our barrack continued the same dull labor, day after day with little change. Every now and then, someone came up with a stick of butter, a piece of dried meat, smoked fish, even, on a couple of occasions, some of the same chocolate that I had shared with Hans on the train from Belgrade to Vienna. The men must have been dealing with the German guards, trading whatever they had hidden—rings, crosses, bracelets, etc.

December 16, 1944: German troops launched a surprise counterattack against the Allies in Belgium, beginning the Battle of the Bulge.

Father asked me one day if I still had the watch and rings Mother had given to me the day we left Belgrade.

"Yes," I said. "I have them sewn into a little cloth. I keep them around my neck, and the watch is in my shoe."

"Good," he said. "Keep them hidden. Don't let go of them. You may need them."

December 22, 1944, Bastogne, France: Brigadier General Anthony C. McAuliffe, commanding the U.S. 101st Airborne defending a major crossroads at the village, replied, "NUTS," in a written response to a German demand for surrender during the Battle of the Bulge.

One afternoon, the German guard announced that it was Christmas Eve and that we would not have to work the following day. Christmas. I had forgotten the holidays. It had been so long since we had celebrated Christmas. I closed my eyes that evening to try to remember. Old Father Frost and his loud, jolly laugh, the gifts, the warmth and beauty of our home on Dr. Kester St., then Dedinye. I began to question whether it had all really existed. Perhaps I had only imagined it all.

I remembered how very beautiful Mother always looked on festive holidays, how happy and gay she seemed. I glanced over to look at her, realizing how pathetic, small, and sad she had become since we were ordered into the camp. There were days now when she didn't seem to understand what was going on. She rarely spoke to anyone. She sat quietly after working on the ditches each day, often weeping, staring at her once carefully manicured hands, now rough with open blisters, nails uneven and broken.

Her black hair had no shine and hung unevenly, revealing strands of gray. She looked old, although she had turned forty-four only a couple of weeks earlier. Often, not always, if someone wanted to speak with her, she would nod and smile faintly, but reply that she wasn't able to receive guests just now. Father's voice interrupted my thoughts.

"Thinking about Christmas, Anochka?"

"Yes, I guess I was. Papa, what's wrong with Mama?"

"I'm afraid she isn't feeling well at all. I don't mean physically. I think her mind sometimes refuses to accept the humiliation. She was always such a proud person. The degradation, all of this, I'm afraid is sometimes just too much for her."

"But why do the rest of us try our best to cope with it?"

"You remember my story about the boat being storm- tossed against a rocky shore? Well, I'm afraid this time the boat may have been broken up too severely to be easily mended. It may take time. I hope she . . ." His voice drifted off, and he went to join Mother. He put his arm around her. She sprang back, startled, desperately tucking away the strands of hair from her face, then straightened her skirt, sat down, and motioned for Papa to sit next to her as her eyes wandered into space. I turned away, as my own eyes began to mist.

The following day, Christmas, was glorious. It was, of course, December 25, not the Orthodox date for Christmas. The soup truck showed up as usual, before sunrise so nobody could sleep late, but nobody had to dig ditches. This time everybody brought their tin cups of soup inside to place them in a pot on the stove. We had hot soup for a change. We were told that there would be a "special" food distribution around 4 p.m.

The men went out into the wooded area to bring in some more fire-wood, while the women stayed behind to tidy up the barrack. Mother seemed almost back to normal, joining in with a pleasant smile. We had no broom, but the floors were swept with an old shirt, the straw was fluffed up, and the blankets were thrown neatly on top. Someone brought a bucket of water, and when it was warmed on the stove the women began to wash. A shirt was torn into pieces to use as washcloths, and all began to dip their piece of cloth into the warm water and to wash as thoroughly as possible in such crowded conditions.

Someone in the group suggested that since we had no toothbrushes or tooth powder or paste, that the next best thing was to dip a finger into the wood ashes from the stove and rub the teeth with it. It worked. The taste was terrible, but after a few rinses with cold water my mouth and teeth did feel cleaner. The wash-up proved to be the ultimate in luxury. Although there was little soap and no towels, all the women felt refreshed, and I think they even felt pretty.

Soon the men returned with armloads of wood and sticks, and a few fresh pine tree branches. The wash water was emptied from the bucket and replaced with fresh water, and the fresh, fragrant pine branches were put into the water. One of the women had a nice lace handkerchief that she placed on top of the branches. With a little imagination it looked like a delicate star at the top of a Christmas tree.

A long wooden table that stood against the wall, unused except to stack some personal items, was cleared and moved to the middle of the room, close to the stove. The fire was roaring inside the stove; an inner warmth began to radiate from each of us, and everyone brought out different items of food from various dealings with the guards.

A few pine branches were strewn on the table, and the food items were arranged among the branches. The table looked almost festive, and every-body decided to wait for the 4 p.m. food truck so that we could combine it all and celebrate the holiday.

Everyone sat on their blanket-covered straw bed and just relaxed, remi-niscing about past Christmases. There was a lot of conversation about the war and current rumors that Allied troops were advancing swiftly and that German defeat was inevitable. It is strange how people in confined con-ditions such as the labor and concentration camps seemed always to have a way to follow the exact movement of troops and the latest news on all fronts.

The slave laborers in the neighboring camp, in spite of being far more strictly controlled and confined than we were, always had the latest information and whispered the news as they marched past our group working on the ditch. Apparently, they had secured or built a secret radio that they were able to tune to the BBC or American Armed Forces Radio broadcasts and follow the movement of Allied forces. These poor men were our link to the outside world. The news was often conflicting, though, and we were never sure of who was advancing toward our location. Bulletins mentioned only "Allied forces," not identifying units, so we were never sure whether it was British, American, or Soviet troops heading toward us.

The conversation that Christmas Day in Blankenburg had a faint flicker of hope that we might all make it through the war alive. But those were just hopes. Because it was Christmas, everyone wanted to feel cheerful. Even Mother seemed more alert that day and came to sit next to me.

"Poor Asinka, you have lost so much weight," she said, stroking my cheek. "You look much too thin. You have aged so much that you would easily pass for nineteen or older."

She said it sadly, but I remember that it pleased me because I could hardly wait to grow up—in actual years, not just in experience. She placed her hand gently on my head and said with tears in her eyes, "You know, Asinka, I was only seventeen when the revolution broke out and they threw me in prison. I was all alone then, just 'Lyena and me rotting in that prison. Both parents murdered, and then," she looked tenderly at Father on the other side of the room, "and then my prince came and rescued me. Yes, just seventeen . . ." Her voice drifted off as she plunged again into her own long-forgotten world.

The arrival of the food truck broke off everyone's conversation, and we all rushed outside to receive the last meal of the day, which was a nice surprise. Not only was the soup hot, but it actually had real potatoes and carrots in it, the first vegetables we had seen since arriving in the camp. In addition, everyone received a double portion of bread and three pats of butter. It was truly a Christmas treat. Everyone was so happy that each of us wished the guards who had brought it a Merry Christmas.

The cups of soup were placed in a pot on the stove to be heated, and

everyone went down on their knees to offer prayers thanking God for having spared us so far, asking his help through the shaky days still ahead,
and special prayers for all our dead. Everyone wished each other a Merry
Christmas, and the food began to be divided very precisely. As everyone
began to relax, the men opened their handkerchiefs and emptied all the
tobacco they had into a single pile and began rolling cigarettes. They
looked as though they thought it the perfect end to the day.

The following morning it was back to the ditch. By this time, the ditch
had been deemed acceptable to the ss, and the group continued to dig
around the compound. I could no longer see them as they worked, but I
was able to watch the slave laborers as they marched past each day. I wondered how they found the strength to go on, to even survive, the way they
were driven by the ss guards.

> December 26, 1944, Bastogne: As the tide turned in the Battle of the
> Bulge, the 101st Airborne was relieved by the U.S. 4th Army, com-
> manded by General George Patton. No man of the 101st has ever
> agreed that their unit needed to be relieved!

The first week in January, we offered special prayers on Orthodox
Christmas. In the middle of January, one of the ss guards appeared to
inform us that we would now be granted permission to go into the village
of Blankenburg once a week from noon to 4 p.m., and we were cautioned
that we were under a curfew. No foreign laborers were allowed outside
the camp after 4 p.m. This was exciting news because none of us had been
allowed outside the compound since we had arrived. The same privilege
was extended to the entire forced labor compound. Each barrack had a
half-day off on different days. I think this had been true all along and that
the privilege was extended to us after some period of probation. At any
rate, it was very exciting, something to look forward to and break the
monotony.

The following morning dawned to the same soup and the same ditch,
but just at noon a German soldier came to the barrack and stamped our
ID cards with the date and the hour. Even the weather cooperated. The
sky was clear and blue, and we didn't notice the cold, anticipating a few
hours of freedom.

We passed the entrance to the tunnel complex that housed the underground munitions factory, and I was astonished to see the size of it and the activity. Groups of slave laborers and their SS guards were all around it. The prisoners resembled ghosts, slowly marching in double lines carrying long iron pipes on their shoulders and not paying any attention to the passing group of "privileged" forced laborers on their way into the town.

Seeing those poor men made me—all of us—realize that things could indeed be far, far worse. We walked briskly past the compound gates and onto the streets where "free" people walked.

Mother held Father's arm, and I walked behind them, all of us silent. I had no idea why we were going into town. I stole an occasional glance at the passing soldiers in their cars and motorcycles and noticed that some of them were rather good-looking and very young. What a pity they all seemed so brutal and unfeeling. I wondered what sort of people they would have been if Hitler and his war had not become a gruesome reality. Oh well, it's all part of life. I dismissed those thoughts, but I did wish that I could be dressed differently, my hair groomed, following a warm bath. What absurd wishes.

A squadron of planes passed overhead as we drew close to the center of the town. At least there was no danger of being bombed in Blankenburg. The bombing in Belgrade and all along the trip from Belgrade to Vienna flashed through my mind, sending cold shivers down my back. I wondered if the war would ever end and if people would ever be able to live normally again . . . if the whole world was at war with everybody existing from day to day as we did. Oh well, I thought. Spring isn't far away. Maybe things will be better in the spring.

What a quaint little town it was, nestled against the Harz Mountains, with crooked cobblestone streets lined with pretty houses and small gardens, untouched by war. As we entered the center of town, we passed small shops. Their display windows were rather bare, but nonetheless they were shops with people going in and out of them, obviously buying things.

I watched my parents as we walked slowly along, remembering how attractive they had been before the war. Mother now had a kerchief covering her once beautiful hair. She wore a heavy jacket that hung on her shoulders revealing cotton stuffing where the seams were split. A rope held the jacket snuggly together at her slender waist providing at least some protection against the cold. A flowered print dress showed below the jacket, and she wore white low-heeled shoes that had one heel crudely attached with a nail.

Father wore a felt hat and a long black coat. The velvet around the collar of his coat was nothing but a shiny, dirty spot, and each time he took a step, a wad of newspaper protruded from one of the shoes. But his shoulders were straight, his head high—the bearing of a military officer. I thought how pathetic they looked, and not for the first time. I remembered Father telling me how they had suffered through the Russian Revolution, and I wondered if we would make it through this war.

"Look," Father said as we walked on a bit, "there's a large nursery. I'm sure they aren't cultivating flowers but vegetables and potatoes. Shall we give it a try? See if we can talk some business to the owner?" Father was addressing both Mother and me, but we didn't respond, just followed him.

He asked us to remain outside while he went into the hothouse. There was an old man inside, and we watched as Father began talking to him and reaching inside his coat. A handshake followed, a smile, and Father came to the door to call me inside. The old man stuffed potatoes and onions into our pockets, carrots into my jacket, and a half loaf of fresh bread into Father's coat. We shook hands and walked out to the sidewalk.

"What did you trade for this time?" Mother asked.

But Father only kissed her forehead, smiled, and assured her that "Everything is in order."

Once back in the camp, everyone scurried around. The kitchen truck showed up shortly after we got back to the barrack, and the usual ration of "soup" was brought inside. The tiny stove was lit, sending smoke throughout the room, but nobody seemed to mind, knowing that it would soon get warm. Everybody emptied their soup ration into one large kettle, and the potatoes, carrots, and onions began to appear from everyone's pockets, along with two half loaves of fresh bread. Everyone tried to pitch in, peeling the potatoes and slicing the onions and carrots.

Even Mother joined in happily, wanting to help, but when someone suggested she peel some potatoes, she looked lost, unsure of where or how to begin, although she managed. The stove had stopped smoking, and the warm air began to spread as everyone moved closer to it, eagerly watching the pot and anticipating the soup.

Soon our tin cups were filled with real soup, thick and flavorful. Everyone was silent, chewing the precious vegetables slowly, trying to keep it in their mouths as long as possible. The dark bread, fresh and with at least a little butter, tasted even better than the most delicate Viennese torts.

"Maria Petrovna, guess who we think we saw in town today," someone said to Mother. "We were sure it was Max and Olga Zengovitz with their daughter."

"But how could that be?" asked Father. "The last time we saw them they were still in Belgrade."

The conversation became lively, but I didn't listen. I was lost in my own thoughts, wondering if it were true. They had pretended not even to see us in Belgrade. Why would they be here?

"Was he wearing his uniform?" someone asked.

"No," another replied. "He was in civilian clothes. Perhaps because he was married to a Russian, he encountered some problems, or maybe when the Germans retreated from Belgrade he had to flee and get his daughter out of the academy. But why would he not wear his uniform? Why would they be here?"

"Well," someone speculated, "if they were trying to escape the Soviets, this is the only sensible route to take, north and west."

The conversation and speculation went on and on. I kept thinking about the "solid foundation" stories Father had told me so very long ago. Father had always told me that in the end, the *very* end, my moral foundations would help me to hold steady through all the tremors and devastations that might surround me. I wondered if he was right. But what "end," "very end" was he talking about? When you die and go to heaven, or must one keep strong for rewards right here on earth? But what rewards? Tomorrow we might all be dead. If so, then maybe he was referring to heaven.

"Asya, are you still hungry?" Father asked. "There's a bit of soup left."

"No, thank you, Papa. I'm full."

The men lit their cigarettes and lay down on the straw beds, and we women began to wash the cups and pot.

"I wonder how long all of this will last? I haven't been able to talk to any of the concentration camp prisoners lately to find out troop movements and the general situation," someone said.

"Well," another retorted, "we'll be much better off if you don't try to contact those prisoners. The guards might get suspicious, and besides, you've heard the Germans. You know Goebbels said new territories have been taken and the German armies are victorious."

"Goebbels also said that they were victorious while they were running like rats from Belgrade," the first responded.

"Hush," said a woman from the other end of the room. "I wish you would stop wondering out loud, or we will all be wearing striped pajamas."

The conversation died away, and someone brought out a book of Chekhov short stories and began to read aloud. God, how many times we had heard these same stories. They were the only reading material we had. Someone had brought them along from Belgrade, and we were happy to have them, but Chekhov's stories were rather morbid, and I wished I could hear something cheerful.

"Asya, are you listening?" Father asked.

"I am, Papa, but I wish we could read something romantic, something cheerful."

Father began to recite from Pushkin's novel in verse, *Eugene Onegin.*

> Onegin, I was younger then,
> Better, it seems to me,
> And I loved you; and you?
> What did I find in your heart?
> What response? Severity alone.
> Is it not true? The surrender of a young girl's love
> was nothing new to you?
> And today—good God—it chills
> One's blood just to recall that cold glance
> And that preaching. . . . But I did not
> Blame you; in that terrible time
> You acted nobly,
> You were righteous before me;
> I was grateful with my whole soul.

Now, that was more like it. Soon the entire room was reciting line by line, each picking up as one finished a line. I believe every educated Russian could recite *Eugene Onegin*, perhaps not in its entirety, but certainly the most romantic and tender parts. It was a nice end to what had been a nice day. Slowly the room grew quiet. The oil lamp was turned way down, and I could hear people shifting in their straw—a sigh, a cough, a light snore from the far end of the room. Everyone said a quiet goodnight, and each retreated into their own world of dreams.

Days and weeks followed without any changes. Same work, same "soup," same reading of Chekov and reciting of Russian poetry. Mother grew quieter, often sitting in a corner without speaking much to anyone, often carrying on conversations with herself. More and more often she seemed to be living in a world of her own. When she was herself, however, she insisted on trying to find Max and Olga Zengovitz in Blankenburg.

I think that Olga was Mother's last link to her past as a young, carefree girl. Mother was never critical of Olga for seeming to turn against her own kind during the occupation of Belgrade, or if she was, she never showed it. She learned that Max and Olga Zengovitz were living in the town and managed to visit with them.

January 12, 1945: Soviet armed forces began a major offensive against the German army in Eastern Europe.

The winter of 1944–45 was terrible, or perhaps it only seemed that way to me because of our living conditions. The final fury of a long winter blasted in with the last week of February. The air was damp, the skies gray and unfriendly, and icy cold winds blew fiercely. One of those winds blew our outhouse down. Father sent me to the Bentin office to ask for nails to repair the outhouse.

January 27, 1945: The Soviets liberated Auschwitz and Birkenau Con- centration Camps.

February 13, 1945: Allied planes began incendiary bombing over the city of Dresden, creating a firestorm on the ground that destroyed the city and killed many thousands of civilians.

I entered the office slowly and rather timidly, not knowing what to expect. A very slender, middle-aged man sat behind a desk. He had large, sad eyes and sunken cheeks. He looked up and spoke very mildly as I entered the office.

"Yes? What can I do for you?"

"Well, our outhouse fell down, and we need some nails to repair it."

"How is it that you speak such perfect German? You're not German, are you?"

"No, I'm Russian, but I speak several languages."

"What are you doing here? Are you in the labor camp?" He motioned toward our barrack.

"Yes."

"What is your name? I am Herr Mueller."

"My name is Asya. It's really Anastasia, but I'm called Asya."

"Now, you want some nails, you said?"

"Yes, please."

"Say, since you speak German— Oh, by the way, can you also type in German?"

"Yes."

"Well, since you can type, would you like to work here in the office, to help me out with my paperwork? I'm sure I can get permission from the commandant and the chief engineer. It would be much easier than working in the ditch, and it would be a big help to me."

"Oh, I don't know. I don't think my parents would like me to help in a place like this. I mean, you are in charge of all those poor prisoners and—"

"I'm afraid I'm not in charge of anything," he interrupted sadly. "I too am a prisoner of sorts."

"But aren't you German?"

"Yes. But, you see, my wife is Jewish. I was told to obtain a divorce or else be shipped off to work in some camp. And so here I am."

"But where is Frau Mueller?"

"In a camp somewhere, I guess. I hope she is still . . ." His sad eyes filled with tears, and he rubbed them lightly. "Well, would you like to help me?"

"Yes, but I must ask Papa first. Oh, and I can't forget the nails."

Herr Mueller went to a cabinet and returned to hand me about a dozen large nails and a hammer.

"If that's not enough, I have some more. You let me know. Oh, wait a minute, Anastasia. It's almost your dinner time, isn't it?"

"Yes."

Herr Mueller went to an adjoining room and returned in a moment, carefully looking out the window, clutching something in his hand.

"Here, it's butter. Put it inside your shirt and don't let anyone know about it."

I ran out, whispering thank you and clutching the hammer and nails. As I left the office, I remembered several papers that had been on Herr Mueller's desk when he was asking me about working in the office and about my typing. They were shipping papers addressed "Klosterwerk— Blankenburg" ("Cloister Works—Blankenburg"). It seemed such an odd name, "Cloister Works." Years later, I would learn that the Nazis had given the name to the camp compound as a cover. A monastery, or cloister, stood in the mountains just above the town, and by calling the slave and forced labor camps the "Cloister Works," they implied that the camps and laborers were there to work on rebuilding and restoring the monastery. The underground tunnel complex and munitions factory were hidden from aerial view.

With the butter cold against my body, I ran back to our barrack. Everybody was already gathered awaiting the daily "soup" delivery.

"Papa, here are the nails and a hammer and—" I stopped in midsentence, confused for a moment, remembering that Herr Mueller had asked me not to tell about the butter, and I was afraid to say anything in front of the others.

"Good. After we have eaten, we will go and nail the outhouse back together."

We all ate our regular soup and bread allotment, the butter still cold against my waist inside my shirt. Father and one other man started toward the outhouse, and I dragged behind, unsure of what to do with the butter and beginning to be a bit uneasy about it. Finally, as the other man walked a bit ahead, I whispered, "Papa, I have a stick of butter in my shirt. What am I to do with it?"

"Butter?" Father whispered back. "From where? Who gave it to you?"

"Herr Mueller gave it to me."

"And who is Herr Mueller?"

"He is married to a Jewish woman."

"What Jewish woman?"

"She's in a camp someplace, and he too is in a camp."

The conversation obviously made no sense at all to Father, so he took me aside and asked in detail about the butter. I described my conversation with Herr Mueller, and we decided to share the butter later on with everyone. When we returned to the barrack we all had a small piece of bread with the butter. Nobody cared where it came from, of course. We all just enjoyed the unexpected treat. I told Father about the conversation with Herr Mueller and the chance to work in the office and asked if he thought it would be all right.

"I think so, Asya. I think so, but let me think about it for a while."

Over the next week or ten days, I went back to visit with Herr Mueller when I had finished polishing each day's allotment of boots. Each time I visited, I left with a stick of butter, some bread, or some chocolate for the barrack. Everyone in the barrack knew about it and was grateful for the extra food.

As the first two weeks of March passed, the terrible wind and cold that had started the month began to weaken. The snow began to thaw, the skies became noticeably bluer, and the days grew longer. The ground around the camp slowly turned from a hard frozen surface into deep mud. March in our forced labor camp was miserable, but it was far worse than I could know in other camps. At about the same time, another girl who the whole world would one day hear about, who was just about my age, struggled under far worse conditions.

In early March 1945, a typhus epidemic swept through the Bergen-Belsen Concentration Camp, killing many camp prisoners. Margot Frank soon died; her younger sister Anne Frank, died two days later.

One morning, the usual line of slave laborers halted in front of our barrack and began to dig a narrow ditch right next to the road and to lay pipe into it. The ground was so muddy that their feet sank deeply as they worked. The wind was icy and the air damp. While I sat on the step, polishing the endless line of boots, I noticed a boy in the line. He was clad in the usual striped pajamas, and he stopped for a moment to rub his hands together, trying to warm them. Our eyes met and held for an instant.

He was about my age, not much older certainly. He was so very thin and shivering violently with the cold. His large brown eyes were sunken deeply into his thin cheeks, and I watched him shivering almost uncontrollably. I looked quickly and saw that the ss guard was walking toward the other end of the line, his back toward us, and on an impulse I ran toward the boy in the line, tore away the soft, bright red angora scarf I was wearing, and while it was still warm put it quickly around his thin neck, stuffing the red ends inside his shirt so that it wouldn't show.

He smiled a bit and managed only a "Merci" and a few words. I know that I answered in French, but only one or two words when the SS guard shouted at me. The guard was there in an instant, tore the scarf from the boy's neck, and began to rip it up, cursing. I turned quickly, and as I ran back to my boots, the guard was directly behind me, his rubber hose raised high and swinging in the air.

"Damned 'Untermenschen.' Can't you stay where you are supposed to stay? What was the conversation between the two of you? Would you like to join him? We have plenty of stripes to put you in."

"You are a beast." I turned to face him, yelling at him. "You call me 'Untermenschen,' but you are a monster, a killer, a torturer. I wish you would all die . . . someday."

I stood there screaming at the guard, tears running down my face, when I saw the rubber hose being raised and aimed at me. I turned as quickly as possible and began to run up the steps when suddenly I felt a sharp, hot sting on the back of my calf.

I ran inside, relieved that the guard didn't follow, and felt something warm running down the back of my leg. I looked down at my leg, amazed that it didn't hurt when I saw blood flowing freely, and a piece of flesh hanging from a deep wound. Quickly I found a piece of cloth, something we were using as a dish rag, and wrapped the calf tightly, but bright red blood soaked through almost immediately. I found another rag and tied it tightly over the first one and lay down on the straw, elevating the leg until the bleeding slowly subsided.

I laid there on the straw crying bitter tears, not because my leg hurt—I didn't feel any pain from it—but because of the frustration and humiliation. I cried for the boy who had worn the scarf for only a moment before the guard ripped it to shreds. He had managed only a word or two before the guard was there, enough though for me to think his accent was Belgian. I hoped he understood that I just wanted to show him kindness and compassion. I didn't understand why the guard wouldn't let him wear it or why he had ripped it to shreds. Now the scarf was of no use to anyone.

Soon the group from our barrack returned from their daily work on the ditch. Father was very upset when I explained what had happened, and someone in the group began to complain loudly that we would all wind up in the concentration camp because of "Asya's mouth" and wishing aloud that I didn't speak German. Everyone began to speak in whispers.

New rumors were circulating that the German army was in real trouble, that it was retreating, and that Allied troops were steadily advancing. Still, nobody knew who the "Allies" were—American, British, or Soviet. There was some speculation about whether the Americans or the British would be better, but everyone prayed that the Russians were not headed for us.

I still did not understand. We were all Russians, yet so afraid of our own people. We were afraid of the Germans, afraid of the Russians, yet knew nothing about the Americans or the British. So how could we know which would be best?

What difference does it make? I thought. Why are they all so anxious to live anyway? They fret constantly about all that they've lost, nothing to look forward to. Why are they so afraid to die? Everyone here has lost everything except the rags on their backs and a few trinkets jealously kept in their ragged suitcases with ugly ropes holding them together. I looked around at all our companions. They all looked so haggard and worn, and I imagined them all jealously clinging to those ugly suitcases.

I looked over at Mother, seated alone in a corner, polishing her finger-nails with a rag and smiling that mysterious smile that she displayed lately, not speaking to anyone, but mumbling to herself almost constantly. I won-dered if she wanted to go on. I wondered what thoughts she had, what hopes or dreams. She spoke so many languages that it wouldn't matter who defeated the Germans. She would get along, just as I would. But how much longer could she survive? I remembered how helpless she had looked when we brought some vegetables back from our first trip into town. She readily pitched in to help, but when someone suggested that she peel the potatoes, she looked lost. My leg began to throb and hurt, but I didn't complain. I didn't want anything to eat that night. I simply lay down on my straw and tried to lose myself in sleep.

The following morning my leg was badly swollen and very painful. Father suggested that I go to the office and ask Herr Mueller for an aspi-rin or something to help fight the infection that was obviously starting. I limped across the muddy ground to enter Herr Mueller's office.

"Good morning, Asya," he said, smiling at first, then frowning. "You look so pale today. Don't you feel well?"

"Oh, I feel fine, but my leg hurts."

"What happened?"

"This ss—" I suddenly remembered the people in the barrack saying that I would get them all thrown into the concentration camp. Herr Mueller *was* German, after all. "This ss guard caught me not working, not polishing the boots, and I was afraid he would get angry. So before he got to me, I tried to run up the steps, but I fell down."

"Well, let me see." He looked at the dirty rags that had by then stuck to the wound, then he jerked them off with such speed that I didn't have time to think about how painful it would be to remove them.

"Hmm, it does not look good. How did you manage to tear off a piece of flesh? Let me wash it with some disinfectant. I have some bandages here, and we'll try to fix that leg up. You know, Anastasia, that looks like a perfect rubber hose mark. I've seen too many wounds like that before."

"And just because I gave my scarf to that poor boy, that ss swine—Oh, my God, it's done. Now we will all rot in the concentration camp." I stood there with my hand covering my mouth, staring at Herr Mueller, my eyes wide, not knowing what to expect.

"Hush, my child. You don't have to tell me. I know. I know much more than any of you can guess. But soon, soon I hear . . . it shouldn't last much longer. I pray my wife will come out of it all right. Oh, God, I wish I knew where she is, if she is alive."

I sat there on a chair as he worked on my leg wound, trying to listen carefully to his words and to make sense out of them. I knew that this poor man carried an enormous burden and that he was no better off than we were, despite the fact that he was German. I wondered if he had heard the same rumors—that Allied troops were closing in and the German army was retreating. I didn't understand anything, only that everyone around me suffered, living from day to day with foolish hopes locked in their hearts.

"Asya," Herr Mueller said, "I think the wound will be all right, but we should have the doctor look at it. You wait here, and I'll be right back."

He returned in just a minute—the doctor's office must have been in the same building—and was accompanied by a middle-aged woman whom he introduced as the doctor. I was amazed when the doctor addressed me in Russian. As she examined my leg, I peppered her with questions, and she explained that she was a Soviet military doctor. Her unit had been captured, she said, adding that there were other Soviet military prisoners in the slave labor camp section.

Speaking Russian, she told me that Herr Mueller had done an excellent job of cleaning the wound and that she was sure it would heal properly.

"But you must be very careful to keep it absolutely clean until it scabs over. We have no medicine available."

She left, explaining to Herr Mueller what she had told me. I never saw her again, nor did I ever see any other Russian prisoners.

"Asya," Herr Mueller said when the doctor had left, "tomorrow morning early, around 5:30, our weekly vegetable delivery will arrive. I hope they get here on time. It's supposed to snow and be colder, but maybe that's better because the ground will be frozen again. It's so easy for these trucks to get stuck in the mud. Anyway, why don't you come early, around 5:00, and I'll be able to give you some potatoes and whatever other vegetables they deliver for the kitchen before they are all checked in and stored. Maybe we can pick out some of the nicest ones, and you can take back whatever is available. I'll get you some butter, too, and your people can fix a nice meal. But don't tell anybody. I'm not allowed to do that. You should bring your Papa with you to help carry them because your leg has been hurt."

"Oh, I will, I will. I'll come early. I'll come even before they march the prisoners to the tunnel factory."

"Yes, they usually march past about 6 a.m., but the truck would have been here already and we can get the vegetables before the guards show up. You should be here even before the truck comes. Now you should go back. Or would you like to help me here in the office?"

"Yes, I would, but they'll bring all the boots for me to shine in a few minutes."

"Well, then when they bring the boots, why don't you bring them in here. At least it's a little warmer. I'll tell the guard that your leg is badly infected and you can do your work in here. Yeah, I'll do that. No," he continued thoughtfully, "it's better if I tell them that I need you to work in the kitchen and they should bring the boots in here. That way no precious time is wasted. Progress, hard work—they like to hear that."

Herr Mueller walked with me back to our barrack, just as the same motorcycle drove up with its side-car filled with dirty boots. I was glad that it was cold and the ground had frozen again. At least the boots wouldn't be as muddy as they had been in the past several days. When a hint of spring was in the air, the ground began to thaw and the camp was surrounded by thick mud. How very different my attitude toward spring had been only a year earlier. Herr Mueller helped me to carry the boots back. I sat on the floor of the tiny office and began the chore I had truly learned to hate.

Herr Mueller went into the next room, which I knew was the supply room for the laborers' kitchen, and returned in a moment with a piece of dark German bread with lots of butter on it and handed it to me without a word. I thanked him and ate eagerly, remembering that I had gone to sleep the night before without eating. It tasted so good that just for an instant I felt guilty because I wasn't sharing it with the rest of the people in the barrack. Oh, well, I thought as I swallowed the last bite, it wouldn't have been enough anyway.

"Why is your wife in a camp?" I asked innocently.

"Please whisper. Someone might hear you."

"Oh, I'm sorry," I whispered. "Why did they take her away?"

"Because she is Jewish, and I did not want to divorce her."

"If you did divorce her, would they still have taken her away?"

"Yes, but then I would be holding some important position in the army or in the party. You know, my brother is with the Gestapo and has a big job someplace."

"If he's so important, why doesn't he help you?"

"Because, my child, he was the one who told the authorities that Hanna, my wife, is Jewish. He *hates* Jews."

"Your own brother?"

"Yes, brother against brother. The whole world is upside down. Something must give. God must be watching all this insanity, and He must, He *has* to put a stop to all of it. You are Russian. You must know what would happen if the Russians suddenly came. Well, for you I suppose it wouldn't make a difference. But just look at what my people have done to your people, and you are not even Jewish. Not even Jewish. You are just not German, and that's what is so wrong. Only Germans, no, only Nazis have the right to survive, to rule the world. Do you hate me because I am German?

I don't hate you because you are not." He paused and looked at me then, and I could see that tears filled his eyes.

"Oh, no, Herr Mueller," I whispered. "I don't hate you. I really don't. You weren't in Belgrade. You didn't bomb our city. You didn't kill our friends. You didn't. *They* did."

"But *they* is me, although I don't feel the way they do," he answered, still whispering, but now pacing the floor, holding his head with both hands. "They, you, me . . . Jews, Russians, French, Greeks. What gives them the right to crush nation after nation, to exterminate, eliminate, destroy? What right? God must see it all. Maybe God doesn't exist."

He continued pacing the floor in silence, still holding his head.

"Do you believe there is a God, Herr Mueller?"

"I don't know, Asya. I just don't know."

"I don't think so either. There used to be a God, but not anymore. I remember at home, whenever I was afraid or lonely or sad, I used to talk to God while looking at the clouds, or in church with Aunt 'Lyena. I always talked to Him, and I knew He was there and that He listened. I always felt so good after the talk, but lately I've been talking to Him, calling Him ever since we fled Belgrade and on the train. He just doesn't answer me. He doesn't hear me anymore. So many people have died, people who I know believed in Him and loved Him, and yet He let them die. He let them die such horrible deaths, not just plain die of old age or illness, but let them be killed . . . horribly killed by Germans."

"You see," Herr Mueller whispered, "you must hate me. I am German."

"No, not you, *them*."

"Yes, *them*," he whispered. He grew silent then and began working on some papers. I understood that the conversation had ended, and I returned to polishing the boots.

A bit later, when I had finished my task, I got up from the floor and reported to Herr Mueller. "The boots are finished."

"Oh, well, just leave them here and go on back to your barrack. Here, Asya, here are some aspirins. Take them before you go to bed, and here is a piece of chocolate for you."

He reached into his pocket and handed me a piece of chocolate with a bite already taken out of it.

"I'm sorry," he added sheepishly. "I bit into it and then remembered that you were here, and I want you to have the rest. Go now and come back early in the morning for the vegetables. Thank you for listening, and don't forget to bring your Papa," he said and again immersed himself in his paperwork.

NINETEEN

Brutality and Murder

March 7, 1945: American forces captured the bridge at Remagen and quickly crossed the Rhine River to enter the German heartland.

The wound from the ss Guard's rubber hose was still painful, and I limped slowly from Herr Mueller's office back to our barrack, arriving before the others returned. The room was neat. The floor had been swept between the straw beds; old blankets covered the lumpy, uneven straw, and the rope stretched across the room held several damp shirts, socks, and rags. The wood stove was almost out, but still offered a little heat, and I moved closer trying to get as much of the warmth as I could.

"Britain is a Kingdom, America is not," said a voice behind me. "If the British are victorious, then I could perhaps tutor the children. But what language would interest them? If America is victorious . . . oh, I just don't know . . . how I long for the steppes and the wind across the fields back home . . . the balls . . ."

I turned and saw Mother crouched in a corner, her eyes wide open but not seeing me—a faraway look and that mysterious smile on her lips again.

"Mama, are you all right?"

She paused then, looking at me.

"You, on the other hand, you don't know the steppes, the rush of the wind in your hair." At first I thought there was a mocking tone in her voice, but it was simple sadness. "You never did become a lady. Look at you, dirty, your leg swollen, hair dirty, uncombed." I saw tears in her eyes then. "You didn't even want to play the piano. You always fought when the piano tutor came. I just don't understand that. When I played, yes, I saw you many times, when I played, you sat as though in a trance. You *love* music. Why didn't you ever want to learn how to play . . . how to glide through a room, not to walk or run like a peasant? You just wouldn't listen to me, and look at you now. Even Kristina looked better."

She shook her head sadly in disapproval and began to examine her own nails, seemingly unaware of how broken and discolored they had become.

"No," she sighed, "you'll never amount to anything. I must go into town tomorrow and listen to a radio. There are these rumors, you know, that the Germans are retreating rapidly . . . that we will soon be liberated. But they're just rumors. People don't know what they are talking about. Adolf Hitler's birthday is coming very soon, and the German armies will be striving to present him with major victories on his birthday as they always do. Nobody is coming. We are just going to rot here and die. How sad that you may die without ever knowing what it means to be a lady, to be admired," she said, brushing a strand of hair from her eyes.

"Mama," I asked, "are you cold?"

"No, I'm fine, thank you." She switched to French and glanced toward the door. "I do wish someone would bring tea now."

"Mother?" I began. "Mama?" But no answer came as I sat down next to her. I wanted to hold her hand or embrace her, but she sat very stiffly then and erect. I didn't dare reach for her. I knew that aloof look too well. For an instant, I was back in Belgrade, waiting for the sound of that old automobile horn, waiting for Mama to come back for me, trying so hard to remember her face and failing. All I could remember was the sound of that old horn. Suddenly I realized that the camp whistle was blowing. Perhaps that was the sound that triggered that old "memory."

The whistle was signaling the end of another workday, the end of another shift in the tunnel. At least they were not air-raid sirens. The skies now seemed filled with American bombers flying overhead in what seemed like wave after wave. Thankfully they never paused over Blankenburg.

Soon the room would fill with people exhausted from another day of ditch digging.

March 21, 1945: Allied bombers began four days of continuous bombing raids over Germany.

I told Father about Herr Mueller and the vegetables and that we had to be up very early to be at his office before the slave laborers marched past—even before the truck arrived. I just drank my cup of the usual soup and went to bed, while everyone sat around the stove, whispering about the latest rumors they had heard from the slave laborers. I fell asleep lulled by low, whispered murmurs.

"Asya, get up." Father was shaking my shoulder gently. "Time to go to the office." I dressed silently and quickly in the dark as Father shrugged into his coat and helped me to find my jacket. It was still very dark outside, only faint light visible to the east. Herr Mueller was already at work and cheerful.

"Good morning, Asya. Ah, good, you brought your Papa." He turned to Father. "I was afraid this little girl couldn't carry the vegetables—enough for all of you, I hope—not with her leg injured. I wouldn't dare help her. You understand," he said with an apologetic gesture.

Within minutes a large truck drove to the front of the office; two prisoners jumped down and brought two huge barrels from the storeroom. They began shoveling vegetables into them and then carried them back into the storeroom. From the storeroom they would be taken to the kitchen building as needed. The vegetables looked dirty, as though just dug from the fields.

The truck drove off, leaving several carrots and potatoes lying on the frozen ground, some pressed into the tracks left by the truck. Herr Mueller returned from the storeroom and handed us two large buckets full of muddy vegetables.

"You had better wait until the prisoner column walks by. They should be on their way now to the tunnel. I don't want the guards to catch you with the vegetables."

Father stood by the stove in the office, warming himself.

"Hope the spring will be here soon."

"Yes," Herr Mueller answered, "a couple more weeks and we'll have warm weather coming. It's pretty here in the spring. There is a certain breeze that comes down from the Harz bringing with it a wonderful scent of spring. You'll see. It won't be long."

I stood by the window, concealed behind a worn curtain. The east was now light, and the new day looked clear. The sun hadn't risen, but its first light illuminated the eastern sky. The gray dawn revealed a procession of slave laborers in their striped pajamas and black head coverings. They marched slowly past the office, harsh German voices yelling, "Hurry! Keep moving." How shiny the boots of the guards were. I was ashamed at how hideous they looked alongside the tired, almost bare feet of the prisoners, ashamed that I had a part in the hideous comparison.

Suddenly, four of the prisoners broke from their line and threw themselves to the ground right in front of the office, grabbing at the vegetables pressed into the tire tracks, clutching them in their weak hands, trying to devour them dirt and all, desperately trying to protect their find with their skinny bodies. As I watched in horror, shiny boots appeared, kicking the prisoners. Rubber hoses began swinging in the air, with more kicking as groans and screams began.

"Get up, swine!" a guard was yelling. "You haven't worked yet. You haven't earned any food. Up with you!"

The kicking and beating continued, and other prisoners started to move toward the guards to try to stop the beatings. Shots were fired. Those who had thrown themselves on the ground remained there. The others hurried back to the long line of human beings who seemed indifferent to the horror that had just taken place. The line was formed again, and rubber hoses and shiny boots appeared alongside the prisoners as they resumed their march to the tunnel.

The whole thing had taken only minutes—three or four at the most—but to me it had seemed an eternity, everything happening in slow motion. I stood there, staring in abject horror, unable to comprehend what I had just witnessed. My face was pressed against the window pane, unable to believe what I was looking at. The gray ground. Frozen vegetables now lying in pools of blood, steam slightly rising from them. Four bodies lay there, two still clutching a hideous frozen carrot.

Without thinking I ran quickly from the office and knelt on the ground, feeling the men, hoping that they had only been wounded, that perhaps

I could help. None of the men moved. There were no more groans. Their horror had ended. They would never again wonder what the new day would bring for them. They never even saw the sunrise on their last day.

I knelt there on the ground, next to one of the bodies, clutching the cold hand of one of the men, holding it tightly against my chest, rocking back and forth and crying. I didn't yell or scream. I cried quietly, tears pouring as though a dam in my soul had broken. Herr Mueller and Father came running from the office to drag me away from the bodies.

"Please, please bring her into the office," Herr Mueller was saying. "Quickly. They'll be back within minutes to clear the bodies, and they will shoot her, too. You cannot show sympathy. Oh, God, bring her in quickly."

"Yes, yes, of course," Father replied in a whisper.

My dress was covered with blood, and I half collapsed into a chair Herr Mueller offered. Suddenly I was violently sick and ran out to the steps to vomit. Father quickly pulled me back inside.

"Asya," Herr Mueller said softly, his hand on my shoulder. "I'm so sorry, so sorry you had to see it. But this goes on every day. You haven't been to the munitions factory in the tunnel. You get used to it. They are shot daily. If someone is unable to work or to get up on command after falling down from exhaustion, they just shoot them. Remember our conversation of yesterday? You said them, yes, *them*. They just shoot them."

I ached all over, as though I had been beaten with the rubber hoses. Every part of my body ached as I turned to Herr Mueller.

"You see, I was right yesterday. There is no God. There never was." I turned to face Father then, still speaking coolly and calmly. "And you, Papa, you've been telling me lies all my life. You told me, you and Aunt 'Lyena, how good God was. How he held the entire universe in his hands. You lied, Papa, *lied*. There is no God, only evil in this world. How *could* you have lied to me? This isn't the first war for you, Papa. You told me about terrible things in the revolution. You knew even then that there was no God. I hate you, Papa. You lied to me."

Father walked slowly toward me, took my head, and pressed it gently against his chest. "Go ahead, cry, my angel. Cry, my little bird. I would never tell you a lie. That is what I have always believed, still believe. There is God, there is good in the world. Someplace there is. I only pray that you will find love for God and peace for your troubled soul. You are so very,

very young." I felt a hot tear fall on my head, and Father began to tremble as he, too, cried quiet tears, holding my head tightly to his chest.

A truck drove up to the front of the office. One soldier sat inside the truck and two others with rifles stood in the back of the truck with two prisoners. The two prisoners jumped down to pick up the bodies from the road. With one holding the feet, the other holding the arms, they tossed each body into the truck with a light swing. One of the guards whistled "Lili Marlene," and another shouted, "Let's hurry it up. Let's get going. We have more trash to pick up over at the tunnel." The truck drove off with its new cargo, wheels spinning in half-frozen ground now softened by warm blood, the scene frozen forever in my memory.

"Thank you for the vegetables, Herr Mueller," I heard Father say.

"Wait," Herr Mueller answered softly. "Wait just a minute. I have some lard for you. We ran out of butter, but the lard isn't bad. It will give some substance to the vegetables and stick to your bones. Enjoy it."

Father put the lard on top of the vegetables in one of the buckets and motioned for me to go.

"Papa," I asked outside, "how can you take those vegetables and the lard?"

"You heard Herr Mueller. The lard will add some flavor."

"Papa, those vegetables are stained with blood. Four people died because they wanted only one frozen carrot, and we're taking two buckets full."

"A lot of people are depending on this food, Asya. They have to sustain themselves. They have to hold onto life the best way they know how."

"Papa, why do you want to live?" I asked suddenly. "What do you expect from tomorrow? What's left for you? Why do you expect anything? Why do you even want to live? For what?"

"I know this is difficult for you to understand. We will have to talk seriously again. You are so young."

"What does my being young have to do with all of this? Tell me! Why do you and all the others want to live? For what? Tell me!"

I was almost screaming at him, tears streaming down my face. I turned to leave Father to carry the vegetables to the barrack, and I ran toward the outhouse. I wanted to be alone. I didn't want to see or talk to anyone, and the outhouse was the only place that sometimes offered some privacy.

There were three seats and none in use. I was thankful for that. I locked the door and sat there for a long time, trying to figure things out, the horrors of a short time before still vivid before my eyes. At one point, the memory of Hopova and the lovely face of my favorite little nun flashed into my mind, but even her peaceful image was no help. I put it out of my mind.

"Are all the seats taken? I really have to go," a voice said as the door rattled.

I unlatched the door and went out.

"Well, the nerve! Taking all three seats for yourself. That's what's wrong with the world today. People just don't care for anything but themselves."

Yes, I thought as I walked away. *Maybe that's it. Maybe that's what's wrong with the world—no private toilets.* I was disgusted. Then suddenly I felt like laughing. *Maybe there is hope. Maybe there is something to look forward to. This woman, for example, had no complaints other than not having the outhouse available in a moment of need.*

When WWII ended in Europe, the names Auschwitz, Buchenwald, Dachau, Bergen-Belsen, Mathausen, Sobibor, and many others became well known throughout the world, defining the evil that had characterized Nazi aggression. Less well known is the existence of thousands of small camps such as the Klosterwerk, often nameless, spread throughout Germany and German-occupied Europe, which supported and encouraged that evil.

The sun was now shining brightly, and it was warm. I thought I heard a bird chirp. Yes, there it was again, and a bird flew from the ground just ahead of me, a worm in its beak. I wondered if it was flying back to its nest to feed a chick. Then another flew past. The world seemed just a bit brighter as I continued to walk toward the barrack.

"Asya," Father said as I entered, "there will be no boots today. They came and said that you should report to the kitchen. No boots to shine today."

"All right, Papa."

As I went out to walk to the kitchen, some twenty prisoners were working in the same place, digging the same ditch, and continuing to lay long pipes in the bottom. I looked along the length of the line, but didn't see the boy to whom I had given the scarf. "Oh well," I thought, "perhaps it's a different group."

But the guard was the same. He walked toward me grinning, swinging his rubber hose.

"What happened to your leg?" he asked, his grin growing broader as he struck his palm lightly with the hose.

"I fell," I answered coldly, staring into his eyes.

The guard turned his head, spat on the ground, and looked away. I turned and limped quickly toward the kitchen. As I passed the office, the blood stains were still visible, although the ground had softened enough for it to have soaked in. The bright blood from the morning was now brown. Like so much in life, in just a few more minutes, no visible trace of the tragedy would remain.

Inside the kitchen building, a huge iron stove with many burners stood in the center, with firewood neatly stacked at the side. Mounds of potatoes, carrots, and turnips were piled against the walls. Tiny three-legged stools stood in front of the mounds of vegetables with men sitting on them, humming a tune or whistling and peeling vegetables. The cook, an Italian I thought, pointed to an empty stool and handed me a small knife.

"A lot of potatoes, eh?" he said in poor German.

As I looked around, I realized that I had never seen any of these men. Of course, each barrack kept to themselves with no visiting or mingling, everyone tired at the end of each day, happy just to return to their own place to rest. I began to peel the potatoes, many of them half frozen and partially mushy. Most of the men were young, with dark hair and olive-toned skin, and I thought they must all be Italians. I could hear them speaking among themselves and knew they spoke Italian. I wished I could speak Italian. I couldn't understand a word, but I enjoyed the musical sound of it so much.

I glanced around the room to notice a young man with dark eyes and curly hair. His smile revealed a row of white teeth as he looked back at me. Oh, how I wished I were dressed differently, my hair combed, and my toes not sticking out the ends of those ugly shoes. I felt a hot blush spread over my cheeks as the young man began to hum. What a sight I must be, I thought, remembering that I hadn't looked at a mirror for weeks.

Suddenly I remembered that less than two hours earlier, I had knelt on the bloodied ground amid four bodies, desperately clutching the hand of one of the dead men, trying to wish life back into him and crying. What was wrong with me? I was devastated at what I had witnessed, yet now I was blushing as a strange boy looked at me from across a room.

I began intensely peeling the potatoes, refusing to look in his direction again. These people seemed so cheerful compared with our group. I heard casual conversation all around the room, humming and laughing. I suddenly hoped that they were not laughing at me, at the way I was dressed, and again I began to blush.

I was happy when the ordeal of peeling potatoes was over. My back was stiff from sitting hunched over on that tiny stool for so long, and I was happy to finally get up and walk toward my own barrack. I stole a quick glance at the young man who was now singing loudly and saw that he was watching me.

Outside the birds were singing, the sky was blue, and the air was warm. It felt good to walk. A few hours earlier I had wished I were dead, but now I was glad to be alive. The sound of a Neapolitan song could still be heard coming from the kitchen building. I wondered where the Italian barrack was and why I had never heard them singing before. Maybe, I thought, they didn't sing before, but with the first sign of spring, like today, they just feel happy.

April arrived, and the breeze from the Harz brought a scent that only nature can provide. The buds on the trees and shrubs were full, just waiting to burst, reveal their inner beauty, and bathe in the warm sunlight. We were told that April in the Harz had never been as warm and bright as that early spring in 1945. Songbirds, it seemed, were everywhere one looked or listened.

The endless procession of slave laborers marched daily to the munitions factory in the tunnel and trudged back in the evening. Their faces did not reveal any new hope, any thought of a new beginning. For them there was no spring. The sun did not warm their exhausted, emaciated bodies. Their eyes and sunken cheeks reflected only pain and sorrow. The songs of birds did not lighten the heavy stone each of them carried in his soul.

April 11, 1945: American forces liberated Buchenwald Concentration Camp.

April 12, 1945: President Franklin D. Roosevelt died of a cerebral hemorrhage; Vice President Harry Truman was sworn in as president.

April 15, 1945: British and Canadian forces liberated the Bergen-Belsen Concentration Camp, where Anne Frank had perished only a few weeks earlier.

We, the forced laborers, however, seemed to have perked up a little. The straw beds were fluffed up, and the blankets hung outside to air in the fresh spring breeze. The drainage ditch which we had dug around the compound now ran constantly with clear water as the spring warmth thawed the hills. The bottom of the ditch was now sand and stones, and the water gurgled as it flowed past our barrack as happily as a clear mountain stream. We even enjoyed washing our hair and our laundry with the clear "running" water instead of the melted snow we had grown used to.

I visited the office to see Herr Mueller several times in early April, but he was very busy, so I often didn't have an opportunity to talk with him. Often I could see an ss officer in the room, and I didn't even approach the building. Once, as I approached the office, a young girl about my age stepped out to the front steps. As I drew near she smiled and greeted me, and I stopped to talk with her for a few moments, embarrassed because she was so nicely dressed while I stood there in rags.

"Good morning," she said politely.

"Good morning. Is Herr Mueller here?"

"Yes, but he is busy just now. Do you live in the labor camp?"

"Yes."

"My name is Lilo, Lilo Palmier," she said pleasantly.

"My name is Anastasia. Do you live here, too, Lilo?"

"No," she answered, "well, yes, in a way. My father is the commandant of the camp."

We chatted for a few minutes, but I was uncomfortable, dressed as I was, and excused myself to return to the barrack. I would not see Herr Mueller again. He seemed always to be very busy then, and as April progressed, I saw many papers being burned outside the office. I never noted the similarity with the burning of papers at Luftwaffe headquarters during my final days in Belgrade.

The news from the slave laborers was encouraging. The Allies were advancing steadily and had already entered Germany. They were even nearing Berlin. Large flights of Allied planes now flew over our heads several times daily in the direction of Berlin or Magdeburg, a large industrial city not too far from Blankenburg.

Blankenburg had never experienced an air raid, but there was nothing of military value with the exception of the underground factory. Fortunately for us, the Allies were not aware of its existence. For me, the constant drone of the bomber squadrons above blended with the bustling sounds of nature around me. The birds, the bees, the brook—all were rushing about us as April progressed.

On April 18, 1945, the concentration camp prisoners didn't march past our barrack to the tunnel. Instead, they were all marched toward a line of freight cars that stood motionless in a field close to the slave labor camp. They were loaded into the rail cars, each of which had a red cross painted on its roof.

There was no work assigned to the forced laborers either. No ditches to be dug, no boots to be shined, and no ss guards in sight. With unexpected free time and no guards evident, everyone ventured off during the day and walked around the camp grounds, surprised at the large expanse of the compound. Bored, I returned to our barrack and went to the "brook," the ditch we had dug, to dip my feet into it. The water was very cold, but it felt so good to feel the running water tumbling about my feet. I wanted to jump in and feel the tingling of the water over my whole body, but that wasn't possible. Besides, the water was much too cold, I thought.

"Hello, my name is Umberto, Umberto Pallovicini," a voice from behind me said. "What is your name?"

My heart sank to my cold feet in the water. It was that handsome young man from the kitchen. Oh, God! I must be a sight. I moved quickly to try to hide my torn ugly shoes from his view. He laughed and removed his shoes to show me that his were in much worse shape.

"May I join your feet in the brook?" he asked in badly broken German.

How sad, I thought, that we had to converse in German. Italian sounded so beautiful, and I again wished that I could speak the language. "Do you speak Russian or Serbian or English or French?" I asked.

"English, a little," he replied in German, "but it's a no-no," and he smiled as he put his finger across his lips and looked around.

"My name is Asya, and I'm Russian, but we were brought here from Belgrade. Well, not really Belgrade, but from Vienna," I said, and then stopped quickly, realizing that I was talking too much.

His dark eyes were smiling, and he kicked tiny pebbles with his feet while dangling them in the water.

"I've been to Yugoslavia many times," he said lightly. "We're practically neighbors."

"I went to Italy once with my father," I said, "but when I was a very little girl. Do you always sing?" I asked, remembering his singing when he was peeling potatoes.

"Yes, it seems that music makes everything almost bearable."

"In our barrack we just read and recite poetry. Nobody feels like singing. But maybe . . . well, I'm sure . . . nobody sings well enough to make it sound pleasant."

Umberto smiled and began to hum.

"Do you know 'Torna Piccina'?" I asked, "My Papa used to sing that to me when I was little."

He began to sing that lovely old Neapolitan song that Father had sung so often to me. It seemed so very long ago—at least a lifetime. Tears came to my eyes then, tears of happiness and sorrow. Happiness that I was there, on a quiet spring day, alive and listening to the song. Sorrow because I realized my childhood was gone and that I would never again be "Papa's little girl." I knew it was silly to feel that way, but I missed my home, my gardens, "my" Belgrade so very much. I hadn't looked at clouds for so long, hadn't lain in cool grass listening to the little buzzes and noises that one can only hear while lying deep in the grass, very still, with no one else around.

"I'm sorry, Piccina. Did my singing make you cry?"

I opened my eyes to see Umberto looking at me as one would look at a child who had been hurt and no one knew what to do about it . . . no one knew how to help.

"Oh, no," I answered quickly. "I loved your singing. It's beautiful. It's just that . . . I think I'm homesick."

Umberto bent very close to me and whispered, "I think that very soon now . . . very soon we will be able to go home, if they don't kill us first. But hush, not a word. It's something we just heard this morning." He paused, looked around, and whispered in my ear, "Have you noticed there are no guards around? Something is going to happen soon, very soon."

The sound of the bubbling water and the singing of the birds suddenly became much louder. My heart began to pound as I felt his breath on my ear as he whispered, "Something is going to happen soon." There was an excitement in the air that one only experiences before an anticipated "unknown" is about to take place.

Just then, Father's voice came from behind me.

"Asya, I've been looking for you all around the camp. You should let us know where you are going."

"Papa," I said quickly, answering him in German. "This is Umberto. He's from Italy, and he sang "Torna Piccina" for me."

I said it all in one breath, embarrassed that Father had found me sitting with a young man, dangling our feet in the water.

"It is nice meeting you, young man," Father said.

Umberto removed a blade of grass he was chewing, stood, and stretched out his hand to Father.

"It is very nice meeting you, sir."

"I'll expect you back in the barrack in a short while, Asya," Papa said as he turned to walk inside.

"Yes, Papa."

"Thank you so much for the song." I smiled as I got to my feet and turned to walk away.

"Here, Asya," Umberto said, smiling, "your ball slippers. You'll need them for a few more days."

His outstretched hand held my ugly, grotesque shoes, newspaper protruding from both, and I felt ashamed as I took them. Then he held up his own shoes, holes in both soles, and held together with ugly string, newspaper protruding from them as well.

"We'll make the best dressed couple at the ball," he said, as both of us began to laugh, the laughter mingling with the sound of the water running in the "brook."

That night the lights surrounding the concentration camp were not turned on. All of the prisoners had apparently been loaded into the freight cars, and ss guards and their dogs patrolled up and down the dead, silent track. In our barrack nobody read Chekov or recited Pushkin's poetry. Everyone whispered about the rumors of the possible surrender of German troops and the general situation on different fronts. The Allies were rumored to be very close to us, and the Soviet army was said to be approaching Berlin. I didn't listen to the discussions. I wasn't at all interested. All I could think of was Umberto, his singing, the brook, the birds.

Will I ever see him again? I wondered.

I remembered how often Father had sung "Torna Piccina" to me when I was small. Now I hoped he would never sing that particular song again. It would be Umberto's and my song from now on. Slowly, the whispering stopped; the oil lamp was turned way down, an occasional cough yielded to soft snoring, shifting in the straw, then finally silence.

Everyone must have fallen asleep, I thought, as I began to feel sleepy, too. *But what was that?* I lifted my head to listen. *Is it a mandolin, or am I dreaming? Yes, it is. It must be coming from the Italian barracks. No,* I thought, *it sounds much closer than that. Torna Piccina. Oh, no, it's him. It's Umberto. Torna Piccina means "Come back, little one." Does he want me to come out? Of course not. How can I? It's dark. It's nighttime, and Mother and Father are right here. What would Mother think? A "lady" would never come out.*

I slowly crept to the window and knelt by the opening. Yes, there he was. I could only make out a silhouette in the moonlight. "Torna Piccina mia, come back, my little one." I wanted to jump out of that window, rush to Umberto, and never to see the camp, my parents, my ugly shoes, the rotten soup and dark bread, never again to hear the frightening roar of bombers overhead. Suddenly, inexplicably, I was almost happy that Belgrade was behind me! In that moment I knew that I would marry an Italian. No one else would do. How stupid of me, I thought. I'll never see him again. He said something was about to happen. Whatever that "something" was, I would never see him again.

A couple more songs followed, and as my eyes filled with tears I could no longer make out the dark silhouette in the moonlight. The mandolin died away along with the singing. The night became still once more. I quietly crept back to my straw bed, covering my face with the blanket, trying to preserve the vision of Umberto and to protect the lingering sound of his voice, wishing I had gone out to sit beside him.

The next morning, April 19, before sunrise a loud explosion awakened everyone and was followed quickly by a series of explosions. The eastern sky was just beginning to lighten. It must have been about 5:00 a.m. Everyone in the barrack jumped to their feet, dressing as hurriedly as possible. Everyone wondered if the camp had been bombed or if we were under an attack of some kind. As soon as I dressed, I rushed outside to see huge billows of smoke by the railroad tracks. All the freight cars were ablaze and in ruins. There were no guards or dogs in sight. Another and yet another explosion followed as I watched.

"Dear God. They have blown up all those prisoners," someone said with a gasp. I heard a scream from somewhere. I'm not sure if it came from our group.

"What is happening?" someone asked. The Bentin office was empty. "Where are the Germans going?"

The road leading into town was alive with military vehicles. The forced laborers stood around the camp in a daze. Nobody knew what was happening. People ran to the kitchen and storeroom carrying foodstuffs out, and the small office that Herr Mueller had occupied was on fire. Some men rushed and tried to put the fire out. Another building caught fire, and some of the men formed a bucket line and brought it under control.

Just then the commandant of the camps drove up to the building with a man I believe was the chief engineer from the tunnel. The commandant used the loudspeaker system to announce that an "unfortunate accident" had taken place at the railroad track and that again there would be no work assignments for the day.

"Please," his announcement continued, "everyone is to remain in their barracks while the accident is dealt with. Anyone seen outside the barracks will be shot."

That was a sufficiently clear command to get our attention. Everyone immediately returned to the barracks. A larger than usual flight of Allied bombers passed overhead just a few minutes later, buzzing lower and louder than before, and the flights continued at regular intervals.

It was April 19, and everyone knew that the following day was Hitler's birthday. Everyone expected that the news reports from the OKW and Goebbels's speech about new victories would be broadcast over the camp loudspeakers today or tomorrow. Throughout the years of the occupation, if one listened to the radio, "new victories" were always announced for Hitler's birthday. New country, new territory, countless lives sacrificed to the ego of a madman. And here in the camp, the loudspeaker system frequently broadcast OKW announcements, German advances, or victories—real or imagined.

Tension continued to mount in the camp. German personnel were seen in the office, but the SS guards were conspicuously absent. The laborers stayed in or by their designated barracks, expecting the guards to return at any moment. No food was served throughout the day. Some of the vegetables Father and I had brought the day before were still left and were boiled, but few people ate.

As the afternoon wore on into evening, the sound of artillery could be heard drawing closer, and fiery blasts lit the hills. Allied air flights continued almost without interruption. The freight cars were still smoldering, sending a terrible odor throughout the April air.

Nobody in the barrack slept. German military vehicles kept moving all through the night. At about 2 or 3 a.m. on April 20, the camp loudspeaker system announced that all barracks should prepare for possible relocation. Everyone began to gather their few remaining belongings together. The blankets were neatly folded and the oil lamp was turned out to comply with a complete blackout order. "Does that mean that we are going to be bombed?" someone asked. No one knew the answer, of course, but there was no sound of planes. Harsh German voices, military commands, and vehicles were heard constantly from the road.

At about 8 a.m., a single Allied plane flew over dropping leaflets. They looked like tiny dots against the sky as they began to glide toward the ground. We ran, reaching into the air, trying to catch them. They were printed in German and demanded German surrender, stating that Allied troops were just on the other side of the hills surrounding the town and would enter Blankenburg that afternoon. The leaflets issued an ultimatum: all firing was to cease. If even one antiaircraft shell was fired at Allied planes after noon, the area would be leveled before the troops marched in.

"So it's really happening," someone said. "The Germans are losing. The information from the concentration camp prisoners was correct." But no one answered. We looked at each other, realizing that for those prisoners it was all over. Their charred bodies were lying somewhere amidst the tracks and mangled freight cars in the field.

Remaining German personnel and guards were frantically burning papers and documents. Their trucks were packed and ready to retreat, but there was clearly no planned relocation of the forced laborers.

Suddenly I heard Mother's voice, as calm and self-assured as I remembered her before the war. "I simply can't believe that it is all over. It's just too sudden. I'm going into town to listen to the radio."

They were the first words I had heard her speak normally in weeks, and she sounded perfectly sensible.

"It's insanity to go into town now," Father tried to reason with her. "Max and Olga may not even be there."

"Well, I'm going. Besides, they're Germans now. I will probably be safer with them than here in the camp. Who knows what the guards might do before they leave? They could decide to kill us all. I'm just as safe there as here."

Father knew it was useless to try to argue with Mother when she sounded so in control and had made up her mind about something. "If you must go, fine," he said with resignation, "but if you aren't back before noon, I shall have to go looking for you. So please try to be back by then."

"Papa," I asked, "are you going to just let her go?"

"What can I do?" he said with a shrug. "She is so stubborn. Besides, she speaks German like a native. She'll get by fine, I'm sure."

"Try to listen to Goebbels's speech. Find out what's going on," someone ventured.

"Well," Father said, "if you have to go, go now. God only knows what will happen after the noon deadline. I pray that the German antiaircraft guns won't fire after noon. Go on, go on," Father kept repeating as he helped Mother to get her things together. As soon as he helped her into her coat, she began to walk briskly toward the road into town, still crowded with German military vehicles.

Just over the hills, black smoke could be seen rising everywhere, the artillery sounding only a mile or two away. Allied bombers were buzzing high in the sky, too high for the German flack to be effective. The bombers usually flew over Blankenburg toward Magdeburg, but today they just circled. A few flack bursts could be seen and heard, leaving only a round puff of smoke against the blue sky. The planes were staying out of range.

Father grew more upset and nervous with each passing moment, now saying he wished he had used force to restrain Mother from going into town. Everyone's head was turned toward the sky, trying to figure out what the bombers were going to do. Our forced labor camp had been emptied of German personnel—no guards, no engineers, no soldiers. It looked as though the entire German army had assembled on the road heading into town.

Suddenly the bombers disappeared, the buzzing sound of aircraft ceased, and there was an eerie silence. Only the sound of motors, brakes, and shouts in German were heard from the road. In a few minutes more, the artillery in the distance grew quiet. The antiaircraft flack guns were silent, and even the military vehicles on the road stopped moving. Everything stood still, as if the world were holding its breath. The breeze could be heard whispering, swaying the young buds on the trees. Even the birds grew quiet as an awesome silence filled the atmosphere. Church bells rang from the town, the only time in the camp I remember hearing them ring the hour: one . . . two . . . three . . . twelve. Noon! Some of the people in the barrack were on their knees, praying, holding the crumpled leaflets in their hands.

The low hum and drone of bombers began then, growing slowly louder. I looked up to see them flying much lower this time, as everyone held their breath. Then the sound of explosions filled the air as the antiaircraft flack guns opened up from positions in the hills around the town. Within seconds, bombs began dropping like hail on the hills, trying to blow up the gun installations. One plane was hit and was falling, whining, twisting, and turning in the air trailing black smoke. Then a loud explosion. I saw parachutes, then another bomber began to fall, more flack, more bombs. Artillery shells were whistling just above our heads. The whole world around us became a crazy holocaust all at once.

Several bombs hit the military convoy on the road, and now the vehicles began to move again, pushing damaged vehicles to the side. Tanks appeared from nowhere, cutting across the fields. I had no idea whether they were Germans or Allies. A lot of the vehicles on the road stood still then, and German soldiers began running, many tearing their uniforms off as they ran in every direction, while others ran along the road now littered with equipment and bodies. Several of the forced laborers picked up rifles and other weapons dropped by Germans and began shooting at the fleeing soldiers.

The air was filled with smoke and human cries and the roar of tanks. The laborers were almost hysterical, and screams of pain from wounded soldiers mingled with shouts of happiness and joy from prisoners whose freedom had finally arrived. Many of us ran to enter the tunnel, hoping the thick walls of the munitions factory would withstand the bombs. Then the planes disappeared as quickly as they had appeared.

As we ventured outside the relative safety of the tunnel, we saw that the entire forced labor camp was engulfed in flames, every single barrack ablaze. I ran toward our barrack, hoping to save something—blankets, pots, something—but it was too late. We now had only what was on our backs: torn, dirty clothes and the tin cup and spoon we always carried in our pockets. The jealously guarded suitcases were now lost. We would learn later that the Italian prisoners had rioted and set the entire camp on fire during the general hysteria. I lost track of time and was surprised to notice that it was growing dark. The sky was red, flames all around me, and in the near distance I could see fires lighting up the sky above the town.

Somehow I became separated from Father and the rest of the Russians in the chaos of running to the barrack. I decided to walk closer to the road because of the burning camp buildings around me. I was afraid the flaming structures would collapse on top of me. The roadway was dark, but from the light of the fires I could see it littered with equipment and bodies. A huge tank suddenly loomed in front of me, smoldering, looking like a monstrous fortress against the flames and the red sky.

Seeing bodies around me, I began to worry about Father. Was he alive? I began calling "Papa, Papa," and running back toward the tunnel. Someone stopped me to say that it would be very dangerous to go into the tunnel again because of the danger of explosion from stored ammunition. So I stood there, in the middle of the road, alone, crying and calling to my father. The artillery was still blasting everywhere, and it seemed so useless to call. Nobody could hear above the whistling shells.

Planes appeared again, but this time they were flying so low that I could see the silhouette of the pilot against the crimson sky. They were fighter planes that seemed to fire at everything that moved on the ground below them. I found myself sitting on the ground, stunned with sheer terror. The shrieking of the engines of the fighter planes, the shrill whistle of bullets flying all around me, the boom of the heavy guns on tanks that were now moving from all directions again, the human screams—it all sounded so unreal. I stood up to look around.

It was as though I were a spectator at a horror show, not feeling a part of it all. It was a nightmare with all the demons unleashed at the same time. I felt a shiver go through my entire body. I felt an inexplicable excitement running through every nerve in my body like an electric current! Was it all real? I wondered, just as a strong wind knocked me to the ground. But how strange, because there is no wind. As I laid there on the ground, I realized that the wind had been caused by a fighter plane that flew almost over my head, machine guns blazing.

I began to crawl off the road toward a ditch to escape another plane I could see diving toward me. As I rolled into the ditch I stopped, not daring to move any further, as I felt something warm beneath me. I touched my dress and felt that it was warm and sticky. Had I been hit? Was it my blood? I moved my hands about slowly in the darkness and felt hair, coarse hair—a horse's mane. I continued feeling with the other hand—a human form. A soldier. Was he dead? I heard a faint moan, wondered if my body weight was hurting the man or the horse, and slowly rolled to the side, away from whatever I was on top of. I was lying on my back, my blood-soaked dress sticking to my body. Suddenly, foolishly, I wondered what Mother's reaction would be if she saw me at that moment.

I was lying on my back, looking upward, and I saw the moon appearing behind the smoke and the hideous red glare of the fires around me. Fighter planes crossed the moon resembling monstrous birds of prey searching for something to attack. The air smelled foul. I could see a few stars where a gentle breeze pushed the smoke clouds aside.

I wondered if the stars cared what was happening here below. I remembered Aunt 'Lyena telling me once, a lifetime ago, that the universe was held in God's hand. Well, He had certainly let it slip tonight, I thought. Tonight was definitely Judgment Day. I wondered if Mother had had a chance to listen to the news and if Goebbels knew what was happening. Or was he reassuring the Fuehrer of new victories for his birthday today, April 20, 1945?

I heard a soft moan next to me. I had forgotten that I was lying between a blood-soaked horse and a dead or dying man. If it's a German soldier, I thought, "Good! Let him die!" I slowly turned toward the sound. My eyes had become accustomed to the darkness, and I clearly saw a German soldier and put my hand on his forehead. Oh, how stupid this all is, I thought. How can I wish him dead? He too has someone, somewhere, waiting for him. He too has plans, hopes, dreams. His eyes were closed, and his lips moved slightly as he tried to say something. I bent closer, placing my ear next to his lips, but only a deep sigh reached my ear, a very gentle breath against my ear lobe, then silence.

I guess he's dead, and I don't even know his name. He died next to me, and I don't even know his name. But what does it matter? I drew back and noticed that his eyes were now open. I brought my face close to his and made a terribly silly face at him, to reassure myself that he was really dead, and then gently pulled his eyelids closed.

The blood on my dress, all over me, was beginning to dry, and my dress was a crusty, stiff mess. I crawled, inched myself out of the ditch, and began to make my way back to the tunnel, desperate to find living people. As I drew close to the tunnel, it seemed that people were everywhere. I heard someone call out to Father, telling him that I was here, but that I was badly wounded. As I approached the tunnel entrance, Father rushed toward me, his eyes filled with unspeakable terror.

"I'm all right, Papa," I called. "I'm not hurt, just terribly tired. Has Mama come back yet?" But I knew the answer before he had a chance to speak. I looked toward the town to see the glow from fires burning there as well. She was someplace in a burning hell like I had just left.

Someone put a blanket over me and then changed their mind as it became clear what a mess I was. The women formed a ring around me and took my dress off. Then someone suggested that they take everything off since the tunnel factory had cold running water. They stripped me of all my clothes, helped me with a sponge bath, and rewrapped me in a blanket. Someone washed all my clothing and hung it to dry on a tree branch just outside the tunnel entrance.

My dress looked funny hanging there, swaying in the breeze and out-lined against the red sky. I was completely exhausted, and suddenly I thought of myself as Joan of Arc: It's me hanging there against the crim-son sky. I'll soon burn, and the gentle voices of all the slave laborers will come out of the tunnel to mourn me. Or will they? What's one more dead among so many? I think that was my final thought that night, as I fell asleep leaning against Father's arm, tightly wrapped in a scratchy blanket.

I awoke to the sound of strange voices coming from the road leading into town. Everyone else stood at the entrance to the tunnel, staring in amazement. I ran to join them, clutching the blanket tightly, and could not believe my eyes when I saw foreign troops marching along the road and driving foreign-looking vehicles. Who were they? Everyone hoped and prayed they were not Russian.

I listened carefully to the voices and shouts of the soldiers and thought, Oh, thank God they are not Russians. I heard some English words, but they were not British, even though the language sounded familiar. Of course, it must be the American troops.

"I think it will be safe for us to go into town now, Asya" Father said softly. "We need to look for Mama."

Father retrieved my clothes from the tree where they had been hung to dry and brought them to me. Two women held the blanket for me so that I could dress. The freshly laundered clothes smelled so fresh. The blood stains hadn't come out completely, but the clothes were all fresh. I felt clean again.

TWENTY

The Price of Liberation

Father took my hand, and together we left the tunnel. Father looked grim, worry creating deep lines in his forehead. His grip on my hand grew noticeably firmer as we began the long walk into the village, walking alongside American troops and their vehicles.

The jeeps, speeding along and weaving in and out to avoid obstructions, were something I had never seen. It was exciting to walk next to the Americans—the strange sounding language, the smudged faces of tired soldiers. Strangest of all was seeing almost all of them chewing something but never swallowing.

Father struck up a conversation with one soldier, and it seemed that Papa felt young again, back in uniform himself, as he quickened his pace, matching the soldier's and pulling me along by the hand. The soldier offered Father a cigarette, and they paused for a second to light it. He asked Father what the yellow armbands that we wore meant. Father explained that we were from Yugoslavia and had been held as forced laborers, that the yellow armbands were required by the Germans as identification, that we had all been "branded in a way."

"You should have shot the goddamned Kraut that put it on you," the soldier said, and turned his head to spit out a big wad of something. I turned to see what it was, but couldn't figure it out. The soldier gave Father several more cigarettes and sped his pace, leaving us behind. As we walked, Father now tore off the yellow armbands we had been forced to wear.

"Papa," I asked, what was that ugly mess the soldier spat out?"

"Oh, that was chewing gum. Remember it was being sold in Belgrade and we would never let you have it?"

I remembered. I had always wondered what it tasted like." Oh, well, I thought, if it were tasty, he surely wouldn't have spat it out.

I was almost skipping, trying to keep up with Father's brisk walk as he kept pace with the soldiers. I listened to the conversations of the soldiers as we walked alongside, but couldn't understand much of it. It was so different from the British English I knew and had spoken at home.

We had to cross the street to get to the Zengovitzes' house, but we waited, unable to cross because of vehicles, tanks, and an endless double line of German soldiers marching after the vehicles, their hands clasped on top of their heads, some clad only in shirt and trousers, some in full uniform. They were prisoners of the Americans now.

It was a strange experience to watch this once invincible, mighty army looking so pathetic. Some of their faces clearly showed great relief, others displayed anger, and some held their heads high, defiant. There were many wounded from both armies, bandages revealing blood spots, some limping.

American soldiers marched on each side of the prisoners, guns held in front of them, but there were no shiny boots and no rubber hoses. Finally there was a space between units, and Father and I quickly crossed the road. It was just a few steps then, until Father stopped in front of what had been a two-story building.

"Well," he said, "here we are. But dear God . . ."

Half of the building was collapsed on the ground. Father asked someone where the occupants of the building were.

"If they survived, they will all be in the village square reading the new ordinances and rules posted by the American Occupation Forces."

Father turned to me, worry and concern showing on his face.

"Asya, will you please stay here just in case you should see Mama or Max and Olga. I'll go to the village square to look for them."

I sat on the curb, in front of the building, fascinated to watch as heavy tanks passed on the narrow village street, raising clouds of dust. Once a tank moved back and forth several times to crush debris in order to allow other vehicles to get through. As one unit of American troops passed, they were singing or chanting something that made no sense to me. I would later learn that they were "counting cadence," a marching chant meant to keep everyone in step.

Father returned in a short time to tell me that he had found the Zengo-vitz family. Max, Olga, and their daughter, Tanya, were in the village center, alive although their apartment was gone. Mother, they believed, might be in the basement of the building.

"Didn't Mama stay with them?" I asked, alarmed. "That's why she came into town, to see them and to listen to the latest news on the radio."

"Well," Father answered, "at noon the air-raid sirens warned people of the approaching bombers, and the villagers all rushed to the shelters. The Zengovitz family went, too, and Mama went with them, but when they reached the shelter she was stopped because of her armband. The shelter was for Germans only. Mama was turned away.

"Mama ran back to the apartment building to take shelter in the basement, and when Olga returned she saw that the building had received a direct hit and half of it had collapsed. She hasn't seen Mama since."

"But why aren't they here? Why aren't they here looking for her? What are they doing?" I demanded.

Father shrugged, a faint smile on his face, a smile that people have when the situation is all too tragic, all too sad, and there is nothing left but to smile helplessly.

"It's hard to believe, but they're standing in line to receive special food rations for foreigners. Apparently the Americans have issued an order to provide extra food rations to all former occupants of the camps . . . because the camp prisoners have been deprived for so long."

"But," I stammered, "but . . . I thought they had decided to become 'German.' They weren't in the forced labor camp. Don't you remember how they ignored us in Belgrade? How Tanya was sent to school in Germany and joined the Hitler Jugend? How Max paraded in his brown shirt with the swastika armband?"

"There are opportunists in every war, Anochka. The Zengovitzes have become Russian once again. People look out for themselves the best way they know how." Father's shoulders slumped as his voice trailed off.

"Aren't you angry, Papa? How about all those principles and the strong, sound foundation . . . the ship in stormy waters . . . remember all those things you told me?" I was in tears, unable to understand how Father, who so solemnly believed in human decency, pride, and high principles, could treat this incident with such ease. These were "friends," after all, once close friends.

"I am glad to hear that you remember all those things," Father answered slowly. "Never allow a single incident or disappointment to change your own convictions. Never! As I said before many times, people look out for themselves the best way THEY know how. But not you! Remember that."

Father had a habit of setting his jaw and compressing his lips in a certain way when he had said all he had to say about a subject, when he would not discuss it further. I had grown to know that facial expression well. It was there now, and I knew the conversation had ended.

We stood together in front of the bombed-out structure where Mother had been seen. Father put both hands on the back of his neck, moving his head back and forth slowly, eyes closed, his face revealing pain and fatigue.

"Let us begin now," he said, "we shall first try to determine where the bomb originally hit. It must have been almost in the exact middle," he was talking to himself as he looked carefully up and around the remaining structure. "Then we shall very carefully try to remove the largest beams. But we must be very cautious, because the whole thing might collapse."

Father kept steadily talking while frantically digging around a large beam that lay across what looked like an opening of some sort. Fine dust rose to form a cloud around him.

"Here, Papa," I said, wanting to help. "Let me hold up this end of the beam so that you can dig underneath to see if there is an opening going down." Just then, a rumble was heard behind us, and a piece of wall toppled down.

"Asya, please," Father said wearily. "Please, let me do it. I couldn't stand it if I had to dig for both of you in the rubble. Please . . . go and sit on the curb and watch the remaining part of the building for me. If it should begin to shift, call out to warn me. Really, please go and let me do it." And he gently pushed me aside.

I walked away, carefully stepping over the rubble, and sat on the curb in front of the ruins. The half of the building that remained standing revealed the partial remains of once homey apartments. The building was still settling, and dust billowed up following slight rumbles. The house, or building, next door was completely gone, just a pile of rubble, a dog whining and digging furiously at the debris.

On the street in front of me, the military formation continued seemingly without end. Roaring tanks continued to crush any rubble in the street, clearing the way for trucks, jeeps, ambulances, and marching soldiers. The American troops were jubilant, high spirited in spite of deep lines showing on their faces, reflecting the horrors of the battle the night before.

Most of the Americans looked grim but determined. I watched them and wondered how many battles they had been through and how many of them had been left in a shallow grave along the way. Every now and then one of them would smile, teeth appearing exceptionally white because of the dark smudges on their faces. I noticed that almost every one of them was chewing a big wad of chewing gum.

The inner columns were German soldiers—now POWs—looking pathetic as they marched between columns of armed American troops. They marched with their hands on top of their heads, uniforms in disarray, staring straight ahead. So different from the brutal, overpowering arrogance of the guards at the labor and concentration camps. Although certainly deserved, it must have been a crushing humiliation to have suffered defeat and capture in their homeland.

One of the passing Americans tossed something in my lap without a word. A Hershey bar. I had never seen a Hershey bar before, and I held it tightly in my dirty hand, afraid to lose it or have it taken from me. I wanted to share the bar with Father, and I looked back at the ruin wondering what was taking him so long. The roar of the tanks, screeching of brakes, singing and shouting of troops, and now the hysterical cries of a woman next to a neighboring ruin, all blended into continuous noise. A nightmare.

Finally, I heard Father calling to me and I saw him standing at the opening in the ruins. His hands and face were scratched. He was completely covered with plaster dust. His usually erect, proud figure was now bent, his bright blue eyes revealing deep pain and sorrow. Suddenly he looked like a very old man.

"Asya," he said, "I've found her. She is somewhat dusty but just as beautiful as ever. Come and help me remove the beam from her legs. I think both of her legs are broken."

I ran toward him, thinking as I ran, "Thank God she is alive. Her legs will heal in time. I clutched the Hershey bar tightly in my hand, hoping it was big enough to split three ways now that we had found Mother, and I placed it in my pocket. I quickly glanced down at my dress. He had said that she looked as beautiful as ever, and I wondered what she would say about my appearance. My hair hadn't been combed or brushed in a couple of days. It will be dark in the basement, I thought. Maybe she won't notice.

I followed Father, stepping carefully on the remains of people's possessions. We made our way into the cellar, and the smell of dust, smoldering wires, and pickling juice filled my senses. The only light in the cellar streamed through the opening into which we had slowly descended. There, among tangled wires, plumbing pipes, and broken jars, I saw my mother.

She was lying on her back, her head turned slightly to the side, facing away from me. A tiny trickle of dried blood traced a thin line from her temple down her pale cheek and down her neck. Her black hair was covered with fine dust, giving the appearance of heavy graying. Her hand rested on a large beam that lay across her legs, and a large pipe and steel wires were lying on top of her stomach. Her dress beneath the pipe and wires was torn and heavily caked with dried blood. I thought her hand moved, but then realized that a light from outside fell on her diamond ring, reflecting brilliant colors of green, red, and blue.

"Papa, is Mama . . . alive?" I asked, not daring to say "dead."

"For me, she will always be alive," he answered, as a tender smile crossed his lips.

We slowly began to move the heavy beam that had fallen across her legs, Father carefully calculating each movement because of the danger of causing additional collapse. I don't know how long it took us to free Mother from the ugly tangle of wires, pipes, and beams. Her legs had been shattered. We found what looked like a torn sheet, and Father gently wrapped her legs and stomach. I picked her up under her arms, Father took her legs, and slowly, almost dragging her body, we brought her out into the light.

Outside, the sun was shining and a gentle breeze felt good against my dusty cheeks. We laid Mother on the sidewalk. I sat next to her on the curb, placing her head in my lap, while Father walked to a nursery, a few houses away, to try to borrow a cart of some kind. I sat there stunned. Suddenly I had become a part of the nightmare.

I was trying to fully comprehend what was taking place. I sharply remembered what she had told me that day in Belgrade, standing atop the ruin of General Nazimov's house. "Never look for me in that," she had said, shuddering, pointing at the ruin. "I would never go into a basement. If I have to die, it will be out in the open or in my own home, but never in the basement. I hate the feeling."

How terrible that the thing she dreaded so much was where she had met her end—alone! This woman, my mother, who was so beautiful, so very talented, so very accomplished, was lying covered with blood, her head cradled in my lap, legs crushed, covered in plaster dust, and wearing an old and torn dress—the exact opposite of everything she had striven for all her life, killed before her forty-fifth birthday.

I looked up just then to see an American soldier taking a picture of me holding Mother on the curb. I wanted to yell at the top of my lungs at the soldiers. What was wrong with them. Couldn't they see that my mother was dead? How dare they continue marching and singing. Isn't everything supposed to die with her? I had seen so many people die a tragic, violent death, and I had been so certain that if Mother were to die, everything would cease to exist for me. I was angry and bewildered by everyone's indifference. Why do I feel this way? I never felt the same deep love for her that I have always felt for Father, I thought.

I tried to remember when Mother had ever bent to kiss me. I suddenly had an urge to kiss her, to embrace her as I had never been allowed to as a child. As I bent closer to her, my tears fell on her face, dissolving and smearing the dried blood on her temple, and the coldness of her cheek brought back the memory of the cold, dead body Aunt 'Lyena had pushed my head to kiss when I was still a toddler. My lips felt that same "death" coldness once more and I could not kiss her again.

With my tears continuing to fall on her cheek, I gently stroked her hair and then tightly pressed her head between my hands. Somehow I was again holding the chocolate bar, and it was now melted in my hand and smeared on her hair. I threw away the melted bar and sticky wrapper, and wiped my hands on my dress.

I was angry; I no longer cared if my dress was messy. She can't see it anyway. Why, why couldn't I do this, hold her like this, when she was warm and beautiful? I bent close to see if I could smell the familiar fragrance of her perfume that always excited me when she walked by. But all I was able to smell was dust, pickling juice, and singed hair. I began to shake with sobs. I had always longed to embrace her, to bury my face in her neck or her breast, to smell her fragrance, to feel her softness and her warmth, only to be held at arm's length. Now she was cold and clammy and had a smell of death about her, and I knew I would never again have a chance to embrace her.

I heard a noise and turned to see Father coming toward me, pushing a rusty old wheelbarrow in front of him. His once white shirt neatly tucked in, his old, dirty tie hanging crookedly on the collar, now too large, making him appear even skinnier. His pants were baggy and torn at one knee, with another old tie serving as a belt. He held his old felt hat in one hand as he pushed the wheelbarrow.

In spite of his pathetic appearance, his great loss, and the crushing pain of the past few hours, Father's head was high as always, his shoulders straight, and for a moment I saw him in his beautiful tsarist uniform holding a bouquet of flowers for his lady—just a flash from the family album. With an apologetic gesture and a faint smile he turned to me.

"I am going to put my hat beneath her head, because the streets are so uneven, and there is debris everywhere. It will be softer for her head."

We placed Mother's lifeless body in the wheelbarrow, Father gently placing the hat beneath her head. Lovingly, he rewrapped her legs and stomach in the dirty sheet and began pushing the wheelbarrow toward the cemetery chapel where she could stay until final arrangements could be made. I walked at the front, a few steps ahead, moving quickly to keep Mother's head from bouncing whenever Father maneuvered the wheelbarrow over bumps and around obstacles.

We were silent and walked slowly, each of us immersed in our own thoughts. I suddenly wished I hadn't thrown away the melted Hershey bar because I was so hungry. We hadn't eaten anything in a day or two. The confusion of the last day of the war, at least for us the last day, the sounds of victorious American troops singing and shouting to one another, the muffled roar of something collapsing and sending clouds of dust into the air, the cries of people digging through the rubble, the rumble of a tank . . . all again was detached from me. Once again, I did not feel a part of it all, only a spectator.

Father began conversing with Mother as though she was taking a walk with him, and suddenly I felt so terribly alone. My thoughts wandered and once again I was back in "my" Belgrade before its destruction, in my favorite spot where, lying on my back nestled in deep grass, I watched fluffy white clouds against the deep blue sky, building endless dreams, seeing not clouds, but castles, animals, angels, ships . . . handsome brave warriors who would conquer the world for me, take me far away . . .

A screech of brakes startled me as a hand pulled mine, and I slipped, almost falling from the curb.

"Fraulein, what have you to trade for a candy bar?"

I jerked my hand away, and Father was instantly between me and the jeep with the soldier in it.

"Goddamned Krauts, we should have killed every one of you," the soldier said with a sneer as the jeep sped away.

Father's firm, gentle hand was on my shoulder then. "They have no way of knowing that we are not German," he said firmly. "Perhaps we should not have discarded our armbands. Soldiers are soldiers. Always remember that, and always keep your distance from them."

I wondered how long this would last. First we were spat upon and humiliated by the Germans, and now we had been liberated from the Germans, but we were still treated like dogs. I looked at Father, whose head was high and proud. No, I realized, one must remain strong in spite of everything. One must retain one's human dignity under any circumstances.

We walked even slower then, Father finally experiencing the heaviness of the wheel barrow, the tragedy of the day, and hunger. Both of us were exhausted. Father was silent, and as I looked at his face I knew that he was reliving his life with Mother. That now, with her body in this pathetic wheelbarrow, he was saying good-bye to her, to his life, to his very reason for living. His entire reason for being was now a lifeless bundle in a wheelbarrow. His eyes were wide open, and I saw a large tear roll down his cheek and nestle in his moustache.

Strangely enough, I felt no pain then, no loss. I was only puzzled that nothing had stopped, that life simply went on. I guessed that the war must be over, at least for us. I thought it probably meant that we no longer had to worry about seeking shelter from bombs or artillery or to be at the mercy of German soldiers.

I looked at a new group of prisoners now marching past us, hands clasped on top of their heads. At least no one was spitting at them, calling them names. At least they were regarded as human beings by their American captors, not "Untermenschen." And I knew that nobody would force them into a train of freight cars and blow them up.

I wondered if the American soldiers knew what horrors had taken place two days earlier, if they cared, or if they regarded all those things as just a part of war. But as I remembered the first soldier we had spoken to, and his comment, "You should have shot those goddamned Krauts!" I knew they would be shocked and angry.

"Asya, here we are," Father said, turning the wheelbarrow into the entrance of the town cemetery and the last few yards to the front of the chapel. Gently, we lifted Mother's body from the wheelbarrow to carry her inside the chapel and place her on the floor in front of the altar.

We knelt together before the altar, and Father began to pray quietly. What is he praying for? I wondered. I know that I was kneeling there deep in my own thoughts. What is to happen now? Where will we go? What is to become of us? When so many people have died, when even Mother has died, why am I still alive? No answers came, of course, and I didn't expect any. I crossed myself and rose to follow Father out of the chapel. Outside, on the steps, he put his arm around my shoulders to say gently, "Wait just a minute, Asinka. I'll be right back."

Father went back into the Chapel, returning in a minute with a leather pouch.

"I almost forgot," he said in answer to my questioning look. "Mother wore this pouch inside her dress ever since the Germans took our home. This will come in handy, now that we have nothing."

I looked in bewilderment at the pouch which Father now put around his neck and inside his shirt.

"She slipped these jewels into her dress" Father replied to my silent question, "just as the Germans walked in to take our home in Dedinye. They were on her dresser . . ."

We walked aimlessly then, not taking any notice of the hectic pace of life around us. We returned the wheelbarrow, and slowly made our way back to the tunnel, the only place we had to spend the night. As we walked, Father asked how I had become so covered with blood the afternoon before, during that last battle at the forced labor camp. I told him about the battle and the ditch I crawled into to try to escape the planes, and the dying soldier and dead horse I was lying on. As we drew near to the tunnel, he asked me to show him where I had seen the horse.

Father drew his pocket knife, opened it, and cut large chunks of meat from the flank of the dead horse. We slowly walked back to the tunnel to spend the night there with the others from the camp. Father built a fire in one of the iron carts that ran on tracks inside the tunnel and roasted the meat for all to share. I didn't realize how hungry I was. I thought it the best meat I had ever tasted.

I could still hear vehicles, tanks, and the shouts of American troops from the road and occasional low flying fighter planes apparently patrolling the road from above. As I looked around that night, I saw that all the faces around me looked relaxed. Safe and secure for the first time in a very, very long time. But, I realized sadly, Mother's face would never again be among them.

Early the next morning, Father and I returned to the cemetery to make burial arrangements and found the chapel floor covered with bodies— German soldiers. The bodies were placed very close to one another because of the number of dead. Mother was at the front, directly in front of the altar, and we had to make our way through what seemed a sea of bodies. About halfway across the floor, I came to the body of a dead German soldier lying on his back with his eyes wide open, and I realized that I had no choice but to step over his head because of the crowding. How can I do this and remain graceful, I wondered, not even thinking that he could no longer see.

I gathered my dress between my legs, held it tightly, and stepped over him. There, I thought, I did that modestly and quite gracefully. I'm sure Mother will be pleased. But what am I thinking? Why do I care? Everybody here is dead. What difference does it make if one is graceful or not? Why do I care now what Mother will think?" A cold chill ran down my back as I became sharply aware that I was surrounded by death.

Father encountered a problem in securing a plot for Mother's burial. The German authorities initially refused permission, stating that the cemetery was reserved for citizens only. They indicated that as a resident of the labor camps, she should be buried there, in an area already containing the bodies of slave laborers who had died constructing the tunnel.

Father was adamant that she would not lie in some anonymous field, and he appealed to the American commander. It took an extra day or two, but permission to bury Mother in the Blankenburg city cemetery was soon arranged. That first day, however, we returned to the tunnel to await the assignment of a burial plot.

When a burial plot was assigned, we stopped at the nursery to once again borrow the wheelbarrow. At the chapel we placed Mother's body in the wheelbarrow in order to carry her to the gravesite. I was amazed at the number of freshly dug graves, and wondered who had dug them all—in two rows. We passed those and turned left down a pretty pathway to see an open grave on the right side of the path.

The casket, a hastily made, plain wooden box, stood next to the open grave assigned to Mother. Father and I lifted Mother's body from the wheelbarrow to place her in the casket. Father lovingly covered her legs and stomach with the same old sheet we had found in the ruins.

A handful of people from our barrack came to the burial to say goodbye. We had no priest, of course. There were no Russian Orthodox churches in the area. Father and I stood at the head of the open casket as he began saying prayers, and the others joined in. For a moment, God forgive me, I suddenly envisioned Aunt 'Lyena standing at the side of the casket and laughing.

Then, as if on command, everyone began to cry loudly, looking critically at me. I could not cry. I had no tears left. I had cried ceaselessly when I held her head in my lap on that sidewalk. But now, inexplicably, I felt a strange sort of relief . . . a certain twinge of freedom that produced a sort of gladness in my heart, not tears.

Two men in the group picked up the casket cover, and Father held a hammer. Someone in the group said to Father, "It's a shame to let those rings go to waste. You know, rings like that . . ." Someone nudged the person, and they resumed crying. The casket was still open, and each in turn bent to kiss Mother for the last time. A chill ran down my back. No. Not again. I don't want to feel the coldness of death again; I don't want that to be my last memory of her. I'm alive, free . . .

"Asya, Mother is going now." I felt Father's hand firm on my shoulder, but I jerked away. The day was bright and lovely, and the cemetery grounds were alive with bright new flowers and buds and the promise of spring, the promise of new life. I jumped over the open grave and ran from the cemetery and onto the road.

The April air felt warm and fresh on my face. The sky was the bluest I thought I had ever seen, the air filled with the songs of delightfully chirping birds and the sweet smell of new flowers. It seemed the most beautiful spring I had ever seen.

I came upon a German military motorcycle with its key in the ignition, and without thinking I half sat on it and turned the key. I had never been on a motorcycle before, of course. The bike made a jump as it tried to start, and I fell forward on my knees. Tiny pebbles were imbedded in my knee. It didn't hurt much. I was glad to feel the pain, to see the blood, proof that I was alive. I could see and hear and feel . . .

I walked slowly back to the grave, overwhelmed at the beauty of the spring everywhere I looked. Father now stood alone. Freshly mounded earth covered the grave, and a wooden cross stood at the head, carved with Mother's name and dates: "Born 1900—Died 1945." Well, I thought, forty-four is pretty old. I gathered some wildflowers, saying one final, silent good-bye, and placed them on the grave, next to the cross. I looked up at Father then. This time he did not look at me with the same loving blue eyes, now red from crying. He didn't hold my hand. He simply turned and began to walk from the grave. I felt free. I felt no pain, no regrets. That would all come much, much later. Even today I can brush my finger over the scar from the ss rubber hose, or look and see tiny bits of black gravel still imbedded under the skin of my knee, and be transported right back to the Klosterwerk camp and to Mother's death.

The following day we returned to the town center to get identification papers from the American headquarters set up in the town hall. Father left me to sit on the steps to the hall, and he went in, returning in a moment to say that I had to accompany him to get our papers. He cautioned me that if anyone asked, I was to say that I had been born in 1926, that I was eighteen.

I was thrilled, though no one asked, and we were issued our first ID papers. They indicated that we were refugees, forced laborers brought from Yugoslavia. Mine indicated that I had been born in 1926. Father had done this, of course, because it would allow me to get adult food rations, but more importantly, extra cigarette rations for him. But I was very pleased to be "an adult." They would remain the only identification papers I had and would prove very useful for my survival in the months immediately ahead.

We left the town hall and walked to the cemetery. Father was unable to be away from Mother's grave for very long. We walked back to the tunnel that evening in silence, Father's shoulders slumped in grief. Over the next several days we made daily trips to the graveside, usually walking in silence.

April 25, 1945: U.S. and Soviet forces linked up at the Elbe River in Germany.

April 28, 1945: Italian dictator Benito Mussolini and his mistress Carla Petacci were intercepted and executed by Italian partisans as they were trying to flee Italy.

April 29, 1945: American forces liberated Dachau Concentration Camp; Adolf Hitler married Eva Braun in his Berlin bunker.

April 30, 1945: Adolf Hitler and Eva Braun committed suicide in the bunker as Russian troops closed in.

TWENTY-ONE

Blankenburg am Harz

Father could not bear to be away from Mother's grave for very long, and he went every morning, not returning until dark. On most days, I went with him, but not always. I had no ambition to do anything or go anyplace. Mother's death wore on me in spite of my fascination with the beauty of nature that spring. Everywhere I looked, new life simply burst out, flowers in abundance and an array of colors such as I had never seen, as if God was trying to tell the world, tell *me*, that a better day had arrived. It was just what I needed. It helped me to put the events of the past four years and Mother's traumatic death aside when I needed so much to heal. But as I admired the new spring beauty all around me, I remembered her telling me that she wanted to die in spring, when the world was lovely, when the natural beauty could console people. Then one day Father returned from visiting the grave and joined me.

"Asya," he said, "we have an opportunity to live in a real house, that is, to have a couple of rooms in a house. It is owned by an elderly widow and needs a lot of repair. I have offered to help her clean up the place and do as much of the repair as I can, and in exchange she will let us live there free . . . and it is very close to Mother. Asya?"

"Yes, Papa."

"Well, what do you think?"

"Papa, I don't care. It sounds fine." Poor Papa. I knew he wanted only to be close to Mother, but I was uneasy, unsure. In the tunnel we were still among other people.

The following morning Father took me to meet the elderly lady. The house was on a delightful narrow, crooked village street, only a couple of blocks from the cemetery. It had a large garden area that was covered with debris from a summer house or large shed that had been destroyed. The lady came out to greet us.

"Oh, what a lovely child she is, and the poor thing has no mother," she said. "Well, so many lives have been lost. I would love to have a young, cheerful voice in the house again. You poor, poor girl . . ."

She extended her hand to stroke my head, and I quickly ducked away. I didn't want anyone feeling sorry for me. Why should they feel sorry for me? I thought. I'm alive and free, and the sun is shining so beautifully. I followed her and Father into the house, a very modest but homey place. My God, how long has it been since I've seen drapes and carpets and a real couch? I thought, realizing for the first time how long it had been since we had those things. The house was intact. Only a part of the sun porch was gone, and a part of the kitchen was damaged, but everything else stood orderly in the dark but cozy house.

Father had a small guest room for himself, while I shared a bedroom with the elderly woman, sleeping on a small cot. On perhaps the second or third day after we moved in, Father and I had to go to the Burgomeister's office to register for ration cards. German residents had been informed that, in accordance with the rules of the American occupation forces, and with the cooperation of the Burgomeister, all foreign nationals from the camps were to be allowed larger rations than the Germans.

Perhaps it was unfair, since there was so little food available, but the reasoning was that the camp residents had been on short rations for so long that they needed the extra calories, while the German citizens had kept themselves quite well fed. We now had more than we needed, since I was receiving adult rations. At any rate, we shared the food with the elderly owner of the house, so she benefited at least a bit.

The trip to the Burgomeister's office became unpleasant for me because the Zengovitzes were among the people waiting in line. They needed us to vouch that they were indeed Russians from Belgrade and had lived in the camps as well. It was such a chaotic time that no one had a way to check the validity of such things except through the identity cards we had been issued at the camp to be able to go into town or to be vouched for by someone who already had been proven to be a camp resident. The Zengovitzes declared that they had lost the camp cards, and Father vouched for them.

I was upset at the lies, but then Father had coached me very carefully to state that I had been born in 1926 and that I was eighteen years old in order to get cigarettes. So, by being asked to lie myself, the untrue statements by and about Max and his family didn't bother me too greatly.

A few days later Father fell from a ladder while working on repairs to the sun porch. It was a bad fall, and he broke his right arm. For the next couple of weeks he continued working on the house, but he was unable to do anything requiring two hands or heavy lifting. I helped him, of course, but his progress was slowed. I had to learn how to shave him with an old-fashioned straight razor. I was a bit nervous using it the first time, but quickly learned, and did so quite well.

While cleaning his room one day, I found his service revolver and the three bullets he kept with it. I remembered when he had shown it to me in Belgrade, and what he had said about refusing to allow Mother or me to fall into the hands of the Soviet army, and shuddered. How he managed to keep a revolver all through the occupation, the flight from Belgrade, and especially here in the Klosterwerk camp is something I will never understand. Surely it would have meant his death if the Germans had ever found it. I had no way of understanding how he and Mother felt about the Soviet "Hooligans," but I was certain that I would choose life in Russia over death.

We visited Mother's grave daily and planted spring flowers. Father spent a lot of time relaxing while his arm healed. One evening the owner of the house was out, and Father and I were alone. Father sat in an armchair, enjoying the comfort of the soft upholstery and puffing on a cigarette.

"You know, Asinka," he began, with a faraway look in his eyes, "I wish there was a way for you to go to America. When you were a little girl, Mother went to Boston, in America, to visit some friends. You must remember Dyadya Shura, Alexander Borovsky, the concert pianist who visited us on his European concert tour. Mother liked America very much. She said that the people were very friendly. Of course, you've seen that for yourself—the American officers and soldiers we have met are all friendly and very courteous. At any rate, I think perhaps it would be a good idea, something to think about."

"Why America, Papa?"

"Well, Europe is in such turmoil. It always has been. We can't stay in Germany. We can't go back to Belgrade. It's in the hands of the "Hooligans," and besides, we have lost everything back there. And France . . . well, I don't know. I do have very good friends in Paris. In fact, my second in command during the Russian revolution is in Paris. He entered the priesthood. You could perhaps go there to Father Gregórii. But France is still Europe, and I'm not so sure."

"Why can't we stay in Germany?"

"Well, I'm sure the Germans aren't too happy to see us around. You know, it's like a bad tooth. If you extract a bad tooth, you don't keep it around to remind you of the pain it caused. In a sense we would be like a bad tooth. Despite the overtures they are making toward us now, when things get back to normal they'll reject us as foreigners, discard us like a bad tooth."

"You're saying that I should go to America or Paris, Papa, but what about you?"

"I'm tired, Asinka. I ran in 1920, first to Shanghai, then to Constantinople, and finally to Belgrade, and look at me again . . . on the run to Vienna, Halle, and Blankenburg. Where to next?"

"Is it because Mother is buried here?"

"Yes. Someday I want to set a nice headstone for her. The wooden cross we placed there will just rot away in no time. She didn't even have a proper casket. Look how we lived while we were in the camps. And I had promised her that I would give her the best for the rest of her life."

I knew in my heart that he could not even think of leaving Mother's graveside. I rose and went outside to sit on the front step of the house. It was dusk, and music and voices from American encampments were heard. I thought I heard very distant artillery and wondered, "Isn't the war over yet? Where are all the soldiers going, and why can we still hear shooting? Only yesterday I thought I heard someone saying that Berlin had fallen."

May 2, 1945: The Soviet Union announced the fall of Berlin, and the Allies announced the surrender of Nazi troops in Italy and parts of Austria.

It was strange not seeing shiny German boots anymore. The Americans had such a casual appearance compared with the uniformed, stiff discipline of the German army. I felt tired and suddenly wanted to go to bed. I peeked into the sitting room and saw that Father had not moved. A tiny table lamp was burning by his easy chair and a trail of smoke was rising above the lamp shade. Father's fingers held a cigarette, his thoughts wandering into space.

"Good night, Papa." There was no answer. He was off in his own world.

Several days later, I saw Father talking very seriously with an American officer. Whether German, Italian, American, or British, Father always seemed to strike up acquaintances with an officer. I decided there must be some special courtesy or camaraderie that existed between military officers that helped them to establish respectful relations.

I had seen Father talking with this officer once or twice before, but this time the conversation looked serious. Not just a smoke and a friendly chat. I was sitting on the front step as Father came to the house saying that the situation was changing. It didn't look good, and we should prepare ourselves for the worst.

"What do you mean the situation is changing?" I asked.

"Well, the Americans are leaving."

"Does that mean that they have been defeated by the Germans?"

"Oh, no, no, they are just moving on. Tomorrow British troops are taking over Blankenburg."

"Why is that bad? At least it will be easier to speak with them. I still have a little difficulty understanding the Americans."

"It just means that the war is not quite over yet," Father said thoughtfully. "The troops are still on the move, and apparently the Soviet army is not too far behind."

The following morning, all the American forces pulled out, and the British army marched in. The language was very familiar to me then. They sounded just like Mother and Miss Spencer back in Belgrade, but their presence made me terribly homesick. The British were very reserved.

They took the war seriously and did not mingle with the civilian population. Their reserved nature was nothing new. I remembered several British friends who visited us when I was a small child, and they were all, just like Miss Spencer, very reserved and proper at all times.

May 7, 1945: Germany signed an unconditional surrender.
May 8, 1945: President Harry Truman announced VE Day, Victory in
   Europe Day.

I found my existence sort of useless. I had not been in school for so very long, and I was amazed to find myself missing my tutors and the structure and discipline that school and my tutors had brought into my life.

I read every book I could find in the house: Goethe, Schiller, Mann, and scores of outdated German newspapers. Reading those papers was so strange. Each issue displayed a headline highlighting a new victory, never a word of defeat. Reading the newspapers always reminded me of hearing a harsh German voice, blaring from the camp loudspeakers, announcing the latest official news bulletins from the OKW.

I wondered where our Russian friends were with whom we had spent so much time in the forced labor camp and who had cried at Mother's graveside. I had seen only one or two of them in town. The Zengovitz family came once to visit, but I pretended to be sleeping when they came. Two of the engineers who worked for the Bentin Company were still in town. I saw Father speaking with them several times and wondered why he would be talking to them?

I never saw Herr Mueller again after the night the office burned down, and it saddened me. I don't think people can share an event such as happened that terrible morning in front of his office without forming a lasting bond. I prayed for him and prayed that he had found his wife.

The town of Blankenburg had taken on a different atmosphere when the American troops left. When the Americans had been in town, there had always been music and laughter. The British troops, with their rigid ways, reminded me of the highly disciplined Germans. Of course, there was no comparison, but the light ways of the Americans had gone.

I remembered what Father had said about me going to America, and I began to think that perhaps I would like that idea. Of course, it was impossible. We had no one in America, and we had no money—not even a change of clothing. Well, I could dream nonetheless. I even missed their constant gum-chewing, although I found it so terribly ugly when I saw them doing it.

A short time after the arrival of the British, I saw Father one day speaking with a British officer. Once again he had formed a friendship with a military officer. He came home that evening obviously distraught.

"This is it, Asya," he said. "They are leaving, too. The British are moving on, and this area is being turned over to the Soviet army. Now I have made arrangements with those two engineers—you remember the two who worked at the Bentin office in the camp—well, their main office is in Hamburg, and their homes and families are in Hamburg also. They have agreed, not out of the goodness of their heart, but for a price."

Father's face looked distasteful, and his voice took on a sarcastic tone.

"For a price . . . yes, they have agreed to take you along to Hamburg. That seems to be the only safe place right now. The Soviet army will not go that far north and west. I have learned that the British have opened a displaced persons camp in Hamburg for Yugoslavian citizens. The engineers will take you there, and if they cannot have you admitted to that camp, then they have assured me that they will find you a place to live and will help you to find work. At any rate, no matter what results from this trip north, it will be far better than taking a chance of falling into Russian hands."

"Papa," I said, "I don't understand any of this. You know that we are Russian. We have been mistreated by the Germans for that very reason, and now we are trying desperately to avoid our own people."

Suddenly Father straightened in his chair, has face assuming a very stern expression, and he shook his finger at me.

"Don't ever, *ever* let me hear you say that the Bolsheviks are 'our own people.' They are monsters who have defiled the Russian earth and destroyed the most inner part of the Russian Soul! Their souls are possessed by a demon. Oh, no, I would rather kill myself *and* you than to let you fall into their hands . . . to have your soul destroyed and your mind poisoned."

He rose from his chair and began to pace the floor, his forehead lined with deep wrinkles, his eyes stern but filled with pain.

"Don't ever forget . . ." He stopped pacing and turned to face me with almost pleading eyes, his shadow so huge on the wall behind him. "Don't ever forget what they have done to your aunts and uncles, your grandparents on both sides. Even though you never met them, their memory should forever live on in your heart."

He broke off then, his voice filling with emotion, not wanting to relive the stories of the murder and rape of family members and the horrors of the Russian revolution. I had heard those stories many times, but they never stirred any great emotion in me. After all, those aunts, uncles, and grandparents were only pictures in the family album. I had no way of relating to them or to the horrors they underwent. It had all happened so long ago, long before I had even been born, but I knew that the pain of the revolution was still fresh in Father's memory.

My God, I wondered. How can Papa live with all that pain and hatred in his heart for so long? Does that mean that I will forever relive the horror of the Nazi invasion and occupation, and the trials of my trip to Blankenburg and the camp? Suddenly, the lovely face of the little nun in Hopova came into my mind. How I longed to be back in the cloister, feeling green grass beneath my feet, to be able to cry over a crushed flower and be assured by the nun that "nothing ever dies," to fall asleep watching the icon and the nodding shadow of the nun on the wall. I wished that I had never seen death, felt hunger, never held my dead mother's head on my lap. I wished with all my heart that I could still believe every word those nuns had told me . . . to look at birds, clouds, flowers and see only God's creative hand, to truly believe again that "nothing ever dies."

"Papa," I asked softly, suddenly looking at Father, "do you think the Germans harmed the nuns at Hopova?"

"Hopova?" Father's shoulders sank down. "Haven't you heard a word I said about your grandparents, your family? Were you listening to me?"

"Yes, Papa, I've heard every word."

"Then," he asked, strong annoyance in his voice, "what do Hopova and the nuns have to do with our present conversation?"

"Nothing, Papa, nothing at all," I said softly. "Goodnight, Papa."

There was no answer again. Lately Papa didn't answer my goodnights. More and more he was preoccupied with his own thoughts, his own memories and pain. A wall had begun to grow between us since the day of Mother's funeral, when I ran from her grave. In a way, I welcomed the distance. Since that frightening day in our garage rooms in Belgrade so long before, I had gradually begun to trust Father again, to rely on his judgment and strength. He had again been the strong model father I loved, and I became confused remembering the garage.

Since Mother's death, I had begun to feel uneasy and to maintain a little distance from Father. I think that without realizing it, I perhaps felt that Mother had always been there between us. I missed her more than I would realize for a very long time. I tried to sleep that night, but could not. I lay there wishing that the icon candle was casting a light and shadow on the wall, that I could fall asleep knowing that tomorrow the peaceful face of a nun would be there to guide me through another day of beauty, flowers, and gentle people God had created for us to cherish and to love.

Morning came all too soon. Father and I walked into town to receive our weekly rations.

"Now," Father reminded me, "don't forget that you're eighteen years old if anyone should ask. But I have your identification certificate right here if anyone should," and he patted his pocket to reassure himself that it was there.

Funny, I thought, as we walked along, I've never seen this phony identification certificate. Oh, well, who cares? I certainly don't. If they want me to, I'll tell them I'm forty years old. We spent almost the entire morning standing in line. I don't recall any conversation between us as we walked back to the house, each probably thinking about the separation that lay ahead.

When we returned to the house, the elderly owner led me into the bedroom to try on some dresses she had found in her closet and an old fur coat. I tried a dress on and found it to be about two sizes too large. The fur coat was hideous. The fur had worn off the elbows and collar. Father had told her that he was sending me on to Hamburg and asked if she had any clothing I might use.

She produced an old suitcase and half-filled it with some underwear, a skirt and blouse, a dress, and a pair of shoes. The clothes were old and very dark, ugly, but I didn't care. I had absolutely no interest in what went into the old suitcase. I never knew what it cost Father, if anything, but I thought I saw one of Mother's rings on the woman's finger later that day.

Early the following morning, Father and I sat on the front porch, my head filled with a sense of foreboding and full of questions, "How far is Hamburg? Where will I go when I get there? How will I live? With whom and where?" Father had no answers to my questions. His only concern was that I not be allowed to fall into the hands of the Soviet army, now only a few miles away.

"Anochka," Father said, "I have given money and a couple of Mother's brooches to the engineers for you. They are going to give these things to you as soon as you are settled so that at least you will be able to pay for food and immediate necessities, a room or whatever."

"They will give me those things when we get to Hamburg?" I asked. I still kept the rings and brooch that Mother had given to me the night I left Belgrade tied around my neck, the watch in my shoe.

"Yes. They have your things locked in their briefcase along with some important papers from their office. I'm sure it's the safest way. There is no lock for your suitcase. They are going to take you to the Yugoslavian displaced persons camp, and if the camp is filled or for some reason you can't stay in the camp, then they will arrange a room for you and help you to find a job."

"What about you, Papa? What are you going to do?"

"I'm going to stay here and hide for a while. Hope the Soviet troops don't find me. Try to save enough money to set a nice headstone for Mama. And if everything fails and they do find me, well, I always carry my trusted friend now." he said, patting his side pocket.

"What 'trusted friend'?"

"My service revolver. Small, but powerful. Big enough to do the job."

"What 'job'?" I asked. "Surely you aren't going to kill someone."

"Just me," he said calmly.

"Papa!" My mouth fell open in disbelief. When he had shown me the gun in the past, speaking of never allowing Mother or me to fall into the hands of the "Hooligans," it had been abstract. Now there was no mistaking his intention.

"Now, now, don't you worry," he said, trying to reassure me. "It would be a relief not to have to run anymore, to seek a new life, to start over again in some new country. I just can't run anymore, Anochka. I'm tired. I need a rest." He paused and took my head in both his hands and kissed my forehead. "Don't think about it. Just try to remember what I have always told you about a strong foundation, about honesty, dignity, and pride. Yes, pride in who you are and what you are."

"Who I am and what I am? Who am I? What am I? I look like a beggar. I have no home, no family. I live in a country that despises us. What is there to be proud of?"

"Your soul!" he answered firmly. "Your basic goodness, dignity, and respect. Respect for yourself above all. Remember that! It looks very bleak right now, I know, but your mother and I were not very much older when we had to start all anew in a strange land."

"Yes, but you had each other."

"That's true, but you have God and love in your heart, which is more important than another person on such a journey."

"Papa, I'm frightened. I don't even know these two men."

"They are all right," he said, trying to reassure me again. "They gave me their word of honor that they will see to it that you are well taken care of and set on the right path. After all, a word of honor is a very serious thing. Now, you must give me *your* word of honor that you will always remember and be proud of who you are. That you will always listen to your inner voice, always listen to your soul, because that is where God is, and as long as he is there, there is nothing you cannot overcome and nothing ahead of you to fear."

He embraced me then and rocked me gently as he had so many, many years before. I could feel his tears falling on my head. A car pulled up in front of the house, and two men got out. Yes, I remembered seeing them once or twice at the forced labor camp, around Herr Mueller's office. They were engineers for the Emil Bentin Company.

Father introduced me to them. Herr Behrens, the chief engineer, is the only name I remember. Father took my suitcase and placed it in the back seat. I sat next to it and placed the ugly fur coat on my lap. Father blessed me and shut the door. He stood outside and spoke to the two men for a few minutes, then the men got into the car and we pulled away. I turned back to wave good-bye to Father. Tears were streaming down his face, but in an instant my vision was blurred as tears filled my eyes, and I could no longer make out Father's figure.

I turned and began to dry my eyes, choking back more tears, realizing that I was also leaving Mother behind, that even her grave was being left.

TWENTY-TWO
Hamburg

I sat back in the seat, looking all around, trying desperately to put my last view of Father, tears streaming down his face, out of my mind. I remembered when I arrived in Vienna and felt so confidant, so determined to get by on my own without Mother or Father, and how disappointed I had been when reunited with them. But I was far less confidant now. My experiences in the forced labor camp and the horrific death of Mother left me far less sure of the future and of myself.

The large Mercedes-Benz sedan in which we were riding was extremely comfortable, and the radio was playing American tunes. How strange it was to be sitting in a typical Nazi automobile listening to American music, when a few weeks earlier, radios played only victorious marches, Goebbels's unpleasant voice spewing lies, and Hitler's raving, guttural speeches, exhortations to "final victory." All that was history now.

The two men talked to each other as we drove, but I didn't listen or speak to them except for a polite "Oh, how terrible, not a house standing" or "That's a nice song on the radio" without ever receiving an answer. As it grew dark, the chief engineer, the only one of the two that ever spoke to me, turned to say.

"We are going to stay at this inn tonight."

The car pulled to a stop in front of a Gasthaus. The men checked in, and after eating a bowl of soup and a sandwich, I went up to my room while they stayed behind to drink some beer. The room was tiny, and I quickly washed up in a bathroom down the hall. Exhausted, I didn't even remember falling asleep when a knock at the door told me it was time to get up. We left right after a quick breakfast, the men anxious to reach their homes before nightfall.

After several hours we began driving through endless mounds of rubble, and the broken, uneven skyline made me believe we must be entering Hamburg.

"Are we in Hamburg now?" I asked.

"No," the chief replied, "we are just entering Altona, a large settlement on the outskirts of Hamburg."

It looked menacing with almost every building destroyed and only jagged ruins to be seen. The air was chilly now, and I was grateful for the ugly fur coat.

"How terrible, everyone must be dead. Is Hamburg just as bombed-out as Altona?"

"Worse," replied the chief, "but the people aren't dead. They learned how to survive the bombs. Only the buildings have been destroyed, not the German spirit."

Suddenly I was aware of the ugly, guttural tone of his answer. I didn't respond, but I remembered Father's warning a few days before—"We'll be like a bad tooth. They won't want us around anymore"—and it made me uneasy.

It had grown dark by the time we stopped in Hamburg, in front of a damaged building located next to a train or trolley overpass. The dim glow from street lights made the neighboring ruins look bigger, more menacing. A Gasthaus sign over the front door was dimly lit.

"Well, here we are," one said. "You wait here, and we'll make arrangements for the night."

The other man took my suitcase inside. They were gone for only a few minutes and as they returned, the chief engineer said, "All right, everything is arranged."

"Aren't you staying here, too?" I asked, alarmed.

"No, our homes are a bit less than an hour's drive from here. So we'll just get going, but we will be back in the morning to look in on you and make sure you get settled. Maybe we can help you find a job or something."

"Oh," I said, "that's very nice. Thank you very much. You'll see your families tonight and come back in the morning to check and help me?"

"Yes, yes," said the other man, the one who had carried my suitcase in. "Oh, and here are a few marks so you can get yourself something to eat."

"But you did pay for my room, didn't you?"

"Yes, yes, and tomorrow morning we'll be back and settle the whole affair. The money, the jewelry, and whatnot that your Father gave us to keep for you. All that we'll straighten out tomorrow, but for now you get a good night's sleep. We had better be going. Our families are waiting for us."

The car drove quickly away into the night, leaving me standing on the sidewalk holding that ugly fur coat in the dim glow of the Gasthaus sign. "What nice men," I thought. "They've found me a room for tonight and they'll be back in the morning to help me begin to face the world all on my own." I turned to walk into the building.

It looked as though it once had been a pleasant place, but the war had clearly taken its toll. The plaster had fallen from some of the walls, and the ceiling had been patched in several places. The furniture looked comfortable but badly worn or damaged. There were several tables in the room, and a floor lamp in each corner provided dim light for the entire room.

Just ahead of me was the desk. Swinging doors behind it led to the kitchen. To the left was a staircase, lath showing on both walls now almost bare of plaster. My suitcase stood on the floor by the staircase, and I walked to it and placed the fur coat on top of it.

"I suppose you're hungry and want something to eat before you go upstairs?" a voice behind me asked.

"Yes, I would like something to eat." I answered, turning to see an enormous fat lady standing with her hands on her hips. I had never seen such heavy makeup, never such red-painted lips. Her face was covered with a heavy layer of powder, and black hair was piled on top of her head with a few restless strands hanging over the fat neck. I looked around the room then. An old man sat at one table with a younger man, and a couple sat at another.

My eyes had become accustomed to the dim light, and I could see the faces of the people sitting in the room. I felt that everyone was staring at me, and I was ashamed because my clothes didn't fit. My legs looked as white as the fat lady's powdered face, and my shoes were two sizes too big.

I tried to smooth my hair, wishing I had a mirror so that I could see myself, but immediately decided I was glad I didn't have a mirror. I was certain I looked ridiculous and out of place. The other customers were dressed modestly, but at least their clothes all fit them, and the fat woman and the only woman customer both wore stockings. I walked to the far end of the room where no one was sitting.

"We have soup, and I'll bring you some sausage and bread," the fat woman said. "Do you want beer with it or schnapps?"

"Neither, I don't like it. Maybe just some water." I didn't want to say that I had never tasted beer or schnapps.

"She doesn't like it," the fat woman said, not to me but to the rest of the room in general as she waddled off. "Water is probably contaminated. You'll get sick. Nobody drinks water."

She returned with a tray in few minutes, and the smell of homemade soup, dark bread, and sausage made me terribly hungry.

"Neither. I don't like it," she said with a laugh. "Well, maybe a little champagne would be all right. I don't know why people are so fussy. They should be glad there's still some beer left to drink, ha, ha."

Her heavy body swayed from side to side as she walked back toward the serving counter. She didn't address anyone in particular. Evidently whoever wanted to listen, it was fine with her. I ate quickly, anxious to go to my room.

"Where is my room, please?"

"It's one flight up," the woman answered noncommittally, "second door to the left. There are no lights in the hallway, so watch your step. The stairs are old."

The stairway was unlit, except for the light from the dining area. The hallway above was lit only by a window at each end through which dim light from the streetlights entered. I stepped carefully and found the second door to the left, opened it, and turned the switch on. An iron bed with a thin mattress and a thin blanket stood against one wall, a night table next to it. The floor was bare. A porcelain basin and matching pitcher stood in front of a mirror on an old dresser, a wooden chair next it. A bare light bulb hung from a wire in the middle of the ceiling. A single window with no shade or curtain overlooked the ruin next door.

The water pitcher was filled with ice-cold water, and I poured some into the basin. A small piece of brown soap and a thin towel were next to the basin, and I washed my face. I got my comb out of the suitcase, and wished that I had a toothbrush. That was a luxury I hadn't had in a long time. I rubbed my finger over the brown soap and then across my teeth, rinsing my mouth into a bucket next to the dresser and emptying the basin into it as well.

I looked in the mirror, noticing how very thin my face had become, making my dark eyes appear even larger. I was skinny, my hair hung lifeless over my shoulders, and I noticed for the first time that it was beginning to darken. "Good," I thought, "at least I won't be asked about my 'Aryan' blood anymore." The room was cold, the floor very cold, and I shivered from the chill and loneliness. I crept to the bed, and sleep came almost immediately.

The next morning after a breakfast of tea with bread and a little cheese, I asked if the men from Hamburg had returned yet. The man at the desk, the proprietor and husband of the fat woman from the previous night, didn't know what I was talking about. He walked over to his wife, who stood at the other end of the counter looking as though she had never been to bed and wearing the same scarlet lipstick and thick face powder.

As they finished conversing, she came over to say that I should just wait for a while.

"Some other girls should arrive soon," she added, ignoring my inquiry.

"Aren't the two engineers coming back soon? Did they t̶ you what time they would be back?"

"You mean the two men who paid for your room last ̶ht?"

"Yes."

"All they told me was that you were looking f̶rk and that they would pay for one nights lodging, and then they off."

"Why, yes, I am looking for work, but they̶posed to come back this morning and give me the money and th̶at my Papa gave them to keep for me."

next to it. The floor was bare. A porcelain basin and matching pitcher stood in front of a mirror on an old dresser, a wooden chair next it. A bare light bulb hung from a wire in the middle of the ceiling. A single window with no shade or curtain overlooked the ruin next door.

The water pitcher was filled with ice-cold water, and I poured some into the basin. A small piece of brown soap and a thin towel were next to the basin, and I washed my face. I got my comb out of the suitcase, and wished that I had a toothbrush. That was a luxury I hadn't had in a long time. I rubbed my finger over the brown soap and then across my teeth, rinsing my mouth into a bucket next to the dresser and emptying the basin into it as well.

I looked in the mirror, noticing how very thin my face had become, making my dark eyes appear even larger. I was skinny, my hair hung lifeless over my shoulders, and I noticed for the first time that it was beginning to darken. "Good," I thought, "at least I won't be asked about my 'Aryan' blood anymore." The room was cold, the floor very cold, and I shivered from the chill and loneliness. I crept to the bed, and sleep came almost immediately.

The next morning after a breakfast of tea with bread and a little cheese, I asked if the men from Hamburg had returned yet. The man at the desk, the proprietor and husband of the fat woman from the previous night, didn't know what I was talking about. He walked over to his wife, who stood at the other end of the counter looking as though she had never been to bed and wearing the same scarlet lipstick and thick face powder.

As they finished conversing, she came over to say that I should just wait for a while.

"Some other girls should arrive soon," she added, ignoring my inquiry.

"Aren't the two engineers coming back soon? Did they tell you what time they would be back?"

"You mean the two men who paid for your room last night?"

"Yes."

"All they told me was that you were looking for work and that they would pay for one nights lodging, and then they took off."

"Why, yes, I am looking for work, but they are supposed to come back this morning and give me the money and things that my Papa gave them to keep for me."

The fat woman's brows shot up as she broke into loud laughter. "Do you know their names?" she asked. "How much money did your father give them?"

I felt as though someone was squeezing, crushing my heart. Dear God, I don't know their names, only that they work for a large firm called Emil Bentin. I could perhaps try to call the firm, but I don't remember the name of the man that had the money. Was it Behrens? How can I ask for them? I felt panic sweeping over me.

"I know the name of the firm," I said. "Emil Bentin."

"Child, there isn't a thing left standing in Hamburg, and if it's an industrial firm it's been leveled. Everything in Hamburg has been leveled. The phones are out of order. Only a few emergency numbers are working. It has been a hell of a war. I don't even know where my own mother is, and you want to find two men from a firm that is probably no longer . . . ha, ha."

Suddenly her mouth looked like a huge bloody hole, and I felt repulsed and frightened. Her husband tugged at her sleeve, pulling her toward the kitchen, and they began to speak in low voices. I moved to sit at a table, trying to think what to do next. They gave Papa their word of honor that they would take care of me and help me find a job, and they said themselves last night that they would be back this morning. Well, maybe they are just a little late. A word of honor is a sacred thing. You never give it unless you sincerely mean it and are going to follow through . . . to keep your word. I grew a little calmer then, believing in the seriousness of a given "word of honor."

"What is your name?" a voice asked, and I looked to see the proprietor standing next to me.

"Asya," I answered. "Well, it's Anastasia, but it's such a long name that everyone uses the diminutive."

"You aren't German, are you? No, of course not. Look, have you ever worked in a place like this?"

"No, but I'm willing to wash dishes or sweep floors or whatever. Maybe make up the beds in the guest rooms."

"Look," he interrupted, "this is no longer a hotel . . . not as you know it. This is a place where men come because their wives are dead or they are lonely and have no one. They come here looking for a girl, and we provide girls with room and board who entertain them." He broke off then, noticing that little was registering with me.

"This is like a brothel, a whorehouse. Do you understand what I'm saying? Look," he said, "get your suitcase and get out of here. Dear God, you're just a child. I should have been here when those two dropped you off. I would have shoved them out of here."

I sat there stunned, my eyes wide, unblinking. I couldn't move. Mother's words, "like a dirty little prostitute . . . like a dirty little prostitute," were running through my mind over and over.

"Where were those two supposed to take you? What nationality are you?" he asked. "Where are you from?"

"Yugoslavia" I answered absently, almost in a whisper, unable to move, frozen in my chair.

"Now listen to me," he said. "Come now, listen to me," and he patted me gently on the shoulder. "There is a Yugoslavian displaced persons camp not too far from here. I don't know exactly where, but I'll find out. Listen," he shifted in his chair, still patting my shoulder, "I'll get your suitcase down, and we can take a trolley. Some of them are running again, and I'll help you find the camp. It's not too far from here. We can get there in a couple of hours. I know approximately where it is. Oh, this damned war."

I sat there, unable to move or to say a word. I was in shock, my mind a complete blank, unable even to think. He returned in a moment with my suitcase, and putting the ugly fur coat over my shoulders, gently pushed me toward the front door, his wife grumbling behind us as we walked out.

After a long trolley ride through nothing but ruins lining both sides of the street, we walked for about an hour. Morning fog was just lifting over the area we were walking in, and the wail of a ship's horn added to my gloom. I was very cold, despite the fur coat that almost dragged the sidewalk.

"There, you see those wooden barracks just ahead of us?" the proprietor said, breaking the silence. "You see where the British troops are? That's where your camp is. Good luck to you, and I'm sorry that you were so misled. Well, good luck," and he turned and walked away.

I didn't know if he heard my faint "thank you." In truth, of course, he was a very good-hearted man who helped me in a time of desperate need.

I reached into the pocket of the fur coat and took out the identification paper that Father had obtained for me in Blankenburg.

"Is this the Yugoslavian camp?" I asked the guard at the gate.

"Yes," he answered. "Just go to the barracks on your left. That is the main office. They will admit you there."

"Thank you."

"I say, it's jolly good to hear at least one of you who speaks the language. It will be a great help, I dare say," the guard's voice trailed behind me as I walked toward the office.

There was no difficulty establishing that I was from Yugoslavia, and after a few questions—"Are you married? Are you traveling alone?"—I was assigned to Barrack B. This was for single women and was about three-fourths filled with women, sitting on the beds, alone, or in small groups, chatting rather happily.

Hearing the Serbian language all around helped me to relax, to feel secure. I found an empty bed, lifted my suitcase onto it, and as I looked around, there were welcoming smiles from all the women. The other women were very helpful, explaining that hot showers were located in the building next door and that the next meal would be served at 6:30. I had just missed lunch. They offered me cigarettes, chocolate, and some cookies, but I declined. All I wanted was a hot shower, to feel a stream of hot water flowing over me. I was exhausted and felt terribly dirty, but at least I felt safe.

The shower building had six shower stalls and as many sinks, with mirrors and lots of soap. The room was deserted, and I took advantage of it, scrubbing myself several times, just letting the hot water wash over my body. I washed the clothes I had been wearing in a sink, shocked at how filthy they were.

I hung my wet clothes on the line and hurried back into my barrack. It was getting chilly. I think this was late May, but the weather was quite cold this far north. After the evening meal, I took another hot shower, went to bed, and pretended to sleep as most of the other women sat and chatted, the sound of their voices and the familiarity of the Serbian language helping me to relax.

I thought of Father and prayed that he was all right. I knew that he was happy as long as he was close to Mother's grave, but I could not understand how he could have sent me to Hamburg with those two men. He had let me down again when I had relied on him. Of course, he had no way of knowing they could not be trusted. They had given him their word of honor. "A word of honor is a sacred thing."

It took several days in the camp before I began talking to the others. I learned that there were separate barracks for married people, for married people with children, for single men, and for single women. During evening hours most gathered in the mess building for singing, guitar playing, and just friendly conversation.

I was called on several times over the following weeks to act as translator, but not often enough to relieve the boredom. Camp life was incredibly boring. There was nothing to do other than take turns cleaning the barracks, helping in the kitchen, and tidying up the camp grounds. It was a very clean place, and the people were particular about their own appearance as well.

July 16, 1945: The United States exploded the world's first experimental atomic bomb in Alamogordo, New Mexico.

There was no word from Father. I had written to him twice, but didn't know if my letters had gotten through or if he could have sent me an answer. I learned that UNRRA (United Nations Refugee Relief Agency) was working with the International Red Cross and had established a system for refugees to register their name and current address in a central bureau, helping people to locate friends and family members who had been separated by the war. I registered right away, listing Father as the person I was seeking, hoping Father would do the same. But I couldn't help remembering his service revolver and what he had told me.

July 30, 1945: The USS *Indianapolis* was torpedoed and sunk by a Japanese submarine in the Pacific Ocean on the return trip after delivering the first atomic bomb to an island airbase. Only 316 out of a crew of 1,196 men survived days of relentless shark attacks.

August 6, 1945: The United States dropped the first atomic bomb on the Japanese city of Hiroshima. An estimated 140,000 people died.

August 9, 1945: The United States dropped the second atomic bomb on the Japanese city of Nagasaki. An estimated 80,000 people died.

August 15, 1945: The Empire of Japan surrendered unconditionally, bringing an end to World War II.

By the end of the war, 50 million people worldwide had been killed. Germany had organized and conducted genocide on a scale never imagined, claiming the lives of some 6 million Jews from throughout Europe. The United States unleashed the first use of atomic weapons when it dropped two bombs on the Japanese cities of Hiroshima and Nagasaki to avoid the human consequences of an invasion of Japan and bring the war to a swift, terrible, final conclusion.

Time passed slowly in the camp. The wind blew in off the North Sea, bringing biting cold, and snow began to fall. Someone mentioned that it would soon be Christmas, and I realized with a shock that I had turned seventeen a few weeks earlier. Funny, I didn't feel any differently. Seventeen seemed like such a child. It couldn't have been me.

Christmas passed and 1946 began with hope for the future, but in truth, people simply lived from day to day. The men of the camp always gathered on one side of the mess building to discuss politics in the evening, the women and children on the other side. The women were usually sewing, patching torn clothes, and reminiscing about home before the war. Then one day the men began to argue violently while discussing politics.

The camp became divided between Tito supporters, or Socialists, and supporters of the young King Peter, or Loyalists. Tito had issued a decree for all Yugoslavs who wished to return, to do so by a certain date. They would be accepted back as citizens of Yugoslavia with no questions asked. Those who chose not to return by that date would lose their citizenship, no longer permitted to return. Endless discussions took place every night, growing more and more heated, and several times British soldiers had to break up serious fights. The tranquility of the camp was gone.

Many people chose to return home. I didn't really know where I belonged and had no one to discuss the problem with. Father had made it clear that he could not, would not return to Belgrade because of the Soviets. I remembered his last word on the subject, "I would rather kill both you and myself than let you fall into the hands of the Hooligans." Aunt 'Lyena was the only other family member left, but I had no idea if she had gone to a different town or city with Sonya and Sergei, or if any of them had survived.

Almost all our friends had fled ahead of the Soviet army as they advanced on Belgrade. I had no idea if anyone I knew was left. What if Father came looking for me in Hamburg? Perhaps I could go on to Paris and find Father's friend, Father Gregórii, the priest. I knew Papa would contact him, but I had no money to travel to Paris and no idea how to find Father Gregórii—and the train to Belgrade was free.

I was deeply depressed and couldn't decide what to do. The camp was built next to a railway siding, and train cars waited at the side of the camp for those returning to Yugoslavia. Finally, still undecided and deeply conflicted, I packed my suitcase, boarded the train, and found a seat in an almost empty car.

As I sat looking out the window, a fight started between Socialists and Loyalists, and a building next to the tracks was set on fire. Only weeks earlier these men had shared meals and singing, exchanging stories of home, but now they fought like dogs! I remembered the terrifying fight between the same groups on the train from Belgrade to Vienna, when the baby's skull had been crushed. "No! I will not go back to that insane fighting of Serb against Serb!" I grabbed my suitcase and left the train moments before it pulled away and walked slowly back to my barrack.

I was sad, crying, and felt totally alone as I made my way back to my spot in the barrack. The women who remained tried to help, asking what was wrong and why I had changed my mind, but I had no explanation. Unwilling or perhaps unable to try to think things through, I grew weaker over the next several days, more and more depressed. I refused to eat and grew even weaker, finally even refusing to get out of bed.

"Aren't you going to eat?" a voice beside the bed asked. "You know, you haven't eaten anything for a couple of days now. You'll get terribly sick." I opened my eyes to see a friendly young woman named Nina looking down at me as she placed her hand on my forehead. "My God, you have a fever. We need a doctor to look at you."

She left and returned with a British soldier who placed his hand on my forehead and said that he would get a doctor from the international camp. In about an hour, a very friendly man in dark-rimmed glasses stood next to my bed.

"Let's see what's making you ill," he said in English, but with a strange accent.

He examined me, carefully checking my lungs, and diagnosed pneumonia. He said that I must remain in bed for complete rest, gave me some pills, and left. I slept fitfully that night, tossing and turning, coughing and waking frequently with chills, yet soaked in perspiration. The doctor returned the next day and became concerned that he was unable to bring the temperature down.

"You should go to the international camp. They have good hospital facilities there," he said with concern. "But of course it is difficult because you are Russian, or rather from Yugoslavia."

"Why is it difficult?" I asked in a weak voice, my lips hurting, dry and almost cracking as I spoke.

"Because," he explained, "that camp is only for westerners, that is North and South Americans, Australians, British and Irish people, people who became trapped here during the war. Now they are free and waiting to return to their homes."

"But I was trapped here, too."

"No, no, it's different. You were brought here as a forced laborer, and the other people were just visiting Europe and got caught up in the conflict. Now they are free and returning to their homes."

"Are you an American?"

"No, I'm from South America, from Colombia. I, too, am waiting for my papers to be processed and shall return home."

The following day was the last day a train would be provided to meet Tito's deadline for all Yugoslav expatriates who wished to return. No cars waited on the track next to the camp, perhaps because of the fights and fire the day I had thought of leaving. Everyone who wished to leave gathered in the yard in front of the barracks to board waiting military trucks for the ride to the train depot.

Years later I would learn that Tito's promise of amnesty had been an empty one, that the Yugoslav authorities checked everyone returning, and that many were separated and punished for past political differences. The camp fell silent then, as only a handful of people remained. I was still very ill. Only four women remained in my barrack. They continued to be concerned and brought me water, but I refused to take anything to eat. The doctor continued to visit, obviously concerned.

"You have to get better. You have to start eating, or you aren't going to make it," he said sympathetically one day. "Did you want to return to Yugoslavia?"

"No," I answered. "Well, maybe. I don't know. I don't care."

"Do you have anybody back in Yugoslavia?"

"No, I don't think so."

"In Germany?"

"Yes, my father. But I don't know where he is now. I've written twice but never received an answer. I think he is dead."

He gave me another pill and covered me with additional blankets.

"Look," he said gently, "the medicine alone will not make you well. You have to eat and drink. You want to get better, don't you?"

"I don't care. It doesn't make any difference to me."

The doctor looked at me, stroking my hair, which was soaked in perspiration. He asked someone if there was a change of nightshirt so that they could put something dry on me. They found an old, oversized dress in my suitcase and changed my clothes, but within minutes I was soaking wet again. The doctor left, saying that he would return that evening. In a few minutes, I went to take a shower because of my heavy perspiration, and then became terribly chilled returning to my barrack. When the doctor returned I was shivering violently, apparently burning with fever. I no longer perspired but was incoherent. He made his decision. I was going to the international camp and into the hospital!

When I next opened my eyes, I couldn't believe the change in my surroundings. The camp was gone. I was in a spotless room with a beautiful bed and thick mattress, snowy white sheets, and pictures on the wall. The windows had white curtains, and I found a large pitcher of orange juice standing on the bedside table. I reached to pour myself a glass of juice and was drinking it when the door opened and the doctor walked in.

"Well," he said with a broad smile, "I thought you had decided to give up, but I was just as stubborn. I wouldn't let you go. See, now aren't you glad to be here?"

"Where am I? This is so clean, so pretty."

"You're in one of the hospital rooms in the international camp."

"But since I'm from Yugoslavia, is it all right? Is it legal for me to be here?" I asked, remembering what he had told me, dreading the thought that I might have to leave.

"You let that be my concern. You just concentrate on getting your strength back. Look at you. You're down below a hundred pounds."

I felt my ribs beneath the blanket. It did feel pretty bony. Oh, well, it didn't matter. I looked out the window and saw bright blue sky and sunshine.

"Is it warm outside?"

"Yes, it's a beautiful day. Spring will be here very soon now, and you better get well soon so that you don't take up any more of my time giving you weather reports. Doctors are very busy, you know." He winked and walked out.

I looked around the room and saw a little table in one corner with magazines and newspapers. They were British and American magazines, and I looked at them in disbelief. So many colors, such pretty pictures. There were horrid pictures of war as well, but I had seen worse in person. They were of no interest. I wanted to see only pretty things. A light knock at the door sent me jumping back into the bed.

"Ah, ha, getting rather frisky, aren't you? Good. I've brought you some breakfast," a young woman said as she walked in with a tray of food.

As soon as food was mentioned, I suddenly was starving. She left the tray with instructions that I must eat everything. Heavens, what food! Eggs, hot biscuits, and jam. I haven't seen food like this in years. I cleaned the plate, wishing there were more. From that day, my recovery was so rapid that the doctor could scarcely believe it. I took daily baths with heavenly smelling soaps and thick towels. Everything was too good to be true. I was afraid to leave the room for fear that they would see that I was better and send me back to the Yugoslavian camp.

Once, in conversation, the doctor learned that I knew how to type, and he made arrangements for me to become a permanent resident of the international camp. I was given a job in one of the offices typing the endless forms and questionnaires for the camp residents who were preparing papers for their departure. No salary. I worked for room and board, but it was wonderful. I shared a room with a girl from Australia, who was also awaiting repatriation. She kindly gave me two of her dresses, beautiful clothes that fit. It was the first time I had had a dress that fit me since I had left Belgrade—really since we had lost our home in Dedinye to the Nazis.

I went back to the Yugoslavian camp one day, to get something from my suitcase, which now held my many cartons of cigarettes. Since I didn't smoke, I simply threw them in the suitcase when they were passed out, and Nina, the girl who had been so nice, continued to do the same for me while I was in the hospital. I didn't think about them or why I saved them or even accepted them, but I would eventually be very glad that I did.

I blossomed in the international camp and was extremely happy. It was not really a camp per se, but a ten-story building in the center of Hamburg that miraculously had escaped the terrible bombings. Soon, however, people began leaving to return to their own countries, to their homes, and I was sad. The international camp would soon close, and I would have to return to the Yugoslavian camp.

I began to take long walks after I had finished all my typing and office work. There was a park nearby, and although the city was in ruins, the park had been picked up and looked clean and neat. Then one day I found a single, lonely daisy growing in debris near the park, swaying in the wind. I remembered my favorite little nun at Hopova—"nothing ever dies"— and it filled me with new hope.

A dance was announced at the international camp, and the doctor stopped at the office to invite me. Before the dance I took the longest bath, selected my prettiest dress, and even curled my hair with little pieces of torn cloth. I was all prepared for the evening.

We entered a large room filled with people, the women all dressed in beautiful clothes, and the men in suits. There were British and American officers as well, all in uniform. A live band was playing, and we found a small table close to the dance floor. I was amazed as I listened to the strange tunes and watched the people dancing even more strangely.

"What kind of music is this?" I asked the doctor, wide-eyed.

"That's the American jitterbug, and it's a Glenn Miller piece called 'In the Mood.' You've never heard it before, have you?"

"Nooo," I answered in amazement.

"Would you like to try it?"

"Oh nooo, no, thank you."

"Good," he said smiling and laughing lightly. "I'm glad because I don't know how to jitterbug myself."

"You know," he added, "this is a farewell dance. Most of the people are leaving this week, which means that we have to try to make some arrangements for you. This camp will close completely very soon."

"Does that mean I'll have to go back to the Yugoslavian camp?"

"I hope not. In fact, I think it would be a good idea for you, as a Russian, to leave the British zone. It's not that they dislike Russians. It's just that it will be difficult for you to find a job, and I understand that most of the camps in the British zone will be dissolved fairly soon. The Yugoslavian camp as well. People are trying to pick up their lives and begin to live normally again, so the camps will all soon be obsolete."

"Well, where do you think I should go?"

"In my opinion, the American zone would be the best."

"Where is the American zone?"

"Oh, let's see. There is Frankfurt, Heidelberg, Wiesbaden, Stuttgart. All those places are in the American zone. That's the reason I invited you here tonight, so that I could introduce you to some American liaison officers. Maybe they will have some ideas. We'll see," he said with a smile.

"Are you leaving for the American zone also?"

"No," he answered, smiling broadly. "Thank God, my papers have finally come through, and I'm returning to Colombia. You know, my children are about your age now, and I'm afraid they may have forgotten that they have a father. But let's go across the room, and I'll introduce you to some Americans."

We walked across the dance floor to a small group of people sitting at a table. Everyone was speaking English, but as a group, with voices sounding all around the table, it sounded very strange to me. The doctor introduced me, and all I heard was, "Hi ya, Blondie. How are ya?"

"Good evening" was all I could think to say when I realized that I was "Blondie."

After a brief conversation and a few questions about my background and language ability, the liaison officer stated that I would have no problem finding a job in the American zone. People fluent in English and European languages were desperately needed. He told me that as soon as I had a place to live and was settled, I should simply go to the Headquarters Compound and apply. There would be many openings, he said, and he strongly recommended that I move to Frankfurt. That was where the main U.S. Headquarters Division was located, and with my language abilities it would offer the most opportunities.

When we returned to our table, the doctor said, "I've learned that there will be a military supply train to transfer the supplies we have here to Frankfurt the day we close," he said. "If you want to go to Frankfurt, I think we can arrange for you to travel on that train at no cost. What do you think?"

"Yes, that would be perfect. I was trying to think of how I could travel to Frankfurt."

The following week the doctor stopped in the office while I was working.

"Good-bye," he said from the doorway. "I'm leaving tomorrow morning, so good luck. I'm very happy you pulled through. Now be sure to take good care of yourself."

I never saw the doctor again. I hope he had a long and happy life with his family back in Colombia. He was so very good to me, so very concerned, and I know that I probably owe him my life. It's sad to remember that I don't think I ever knew his name. I always addressed him simply as "Doctor."

Two days later, the last of the supplies bound for Frankfurt were loaded, and I went with them to the waiting train.

TWENTY-THREE
Frankfurt

My arrival in the American zone was disappointing; it was not as easy to find a job as I had thought. The problem was me, of course. I had no idea how to go about applying, and I was very unsure of myself. I registered again with UNRRA and checked the bulletin board daily for word from Father.

> May 11, 1946: Care packages began to arrive in Europe for the first time, at the port of Le Havre in France.

There was constant tension in the camp. People felt "displaced." Without fluency in German or English, they couldn't find work. They longed to go "home" but no longer belonged anyplace. Many of them now regretted not returning to Yugoslavia, but of course it was too late. Tito's proclamation had closed that possibility. The refugees remaining in the camp were now classified as "stateless," reflecting the reality of no longer being able to return to their homes, but without legal residency or citizenship in another country. I marveled at Mother's wisdom in selecting the languages for me to study and how she had known that German and English would be so essential. I knew that my language ability was the key to my leaving the camp, but I didn't know where to begin. Finally, about six weeks after arriving in the American zone, I decided that "camp life" was just *not* for me. I simply had to break away.

That day I went to the camp office and told them that I wanted to find a job.

"Well, Miss," the soldier in the office replied, "just go down the street on the opposite side to the main gate of the U.S. headquarters division and tell the guard at the gate that you are interested in looking for work. He will be able to direct you to the employment office."

Can it possibly be that easy? I wondered.

The following day the weekly supply of cigarettes was distributed in the camp. I received my allotment and went to my bed to open my suitcase and throw them in with all the rest. I still didn't smoke, and by now my suitcase was full of them. A young woman watched as I put the new ones in.

"Asya," she said, "you should either learn to smoke or trade those cigarettes for something you want or need."

For the first time I realized that every day the front of the camp was crowded with Germans trying to trade for cigarettes. Apparently cigarettes were not easily available to the civilian population, and they would trade almost anything for a pack of cigarettes.

"Have you ever watched German men on the streets?" she continued. "Have you noticed that almost every one of them carries a cane?"

"No," I answered puzzled, "I don't think I have." "Come outside for a walk with me. I want to show you something."

We walked together out the main gate of the D.P. camp and paused long enough for her to light a cigarette. She took two puffs, threw the cigarette down, and took my arm to begin walking slowly away. Out of nowhere, an elderly man with a cane appeared, his head high, apparently strolling aimlessly. Glancing quickly both ways, he pointed his cane toward the lightly smoldering butt, brought the tip of his cane up, removed the cigarette, hungrily drew the smoke into his lungs, and smoked it quickly down to the very last possible puff. In just a moment, another man appeared with a cane and speared somebody else's discarded butt. They had driven thin nails at the tip of their canes, and instead of suffering the humiliation of bending down to pick it up, they speared the butts with the nail.

"Oh, how terribly sad," I said, almost in a whisper.

"What do you mean sad?" she replied, beaming with inner satisfaction. "They're Germans! Have you forgotten how they treated us? To hell with them! All those mighty, powerful officers are now too proud to bend down and pick up a butt. Typically German, they've simply come up with a tricky solution."

"But the war is over. Why can't we just think about the future and try to make something of our miserable lives?" I said wistfully, not believing there was much of a future for any of us other than another camp perhaps. "I wish I could move out of the camp and live in a real home again, with real furniture."

"Well," she replied, "you have a whole bunch of cigarettes. They are worth more than Marks! Maybe you can use them to rent a room with a German family. You know, they're terribly eager to rent rooms because they have absolutely nothing."

"You know, that's an idea," I said, already thinking.

Back in the barrack, I wrapped ten packs of cigarettes in a piece of newspaper, tied it with a piece of string, and began walking around the area to see if I could spot a "Room for Rent" sign. Within an hour I found one that seemed to be in a good neighborhood—a two-story stone home standing almost alone. Many of the other homes had been destroyed or heavily damaged. This one stood intact and looked inviting.

My knock was answered by an elderly couple who, like most of the German population, were struggling to get by. They had two sons, the woman explained. The eldest lived on the ground floor with his wife and had lost his right leg on the Russian front. The youngest son had been killed when the Russians took Berlin. The elderly couple occupied the second floor.

"We are renting our sitting room," the woman said as she opened the door to a large, nicely furnished room. The furniture, including a large iron bed, had obviously been handed down through several generations. "Are you Austrian, my dear? Is it only you who want the room? I mean, you don't have someone you'll be sharing the room with?"

"No, just me. How much would the rent be?"

"Well, if you are working for the Americans, we don't need the money. If you are working, maybe you could supply my husband with cigarettes and perhaps some coffee and food. Maybe some coal or wood for fuel.

The winter is coming and we have nothing to heat the house with. My husband has arthritis very bad."

"Well, I brought some cigarettes with me," I said, opening the package and holding it for the woman to see. "Will this be enough to start with? I'll see what I can do about some coffee."

"Franz, Franz, look, my dear. Look here. Have you ever seen so many cigarettes?" she exclaimed. "See, I told you we should rent our sitting room."

Her husband, limping slightly, his fingers crooked from arthritis, eagerly ripped open a pack. His hands trembled as he lit a cigarette and slowly exhaled the gray smoke, sighing deeply.

"Thank you," he said simply, as he left the room.

Walking between the DP camp and my new room, I had seen what I learned was the main U.S. Headquarters Division compound, and I noticed a clean, orderly building, which appealed to me for some reason, part of which was the U.S. Military Mortuary Service. The building was part of the main Headquarters Compound, but the entrance to the Mortuary Service was directly on the street where I passed. Death was nothing new to me, and the next morning I walked to the office to inquire about a job. The office was supervised by a U.S. Army chaplain, Captain-Chaplain Goodwin, who interviewed me. This time, however, I introduced myself as *Sonya A.* Popoff. Everyone, especially the Americans, mispronounced Asya or Anastasia, and Sonya seemed a name they easily pronounced.

"Have you ever worked in a mortuary before?"

"No, but I'm willing to learn."

"You speak English very well. Do you know any other languages?"

"Yes, German, French, and Russian. And Serbian, of course."

"The German, Russian, and French could be very helpful," he said as he raised his eyebrows. "Do you know how to type?"

I started to work at the mortuary the next day. My responsibilities were to prepare the paperwork that had to accompany each body, to work as a receptionist, and to translate when necessary in dealing with the German authorities. It was pleasant work; the only difficulty was the hours. I finished after sunset, and in the shortening daylight of autumn I had to walk home alone after dark, always walking in the middle of the street to avoid the frightening alleys and the even darker doorways. I immediately registered my new address at Frau Schmidt's with UNRRA. I still hoped to hear from Father, but remembering his service revolver and what he had said before we parted, I feared he was dead.

One of the GIs, a sergeant who worked in the same office with me, had arranged for his wife to join him. They were both in their very early twenties, and we became good friends. They invited me to their home several times for dinner or to spend the day with them, going for a Sunday drive with a picnic lunch. His wife, Margie, very sweet and about my size, introduced me to Sweetheart Soap. I will never forget my first bath with Sweetheart Soap. She also gave me my first pair of nylon stockings, and I thought I had found heaven. Sweetheart Soap and nylons!

I enjoyed my work at the Mortuary Service very much, even though the "pay" was insignificant, barely enough to manage rent and food. Then one day in autumn 1946, I was swamped with paperwork. A large American troop transport plane had crashed, and many bodies had been burned beyond recognition. They had been sent to our office for processing before being shipped back to the States. The Criminal Investigation Division (CID) at U.S. Main Headquarters was called in. Robert Baker, an agent with the U.S. Federal Bureau of Investigation, then a civilian employee assigned to the Headquarters Division, was in charge and came to take fingerprints to identify the bodies.

I stood by watching him closely as he went through each step necessary to take reliable fingerprints from the badly burned corpses. I tried to hand him things in order to make myself useful so that he wouldn't send me away. I couldn't resist asking questions. Finally, as he finished working on one of the bodies, he looked up at me. "Are you interested in this work?"

"Oh, yes," I said. "I think it's fascinating. Wonderful that you can identify people this way, especially when they are so badly burned."

"You speak English perfectly. Do you know German as well?"

"Yes. German, Russian, French, and Serbian."

"Well, "if you are interested, you might come and see me in our office— CID in the main Headquarters Compound. We have a large staff of German clerical workers, and I need someone who can translate for me and supervise their work. We frequently need to coordinate our work with German or Russian authorities. There will be a class in fingerprint classification starting soon, which you need to take."

The next day, I went to his office to apply for a job with CID. It was still within the same compound, but to get to CID I had to enter the main gate. I received an excellent recommendation from Captain-Chaplain Goodwin at the mortuary, and the following week I started work with Baker and began a short course in fingerprint classification. The course was just sufficient to let me understand the classification and filing system in order to retrieve records from the files and to supervise the German clerical workers, but I was fascinated with the work. I became quite adept at recognizing the whorls and sequences of fingerprint identification. It was a fairly large office, and I worked with Baker and two Army CID agents. My work was both clerical and supervisory, typing correspondence for Baker, filing and retrieving records, and supervising the German clerical staff. At this time CID conducted background checks for displaced persons interested in immigrating to the United States.

I was now eighteen years old, although my papers showed me as twenty. So often I had silently thanked Papa for lying to get that first ID paper with the incorrect birth date. It had helped me to find work. In summer 1947, Bob Baker called me into his office.

"Some changes are coming up, Sonya My assignment with CID European Headquarters is ending soon, and General Eisenhower is moving the U.S. Headquarters Group to Heidelberg.

"CID is moving as well, but the Fingerprint Division is going to be reduced, and there won't be a need for your position. I have a very good friend who is an officer with the Quartermaster Corps, Headquarters Division. He needs someone with your language ability and office skills, and I can give you an excellent recommendation. It would be a good job. If I leave before the move takes place, you could return to the Mortuary Office. I've already spoken to Captain Goodwin, and he would be pleased to have you back for that last few weeks. Think it over, and if you are interested in moving to Heidelberg, I'll arrange an interview for you."

It didn't take much thinking. Even as a child I had heard of Heidelberg as a university city, and I knew it would be much more pleasant than Frankfurt. I had no ties to anyone in Frankfurt, and I had wanted to move, depressed by the ailing Schmidt family. Bob Baker arranged for my interview with the commanding officer of the Quartermaster Corps, Headquarters Division and gave me the highest possible recommendation.

Then one day in late August 1947 Frau Schmidt met me at the door as I returned from work.

"There was an older gentleman here inquiring for you, Fraulein Asya. I told him where you worked, but he didn't want to bother you at work. He said he had to get an early train. But he left a letter," she said, handing it to me.

Papa! The letter said that he had been searching everywhere for me, beginning in Hamburg, and that he had finally obtained my address from UNRRA. He wrote that he was fine, doing well, living in Munich, and that he had found a position as an administrative assistant in a large hospital. I was overjoyed to hear from him, to know that he was alive and well, and I made immediate arrangements to go to Munich and see him. I could only arrange a day trip, but I found that I could get an early morning train to Munich on Sunday, spend the day with Father, and be back in my room by late evening.

Father had aged terribly. I was shocked when I saw him. He was very thin, with a lot more gray in his moustache, his bushy eyebrows almost white, the wonderful spark gone from his blue eyes. Mother's death had taken a terrible toll. We went together to the hospital where he worked and where he introduced me to his close friend, Doctor Shernadze, before we went to Father's office where we could talk privately.

"Thank God, I have found you," he exclaimed as we embraced again. He would not let go of me. "I have looked everyplace. I turned the earth upside down to find you. I never thought I would live long enough to see you again, but here you are. You are older, a young woman now. There is a new expression in your eyes. Are you doing well?"

"I'm fine, Papa. I have a very good job, and I live in a very nice, clean room."

"Are you happy?"

"Happy? Yes, I guess I am. I'm happy that I'm alive, happy that I'm not sick. How about you, Papa? How did you escape from the Russian zone? What are you doing here in Munich?"

"I traveled mostly by night, " he said. "Some of my friends got caught, but I decided that there was still life in me, and I wanted to make sure that you were all right. I guess I just didn't want to die until I made sure. Mama is probably angry with me for leaving her, for not wanting to join her there, but I made one last run . . . and I think I'm pretty safe here in the American zone."

"Are any of our Russian friends still around? I mean the Belgrade group from Dr. Kester Street?"

"Yes, as a matter of fact, a few of them are here in Munich. I haven't heard anything about Lyalya or Borya. General Skorodumov married Nina. You remember her, I'm sure. But I don't know where they are now. General Nazimov's widow, Nadia, is here in Munich with Yura. You remember that the General died in a bombing raid in Belgrade. And poor Sasha . . . oh, well, I don't think you remember him. Anyway, he died, too. Fell from the train trying to flee Belgrade. Right under the wheels, poor soul. But enough of that."

"Do you know anything about Aunt 'Lyena?" I asked.

"Yes, not good news, I'm afraid." Suddenly his face twisted in pain, and he began to choke up. "Aunt 'Lyena is dead," he sobbed, shaking with emotion. "She was hanged! I don't know if it was Soviet troops or Partisans. How could anyone do such a horrible thing to helpless, frail Elyena?" He stopped then, choking back sobs.

"Chuchurovic," I cried, remembering dear sweet Aunt 'Lyena. "Oh, Papa. You should have brought her along. I will never understand how Mama could have left her behind. Never."

Father crossed himself and paused, getting control of his sobbing and wiping his tears.

"Well, remember the camp in Blankenburg," he continued. "Poor Aunt 'Lyena never would have survived that. Perhaps it's for the better. Her whole life was spent in devotion to God, and she is with Him at long last."

"Do you really believe there is a God, Papa?" I asked, drying my tears, "a God who could allow something like that to happen to someone as devoted as Aunt 'Lyena?"

"Oh, hush, Asinka, of course. Don't ever doubt that. I have found *you* with God's help."

He looked at me as he spoke, the same way he had done so often years before, when he had made me believe that there was goodness all around us . . . that we only had to look for it . . . when he would point to a bird, a flower, a bee with its nose buried deep in a flower, and say, "See what beauty God has created for us to share. And we are his creation, just like the birds, the trees, the sky."

It had always worked magically, and I would happily skip alongside, holding his hand and forgetting the hurt or disappointment or doubt. But it no longer worked. I heard his words then and knew that he was trying to explain, soften the news about Aunt 'Lyena, but the words were jumbled, meaningless to me. I was no longer the happy child skipping at his side. I had grown up with full awareness of the hurts, real disappointments, and endless tragedy that this war had brought. I was eighteen years old, but emotionally I felt as old as Father. We both knew that we could not bring back the past. The words and tender looks which had meant so much then could never be reestablished. Too much had happened to both of us.

"What are your plans?" he asked after a moment. " Have you thought of going to Paris? Perhaps to live with my friend, Father Gregórii, and his family and continue your education?"

"No, Papa," I answered. "I've never considered Paris. I have a good job now. I'm going to transfer to the new U.S. Headquarters Division in Heidelberg very soon, and I'm seriously thinking of going to the United States."

"But America is so far away," he said, "and we don't have anyone there."

"That's all right," I answered. "The office I work for processes immigration applications for refugees from all over Europe who apply, and I understand that it's not difficult to get a visa if you are healthy and have no criminal record."

"America—I thought that would be a good thing when we were together in Blankenburg, but now . . ." he said thoughtfully. "Well, I hear that a lot of refugees are trying to get to America. Many have already left. It's just that it's so far away, and we have no money, no friends there. But Paris, well, there are several Russian families there that I know besides Father Gregórii and his family. Well, we can talk about it later," he said, embracing me again.

"Papa," I said without thinking, "why don't you come back with me? We can find a small place to live, and that way we could be together."

"No, Asinka," he said thoughtfully. "You could move here. I have a good job and have established a new set of acquaintances here. And I might still go on to Paris. I think I need the company of my good friend, Father Gregórii. There are a lot of things I can't explain, there is a doubt in my heart . . . divine questions that I cannot find an answer to. I think he must have gone through this after the Russian Revolution, when he left our circle and began a new life as a priest. Perhaps he too went through what I am going through now, although I'm twenty-five years behind him in facing these doubts. Maybe he would hear me, understand my soul and explain."

"Are you thinking of becoming an Orthodox priest, Papa?"

"Oh, no," he answered quickly. "It is too late for that now. My heart is heavy and my soul is troubled. I just want to be close to him, to be able to talk things over. We were very close and shared good times in the Academy, and later during the revolution we shared tragedy. We understand one another. You know," he continued as though talking to himself, "you know, my philosophy of life used to be that there is no such thing as a bad person. Why? We are all the creation of God, and everything God created is good. If by some chance you come upon a bad person, well, there are some miscalculations that God perhaps made in the past. Prehistoric animals, the dinosaurs, for example, could not support life because of their hugeness, or whatever reason, so they died off. But man is such perfection that it is almost impossible to find a bad one. Well, the Russian Revolution and this war have brought out some bad ones. But in general, if I came upon a bad person, I used to say, 'Bank it, it will draw interest. Bank it in your mind and your heart, and from the interest you accumulate you add to your experience and it helps you to grow and mature.' But lately, my philosophy has reversed. I believe it's almost impossible to find a *good* person, someone upright and decent. Of course, I could 'bank' that, too, add it to my total experience.

"But, you see, Asinka, I'm old now. I'm fifty-two and I have no time, no patience to wait for the interest to grow in the bank of my mind and heart and soul. I want to understand where I went wrong. I want some answers from my friend. He's a man of God. But," he paused, his finger raised as the stern expression I remembered from years before formed on his face, "but I still maintain, despite my many doubts about the human race, I still maintain, and I want you to remember . . . that I strongly believe in the importance of a good foundation, in the soul of a person, in the ship tossed about on rough seas that we discussed so many years ago. I still firmly believe that a strong foundation can withstand almost . . . no, not almost, a strong foundation can withstand *all* the storms that life brings. The core, the foundation, the soul is there, and you and you alone can build around it. And if it's imbedded deeply enough—and yours *is*—it can withstand anything and become whole."

He grew silent as I looked at him, remembering all the loving, happy times of my childhood.

"So you want to go to America, eh?" he said after a moment. "Well, maybe it's not such a bad idea. Tell me, Asinka, have you met anyone you really like? Are you still 'Papa's little girl'?"

Suddenly I saw not the Papa I had just been talking to but the vacant stare I remembered from the garage rooms in Belgrade, and I remembered being sent alone to Vienna, then, even worse, to Hamburg. I knew exactly what he was asking. It would have been so easy to answer truthfully ... to answer simply, 'Yes Papa, I haven't met anyone like that yet.' Instead I looked directly into his eyes and replied coldly, "Really, Father, that's of no importance at all now, is it?"

The words were not out of my mouth before I regretted them, wished that I could take them back. The sadness that came over him twisted his face and reflected the deep hurt that he was feeling, and I have regretted that moment all my life. He leaned over then, kissed my forehead, and suggested that we go out.

We ate in a tiny cozy restaurant that Father knew, indulging in only small talk as we sat there. When we had finished, Father took me to the train station.

It had been good to see Papa again, good for *my* soul to have his reassurance and his trust. I had begun to have so many doubts lately that the meeting had been like medicine to my own inner well-being. My own faith had begun to falter, and Father's strong faith had strengthened me. But I was so very, very sorry about the way I had answered his "Papa's little girl" question. Whatever brought about the incident in the garage in Belgrade, I had long ago forgiven him, even if I still did not understand it. In the following weeks we exchanged letters. Nothing important was said. The letters were simply a way of maintaining contact.

I finally understood Papa's determination to keep Mother and me from the Soviets. Aunt 'Lyena's horrible death weighed heavily on my mind for many years. Many Soviet divisions included a political officer whose duties included searching for expatriate White Russians. Of course, I don't know if that led to the tragedy of Aunt 'Lyena. I have never been able to face squarely, to comprehend, and to accept her final days. I hope as was her custom she was deep in prayer at the village chapel when the Soviet troops passed our house in Yaintse, and that she was at least spared the anxiety of hearing the shouts and voices of Ukrainian Soviet soldiers passing so close.

Aunt 'Lyena was the kindest, gentlest person I have ever known. Her entire life had been spent in devotion to God. Thankfully, I cannot imagine the class hatreds that led the perpetrators to commit such a horrible crime, but I know without doubt that in Aunt 'Lyena's final moments, she forgave them. While she did not die in defense of her faith, I believe she received a martyr's welcome in Heaven, and that belief has provided some solace. And I believe that she has watched over me all these years.

My nineteenth birthday would have passed in 1947 without notice, but a letter from Papa wishing me a happy birthday had arrived a day or two before. I moved to Heidelberg with the Headquarters Division and began my new job. The Marshall Plan swung into full action, and the change throughout Western Europe was remarkable. In Germany, rubble removal began in earnest, forests and green areas were picked up and cleaned, and rebuilding began everywhere. I became more and more convinced that I would like to emigrate to America. But I loved Europe so very much. Europe was where my roots were, where I felt so much at home.

Then one Saturday evening in early December I was sitting in the parlor of my new rooming house, reading something when I heard the doorbell. I went to the door and opened it to find a messenger.

"I have a telegram for Asya Popoff."

I stood motionless. Time stood still. I knew the contents of the telegram without looking, and I would not take it. I knew at once that the telegram was from Munich. I felt it.

"Would you please read it to me?" I said softly. "All I want to know is when he died."

"*Your father died at 7:00 p.m. Saturday, December 13, 1947. Funeral scheduled December 16. Dr. Shernadze.*"

I remembered Dr. Shernadze from my visit with Father in August.

The last person in the world had gone. Papa was dead. I was truly alone in the world now.

TWENTY-FOUR

The End of the Beginning

I went to my office the following morning, Sunday, to ask for a few days off. Captain-Chaplain Goodwin was the only officer I could find. He was very sympathetic and offered to help, assuring me that he would inform my boss, Bob Baker. Since my payday was a week away, he gave me Marks so that I could purchase my ticket and have a little money for incidentals.

I called my friends from Vermont to tell them what had taken place and that I would be unable to be at the office on Monday. They picked me up right away, insisting that I come to their apartment to stay until I left for Munich. While Margie did her best to console me, her husband called to find out the train schedule and left briefly to get my ticket for the following morning.

We were unable to reach Dr. Shernadze by telephone. The sergeant sent him a telegram giving him my arrival time the following day and to tell him that I would make arrangements for Father's burial when I arrived. Bless their hearts, they knew that I had little or no money, and they called everyone they knew in order to round up cigarettes that could be bartered for funeral expenses. When my train left, I had twenty cartons of American cigarettes in my suitcase. I had managed to save almost a thousand Marks. That was not very much in 1947 Germany, but I hoped it would help.

I don't know what I would have done without the help of my Vermont friends. My dresses were all showing signs of wear by then, and Margie insisted that I take a suit of hers. We were the same size, and she loaned me a soft, light beige, almost peach colored wool suit. It was the dressiest thing she had, she explained, apologizing that she had nothing in dark colors. She had sewn a black armband which she placed in the pocket of the suit jacket and explained that I could put that on for the funeral. She also loaned me a pair of loafers because my shoes had almost no soles left; even the cardboard liner was little help. At the train station I was overwhelmed with grief and terribly nervous knowing that my suitcase contained American cigarettes.

Seated on the train I looked out at the bleak landscape. Low gray clouds hung over the fields. A mixture of snow and rain beat against the windows, and the compartment was cold. It was a three and a half hour ride, and the bleak December scenery matched my mood and my thoughts. I looked again at the telegram: "Your father died." "It must be true," I thought. "But when I saw him in late August he was fine, so relieved that we had found each other through UNRRA."

In the two years that we had lost track of each other I had begun to accept that he was dead, but deep in my heart I believed that Father was out there someplace, that one day we would find one another. That conviction sustained me, kept me strong, firmly believing that the "foundation" Father always spoke of was beneath my feet and entrenched in my heart. Somehow I knew that, although badly battered during the war years, the foundation he and Mother had helped me to build was still very much intact.

After I saw him in August, I made up my mind to have a talk with him at our next meeting. In the two years of believing he was dead, I had come to understand that Father was just a man, not the super being I had made him out to be when I was a child, simply a human being with human faults and weaknesses.

I had been carrying the hurt in my heart for too long. I had rehearsed how to say it, and I had resolved to tell him that although I could not understand his actions that day in the garage, I wanted to put it behind us, that I had long ago forgiven him and wanted to start a new father-daughter relationship. Yes, that was what I intended to do at our next meeting. But *this* was our next meeting.

My eyes filled with tears as I looked out the window of the train. Mother had been killed just twelve hours before we were liberated and lay buried in Blankenburg City Cemetery, now the Soviet zone, lost to me forever. Aunt 'Lyena, murdered, hanged by unknown persons driven mad by ignorance or some insane class divisions, real or imagined, perhaps buried in Yaintse, was also lost to me forever. Now Father was to be buried in Munich. What was once such a close, small family would now lie in graves scattered throughout Europe.

I looked at my watch. It was the dainty gold watch with six diamonds that Mother had tearfully passed through the iron fence at Luftwaffe headquarters in Belgrade just before I left on the train bound for Vienna in October 1944. I had kept it in my shoe, wrapped in paper and hidden under the arch of my foot, because I was so afraid that the Germans would take it from me. I looked at the watch now and thought it so sad that a man-made object such as a watch could weather war, occupation, and bombing. And yet God's creation, a human being, was so vulnerable, so helpless in war, so easily killed. I wondered how my favorite nun at Hopova would explain this to me. The conductor's voice broke the silence of the car.

"Karten, bitte."

I gave him my ticket, afraid that he would ask me to open my suitcase, but thank goodness he punched my ticket and left the compartment without a word.

The train finally pulled into the Munich station. It was only a short walk from the trolley stop to the hospital, but it was still raining and I was soaked and shivering from the cold when I arrived to knock at Dr. Shernadze's door.

"Ah, you made it, Asya, but you're soaked. Come in, come in. Give me your jacket to hang up," he said, shaking my hand warmly, taking my suitcase, and helping me with my jacket.

"Doctor," I asked, "is Father really dead? What happened?"

"He died of angina pectoris, Asya. It happened very fast. He did not suffer."

"Was he alone when he died?" I asked, silently praying that someone had been with him.

"Not exactly. It was my night off, and he and I were going out to dinner. We were planning to go dancing with two of the nurses later that evening. I was already in my car when your father came out and said that he had forgotten something and that it would take him only a minute. After several minutes, when he did not return, I shut the car off and went to find him.

"Your father was slumped across his desk gasping for air. I removed his coat and jacket, and when I took his shirt off I could see a large dark bruise on the left side of his back. I rushed to my room for my bag and gave him an injection, but it was too late. He expired just then. He didn't suffer, Asya; in fact, he was in very good spirits and looking forward to our night out."

"Where is he now?"

"He is in Room 5, down in the basement. You can go down and have a few moments with him."

I made my way along a dark basement corridor toward the number 5 that I could see lit above one of the doors. I knocked softly, opened the door, and went in. In a very narrow room a single, dim light bulb protruding from the wall above a gurney lit the room. I took a couple of steps toward it, toward Father lying there with his hands folded on his chest, his blue eyes open.

He wore a dark blue suit and a white shirt with a dark blue tie. My heart began to race, "He isn't dead . . ." I thought. He was lying there with his eyes wide open. I stepped closer; his eyes were fixed straight ahead. "Is he trying to trick me?" I wondered as, God forgive me, a picture of him kissing me, pressing against me as I struggled to push him away that day in the garage, flashed in my mind.

"Papa?"

The sound of my own heartbeat thundered in my ears and sweat poured from my forehead as I took one step closer.

"Papa, Papa," I cried, as I reached for his folded hands.

His hands were icy cold and damp, just like the body I had kissed when I was a toddler. Goose bumps covered my body. I felt faint and sweaty and ran out of the room. I leaned against the cold wall of the basement corridor, gasping for air, my heart beating wildly. "Yes," I thought, "now I know. He is dead. Oh Papa, Papa."

Tears were streaming down my face, and I was shaking with sobs as I felt the doctor's arm tighten around my shoulders.

"Come, you must rest now. Tomorrow will be a very hard day for you." he said. "I have an empty hospital room, and you can stay there. I'll send my nurse in to help you, and I'll see you later."

I entered the room he indicated and saw my jacket hanging on the back of the chair. A bathrobe lay across the bed, and I sat on the bed as a nurse walked in.

"The doctor said you might need some help. Do you need anything?" she asked sympathetically.

"No, thank you."

"Of course you do," she insisted softly. "First, take off your wet clothes and put that bathrobe on. Did you bring a nightgown?"

"No," I answered absently. "I'm sorry. I didn't think about a nightgown."

"Of course not, you have too much on your mind. We'll have your clothes all cleaned and dried so that you'll have fresh clothes for the funeral."

She led me to a bathroom down the hall.

"There are fresh towels and a fresh hospital gown in the bathroom. You go and take a good hot bath. The doctor will come to see you in a little while."

The warm water was soothing, but everything seemed like a strange dream: the hospital room, the nurse, my father lying dead in the basement with his eyes wide open. I was moving about as though it weren't me. I felt once again like an observer of myself. I didn't feel myself walking or taking a bath or returning to my room and lying down on the bed. I didn't feel anything. I felt like an empty shell.

I wondered if this was how "dead" felt. *Mother dead, Aunt 'Lyena dead, Kolya dead, now Father dead. Maybe I was dead, too.* A crucifix hung on the wall, and I looked at it and wondered if I should pray. *But why? Aunt 'Lyena prayed fervently all her life and her parents were murdered, her sister was killed, and she was hanged. Prayer didn't help her at all.* I looked at the crucifix again. *Even Jesus died in vain. The world is just as cruel. Life itself is cold and cruel.*

A soft knock on the door brought the doctor in.

"Do you feel any better, Asya?" he asked with concern.

"I don't feel anything. Not bad, not good, nothing."

"How about some hot soup? Get something into your stomach."

"I'm not hungry."

"No, I know you aren't, but you should have something in your stomach."

The nurse brought a steaming bowl of chicken soup, a cup of hot tea, and some Zwieback toast. The doctor began to spoon feed me, then made me sit up on the edge of the bed to finish the soup.

"Asya," he asked, "have you ever met Father Gregórii?"

"No. Papa spoke of him often. He was a good friend and comrade of Papa's in the regiment, and then at the end of the Russian Revolution he emigrated to Paris and became an Orthodox priest. I have never met him."

"Your father spoke of him often to me," he said, "and once in conversation he said that if he should die he would like Father Gregórii to conduct his funeral. Well, I have contacted him, and he arrives from Paris in the morning to officiate at the services. He will stay in your father's room."

"Oh, good, I'm certain Father would like that."

"Yes, and did you know that Mrs. Nazimov and Yura are here in Munich, as well as the von Der Nonnes, and that they will all be at the funeral?"

"No," I answered softly, "I did not."

I didn't sleep well at all that night, dozing fitfully. Eventually, morning light filled my room, and soon the same nurse knocked and entered with my fresh clothes.

"I found a black armband in the pocket of your suit," she said. "I attached it to the left arm of the suit. You'll feel a little better with all fresh clothes. The doctor will come later to take you to breakfast."

"Thank you," I said. "You've been very kind."

I took a bath and dressed. My head ached, and I was so very tired. Doctor Shernadze knocked lightly and entered.

"Good morning, Asya. We have an awfully lot to do. We are going to have a mass in the hospital chapel at 4:00 p.m., but you and I have to go to the cemetery and pick out a grave site. I brought the death certificate with me. Do you have any money?"

"Yes. Well, some, not enough. But I have twenty cartons of American cigarettes here. I understand they are worth a lot of money. Oh, and I also brought three pounds of coffee. I forgot about that. Is there a black market someplace where I can sell it all and get money?"

"Don't worry about that. What you brought will be plenty to take care of the expenses. I'll take care of it. Where are the cigarettes and coffee?"

"They are here in my suitcase. Shall I get them?"

"No, just leave everything here. I'll take care of it after breakfast."

We left my room and walked down the hall to a small lounge. I could smell the coffee. There were five tables with four chairs at each table. A long table set with a white tablecloth stood along the left wall and held a large coffee urn, cups, and pastries. Most of the dining tables stood along a wall with large windows. The light from outside prevented me from seeing the faces of the people, all seated with their backs to the windows. The conversation stopped as we entered the room, and I could feel all eyes upon me. In a moment, a tall, bearded man dressed all in black stood and came toward me.

"So you are Vasilii's daughter." He addressed me in French, without introducing himself, though his dress made it clear that this was Father Gregórii.

"I'm sorry, Father Gregórii. I'm afraid I have forgotten all my French," I answered in Russian.

"Oh? I thought you were going to attend the Sorbonne at one time?"

"Yes, but all that changed . . . because of the war and . . ."

"You know, you have caused your father a lot of heartache," he interrupted, frowning sternly. "He spent two frantic years searching for you. Did you make any effort to find him?"

"No, Father," I answered, "not really. I registered with UNRRA and listed his name as who I was looking for. I wrote to him twice in Blankenburg but never received an answer. I was in the refugee camps at first, and then tried to find work to get out of the camps."

"Yes, but you broke his heart. He was so worried about you." he interrupted sternly.

"I know, and I'm very sorry."

"Well, Asya, you look all grown up." Aunt Nadia Nazimov interrupted the priest and extended her hand to shake mine. "But you should have dressed differently," she said critically. "This is the cold autumn, and after all we are here to attend a funeral. You should have dark clothes."

"I know, Aunt Nadia, and I do feel very badly about it, but I had to borrow these clothes, everything—from an American friend—she didn't have any dark clothes." I felt mortified. I wished that I could fall through the floor, now noticing that everyone in the room was dressed in dark clothes.

"Well, you look like a girl, a very pretty one. The last time I saw you in Belgrade you were skin and bones . . . and dirty, remember? It was the night we found my father in the ruins. But now you look very nice, very pretty."

I turned toward the voice. "Yes, Yura, I remember. That was not a very pleasant night."

Yura walked away after a few moments to get some coffee as Mr. von Der Nonne approached with his son and daughter to shake my hand. They all looked so different to me. So much cleaner, I thought, and then realized that the last time we had all seen each other was among the ruins of Belgrade. There were several more Russians whom I did not know who came to shake my hand—Father's friends he had met in Munich—they were not Belgrade people.

I sat down at an empty table. The doctor sat with me, but left quickly after having a cup of coffee. I took a cup of coffee and one of the small rolls that were on the serving table. I was just finishing a second cup of coffee when Doctor Shernadze returned to say that we had to leave for the cemetery.

Once in the car the doctor handed me a large envelope that contained father's death certificate and 35,000 Deutsch Marks from the sale of the coffee and cigarettes. How he had managed it so quickly I will never know. It was still raining and cold, and we drove the few blocks to the cemetery. The doctor parked in front of a small building, and we entered the cemetery office where I was shown a plan of available grave sites, each priced on the plan with German efficiency.

"The price shown does not include a head marker," explained a person behind a large desk, "Here is a list of head markers with the price above each one."

I looked at the grave site plan; each site had a different set of prices. I looked at the markers, desperately trying to make sense of things. I saw a grave site that I thought I liked and saw that it was priced for ten, twenty or thirty years. If I got it for thirty years, the site would cost 30,000 Marks; the head marker, the cheapest one, a wooden cross with a steel frame and Father's name, would cost 3,000 Marks, the next marker was 7,000 Marks. I could not afford that. I could only point my finger at the site and marker I had chosen. I felt faint and sick to my stomach. Words would not form in my mouth.

"All right, Fraulein, the total will be 33,000 Marks, and we will have some flowers placed on the grave at no extra cost. Do you have the death certificate?"

I handed him the envelope, still unable to speak, and he counted out 33,000 Marks, removed the death certificate, and returned the envelope to me with 2,000 Marks and a receipt neatly placed inside.

"Now," he continued, "if you will sign right here we will have everything ready for you. Well, not for you," he chuckled. "Oh, yes, your father . . . well, ready for him. I understand the body will be here by 6:00 p.m. Our grave diggers are here until 8:00."

I walked out of the office leaning on the doctor's arm, unable to think or to feel anything. We got back into the car and drove to the hospital in silence. As we entered the hospital, the doctor held the door for me.

"I'm sorry the man at the cemetery seemed so cold and impersonal."

"It's the German way," I replied simply.

"Have you noticed that the Germans seem to be even more hostile toward us now than when we were 'under their thumb,' so to speak?"

"Yes." I answered, fighting tears and remembering Papa's warning before we parted in Blankenburg. "The resentment is obvious, especially if you work for the Americans," I said, trying to regain some composure.

"Are you going to continue working for the Americans, Asya?"

"Yes, thank God I speak English fluently. I don't know what would have become of me if I didn't speak several languages."

"Well," the doctor said, "I have patients to see. You should go to your room and try to rest a little. We have to be in the chapel at 4:00 p.m. I hope I'll be able to make it on time."

"Thank you, doctor, for taking me to the cemetery and for selling the cigarettes."

I returned to my room and lay down on the bed, turning my head to look out the window. It had started to rain again. I thought of Papa, lying in the cold basement. I thought of Father Gregórii's words, "You have broken his heart." But it's not my fault that Papa died. Or is it? After all, it was he who sent me to Hamburg alone. Of course, I know that he was afraid of the advancing Soviets and that he thought me safer in the well-established British zone. Oh, God, could it have been my fault? Papa was only fifty-two years old.

I walked to the chapel at close to 4:00 p.m., a small chapel, softly lit by candles. The casket stood on a bier in the middle of the chapel. The candles at the head of the casket flickered, casting moving shadows over Papa's face. His eyes were closed. A large gold Orthodox cross lay across his chest. His face was peaceful; the ever-present wrinkle between his brows was gone.

"Papa, all your worries are over now. You no longer have to be on the run, seeking a safe place for us, no longer wondering what's to become of us," I said to him silently.

The small chapel began to fill. The priest filled the censor and began to slowly distribute incense around the casket, reciting prayers as he walked. I stood by Papa's left side with my left hand on the casket. The priest began to sing "Nadgróbnoe Ridánie" (Funeral Sobbing), the melody of which is extremely melancholy. I began to cry, softly at first. But soon I became overwhelmed and could no longer control my sobs. I held onto the rim of the casket and reached for Papa's hands. Their damp coldness no longer bothered me. My tears fell on Father's face, and I reached to touch it. I did not want to let go of him.

Pictures of my past flashed through my mind. Hundreds of dead on the streets of Belgrade, ruins all around me; parting from my parents as they sent me alone to Vienna with the retreating Nazis; searching for Mother in the ruins and carrying her body out to the sidewalk; the chapel floor with Mother's body laid out with so many others; her funeral; waving goodbye to Papa when he sent me on alone to Hamburg . . .

I had managed to take it all as a part of living, managed to remain at least a little detached from it all, never really let myself feel the hurt inside, never really allowed myself to cry. And now the tears could no longer be held back, and all the pent-up emotions flooded out. I believe that on some level I realized for the first time that I was truly all alone in the world.

Although I hadn't heard from Father in two years and had come to believe that he was dead, somehow there was always the hope, the conviction that he was out there somewhere and that we would one day find each other. Now that hope, that conviction was gone. Now as I stood there holding on to the casket, I felt that the "foundation" he had so often spoken of was collapsing. The Mass ended, and I felt someone pulling my hands from the casket and someone else leading me away as the casket was closed.

I rode to the cemetery in the hearse, along with Papa's casket. The casket was carried to a gaping hole at the cemetery. By then it was pouring rain. I threw a muddy clump of earth on the lowered casket. The ground that was hurriedly shoveled onto the casket sounded like distant thunder. The grave diggers formed a mound of earth that kept collapsing, sliding off, as the rain formed puddles. Flowers had been placed on top of the mound of wet earth, the petals sinking into the mud. I took a bouquet, trying to shake the mud off, but the petals were too wet and muddy. I put the bouquet back on top of the mound, closer to the head. Another deep puddle had formed where they had lain before. I felt someone slip something over my shoulders.

The grave diggers left, and I turned to see that everyone had left. It was nearly dark, and I was alone in the rain. I walked to a nearby bench beneath a tree, but it was bare of leaves. It did not provide any shelter from the rain. I scraped the mud from my shoes on the gravel by the bench and began the long walk to the street. The hospital was not far from the cemetery, but, now soaked and starting to shiver, I took the trolley. As soon as I reached the hospital, I went to my room, and the same nurse who had been so kind came in almost as soon as I entered.

"Well, this is the easiest nursing duty I've had in a very long time," she said with a smile. "Give me your wet clothes and put this robe on. That's mine. It's prettier than the hospital robe."

"Thank you again," I said gratefully.

I washed my face and looked at my image in the mirror. My eyes were puffy, swollen, but I had no more tears. I felt that I would never have tears again.

Outside the wind was howling, a mixture of rain and snow beating against the window. I thought of Mother's funeral and how different it had been. The skies then were blue, the trees full of tender green buds, and the most beautiful wild flowers I had ever seen were blooming everywhere. Birdsong filled the air, and the whole world had seemed to be awakening with new life, new hope. It was, I thought, the most beautiful spring I had ever experienced. Germany had been defeated, and there would be no more death, no more bombs. It had seemed to me then that a new life was beginning. Today it seemed that my world had ended. There was no hope, no promise of new life. I was alone. One person with no ties, no roots—my last link to identity and purpose now lying beneath the cold, muddy earth of Munich.

There was a knock on the door, and Father Gregórii entered.

"Well, what are your plans now, Asya?" he asked.

"I'm going back to my job in the morning. Father Gregórii, I would like to go to Father's room and see if I can find some pictures and personal mementoes from Papa."

"Why the sudden interest?" he interrupted, frowning. "You made no effort to find him in two years. No, no, Asya. I am the executor of your father's things, and I don't think you should seek any mementoes."

"But I know that he had some of Mother's things. He had a very old icon and family pictures. I know he would have wanted me to have those things."

"No, you see, you have already built your life. You've made choices without your father and, therefore, I feel that Aljona should have all those things, should she ever come out of the USSR. In the meantime I'll be in charge of them."

"But she is not my sister," I protested, "not any relation to us at all."

"That's true, but your parents cared for her and sent her with the Red Cross," he answered firmly. "Unfortunately, they were intercepted by Soviet troops."

"But I'm the only one left truly related to Mother and Father."

"You must let me be the judge. I know that your father would have wanted it this way."

"How can you possibly know this, Father Gregórii? You have lived in Paris all these years. I've never even met you before." I could feel tears welling up, but these were tears of anger, and I did not want him to see them.

His hand went up, and he blessed me and held his hand for the traditional Orthodox kissing of his hand to acknowledge the blessing. I refused to do this, and he turned and left the room. *Meddlesome Priest!* I thought. *You know nothing of me at all. You know nothing at all of what has happened to me, to Papa and Mama and Aunt 'Lyena. Nothing at all of what we went through over the past six years. Whatever Father wrote to you, you can never know the trauma, horror, and hurt that we have all gone through.*

I was furious, and perhaps I felt a little guilty for not acknowledging his blessing. I was furious, but I was so young, so emotionally devastated by the loss of Papa, that I could not stand up to him and insist on my right to Father's last effects. "They are only things, Asinka."

I know now that Father Gregórii knew only that Papa, his friend and comrade, had written to him about the destruction of our family and his search for me, about his worry and deep sadness that I seemed estranged from him at our last parting. It was clear that Papa had written about the distance that had grown up between us when we had been reunited in late August, but he had never indicated the reasons for that distance. But this man was a priest. He, above everyone, should have realized that there is always another side to any story. He made no attempt to discover another side. Poor sad, little Aljona had a far greater effect on my life than she ever knew.

A few minutes after Father Gregórii left, Aunt Nadia Nazimov knocked and entered the room. She came to say good-bye, but she said many of the same things Father Gregórii did, complaining about the worry I had caused Mother during the occupation of Belgrade and how Father had been searching for me. I did not even respond. I felt I was back in Belgrade during the occupation, hearing the harangues of the dour-faced Russians who always filled the house at Yaintse. It was getting late. I just wanted to go to bed, get up early, and leave Munich.

In the morning I stopped at Doctor Shernadze's office to thank him for everything and to say good-bye, then left the hospital and took the trolley back to the Munich Rail Station. I never returned to visit Father's grave. The memory of those two days of his funeral, Father Gregórii, and Aunt Nadia would always remain just too emotional!

8/14

DISCARDED

Lucy Robbins Welles Library
95 Cedar Street
Newington, CT 06111